ARCHBISHOP CRANMER'S IMMORTAL BEQUEST

ARCHBISHOP CRANMER'S IMMORTAL BEQUEST

◆ ◆ ◆

The Book of Common Prayer
of the Church of England:
An Evangelistic Liturgy

by
Samuel Leuenberger, D.Th.

Originally published in the German language in Basel
with the title
Cultus Ancilla Scripturae

Translated from the German by
Samuel Leuenberger and Lewis J. Gorin, Jr.

With a Foreword to the English Edition by
James I. Packer

WILLIAM B. EERDMANS PUBLISHING COMPANY
GRAND RAPIDS, MICHIGAN

Copyright © 1990 by Samuel Leuenberger
First Published 1990 by Wm. B. Eerdmans Publishing Co.,
255 Jefferson Ave. S.E., Grand Rapids, Mich. 49503

Printed in the United States of America

Library of Congress Cataloging-in-Publication Data

Leuenberger, Samuel, 1942–
    [Cultus Ancilla Scripturae. English]
    Archbishop Cranmer's immortal bequest: the Book of Common Prayer of the
Church of England: an evangelistic liturgy / by Samuel Leuenberger: translated
from the German by Samuel Leuenberger and Lewis J. Gorin, Jr.; with a foreword
to the English edition by James I. Packer.
        p.   cm.
    Translation of: Cultus Ancilla Scripturae.
    Includes bibliographical references.
    ISBN 0-8028-0474-8
    1. Church of England. Book of common prayer—History and criticism.
2. Cranmer, Thomas, 1489–1556. 3. Puritans—England. 4. Church of
England—Liturgy. 5. Church of England—Doctrines—History. 6. Anglican
Communion—Liturgy. 7. Anglican Communion—Doctrines—History.
8. Church of England. Alternative service book 1980—History and criticism.
9. Religious awakening—Christianity.   I. Title.
BX5145.L4613   1990   90-31015
                                                          CIP

In Celebration of Archbishop Cranmer's 500th Birthday

This translation is published in celebration of the 500th anniversary of the birth of England's great churchman, Thomas Cranmer, Archbishop of Canterbury, who was born July 2, 1489.

Archbishop Cranmer presided over the introduction of the Reformation into England during the course of which he:

1. Secured the authorization for the publication in 1537 of the so-called Matthews Bible which was the first English-language Bible to be legally issued in England.
2. Wrote the preface to the publication of the Great Bible of 1539, sometimes called the Cranmer Bible, in which he called for constant study by all Christians of the Bible.
3. Compiled and directed the issuance of the first edition of The Book of Common Prayer in 1549, the obvious purpose of which was to spread a general knowledge of the Bible throughout the population.
4. Revised and reissued The Book of Common Prayer in 1552 as soon as it was pointed out that certain unbiblical matter had been allowed to creep into the edition of 1549. In 1989, The Book of Common Prayer, still authorized by Britain's Parliament in the edition issued in 1662, is essentially unchanged from Cranmer's 1552 edition in its emphasis on the Bible.

Archbishop Cranmer not only introduced into England a Bible in the English language; he also introduced into the worship of England a prayer book whose content was almost all taken directly from the Bible, and whose evident purpose was to encourage regular study of the Bible. In short he nailed a banner to the mast of England's ship of state, a banner calling for devotion to the Bible, and that banner, though often assaulted in the last five hundred years, still flies.

Among the many who have died in defense of that banner is Archbishop Thomas Cranmer himself, who for his efforts on behalf of the Bible underwent a martyr's death.

All English-speaking people who believe the Bible is the Word of God are under obligation to Thomas Cranmer and owe him a debt of gratitude for the prayer book he has left them as a legacy of his martyrdom.

To my parents,
my wife Eleanor, and our children
Silvanus, Priscilla, and Lukas,
as well as to the uncompromising servants
of the English church:
John Hooper and Edmund Grindal

CONTENTS

Foreword by Dr. James I. Packer   xxv

Preface   xxvii

    1. Hypothesis of the work   xxvii

    2. Explanation of the fundamental concepts   xxviii

       a. "The Book of Common Prayer"   xxviii

       b. "Revivalism"   xxviii

       c. "Puritanism"   xxix

    3. A critical survey of the applicable literature   xxxi

       a. Reference The Book of Common Prayer   xxxi

       b. Reference the revivalism theme   xxxii

       c. Reference puritanism   xxxiii

    4. Statement on procedure   xxxiii

Acknowledgments   xxxvi

I. The Book of Common Prayer of 1549

A. Review of the contents of the divine services under consideration   1

B. History of the origins of this first draft   2

C. Draft of 1549 as a liturgical outgrowth of the church politics of Thomas Cranmer   4

    1. Cranmer's church politics in harmony with Henry VIII   4

CONTENTS

2. The BCP of 1549 with emphasis on its holy communion liturgy   7

II. Cranmer's Most Important Consultants in the Construction of a Genuine Reformation Book of Liturgies: Peter Martyr Vermigli, Martin Bucer, and John Hooper

A. Peter Martyr and the distinctive features of his theology   13

  1. Biographical sketch and general remarks   13

  2. Roots of Martyr's revivalistic theology of the Word,
of faith, and of a rebirth   15

    a. Renewal of the inner man   15

    b. Accent on the depravity of man   16

    c. Accent on God's pure Word and ...   16

    d. Repudiation of perfunctorily used ritual forms   16

    e. Spiritualizing of the ecclesiastical concept   17

    f. Aristocratic mentality   17

    g. Love of the structure of the ancestral church   17

    h. Fondness for ecumenical scope   18

  3. Some principles of Martyr's theology of the
sacraments and their influence on the BCP   18

    a. Objections of Martyr to the BCP of 1549 ...   19

      (1) Communion is a congregation event

      (2) Transformation as inner reality

    b. Further characteristics of Martyr's theology of the
sacraments and their roots   21

      (1) The material symbols in the service as the making
of an analogy to spiritual reality

      (2) Denial of the bodily real presence and the
importance thereof

      (3) Sacramental symbols as auxiliary means
for stimulating faith

      (4) Sacramental symbols as helps to an intensified
experience of the word

    c. Influence of Martyr's revivalistic theology on the overall

ritual of holy communion in the BCP as well as on the
Thirty-nine Articles 24

(1) The three exhortations

(2) Confrontation of the law and the gospel in the
communion service

(3) Predestination

4. Final observations 26

  a. Martyr's importance to the BCP and the
Church of England 26

  b. Martyr's influence on the personalities among the
English church in exile 27

  c. Martyr's patristic knowledge 28

  d. Martyr's recommendations for a new ecclesiastical law 28

B. Fundamentals of Bucer's theology as revealed in particular by
examples from his *Censura* 28

  Introductory remarks 28

1. Measures to be taken for awakening and promoting faith 29

  a. General understanding reference divine services 29

  b. What is based on Holy Scripture is God's doctrine 29

  c. What is spoken in prayers or thanksgiving must
proceed from a heartfelt faith 30

  d. The conduct of the appointed minister during the
divine service requires a devotional attitude 30

  e. Church discipline 30

2. Practices obstructing faith 31

  a. Unnecessary ceremonial 32

  b. Representation in matters of faith 32

  c. Chattering talk in declarations of faith 34

  d. Rubrics which encourage minimalism 35

  e. The prayer for the dead 36

  f. Ritual practices in connexion with consecration 37

3. Faith as an aspect of an edifying fellowship 38

  a. Importance of distinguishing between the faithful
and the unfaithful 38

CONTENTS

b. Responses and those texts spoken by all   39

c. Segregation of choir from congregation   40

d. Fellowship in the sense of a personal exchange of faith   40

4. The church as the form of organization for bearing witness to the faith   41

    a. A fellowship of the faithful   41

    b. Tests of a true church   41

    c. Oneness of the true church   42

    d. Concerning the "infallible church"   42

    e. Overcoming the discrepancy between the clerical and lay church   43

5. Faith in its impact in the social field   44

    a. The responsibility of the born again vis-à-vis their fellow citizens   44

    b. Identification of the chosen congregation with the political inhabitants and the consequences arising therefrom   45

      (1) The bringing to a realization of one's election through the distribution of spiritual qualities

      (2) The bringing to a realization of one's election through the distribution of material goods

    General closing comments about Bucer   46

C. John Hooper as the father of puritanism and the main features of his theology   48

1. Introductory remarks   48

2. His educational tour in Zurich and his digestion of Bullinger's covenant theology   48

3. Reference to Hooper's encouraging and productive contact with king and archbishop   59

4. An analysis of the important elements in Hooper's preaching and writing with reference to content   63

    a. Depravity of man and his frailty   63

    b. The way to personal awareness of sin and repentance   64

    c. Appropriation of salvation through penance and rebirth   65

d. Importance of the Ten Commandments and God's Word 67

(1) "Pura Vita" or sanctification

(2) "Pura Doctrina"

(3) "Purus Cultus"

e. The importance of the soul 73

f. Warning and threat of judgment 73

g. Contrast between a transitory world and
everlasting treasures 74

h. Earthly life as a pilgrimage 75

i. Proclamation of the true church with its various aspects 76

(1) The true church based on the Word and not
on external aspects

(2) The true church is that fellowship which
adheres to the Word of God

(3) The true church possesses a unity effected
through the Holy Spirit

(4) Safety and life also belong to Hooper's concept
of the true church

(5) This church is also at war with the world and the
Satanic powers which is why Hooper calls it the
"church militant"

(6) The true church propagates no heresies

(7) Hooper sees the true church as a fellowship
for the purpose of edification . . .

(8) The true church can assuredly have an external
organization with established structures and
historically developed forms

j. The testifying to faith as a missionary function 80

5. The most important elements in Hooper's sermons
in regard to form 81

a. The direct appeal by speaking in an energetic
and exhortative way 81

b. A manner of speaking which appeals to the heart 82

c. Graphic illustrations 83

d. Utilization of the Bible 84

e. Repetition 84

D. Comments summarizing the contributions of
   Martyr, Bucer, and Hooper   84

   1. Peter Martyr   84

   2. Martin Bucer   85

   3. John Hooper   86

III. Cranmer's Drafting of The Book of Common Prayer of 1552 as the Fruit of His Discussions with Martyr, Bucer, and Hooper

A. Main features of Cranmer's theology   88

   1. Cranmer's understanding of Holy Scripture   89

      a. Holy Scripture is the ultimate authority in reference
         to questions seeking truth   89

      b. Holy Scripture is the instrument for our salvation   89

      c. Holy Scripture can edify people however learned   90

      d. Cranmer understands Holy Scripture as the guide
         to mastering a practical life work . . .   90

      e. Cranmer's understanding of Holy Scripture discloses
         a fundamentalistic approach . . .   90

         (1) The Bible is nourishment without unwholesome
             impurities or indeed any toxic elements

         (2) There are no truths which do not require
             confirmation through Scripture

         (3) Holy Scripture neither lies nor deceives

         (4) Cranmer goes so far as to employ the idea of
             infallibility in his understanding of Scripture

         (5) The Bible is not subject to any council . . .

      f. Revelations by means of occult phenomena are
         to be shunned   91

      g. Cranmer argues for the self-sufficiency of the Word   92

      h. God's Word is also even for children   92

      i. The Word exercises a missionary influence . . .   92

      j. God's Word operates to promote maturity in people   93

CONTENTS

2. The basic principles in Cranmer's hermeneutics . . .   93
   a. Dark passages in Scripture . . .   93
   b. Dark passages in the Bible reveal themselves . . .   93
   c. Cranmer is thereby convinced that the Bible
      interprets itself   94
   d. The soundness of the interpretation of Scripture
      passages   94

3. The three principal liturgies in the BCP of 1552 as
   reflections of Cranmer's compilatory theology   97
   a. The most important dogmatic elements in Morning
      as well as in Evening Prayer with reference
      to sin-grace-faith   98
      (1) Sin-grace-faith in the twelve introductory
          quotations from Scripture in Morning Prayer
      (2) Sin-grace-faith in the exhortations, confession,
          and absolution
      (3) Sin-grace-faith in the Lord's Prayer, opening
          sentences, and Psalm 95
      (4) Old Testament lesson
      (5) In the Te Deum Laudamus . . .
      (6) New Testament lesson
      (7) Benedictus
      (8) Apostles' Creed
      (9) Miserere
     (10) Lord's Prayer
     (11) Closing sentences
   b. The most important dogmatic elements in the
      eucharistic liturgy with reference to sin-grace-faith   105
      (1) Opening collect
      (2) Decalogue
      (3) Twenty offertory sentences
      (4) Prayer for the church militant
      (5) Sin-grace-faith in the three exhortations
      (6) Invitation to confession, confession, and
          absolution

(7) The four comfortable words from the
New Testament

(8) Preface with Sanctus

(9) Prayer of humble access

(10) Consecration prayer

(11) Closing prayers after the Lord's Prayer

(12) Gloria

4. Citations from Cranmer's works for the understanding
of the principal dogmatic elements of sin-grace-faith   112

  a. Justification according to Cranmer   112

  b. Aspects of Cranmer's concept of faith   113

    (1) Faith as the acceptance of the promise and the
forgiveness of sins

    (2) Faith as a matter of the heart

    (3) Faith as a consequence in good works

    (4) Faith as a spiritual sacramental eating

    (5) Faith as consecration

    (6) Faith as an uplifting of the heart

B. Principal differences in the prayer book of 1552 and the
traces of Martyr, Bucer, and Hooper   120

  General comments   120

  a. Elimination or rearrangement of certain
liturgical elements   120

  b. Elimination of symbols and gestures   123

  c. Additions and innovations   124

  d. Modifications with reference to altar and vestments   124

  e. Brief summary and conclusion   125

IV. The Book of Common Prayer of 1662

A. The road to and the fight for the integration of the
prayer book of 1552 into the edition of 1662   128

  1. Forces directly and indirectly involved in the fight   128

a. The Elizabethan puritanism of Edmund Grindal
   and the BCP of 1559 128

b. Independency, presbyterianism, and militant puritanism
   against a background of royalism and episcopalianism ... 137

c. The Restoration and the BCP of 1662 144

B. Evaluation and deductions 149

C. Analysis of the genuine revivalistic elements in the
   three principal liturgies in the BCP of 1662 151

Opening Remarks 151

1. Morning Prayer 151
   a. Introductory sentences 151
   b. Exhortation 152
   c. Confession 154
   d. Absolution 155
   e. Opening sentences 157
   f. Psalm 95 157
   g. Old Testament lesson 157
   h. Te Deum Laudamus 158
   i. Benedictus 159
   j. Apostles' Creed 159
   k. Responsive closing versicles 160
   l. Seven closing prayers 160
      (1) First collect
      (2) Collect for peace
      (3) Collect for grace
      (4) Prayer for the king or queen
      (5) Prayer for the royal family
      (6) Prayer for the clergy and people
      (7) Prayer of St. Chrysostom
      (8) Closing benediction

2. Evening Prayer 163
   a. The liturgical building block 163
   b. Structure 163

    c. The most important differences between the liturgical
       elements of evening prayer and morning prayer   164
       (1) Magnificat and Nunc Dimittis
       (2) Second and Third Collects

   Closing remarks about Morning and Evening Prayer   164

  3. Holy communion liturgy   165
    a. General statements in the opening rubric   165
       (1) Comparison with the Pre-Second Vatican Council . . .
    b. Opening collect   167
    c. Proclamation of the Ten Commandments   167
    d. Two collects for the royal government   168
    e. Rubrics   169
    f. Quotations from Scripture in the introduction
       to the offertory   169
    g. Prayer for the church militant   170
       (1) The emphasis on the divine word
       (2) Transitoriness of this life, with its misery
       (3) Remembrance of the faithful dead
    h. Three exhortations   172
       (1) First exhortation
       (2) Second exhortation
       (3) Third exhortation
    i. Invitation   177
    j. Confession and absolution   178
    k. The four comfortable words   180
    l. Words of distribution   180
    m. First prayer of thanksgiving   181
    n. Second alternative prayer of thanksgiving   181
    o. Concluding remarks   183

D. Consequences of "Pura Doctrina" and "Purus Cultus"
   in The Book of Common Prayer of 1662   184

  1. Ecclesiological characteristics   184
    a. Catholicity   184
       (1) The concept of "catholic" of Ignatius

(2) Vincent's concept of "catholic"

(3) The concept of "catholic" of Cyril of Jerusalem

(4) Cranmer's understanding of "catholic"

(5) An important aspect of "catholic" with Calvin

(6) A few points in the understanding of
    catholicity in the BCP

(7) Comparison of the BCP with the conceptions
    of the earlier-mentioned catholicity of the
    patristic and of the Reformation

  b. The congregation   190

  c. Ecumenicity   191

(1) The abundance of theological streams in the BCP

(2) The variety of theological streams in the
    service of unity

(3) The mission of the streams present in the BCP

2. Sacral aspects   195

  a. Definition of "sacral" based on the Biblical conception   195

  b. Sacrality according to Harvey Cox   197

  c. Adoration   200

(1) In Morning Prayer

(2) In Evening Prayer

(3) In the Holy Communion Service

  d. Romantic peculiarities   206

  e. What serves for adoration   210

(1) The speech used in the BCP in Morning
    and Evening Prayer

(2) Gestures

(3) Liturgical vestments and cloths

    (a) Vestments for Morning and Evening Prayer

    (b) Vestments for holy communion

    (c) Vestments for special occasions . . .

    (d) Symbolism of vestments in East and West
    churches

    (e) The liturgically vested choir . . .

    (f) Liturgical linen

(4) The sacral place and its appurtenances
   (a) The altar-like communion table
     and its accessories
   (b) Choir stall
   (c) Pulpit
   (d) Lectern
   (e) Seating facilities for the congregation
   (f) Church windows
   (g) The sanctuary light
   (h) Baptismal font

3. Effects of the liturgy   224
  a. Spirituality   224
  b. The form as support for the Word   224
  c. The holy communion liturgy as a dramatic
     presentation of salvation   225
  d. Daily Morning and Evening Prayer as a proclamation
     of the self-interpretation of Holy Scripture   226
  e. The true reasons underlying the sacrality
     of the BCP of 1662   227

V. The Oxford Movement (Tractarian Movement) as an Expression of Dissatisfaction with the Principle of Sola Scriptura and Its Consequences

A. The Anglo-Catholic Movement (Oxford or Tractarian
Movement) constitutes the antithesis to The Book
of Common Prayer of 1662   229

1. Introductory remarks   229

2. Its prelude in "The Tracts for the Times"   229

3. Some of the salient features of The Oxford Movement   230
  a. The Oxford Movement's understanding of Scripture   231
  b. Its understanding with reference to reason   234
  c. Ecclesiological features of The Oxford Movement   235
   (1) The true church as a historical, territorial,
     juridical, and ritualistic entity

(2) Doctrine with respect to sacraments

(3) Doctrine with respect to incarnation

d. Consequences of these ecclesiological conceptions   238

e. Remarks in summary   239

4. Newman's Tract XC and The Book of Common
Prayer of 1662   240

B. Fruit of The Oxford Movement in the nineteenth
and at the start of the twentieth centuries   243

1. The BCP furnished with lustre leads to revival   243

a. Robert Aitken   244

b. Richard Twigg   244

c. George Howard Wilkinson   245

d. Arthur H. Stanton   246

2. The Oxford Movement leads to the formation
of monastic brotherhoods and sisterhoods   247

a. The Community of the Epiphany in Truro   247

b. The Society of St. John the Evangelist   247

3. Questions and conclusions   248

C. Charles Gore and *Lux Mundi* as well as
William Temple compose the synthesis   250

1. Introductory remarks   250

2. Several examples of the continuation of Tractarian
traces in *Lux Mundi*   251

a. Incarnation and development   251

b. Church and tradition   252

3. Continuation of the theology of *Lux Mundi*
through William Temple   253

4. The BCP of 1927/28   254

D. The Anglo-Catholic elements converted through
John Robinson into a radically modernistic theology, as
background to the experimental liturgies and the ASB 1980   254

Some important characteristics of Robinson's theology   254

a. The incarnation and its consequences   254

    b. Development   258

    c. Demythologizing for the purpose of concentrating
       on the world   261

E. Experimental Liturgy Second Series and Series 3   266

  1. Partial elimination of Reformation substance   266

    a. Introductory rubric   266

    b. Ten Commandments   266

    c. Nicene Creed   266

    d. Twenty offertory verses   266

    e. Prayer for the church militant   266

    f. Exhortations   268

    g. The confessions in both formulas   268

    h. Preface   269

    i. Consecration prayer   269

    j. Liturgical matter after consecration prayer   270

    k. Agnus Dei   270

    l. Both alternative closing prayers   270

    m. Closing benediction   273

  2. The most important differences in respect to form
    in the two liturgies mentioned as compared
    with the canonical BCP   273

  3. Interpretation of the above-mentioned differences
    between the BCP 1662 and the alternative liturgies
    Second Series and Series 3   274

    a. Introductory rubric, exhortations, confession,
       and closing prayers   274

    b. The twenty offertory verses, prayer for the church
       militant, and the four comfortable words   276

    c. Decalogue   277

    d. Preface and consecration   277

    e. Interpretation of the formal dissimilarities   279

F. The Alternative Service Book 1980   280

  1. Introductory remarks   280

2. Morning Prayer 280

   a. Survey of liturgical components 280

   b. Observations respecting the most important
      liturgical components mentioned in survey (a)
      and their interpretation 281

        Reference 1: Declaration on the meaning
          of the service 281

        Reference 2: A Biblical sentence which is to be
          taken from a given selection 282

        Reference 5: Confession or choice of
          alternative confessions 282

        Reference 6: Absolution 285

        Reference 7: Opening sentences with
          the minor Gloria 286

        Reference 11: The congregation speaks a response ... 286

        Reference 12: Benedictus or the Benedicite,
          Omnia Opera or the hymn great and wonderful .. 286

        Reference 14: Response of the congregation 286

        Reference 15: Opportunity for the sermon 286

        Reference 16: Te Deum or Gloria in Excelsis 286

        Reference 20: Closing sentences 287

        Reference 21: Collect for the day 288

        Reference 22: Collect for peace 288

        Reference 23: Collect for grace 289

        Reference 24: State prayers and freely
          selected prayers 290

        Reference 25: Prayers of benediction 290

      Balance sheet 291

3. The Order for Holy Communion Rite A 294

   a. Survey of liturgical components 294

   b. Observations respecting the most important
      liturgical components mentioned in survey (a)
      and their interpretation 295

        Reference 4: Decalogue or summary 295

Reference 5: The transitional words
to the confession   296

Reference 6: Confession   296

Reference 7: Absolution   296

Reference 8-10: Kyrie and Gloria as well as
collect for the day   297

Reference 17: Nicene Creed   297

Reference 18: Intercessions and thanksgivings:
The great intercessory and thanksgiving prayer   297

Reference 19: Prayer of humble access
and its alternative   304

Reference 20: Proclamation of the peace,
with alternatives   305

Reference 25: Eucharistic prayer, with
three alternatives   305

Reference 27: Words upon the breaking of bread   312

Reference 29: Words of invitation   312

Reference 30: Words of distribution,
with alternative   312

Reference 36: Benediction (with alternatives)   313

4. Apologetical reflections   313

Appendix on the explanation of liturgical terms   322

Bibliography   326

Closing summary   337

Notes   339

General index   376

FOREWORD

Looking at a familiar object from an unfamiliar angle can be an illuminating experience. It is so here. Anglicans like myself are familiar with the domestic approach to the 1662 Prayer Book—the approach, that is, which focuses on sources, craftsmanship, antique models, comprehensive policies, and related historical matters. But Dr. Leuenberger, with a continental heritage behind him, comes at the Prayer Book from the standpoint of dogmatics, spirituality, and pastoral motivation, asking what sort of worship and piety it was meant to express and foster. He calls Prayer Book piety "revivalistic" and "puritanical," meaning that at every point the worshipper's exercise of faith from the heart is called for in response to the continual detection of sin and declaration of grace which permeate the service forms. What he wants us to see is that Prayer Book worship is, first to last, justification by faith set forth in liturgy so that it might be reapprehended and reexperienced in regular acts of devotion. Is he right? He most certainly is. All Reformation piety and worship was pure Augustinianism, purged by being sifted through the meshes of justification by faith, and it was this that cautious Cranmer, egged on, as Dr. Leuenberger correctly explains, by the sharp minds of Martyr and Bucer and the personal force and vision of Hooper, embodied in his maturest liturgical work. Nor was it lost in 1662, however much Puritan pleas at the Savoy Conference were resisted. Reformed Augustinianism is thus the Anglican mainstream heritage of praise and prayer.

Is Dr. Leuenberger right to point to a wide motivational difference between the 1662 Prayer Book and the 1980 Alternative Service Book (to which he might have added the 1977 Book of Common Prayer of the Episcopal Church in the USA)? I am afraid he is, and I fear that Anglicans who trade their Augustinian birthright in worship for such specimens, not to say messes, of modern liturgical pottage will find a decade or two down the line, not that they have dosed themselves into new spiritual vigour, but that they have bled and starved themselves into new spiritual weakness. May it not be; but rational reflection makes me fear the worst.

Because of the importance of these points, I commend Dr. Leuenberger's discussion to Anglicans generally, to all who care about the Reformation legacy in worship, and indeed to all who desire the good of the church and the glory of God.

JAMES I. PACKER

PREFACE

Various periods of study spent in the Anglo-Saxon world have made me aware of the unique impress of Protestantism in its Anglican form. In the present work interest is focused especially on the liturgy book of the Church of England, The Book of Common Prayer of 1662.

1. HYPOTHESIS OF THE WORK

It is worthy of note that the sixteenth-century liturgical formulas of today's "canonical" book of liturgy of the Church of England embody many elements which with respect to substance as well as form are encountered in the revivalistic movements of the eighteenth, nineteenth, and twentieth centuries. These elements occur in a particularly concentrated form in the three principal liturgies for morning and evening prayer as well as in holy communion.

The question arises: whence came these elements which are so typical of the theology of the revivalistic movement as well as for their practical use in evangelization meetings?

Our objective then is to trace the source of these revivalistic elements and to reveal how they reached The Book of Common Prayer of 1662.

Accordingly we intend to present the history of the maturing of this development to its ultimate state, the "canonical" prayer book of 1662. A further objective is to bring to light the prime mover in revivalistic spirituality, namely, puritanism. After a thorough analysis of the revivalistic elements in the BCP[1] of 1662 mention will be made of the fruit which this puritan-based revivalistic spirituality has produced.

In doing this the objective will be illuminated upon its positive side. However, this work also recognizes its obligation to disclose the negative side: what happens when more and more forces gain a success in which the genuine Reformation inheritance of the revivalistic Book of Common Prayer is surrendered to a "complexio oppositorum" sympathetic to Roman Catholic tradition?

For the purpose of giving an answer thereto, this work closes with an analysis of some recent Anglican experimental liturgies and an alternative service book.

2. EXPLANATION OF THE FUNDAMENTAL CONCEPTS

a. "The Book of Common Prayer"

The Book of Common Prayer of 1662 is the subject under discussion. By "The Book of Common Prayer" is understood the until today never repealed liturgical prayer book of the Church of England dating from 1662, which was authorized by the House of Commons. This Book of Common Prayer contains the most important rituals for the ecclesiastical life of the English Church, such as the daily morning and evening services and the liturgy of holy communion. Also included therein are the so-called casuals, which are the rites of baptism, confirmation, marriage, and burial. Even the consecration rituals for deacons, priests, and bishops are present in this all-inclusive prayer book.

As a result, this Book of Common Prayer is not just a concern of monks, as was the breviary, or priests' affairs such as the Middle Ages book of the mass, but instead it belongs to the general public. Likewise The Book of Common Prayer is, so to speak, a home devotional manual which belongs, like the Bible, in every Anglican family.

b. "Revivalism"

By the term "revivalism" is meant that theological concept which emphasizes a conversion and personal acceptance of salvation in Jesus Christ by making a decision, and which also attaches special importance to the gathering of the faithful into a loving fellowship. Revivalistic mentality places missions very much in the foreground and proclaims loyalty to Holy Scripture as a force convicting men of their sins. It is a property of the revivalistic mentality to accentuate repeatedly repentance, rebirth, sanctification, and bearing witness. Biblical piety is here the principal theme.

It is interesting that the term "revivalism" was not yet formally established in the sixteenth century, but as far as the substance goes revivalistic spirituality began to blossom especially in the Anglo-Saxon area through the Reformation emphasis on "sola scriptura" two hundred years before the classical revivalistic movement in Europe and America.[2]

Undoubtedly the most important root in the origin of "revivalistic" spirituality is the evangelistic preaching of the apostles Peter and Paul and others which the New Testament clearly reveals to us. The missionary atmosphere in the primitive church was thoroughly "revivalistic."

Only at the time of the Reformation was the soil again prepared in which the "revivalistic" spirit might flourish.

It is helpful to a clearly understood definition of the "revivalistic" concept to make mention of pietism which arose in the eighteenth century. One great revivalistic movement in Europe, America, and in the mission fields has been reflected in a type of piety which has been designated, particularly in German-speaking areas, as "pietism." Revivalistic theologians of the Reformation period such as Martyr, Bucer, and Hooper, and early puritanism, were rooted solely in Holy Scripture; such was not the case with pietistic devoutness in German cultural circles. Pietism was rooted too in Middle Ages mysticism and in spiritualism.[3] Pietism is a special form of revivalistic theology.

In our context we understand "revivalism" as a dynamic manner of approach setting forth the essentials of Biblical faith in a demanding as well as in an enticing way, so that one is lead, as already stated, to repentance, rebirth, sanctification, giving one's witness, and to a loving fellowship with the faithful. The term "revivalism" thus deals with substance as well as method in promoting faith.

The term "puritanism" also plays an important role in this work. For that reason it is necessary to define that term vis-à-vis the expression "revivalism."

c. "Puritanism"

Puritanism with its many facets first emerged as a movement in a clearcut way in the seventeenth century. Nevertheless the message of puritanism was previously found in the sixteenth century, being particularly evident in the figure of the influential English bishop, John Hooper. We will be concerned above all with the Hooper puritanical stamp. "Puritanism"[4] implies the following attitude: an emphasis on the pure Biblical doctrine without any mixture, hence the "pura doctrina," but also in addition a liturgy for divine services conforming to the Bible without consideration for human tradition, which type of liturgy is called "purus cultus." This belongs chiefly to the battle against paganism, which reveals a Zwinglian influence.

Puritan mentality includes the idea of revivalistic spirituality. Nevertheless the terms "puritanism" and "revivalism" are not identical. The puritanical spirit is generally also revivalistic, but revivalistic spirituality need not in all circumstances be puritanical.

It can happen that great revivalistic theologians accept special doctrines in addition to the basic element of faith, and elaborate further as was partially the case with the Swabian fathers of pietism. Thus theologians like Christoph Oetinger, Michael Hahn, Johann Christoph Blumhart, and others at the end of the eighteenth and the beginning of the nineteenth centuries, who strongly defended the idea of revivalism, defended also universalism. By doing so they have to a certain degree withdrawn from "pura doctrina." On that score many examples could be cited such as the intense interest in occult phenomena of Oetinger, Oberlin, Michael Hahn, and Johann Christoph Blumhart.[5]

One encounters in revivalistic circles of Lutherans generally a great love and reverence for the altar and crucifix as well as for the bodily presence of the Saviour in the host. Thus we see in Wilhelm Löhe[6] and Claus Harms[7] representatives of a revivalistic theology combined with a great love for liturgy and sacramentalism. The Lutheran conception of "finitum capax infiniti" is for puritans with their emphasis on the "purus cultus" an impossibility. A further essential element of puritanism is the "pura vita." It is possible that the "revivalistic" spirit was present to a certain degree among the anabaptists of the sixteenth century, but at the same time the Biblical ethic, the "pura vita," was found to some extent lacking, for example, among the fanatical anabaptists in Munster, Westphalen, against whom Luther in particular had to fight.

Where "pura doctrina" is overly emphasized, orthodoxy eventually becomes rigid, at which point the "pura doctrina" comes off badly. Neglect of "pura doctrina" leads to fanaticism. Where "purus cultus" is ignored, magic-pagan elements throw their weight around.

Puritanism is that great force which on the one hand helped the revivalistic spirit to develop and on the other hand disciplined it with the curbs of puritanism which held itself responsible to church, state, and society and came to an understanding of history. As against it, pietism retains a disposition to retreat from the world and to some extent an indifference vis-à-vis dogma.

Although various types of puritanism have been developed, we lay emphasis on puritanism of the early phase in which in the person of John Hooper the concepts of "pura doctrina," "purus cultus," and "pura vita" were given a special impulse.

3. A CRITICAL SURVEY OF THE APPLICABLE LITERATURE

a. Reference The Book of Common Prayer

The First and Second Prayer Books of King Edward VI, London 1968.

The Book of Common Prayer of 1662, Oxford 1968.

Missale Sarum, ed. by J. Wickham Legg, Oxford 1966.

R. Aitken, *The Prayer Book Unveiled in the Light of Christ*, London 1863.

H. I. Bailey, *The Liturgy Compared with the Bible*, London 1857.

R. T. Beckwith, ed., *Towards a Modern Prayer Book*, Wallingford 1966.

A. Beesley, "An Unpublished Source of The Book of Common Prayer," *Journal of Ecclesiastical History* XIX (1968).

R. P. Blackenay, *The BCP in Its History of Interpretation*, London 1870.

John E. Booty, *The BCP of 1559*, University Press of Virginia 1976.

F. E. Brightman, *The English Rite, Being a Synopsis of the Sources and Revisions of The Book of Common Prayer*, London 1915.

Stella Brook, *The Language of The Book of Common Prayer*, Oxford 1965.

Peter Newman Brooks, "Stewardship in the Great Tradition," in *Ritual Murder*, edited by B. Morris, Manchester 1980.

G. H. Cameron, *Are We Loyal to The Book of Common Prayer and the Principles of the Reformation?* 1917.

E. Cardwell, *History of Conferences about the Prayer Book*, Oxford 1849.

J. W. Charley, "The Draft Order for Holy Communion (Second Series)," in *Towards a Modern Prayer Book*, ed. by R. T. Beckwith, Wallingford 1966.

G. Cuming, *The Godly Order, Texts and Studies Relating to The Book of Common Prayer*, London 1983.

J. J. Cuming, *A History of Anglican Liturgy*, London 1969.

Michael Davies, *Cranmer's Godly Order*, New Rochelle, N.Y. 1976.

G. Dix, *The Shape of the Liturgy*, Glasgow 1947.

J. Dowden, *The Workmanship of the Prayer Book*, London 1904.

T. W. Drury, *Two Studies in The Book of Common Prayer*, London 1901.

G. E. Duffield, *The Work of Thomas Cranmer*, Philadelphia 1965.

G. E. Duffield, "The Language of Worship," in *Towards a Modern Prayer Book*, ed. R. T. Beckwith, Wallingford 1966.

E. Evan, *The Prayer Book, Its History, Language and Contents*, London 1909.

D. Hague, *Protestantism of the Prayer Book*, London 1893.

G. Harford–M. Stevenson–J. W. Tyrer, eds., *Prayer Book Dictionary*, London 1925.

G. D. Kilpatrick, *Remaking the Liturgy*, London 1967.

David Martin, "A Plea for our Common Prayer," in *Ritual Murder*, ed. by B. Morris, Manchester 1980.

B. Morris, ed., *Ritual Murder*, Manchester 1980.

C. Neil, *The Tutorial Prayer Book*, London 1963.

Proctor & Frère, *A New History of The Book of Common Prayer*, London 1949.

L. Pullan, *The History of The Book of Common Prayer*, London 1949.

M. Ramsey, *The English Prayer Book 1549-1662*, London 1963.

C. E. Ratcliff, *The Liturgical Work of Cranmer*, three commemorative lectures delivered in Lambeth Palace, Westminster 1956.

b. Reference the Revivalism Theme

G. R. Balleine, *A History of the Evangelical Party in the Church of England*, London 1951.

Fr. Chr. Beardsley, *History of American Revivals*, New York 1904.

E. Beyreuther, *Erweckungsbewegung im 19 Jahrhundert*, RGG Vol. II, 1958.

L. E. Binns, *The Early Evangelicals*, London 1953.

Ludwig Hofacker, *Predigten* Vol. I, Lahr-Dinglingen 1977.

Gérard Itti, *Dans Quelle mésure Bucer est-il piétiste?* Strasbourg 1936. (Diss.)

E. M. Jung, "On the Nature of Evangelism in Sixteenth-Century Italy," *Journal of the History of Ideas* XIV (1953).

Otto Riecker, *Das Evangelistische Wort*, theol. diss., Heidelberg 1935.

M. Schmidt, "Die innere Einheit der Erweckungsfrömmigkeit im übergangsstadium zum Lutherischen Konfessionalismus," ThLZ 74, 1949.

C. H. Spurgeon, *Twelve Sermons on Soulwinning*, London 1881.

E. H. Sugdon, *The Standard Sermons of John Wesley*, Vols. I and II, London 1921.

Dieter Voll, *Hochkirchlicher Pietismus*, Munich 1960.

c. Reference Puritanism

Josef Chambon, *Der Puritanismus*, Zurich 1944.

Patrick Collinson, *The Elizabethan Puritan Movement*, London 1967.

W. Haller, *The Rise of Puritanism*, New York 1938.

E. B. Hulbert, *The English Reformation and Puritanism—with other Lectures and addresses*, Chicago 1908.

M. M. Knappen, *Tudor Puritanism*, Chicago 1930.

August Lang, *Puritanismus und Pietismus, Studien zu ihrer Entwicklung von M. Bucer bis zum Methodismus*, Neukirchen 1941.

T. Price, *History of Protestant Nonconformity in England from the Reformation under Henry VIII*, 2 Vols., London 1836-1838.

M. Schmidt, "Puritaner," in *RGG* Vol. V, 1961.

H. W. Schneider, *The Puritan Mind*, New York 1930.

H. Schöffler, *Die Anfänger des Puritanismus*, Leipzig 1932.

L. L. Schücking, *Die Familie im Puritanismus*, Leipzig and Berlin 1929.

G. S. Wakefield, *Puritan Devotion*, 1957.

W. M. S. West, *John Hooper and the Origins of Puritanism*, Zurich 1955.

The remaining bibliography follows in the appendix to this work.[8]

4. STATEMENT ON PROCEDURE

The procedure employed in the present work is the narrative of a development in church history which demarcates, so to speak, a framework within which occurs a systematic-dogmatic analysis.

The work will set forth the dynamic process from which as a result has emerged today's still "canonical" The Book of Common Prayer of 1662.

Chapter I treats of the liturgical cornerstone which has led to the emergence of the final "canonical" edition of 1662. This cornerstone or liturgical foundation is the prayer book of 1549. The Book of Common Prayer of 1549 is indebted for its origin to Thomas Cranmer whose church politics activity will be briefly described in order to make the liturgical solution of 1549 better understood as a compromise between Reformation and Roman Catholic theology.

Cranmer, unwilling to stop with a compromise solution, was moved to engage theological consultants from abroad to carry through a consequent Reformation in the Church of England. In Chapter II we set forth the most important basic concepts of theology of three prominent consultants, Peter Martyr Vermigli, Martin Bucer, and John Hooper. In the course of the presentation the hostility to compromise on the part of these theologians, with their accent on "pura doctrina," becomes clear. Hooper[9] in particular articulated Reformation-puritanical concepts in a practical pastoral way, for which reason we want to give an analysis of the elements of puritanism with examples from his sermons. In treating the theological concepts of Martyr and Bucer, their criticism of the BCP of 1549 is given. The theology of Cranmer, bearing the impress of his discussions with Martyr, Bucer, and Hooper, is set forth in Chapter III, with his new characteristic of hostility to compromise. This purified Reformation theology had to speak out in the new version of the prayer book of 1552. In our treatment of the new draft, we investigate Cranmer's theology as reflected in the liturgies for Morning and Evening Prayer as well as in the Holy Communion Service. A comparison between the BCP of 1549 and that of 1552 presents in a comprehensive way the principal differences between the two prayer books.

Chapter IV has the task of introducing those forces or powers which succeeded in preserving the BCP of 1552 and in integrating it into a new version with only a few changes. At the same time, puritanism with its complex influence as well as episcopalianism and the Restoration are mentioned. The BCP of 1662 by reference to its three principal rituals is treated as the fruit of these struggles, and the victory of puritanism can be perceived through an analysis of particular liturgical texts.

Where "pura doctrina" occupies the first rank, as is the case in the BCP of 1662, certain consequences also arise which we investigate. Ecclesiological characteristics such as catholicity, the concept of the congregation, and ecumenicity stand out in particular. These characteristics become understood in the course of the presentation as features bearing the stamp of Holy Scripture: in effect, "pura doctrina."

Because one speaks of "Holy" Scripture, a chief characteristic of the Bible must be its holiness. Indeed the "pura doctrina" as representing the Bible possesses as a consequence the attribute of holiness or sacrality. It then becomes appropriate to elaborate upon the idea of Biblical holiness and to point out how worship implies above all the sacral. Worship makes use of certain means of expression and symbols which reflect the sacred. In this connexion the speech, gestures, liturgical vestments, and place of the service with its important objects as well as the termination of a divine service will be discussed.

Chapter V introduces those theologians and churchmen who interpreted the BCP of 1662 in accordance with their sympathy for the church of the Fathers and the period of the Middle Ages and had great reservations in regards to the Reformation.

Consequently this suggests a brief survey of the origins of the Anglo-Catholic movement and its chief tenets. The Tractarian Movement mobilized chiefly at the beginning of the twentieth century those theologians who wanted to achieve a reconciliation between the theology of the Fathers as well as of the time of the Middle Ages, on the one hand, and the Reformation on the other hand. This "via media" is then briefly considered with its principal effects which are revealed in the emergence of alternative liturgies. The theological prerequisites immediately prior to the experimental liturgies and above all to The Alternative Service Book 1980 will be briefly set forth by reference to John Robinson, the most influential theologian of England in the waning twentieth century, and to the WCC (World Council of Churches). Robinson and the spirituality of the WCC are to be understood in this more as a trigger for the experimental liturgies and the ASB 1980[10] than as their actual cause. The actual cause is seen to be in the "via media" provoked by the Anglo-Catholic Movement.

After reference to the above, a detailed analysis is made of the principal rites in the experimental liturgies and in The Alternative Service Book 1980.

ACKNOWLEDGMENTS

I wish to express my heartfelt thanks to all those who have been in prayer for this work.

I particularly thank my doctor father, Prof. E. Brown, and the co-reviewers, Dr. Prins and Prof. E. W. Kohls, for their most valued suggestions for my work, without whose support and understanding my dissertation would never have been completed.

I wish to thank the entire theological faculty of Stellenbosch most heartily for having given me the opportunity to present my doctoral thesis.

My appreciation in great measure is owed to Prof. G. W. Locher also, who as an authority on Zwingli acquainted me with the Zurich-Reformed heritage in The Book of Common Prayer, and contributed his time and interest to my task.

I express my thanks to Prof. A. Lindt for his criticism which led to profitable revisions.

I am obliged to express my high regard for St. Stephen's House in Oxford where I was permitted to spend my semester abroad in 1966/67 and where the most important impulses to occupy myself with The Book of Common Prayer were received.

I am much indebted to my father-in-law who has devoted a great deal of time to a careful translation into English. I would like to express my sincere thanks to him.

Last but not least I must mention my beloved wife Eleanor who, chiefly by her moral support, contributed greatly to the completion of this work.

I. The Book of Common Prayer of 1549

A. REVIEW OF THE CONTENTS OF THE DIVINE SERVICES UNDER CONSIDERATION

The Book of Common Prayer of 1549 consists of the following formulas for divine services:

1. Morning Prayer or Matins[1]
2. Evening Prayer or Evensong[2]
3. Holy Communion[3]
4. The Litany[4]
5. Public Baptism[5]
6. Private Baptism[6]
7. Confirmation with a catechism[7]
8. Solemnization of Matrimony[8]
9. Visitation of the Sick[9]
10. The Communion of the Sick[10]
11. Burial of the Dead[11]
12. Purification of Women[12]
13. Ash-Wednesdaye[13]
14. Ordering of Deacons[14]
15. Ordering of Priests[15]
16. Consecration of Bishops[16]

In addition to the sixteen formulas for divine services mentioned above, the prayer book of 1549 contains a calendar with a plan for Bible reading for Morning Prayer and Evening Prayer, a table for Epistles and Gospels for each Sunday's communion service with the corresponding collects, as well as the Apostles' Days with the collects, lessons, and Gos-

1

pels belonging thereto. With this brief outline let us proceed with a short historical survey.

B. HISTORY OF THE ORIGINS OF THIS FIRST DRAFT

Britain became Christian in the course of the fourth century. After the withdrawal of the Roman troops in A.D. 402 the old British church, which enjoyed no connexion with Rome, sprang up in the western mountains of the main island. The Scotch-Irish church which was similarly independent of Rome arose in Ireland.

Almost two centuries after the invasion in 449 by the Angles and Saxons an Anglo-Saxon church oriented toward Rome came into existence under the influence of Augustine, the Benedictine monk sent to Britain in 597 by Pope Gregory the Great. The Synod of Whitby eventually in 664 became an important milestone by putting the seal of victory on the triumph of the Latin church institutions over the Celtic.[17]

As a result of the Romanizing of the Anglo-Saxon church the Roman liturgy was able to establish itself although liturgical elements of the former Celtic church structure were assimilated. Nevertheless there was still no strict order in the liturgy. In the same church were to be found various church service books side by side. In order to create some order in liturgical matters certain bishops declared the use of church services of their cathedrals to be obligatory for the entire diocese. The church services of the following three dioceses were particularly influential: the divine services of York, Hereford, and Salisbury. The Cathedral of Salisbury took over the leadership in liturgy.[18] The following important development took place in that spiritual center: the books needed in the celebration of the mass were assembled into one volume, the missal. Thus materialized the so called "Sarum missal." A short schematic description may serve as an introduction to the books in the combined missal:

The sacramentary: contains the unvarying text of the
mass with the canon[19]

The antiphonal or
gradual: contains the text of the sung mass

The lectionary: contains the Epistles and Gospels

MISSAL

2

organized in accordance with the
church year

The psalters framed in the early Middle Ages for the liturgical life in monastic circles received in the course of the centuries important admixtures which found their way into various books and evolved in the eleventh and twelfth centuries into the breviary. The following table sets forth those books joined together in the Salisbury tradition in the breviary:

The psalter	
The antiphonal: contains the sung as well as the spoken text from Scripture or other sources, which prescribed the arrangement of the psalms for the church year, as well as the responses	BREVIARY
Hymns: fourth- to seventh-century poetically composed songs of praise for the enrichment of monastic hourly prayers	

Additional liturgical books are included in the two volumes described below:

Catechumenical service	
Rites for public baptism	
Ritual for private baptism	
Ritual for marriage	MANUAL
Ritual for the anointing of the sick	
Burial liturgy	
Ritual for the purification of women after childbirth (Ordo ad purificandam mulierem post partum)	
Ordering of deacons	PONTIFICAL
Ordering of priests	
Consecration of bishops	

The liturgical books of Salisbury mentioned above, and their arrangement, figured prominently together with other factors in the composition of the BCP at first in 1549[20] and later in the BCPs of 1552 and 1662. Among the other factors which found usefulness in the develop-

3

ment of the BCP were those theological concepts of Reformation thinking which prevailed among Francis de Quinonnes and Hermann von Wied as well as the theological contributions of the well-known savants Bucer, Martyr, and Cranmer, who acted in their own way as heirs of the three principal Protestant types: those of Luther, Calvin, and Zwingli.

The Franciscan Francis de Quinonnes published in 1535 a revised edition of the Roman breviary from which unbiblical elements were eliminated. The psalter as well as the Old and New Testament lessons were to be given full play. Behind this lay the intent to make the breviary palatable to secular clergy so that these would increase their reading of it. This Franciscan's concern is reflected in the preface to all the principal editions (1549, 1552, and 1662) of the BCP.[21]

Hermann von Wied[22] (1477-1552), Archbishop of Cologne, opened himself to the Reformation and participated in the realization of an influential Church Agenda: this refers to the Cologne Church Agenda. This reflected the notable influence of Osiander's (1498-1552) Church Agenda for Nürnberg and Brandenburg to which Bucer also contributed. In the Cologne Church Agenda are found formulas for baptism, confirmation, marriage, communion, visitation of the sick, and communion of the sick as well as a burial liturgy.

Thomas Cranmer (1489-1556), the creative compiler of the BCP, drew extensively for the compilation of this liturgical masterpiece upon the useful ingredients of the divine service tradition of Salisbury and upon the Cologne Church Order. Thus the BCP is a synthesis of Reformation and Catholic elements.[23]

C. DRAFT OF 1549 AS A LITURGICAL OUTGROWTH OF THE CHURCH POLITICS OF THOMAS CRANMER

1. CRANMER'S CHURCH POLITICS IN HARMONY WITH HENRY VIII

Before we deal with the principal differences between the three editions of the BCP of 1549, 1552, and 1662, something should be said about Cranmer's personality so that one can better understand certain decisive key points in the BCP.

Thomas Cranmer, who was descended from landed gentry, grew up

4

under easy circumstances. His rearing in his parents' home had as a purpose, among other things, to make Thomas a man well versed in the ways of the world. The arts of riding and archery, in which Cranmer was somewhat accomplished, served this purpose. Important years of education followed, during which Cranmer studied at Jesus College, Cambridge. There he received his master's degree in the year 1514 for his studies of the ancient tongues and the humanists Erasmus and Faber. Consecration of Cranmer as a priest must have occurred in the years between 1516 and 1520.

Lutheran ideas came into circulation in Cambridge just before 1520. This provoked Cranmer to devote himself to a searching study of Scripture. Something of Cranmer's character is here revealed, in that he wanted to verify fully to what extent the new doctrines were legitimate.[24]

A receptivity to various theological trends which nevertheless remained disciplined by the Bible, as well as readiness to let himself be given political-diplomatic missions to be handled in foreign countries reveals another side of Cranmer. Selected incidents may throw some light on this:

In 1530 Cranmer traveled to Italy on a mission for Henry VIII to determine from professors in several universities what was the impact of the king's divorce of Catherine of Aragon. Henry VIII sent Cranmer in 1532 to Germany to promise Charles V his moral support in the presence of the Turkish danger. At the same time Cranmer had to negotiate with the emperor due to an extension of a trade agreement between England and Flanders. The Archbishop of Canterbury was forced to develop diplomatic ability to a high degree. Cranmer could observe how forthrightly the princely houses of Germany supported the Reformation. It therefore is not by chance that Cranmer advocated the divorce of Henry VIII on tactical grounds in order thereby to obtain the sympathy of the English king for the cause of the Reformation.

The German princes declared themselves to the Emperor Charles ready to help him against the Turks. Thus the princes on the Luther side obtained from Charles V permission temporarily to be able to carry on Protestant practices in their territories. Cranmer found the church political tactics of the German princes a positive confirmation of the correctness of his own diplomatic endeavours.

In Germany Cranmer carried on talks with John Friedrich of Saxony, Spalatin, and others. Cranmer's encounter with Osiander (1498-1552) was however of the most importance. He was able to persuade the latter in Nürnberg of the propriety of the divorce of Henry VIII. Cranmer may also have succeeded in winning one of Charles's court theologians, Cornelius Agrippa von Nettesheim, to endorse Henry's divorce.[25]

5

Cranmer received crucial impulses toward Lutheran theology from Osiander, whose niece he married.

Cranmer proved himself to be a man through whom diplomacy could serve in the Reformation for the accomplishment of scriptural truth. Something akin to the principle that "the end justifies the means" is to be found in Cranmer.

Henry VIII appointed Cranmer Archbishop of Canterbury immediately upon the latter's return to his homeland in the year 1533. In this position Cranmer was much later on to set the course for the welfare of his church when he near the end of the forties summoned some theologians of the highest rank to England. Among these the Italian Peter Martyr Vermigli (1500-1562), the German Martin Bucer (1491-1551), and the Pole John Laski (1499-1560) are particularly conspicuous. With these men Cranmer enriched not only the theological places of learning at Oxford and Cambridge but he also introduced thereby an international breadth as well as variety regarding theological types into the English church. Thus Martyr is primarily a representative of the Calvinistic tradition while on the other hand Bucer belongs to the most influential advocates of the South German Reformation. He envisaged alongside personal sanctification a change of politics as well.

John Hooper (1495-1555) during his studies in Zurich in 1547-1549 absorbed for himself through Bullinger a great deal of Zwinglian theology. After his return he proved himself a proponent of radical Reformation out of which emerged the puritans.[26]

Cranmer also knew how to digest and to make use of the Zwinglian-puritanical spirituality.[27]

The theologians mentioned above all had an effect upon the drafting of the BCP in its second edition of 1552, and hence on that of 1662, although it was Cranmer who knew how to spin with skill the various theological-liturgical threads. Cranmer reveals a further characteristic: his love for synthesis.

The first evangelical Archbishop of Canterbury went through various theological phases, but without their counteracting one another. W. Nyenhuis has produced evidence that Cranmer thought about holy communion originally in a Roman way, then at a certain period in a Lutheran way, and finally in a Zwinglian way.[28]

Cranmer's predilection for synthesis mentioned above became manifest chiefly in the edition of 1549. It is understandable that the first Protestant Archbishop of Canterbury, prior to reaching the summit of his Reformation maturity, would have had in mind in drawing up the first edition the great wide world of the kingdom and seafaring nation of England

and hence would seek to offer a theological breadth which took into account both Roman Catholic and Protestant elements. G. W. Locher expresses this in an apt way when he writes:

> Probably Cranmer has consciously sought (and found) a style which sets forth clearly the liturgical essentials and yet nevertheless leaves room in the church for various accepted theological alignments. . . . The archbishop of a mighty kingdom and of seafaring island folk thinks and leads in other dimensions than those of a middle class republican parish pastor.[29]

The BCP of 1549 was an interim solution which immediately caused Cranmer to feel obliged in discussions with Martyr, Bucer, Hooper, and others like John Laski and Pollanus to search for a fruitful and uncompromising Biblical result.

How earnest Cranmer was in his evangelical faith appears from the fact that he was ready to go willingly to prison because of his Reformation convictions. The three written retractions penned by Cranmer in the prison at Oxford should not cause us to become confused about his character.[30] His "recantations" give an insight into the great battle which the reformer may have fought out inside himself for the sake of truth. Cranmer had been bitterly ashamed of himself because of his recantations and had also given this a written expression.[31] In the year 1556 this great reformer sealed his faith with a martyr's death.

2. THE BCP OF 1549 WITH EMPHASIS ON ITS HOLY COMMUNION LITURGY

In external structure, that is to say in the sequence of its various divine service formulas, the BCP of 1549 is not substantially different from the canonical BCP of 1662. In comparison with the editions of 1552 and 1662 the table of contents of the BCP of 1549[32] indicates that there are some formulas lacking which are added in 1552 and 1662: the baptism of adults[33] and the anniversary of the coronation of the monarch.[34] In addition the psalter,[35] the prayers for various concerns,[36] and prayers for those at sea are lacking.[37]

The first Edwardian BCP[38] still bears middle English features in it. Also more of the church service elements of the Sarum book of liturgies (divine service formulas from Salisbury) are taken into consideration.[39]

Cranmer, following the example of the Lutheran revision of the breviary, selected from the hourly prayer book of the monastic breviary with its eight monastic liturgies (matins, lauds, prime, terce, sext, none, vespers, and compline),[40] two divine services: Morning Prayer and Evening Prayer. Its Catholic framework without a specific Reformation addition is particularly conspicuous in the BCP of 1549.

Cranmer selected for the compilation of his morning service typical liturgical elements of matins, lauds, and prime. For Evening Prayer (the evening service, or vespers) he chose ingredients from the Sarum vespers and compline.

The table below should make this clear:

Morning Prayer
(morning divine service or morning praises)

Lord's Prayer	
Versicle[41]	
Gloria[42]	Matins from Sarum
Psalm 95 (Venite)	(Salisbury)
Psalms for the appropriate day, with Gloria	
Lesson from the Old Testament	
Te Deum[43]	
Lesson from the New Testament	Lauds from Sarum
Benedictus[44]	
Kyrie[45]	
Creed	Prime from Sarum
Lord's Prayer	
Intercession	
Collect for the day[46]	Lauds from Sarum
Collect for peace	
Benediction	Prime from Sarum

Evening Prayer
(evening divine service or vespers)

Lord's Prayer	
Versicle	
Gloria	Vespers from Sarum
Psalm of the day, with Gloria	
Lesson from the Old Testament	
Magnificat[47]	
Lesson from the New Testament	Compline from Sarum
Nunc Dimittis[48]	

8

Kyrie
Creed
Lord's Prayer
Intercessions   } Vespers from Sarum
Collect for the day
Collect for peace
Collect for grace   } Compline from Sarum

In connexion with Morning and Evening Prayer, which later on will be analysed more thoroughly, a noteworthy observation is that in the edition of 1549 there is lacking any confession of sin and any corresponding absolution. (The Sarum breviary, being within the Roman tradition, recognizes for most hourly prayers no true penitence section. We find an exception in the confiteor[49] of compline.) There is here expressed something which reveals a tendency in the thinking of Catholicism in the Middle Ages: man, at his innermost core, is good. This core is the intellect and the spiritual abilities of man which have not become depraved by the fall of man.[50] Sin is therefore understood more as a state of disease. Comparison with the editions of 1552 and 1662 will provide more enlightenment thereon.

In the 1549[51] holy communion many vestiges still remain which reveal medieval thinking of the high scholastic tradition. This shows itself clearly in the complex of prayers which in the eucharistic liturgy is known as the canon. The term "canon" is used there because these prayers, assembled as a unit, remain generally unchanged and thus constitute a fixed ingredient of the communion service. The canon of the BCP of 1549 agrees in its essential elements with those of the Sarum eucharist and likewise therefore with the Roman structure of the mass.

The elements of the Roman canon are:[52]

Introductory dialogue of the Sursum Corda[53]
Preface with Sanctus and Benedictus[54]
Prayer for the acceptance of the sacrifice
Prayer for the living and dead saints
Consecration section with words of institution
Anamnesis with prayer again for acceptance of the sacrifice[55]
Prayer for the blessed receiving of the sacraments
Remembrance of the dead again and prayer for communion with the saints
Doxology

In the Holy Communion Service of 1549 we still find liturgical riches such as the Introitus[56] and the Agnus Dei[57] which are no longer present in the editions of 1552 and 1662. We want to explain some elements contained in the first Edwardian prayer book communion service differing from Reformation conceptions. Thus the prayer for the saints reads:

. And here we do geue unto thee moste high praise, and heartie thankes, for the wonderfull grace and vertue, declared in all thy sainctes, from the begynning of the worlde: And chiefly in the glorious and moste blessed virgin Mary, mother of thy sonne Jesu Christe our Lorde and God, and in the holy Patriarches, Prophetes, Apostles, Martyrs, whose examples and stedfastnes in thy faith . . . graunt us to folowe.[58]

In the prayer for the dead it says in closing:

We commend unto thy mercye all other thy seruauntes, which are departed hence from us, with the signe of faith and nowe do reste in the slepe of peace: Graut unto them, we benede thee, thy mercy, and euerlasting peace.[59]

Immediately prior to the words of institution appears a consecration prayer with epiclesis, i.e., with a prayer to the Holy Ghost for the consecration of the communion elements. At the same time the celebrant in accordance with the rubric[60] makes the sign of the cross over the bread and wine:

Heare us we besech thee; and with thy holy spirite and worde, vouchsafe to blesse and sanctifie these thy gyftes, and creatures of bread and wyne, that they maie be unto us the bodye and bloude of thy moste derely beloued sonne Jesus Christe.[61]

In the prayer for the acceptance of the sacrifice after the anamnesis we read:

Yet we beseche thee to accepte thys our bounden duetie and seruice and commaunde these our prayers and supplicacions, by the Ministery of thy holy Angels, to be brought up into thy holy Tabernacle before the syght of thy dyuine maiestie.[62]

The strong emphasis on Mary in the prayer for the saints reflects the concept of a mediating entity between God and man. An intercession for the benefit of the dead becomes comprehensible upon the postulate that man being at heart good is not wholly dependent upon the expiatory sacrifice of Jesus. Therefore there are also credits such as intercessions which can have an influence on the fate of the dead.

In the consecration prayer with epiclesis the concept is implied that the working of God's benediction depends upon a formula spoken at some particular place in the liturgy.

Confidence in a system of mediation is revealed with particular clarity in the intercessory prayer for the acceptance of the sacrificial offering in connexion with the anamnesis. Angels bring the prayers as gifts of sacrifice before the throne of God.

The formulas for child baptism, visitation of the sick (anointing of the sick) and the service of thanksgiving of women after childbirth reveal yet again a powerful sacramental attitude. A theology based on sacramental thinking understands the affairs of God thus that He binds Himself to particular symbols which appeal to the senses so as to work for men through these. To such symbols as bread and wine, oil, white garments, candles, etc., can be ascribed a particular independent function in the sense of an "ex opere operato."

In the public baptism of children this sacramental approach is particularly evident when the priest, after their answers[63] have been given by the godparents to his questions, wraps the white christening robe about the baptized infant as a guarantee of innocence and afterwards anoints the forehead of the child with the chrism:

> Take this white vesture for a toke of the innocencie, which by God's grace in this holy sacramente of Baptisme, is giuen unto thee.[64]

> He vouchsaue to annoynte thee with the unccion of his holy spirite, and bring thee to the inheritaunce of euerlasting lyfe.[65]

Oil likewise plays a role in the divine service at home beside the sickbed:

> As with this visible oyle thy body outwardly is annoynted: so our heavenly father almyghtye God, graunt of his infinite goodnesse, that thy soule inwardly may be annoynted with the holy gost, who is the spirite of al strength, coumforte, reliefe and gladnesse.[66]

In the first Edwardian prayer book the form for the thanksgiving after childbirth bears a title which betrays somewhat the idea of a ritual cleanliness, or rather uncleanliness: "Purification of weomen." In accordance with this service the mother has to offer her white baptismal garment as a sacrificial cleansing (chrisom).[67]

The misconception that this BCP of 1549 displayed a predominantly Catholic character should however be avoided. In this edition of 1549 Cranmer introduced the spirit of the Reformation throughout, although he

11

at the same time let stand a few vestiges of Catholic thinking as well as ideas currently in vogue. We have just investigated these vestiges briefly.[68]

Thomas Cranmer brought in Martin Bucer to make an appraisement of this prayer book of 1549 which he, Cranmer, had compiled by himself. Peter Martyr Vermigli also expressed his opinion thereon. Bucer delivered a profound critique on the BCP of 1549 in his "Censura." Two prominent Anglican bishops, John Hooper (1495-1555) and Nicholas Ridley (1500-1555) associated themselves with it.

What points then did Martin Bucer criticize in particular? He dealt with those places which we have in part previously mentioned as vestiges of Middle Ages-High Scholastic tradition. Bucer also spoke out against gestures of kneeling and of making the sign of the cross, as well as against the use of eucharistic vestments.

Cranmer took these objections of Bucer in the Censura as well as the critical comments of Martyr, Hooper, and Ridley to heart. Bucer also submitted the Censura in 1551 to the Bishop of Ely for his scrutiny.

Summarizing, we should record the following: the Censura, the critical advice of Martyr, the powerful influence of Reformation church service methods in an early puritanical direction through Hooper and Ridley (Bullinger's substantial influence), and finally the Strasbourg liturgy of 1551, translated into English by Valeranus Pollanus, produced the prerequisites for the second Edwardian prayer book of 1552.

II. Cranmer's Most Important Consultants in the Construction of a Genuine Reformation Book of Liturgies: Peter Martyr Vermigli, Martin Bucer, and John Hooper

In order to be able to understand the source of the historical and theological background of the BCP of 1552 this chapter sets forth only the most important theologians who quantitatively are considered to have had the most influence on Cranmer. Martyr's, Bucer's, and Hooper's influence exceeds by a wide margin the influence of a John Laski or a Valeranus Pollanus. For that reason we omit the last two named from our discussion.

A. PETER MARTYR AND THE DISTINCTIVE FEATURES OF HIS THEOLOGY[1]

1. BIOGRAPHICAL SKETCH AND GENERAL REMARKS

Vermigli, Peter Martyr (1500-1562), born in Florence to a wealthy well regarded family, became, against his father's wishes, in 1516 an Augustine in Fiesole, and from 1519 on studied ancient languages, Aristotle, and Scholasticism in Padua. At 26 he was nominated as reformer of monasteries belonging to his order and in that capacity he went to Naples where he came in touch with Juan Valdes and where he became deeply involved in the evangelical faith. Called as abbot to Lucca, he wanted like Savonarola to combine the renewal of faith with a political revolution in the life of the city, and he established a kind of Bible school. He fled from the inquisition in August, 1542, to Strasbourg, became an Old Testament professor, and got in touch with Bucer. Called in 1547 to Oxford by Cranmer, he became a co-founder of Anglican church doctrine. In 1553 the accession of Mary Tudor banished him again to Strasbourg. In 1556 he accepted a call to Zurich as professor. Vermigli worked through an intense correspondence for the Reformation in Poland and the building of the English church and also took part in the religious discussion in Possy. In the clear strength of the evangelical faith Vermigli devoted himself to an understanding between Luther and Reformed.[2]

Until now only a little has been written about the influence of Peter Martyr on the BCP. Isolated articles in theological periodicals in the Anglo-Saxon world furnish some material for our inquiry. Of more help are the extensive standard works on Martyr's theology which were published some years ago.[3]

Cranmer called Martyr to England as a theological consultant because he had probably received excellent references from Bullinger. Before his move to Oxford, Martyr resided as the guest of Cranmer in Lambeth Palace for several weeks.

Between November 1551 and April 1552 Vermigli stayed twice at the residence of the Archbishop. During this half-year period the outstanding Italian theologian was able to share many suggestions with his host Cranmer. Above all, Martyr exercised an influence upon his students during the nearly six years of teaching as a professor of Biblical exegesis at Christ Church College in Oxford.

Of particular note is the amazing similarity between Cranmer, Martyr, and Bucer touching their concepts and even in their terminology. One can scarcely resist the thought that these three learned churchmen amounted to a theological triumvirate. We find that all three placed an emphasis on the relation between the Word of Scripture, faith, and rebirth. One can easily account for the stress upon the Word and faith as generally good Reformation thinking, but the accentuation here placed on their association with a rebirth as well as the combination of leading Reformation ideas with adjectives in apposition[4] which produce a revivalistic style, seem to be something peculiar to the English Reformation, and to its three chief architects.

2. ROOTS OF MARTYR'S REVIVALISTIC THEOLOGY OF THE WORD, OF FAITH, AND OF A REBIRTH[5]

The typical basic concepts of Word, faith, and rebirth, with their mutual interaction, are clearly expressed in Martyr's works written for the English church. To these belong the exegetical lectures delivered in Oxford on the Epistle to the Romans and First Corinthians.

He produced the very comprehensive work on holy communion, the "Defensio" in his exchange of opinions with Stephen Gardiner. Martyr dedicated the work to Queen Elizabeth I (1558-1603). This long treatise was published in Zurich in the year 1559. We will quote from it later on. For the present its principal theme ought to become evident, so as to reveal Martyr's theology, in a passage taken from his lecture on First Corinthians:

> We hold a twofold knowledge of God: but the one perception is common and by nature, which is thus slight and infirm, valid only to render men inexcusable. . . . The other is that through faith, and depends on the Word of God and divine revelation. And this, which alone brings rebirth through Christ, is thus effectual, to transmute souls and make us partakers of the divine nature.[6]

The connexion between Word, faith, and rebirth becomes clear in the above quotation. These elements are not unusual in the great revivalistic sermons of the eighteenth and nineteenth centuries. We are interested wherein lie the roots to this sort of theological alignment of Martyr. The explanation thereof lies in the decisive years of apprenticeship which Vermigli spent in Naples from 1537 to 1540. Martyr, as an educated Augustine monk, came into contact in Naples with fashionable circles which cherished concerns for the revival of faith.[7] To these circles belonged people like Juan Valdes (1500-1541), Vittoria Colonna (1492-1547), Flaminio, and others.

Some important basic features of Italian revivalistic circles:

a. Renewal of the Inner Man

Informative material on the Italian revivalistic movement is found in an article by E. M. Jung.[8]

Based on her studies E. M. Jung determined that this Italian spiritual movement was not primarily devoted to the outer reform of the church, but rather to a new life within men.

Evangelism was no theological system and no pious organization, but a new religious attitude. . . . It was not so much interested in a dogmatic or ecclesiastical reform, as in the renewal of the interior man.[9]

b. Accent on the Depravity of Man

Acknowledgment of the guilt of man toward God blossomed out anew in these evangelistic circles. The picture of mankind permeated with humanistic optimism was shattered. Mistrust with respect to the ability of man gave place to a strong trust in the immense grace which saves the lost sinner. Something of the Soli Deo Gloria can be said to come to light in this.

> Both [protestantism and evangelism] developed out of the passionate search of individual souls for justification and salvation. Both were reactions against the intellectualism and optimism of the preceding humanistic age. . . . Both distrusted human abilities and the value of human works, emphasizing instead divine grace in order to glorify the omnipotence and mercy of God.[10]

c. Accent on God's Pure Word and the Responsibility of Man

The conviction was championed that the Word of God stands above church doctrine. Equally, the opinion prevailed in these circles that the individual man must rely on his own insight, freeing himself from the priest's intermediate role as intercessor.

> Both placed the pure word of God above the teaching of the Church, and preferred their own inspiration to dependence on the mediation of priests.[11]

d. Repudiation of Perfunctorily used Ritual Forms

As is typical of revivalistic spirituality they objected in these evangelistically oriented groups to the superficiality of the activity in divine services due to a mechanical unrolling of the liturgy. The disciples of this revival movement declared themselves in favor of a Christ-centred piety.

> Both abandoned the out-dated, superficial forms of devotion and tried to restore a simple Christocentric piety.[12]

16

e. Spiritualizing of the Ecclesiastical Concept

This feature is particularly characteristic of revivalistically oriented circles. A mistrust often exists with respect to the concept of the church in which the outer visible structure, with its entire apparatus of canonical rule, becomes the governing factor. In opposition to this should be stressed the fellowship among the faithful as the church constituting factor, in which legitimate aspects of the church as regards its organization frequently become undervalued.

> Evangelism dreamed of a spiritual Church which should be the mother of all the faithful and the community of the saints, rather than an organization of secular power.[13]

f. Aristocratic Mentality

Many cultured aristocrats belonged to this Italian revival movement. Its supporters distanced themselves from any revolutionary action such as iconoclastic measures. Love of the esthetic was present throughout. With this strong individualistically stamped piety was contained a spiritual attitude which accorded well with the aristocratic character. The aristocrats knew better how to remove themselves from a church of the "masses."

> Evangelism lacked all revolutionary character. It was an exclusive religion for the aristocratic elite. . . . Evangelism was basically a religion for the salons of distinguished ladies like Vittoria Colonna, Giulia Gonzago, . . . for the studies of humanists like Valdes, Flaminio, for the palaces of cardinals like Contarini, Sadoleto. . . . The return to the pessimistic view of christianity, as expressed in the Reformation, did not lead the followers of Evangelism to iconoclasm . . . on the contrary, it merged with a high aesthetic culture.[14]

g. Love of the Structure of the Ancestral Church

Despite a critical attitude toward the superficiality of its religious life, disciples of the Italian revival movement remained loyal to their ancestral church. Their program was by no means intended to destroy the historically developed form. They were much more concerned, in view of the growing alienation, to oppose to it a spirituality of introversion.

They thought that the Church could and must be reformed through a return to the spirit of the Gospels, but they did not want to shake its historical structure.[15]

h. Fondness for Ecumenical Scope

E. M. Jung mentions in her article a quotation from Juan Valdes which reflects very aptly the spirit of that movement, in which the lay element received a significantly higher worth. Apparent in this quotation from Valdes is a comprehension of Biblical ecumenicity which is not bound up in the lockboxes of this or that confessional group, but instead embraces all Christians who stand in the faith and in sanctification.

> The Church is not limited to this or that Christian communion: it is wherever Christ is. It has always been, since Christ sent his Spirit among men, because there has always been faith in the earth, and it consists of those Christians who have sufficient faith to be sanctified.[16]

Salvatore Corda alludes repeatedly in his dissertation to the connexion between Martyr's theology and the Italian revivalistic movement:

> An earnest, orthodox religion of the heart: this was the type of spirituality that Vermigli shared in Naples. . . . The point we wish to make is that Vermigli's alignment with Evangelism in Naples basically resulted in a new type of piety and religious sentiment and not in a new theological system implying a rejection of dogma. . . . The type of religiosity embodied by Vermigli when he arrived in Strassburg . . . was basically that of Italian Evangelism.[17]

3. SOME PRINCIPLES OF MARTYR'S THEOLOGY OF THE SACRAMENTS AND THEIR INFLUENCE ON THE BCP

Martyr took an active part in the revision of the BCP of 1549. Cranmer appreciated his support. Bucer submitted his *Censura* to his friend Vermigli. Martyr knew the BCP in the Latin translation of John Cheke.[18] That Martyr concerned himself with the revision of the BCP of 1549 arises out of a letter written by Martyr to Bucer.

a. Objections of Martyr to the BCP of 1549 re the Communion of the Sick and the Theological Conception Revealed Therein

Martyr composed a critical commentary on the BCP of 1549, as may be seen in the letter addressed to Bucer:

> At this time nothing could happen more desirable or agreeable to me than that I should see your "Censura" on the Book of Sacred Offices. I therefore return you infinite thanks for your condescension in sending it to me, that I also would myself state my opinion respecting it. And when . . . the version of Mr. Cheke was given me for perusal, I noted those things which appeared to me worthy of correction, as far as I was able to collect them from that translation.[19]

(1) Communion Is a Congregation Event

It is obvious from this letter that Martyr's lost commentary must have concerned itself exhaustively with the communion of the sick. Vermigli objected that, based on this formula[20] the patient received from the main Sunday service a consecrated host at home without a repetition of the words of institution. In this it becomes clear that for Martyr the celebration of holy communion must be an event in the presence of the congregation. As soon as the celebration is finished one can no longer speak in reference to the remaining bread about "Character Indelebilis" as a result of the consecration. Martyr stands here in the reformed tradition where, to the extent possible, all of that which can interfere with the act of faith through a magical interpretation is avoided. Plainly Jesus cannot be delivered to the patient in the host or in the bread based on a consecration accomplished long before. As an example one may not in keeping an appointment with another person be replaced by simply having one's photograph exhibited. It requires the production of a personal contact through the direct spoken word of speech. The priest must speak the words of institution there at the communion of the sick because Jesus speaks directly to both the pastor and the sick person, and thus wishes to make good his promise in Matthew 18:20. In this connexion Martyr writes:

> I have only wondered how you could have omitted to disapprove the order which is given in the Communion of the Sick, if it shall happen to be on the Sunday on which the Lord's Supper is celebrated, that the minister should in that case take with him a portion of the elements, and so should administer the Communion in the house of the sick person. In which mat-

ter it offends me that they do not there repeat those things which particularly belong to the Lord's Supper, since I agree with you in thinking that the words of the Supper belong more to men than to bread and wine. I stated that it clearly seems to me, that all things that are necessarily required for the Lord's Supper, should be both said and done in the presence of the sick person, of those who communicate with him.[21]

The BCP of 1552 took this criticism of Martyr seriously. Hence we also find later in the prayer book of 1662 that the words of institution are required in the formula for the Communion of the Sick.[22] In this matter consequently we are dealing with an important influence of Martyr on the BCP. S. Corda in his searching study on Vermigli's theology of the sacraments points therein to the character of the eucharist as an event, in contrast to the preservation of previously consecrated bread which is later chosen for the sick.

The sacrament is not a product that you can put aside for later use, but rather something that happens under given conditions.[23]

(2) Transformation as Inner Reality

Pronouncing of the words of institution is thus indeed important to Martyr since for him the transformation must be something inside, something occurring in the spiritual domain. The outer consecration then is simply an impulse in the sense of an analogous proceeding. The outer consecration of the elements through the speaking of the words of institution constitute for the faithful a symbol for that which should be an event inside the heart. Vermigli's objections with respect to the formula for the Communion of the Sick in the BCP of 1549 may have been already definite based on that theology which he some years later developed fully in his *Defensio*.[24] A quotation from that work may clarify Martyr's conception of the transformation as an inner spiritual reality:

Vel quod illa mutatio panis, qualiscunque tandem est, instituta sit in hunc tantum finem, ut efficiat, atque inducat quantum instrumenta possunt mutationem nostram.[25]

S. Corda remarks about the passage just quoted from the *Defensio*:

He improves upon his analogy, however by affirming that we are changed more than the sacramental symbols, both because we were originally

20

created in God's image and also because the sacramental change occurs not for its own sake, but in view of our transformation.[26]

Were the priest to deliver over to the sick some bread already consecrated, based on the view that the element possesses a Character Indelebilis, then clearly in Vermigli's conception the motive for a change of heart is lost.

b. Further Characteristics of Martyr's Theology of the Sacraments and Their Roots

As a former Augustine monk Vermigli is found in the spiritual tradition of the greatest Latin Church Fathers. His communion theology is therefore built upon the doctrine of Verbum Visibile. From thence comes the weighty conception of the proportion of analogy and the relation of proportions which is found in the Aristotelian ethic. Martyr wrote a commentary on the latter.

According to the conception mentioned above a proportion of correspondence is established between the material and the spiritual-sacred spheres. Thus occurs through the material symbols of the bread and wine an analogy to the spiritual reality in which the Holy Spirit acts as the catalyst of the process. Augustine produced the theological substance for this scheme of analogy through his theology of the Word. For Martyr, as a result, the Incarnatio Christi is of great significance.

(1) The Material Symbols in the Service as the Making of an Analogy to Spiritual Reality

Because of our frailty Jesus has become man to show the way to salvation by a material sign. In his commentary on Romans, Vermigli wrote in an illuminating way on this problem:

> For since we are weak, nor easily believe the promises of God, it was needful that his goodwill towards us should be signified not only by words, but also by things that could be offered to our sense.[27]

We men should become alert through analogies in the bodily sphere to certain truths of a spiritual kind. Martyr expresses himself thereon clearly in his commentary on 1 Corinthians 13:1:

> For we are framed in such a way that we are led to the knowledge of causes by their effects, and are trained to certain truths by similitudes.[28]

This analogy between the sensible and the spiritual sphere of divine truth does not function automatically. The Holy Spirit and the Word of God must also so intertwine that the proper relation between these two spheres can occur. McLelland points out with reference thereto that Martyr taught no functioning Analogia Entis independent of Holy Scripture:

> In a very clear passage Martyr points out that there is not sufficient natural analogy for us to comprehend the thing itself, for this there is required a constituting authority, the Word of God, and an effectual signification, the Holy Spirit's work.[29]

(2) Denial of the Bodily Real Presence and the Importance Thereof [30]

The denial of Jesus's bodily real presence in the elements, as well as the rejection of Manducatio Impiorum become comprehensible from the analogy doctrine, which is often connected with nominalistic thinking. The preservation of both spheres, namely the created-material and the uncreated-spiritual, is upheld by this conception of the doctrine of analogy, and the mixture of the two domains should be avoided by all means. The phenomenon of idolatry and pagan elements in general results from the mixing of the spiritual-sacred sphere with the material.[31] It is worthy of note that the Reformed tradition in general thought highly of the analogy doctrine.

The denial of the bodily real presence of Jesus in favour of the presence of Christ in the heart (soul) on the ground of a personal decision for him categorically demands a straightforward personal faith, in the revivalistic sense. A bodily real presence in the elements, indoctrinated independently of the attitude of the individual toward faith, can very easily lead to an understanding of Jesus as a dispenser of power in a magical sense by means of the bread and wine, as a result of which the encounter with Christ as a person proves to be almost imperceptible or nonexistent.

Just as with Cranmer, the belief that Jesus, since his ascension, indeed dwells in his heavenly abode is important to Martyr. The tarrying of Jesus in the glory "above" gives the churchgoer a vertical orientation from which results something of an awakening of faith. The Sursum Corda in the eucharistic liturgy contains a deeper meaning because of this. Martyr expresses himself on this in the following way:

Nos monemus nostros, ut in sacra Communione corda sua sursum subve-
hant: utque admonity symbolis visibilibus, animos ab illis ad coelum trans-
ferant.[32]

(3) Sacramental Symbols as Auxiliary Means
for Stimulating Faith

Although Martyr does not consider the sacraments as necessary to salvation,[33] since quite certainly faith is the absolute prerequisite,[34] they are
nevertheless important and should on no account be scorned. S. Corda remarks thereon:

> In Vermigli's system the spiritual eating begins with the work of the Holy
> Spirit, who uses sacramental symbols as an instrument to stir up man's
> faith.[35]

(4) Sacramental Symbols as Helps
to an Intensified Experience of the Word[36]

By the analogy doctrine of Martyr his pressing recommendation for the
taking of the sacrament as an intensified experience of the Word becomes
for the first time truly comprehensible. S. Corda clarifies Vermigli's conception strikingly when he writes:

> Thus the bodily eating of the sacrament is by no means superfluous or rela-
> tively unimportant for Vermigli. He understands it as a heightened form of
> hearing God's Word. . . . We should keep in mind, however, that according
> to Vermigli, the symbols added to the Word heighten the way of reception,
> but can not give more than the Word.[37]

Martyr's doctrine of the communion sacrament is linked by this
analogy principle as a faith awakening instrument and a seal of faith which
establishes the relatio and the communio between Christ and the faithful.

c. Influence of Martyr's Revivalistic Theology on the Overall Ritual of Holy Communion in the BCP[38] as Well as on the Thirty-nine Articles[39]

(1) The Three Exhortations[40]

Alan Beesley[41] has been able to show that the middle exhortation is, to the extent possible, an exact translation of Martyr's "Adhortatio ad Coenam Domini Mysticam" into beautiful liturgical English. Cranmer had the translation made. The first and third exhortations are conformed organically to the middle one. In the BCP of 1549 one is lacking, since only two exhortations are given. That now a new exhortation, even that of Martyr (in the BCP of 1552 it is located in the first position, in the prayer book of 1662 in the second position), is admitted to the BCP seems to be a corroboration of the revivalistic idea. It isn't out of the question that the exhortations in the prayer book of 1549 traced even then back to Martyr's suggestions.[42] Vermigli was living by 1547 in England where he spent his first three months in Lambeth Palace with Cranmer. Martyr in his lecture at Christ Church College in Oxford on the First Epistle to the Corinthians had dealt in particular with chapters 10 and 11 and their enlightenment respecting the communion question. What was said in that lecture on these chapters reveals an astonishing identity with the third exhortation. The conclusion is obvious that Martyr may also be the author of the third exhortation.[43]

(2) Confrontation of the Law and the Gospel in the Communion Service[44]

The question arises as to whether Martyr could have influenced Cranmer to let the first part of the communion liturgy be based on theological conceptions of the Law and the Gospel. In the BCP of 1552 the proclamation of the Decalogue comes immediately after the opening collect.[45] In this connexion one must refer to John Hooper who as a well-known covenant and Decalogue theologian should definitely share responsibility for placing the Ten Commandments at the beginning of the communion service, as we shall later seek to establish.[46] But the law is also important to Peter Martyr, and in his influential lecture as a professor at Christ Church College, Oxford, on the Epistle to the Romans he indicated those elements which in a Lutheran way accentuate the contrast between the Law and the Gospel, although Vermigli is a Reformed theologian:[47]

The Old Covenant is Law, the New is Gospel. . . . The Law contains the traditional doctrines which God gave to lead men to Christ. The Gospel is the power of God to Salvation: an expounder of the remission of sins through Christ. . . . This must then be the distinction, that those evangelical doctrines which are in the Old Testament Books describe the future and are a counter promise. Those in the New echo the Law and lead to this introduction: there it preaches penitence which the Law before pressed on those who believe.[48]

With Hooper the Decalogue is valuable in itself and not just for its leading one to, and its converting one to, the Gospel. The keeping of the Ten Commandments is a part of the Covenant agreement both in reference to the Old and to the New Covenant.[49]

The question arises did this combination of Hooper's and Martyr's elements in respect to their conception of the Law and the Gospel contain something like a seed from which grew Methodism with its emphasis on the method of a punctilious observance of the divine ordinances?[50]

(3) Predestination

Martyr's lecture at Oxford on the Epistle to the Romans is very rich in reference to the doctrine of predestination. Anderson supposes that Martyr had conversed with Cranmer in Lambeth Palace during the winter months of 1551-1552 on the complex question of predestination. Through this, impulses may have emanated from Martyr on the composition of the Seventeenth Article. The first draft of this brief dogma in the form of tersely compressed articles included forty-two articles. In this draft one did not find in the Seventeenth Article the addition that men are elected "in Christo." This important addition is first found in the second edition of the so called Thirty-nine Articles of 1563.[51]

One could suppose that this "in Christo" is due to Martyr whose thinking in his predestination doctrine was Christ centred. Perhaps Bullinger, with whom Martyr had an active theological contact, was behind this. The Second Helvetic Confession composed by Bullinger called special attention to the "in Christo" under the question of predestination in an emphatic way.[52] The conception of election in Christ is a basic postulate in revivalistic theology. We place the two texts in the Latin form opposite one another:

	Martyr,
Article XVII[53]	**Epistle to the Romans lecture**[53]

Praedestinatio ad vitam, est aeternum Dei propositum, quo ante iacta mundi fundamenta, sua consilio, nobis quidem occulto, constanter decrevit, eos quos in Christo elegit ex hominum genere, a maledicto et exitio liberare, atque ut vasa in honorem efficta, per Christum ad aeternum salutem adducere.

Dico igitur, praedestinationem esse sapientissimum propositum Dei, qua ante omnem aeternitatem decrevit constanter, eos, quos dilexit in Christo, vocare ad adoptionem filiorum, ad iustificationem ex fide, et tandem ad gloriam per opera bona, quo conformas fiant imagini filii Dei, utque in illis declaretur gloria.

4. FINAL OBSERVATIONS

a. Martyr's Importance to the BCP and the Church of England

It is within the area of the probable that Martyr brought to light his Italian revivalistic heritage in conversations with Cranmer. During his half year sojourn as the guest of Cranmer in Lambeth Palace from November 1551 to April 1552 decisive things must have occurred. If you compare the characteristics enumerated by E. M. Jung[54] of the evangelically oriented circle of the Italians of that date, with matters peculiar to the BCP,[55] they display a disconcerting similarity to each other. Additionally, in the BCP a love for the structure of the historically matured with reference to church and liturgy is obvious, together with the purging of the rank growth of pagan elements. There comes too from the BCP an interest in a religion of the heart within the sense of a power to change men through their relationship to Jesus. We find further parallel to the ideas of the revivalistic circles of Italy in The Book of Common Prayer in its stress on the absolute sovereignty of the Word of Scripture. Nor should one forget the esteem for the esthetic in The Book of Common Prayer, which reminds one of the aristocratic atmosphere of Italian revivalistic circles. Not to be overlooked is the ecumenical breadth of this common prayer book, which was also a typical feature of the evangelically oriented circle of Italian aristocrats.

We would like to add to these assertions made by E. M. Jung by putting the following question: Has Martyr truly passed on in innumerable stimulating conversations the Italian revivalistic spirituality which he has integrated into his theology?

b. Martyr's Influence on the Personalities among the English Church in Exile

Vermigli even after his flight from Bloody Mary still considered himself committed to England. Thus he sought contact with prominent personalities who during Mary's reign studied on the continent. Some of these fugitives later held the position of bishop under the Protestant Queen Elizabeth I (1558-1603). Among these are important personages such as Edwin Sandys (Bishop of Worcester), John Jewel (Bishop of Salisbury), Edmund Grindal (Archbishop of Canterbury), and John Parkhurst (Bishop of Norwich). Martyr corresponded with these personages who cherished and preserved the merits of the Reformation. Martyr was thus able to maintain his theological influence on the English church.

In Martyr's letters, so far as they have survived for us, the revivalistic concerns of Vermigli have not been directly expressed. However there are indirect inferences possible from those letters which important bishops like Sandys and Jewel have addressed to Martyr. These letters written in the years 1559-1562 express in various ways how greatly esteemed Martyr had become as a theological teacher in England. Thus John Jewel writes in a letter dated November 2, 1559:

> Yesterday, as soon as I returned to London, I heard from the Archbishop of Canterbury that you are invited hither, and that your old lectureship is kept open for you.[56]

John Jewel assured Martyr that even Queen Elizabeth was very interested in his return to England.

> She was altogether desirous that you should by all means be invited to England, that as you formerly tilled, as it were, the university by your lectures, so you might again water it by the same.[57]

The laudatory and appreciative words of Bishop Jewel indicate that it must not have been simply a matter of dry theological lectures with Martyr, but it had been a matter of mediating a knowledge which granted life and changed one's attitudes. The expressions "tilled" and "water" used by Jewel seem to point to lectures in a revivalistic spirit. It is interesting that later on Jewel in a letter of November 16, 1559, expressed what Martyr could expect in the event of his return:

> Both our universities, and that especially which you heretofore cultivated with so much learning and success, are now lying in a most wretched state of disorder, without piety, . . . without a teacher, without any hope of revival.[58]

Of particular note are the expressions "piety" and "revival" appearing in the above quotation.

c. Martyr's Patristic Knowledge

That Vermigli, with his immense knowledge in the field of the patristic, encouraged Cranmer to remain true to the Church Fathers is not insignificant. Anderson calls attention to the fact that Cranmer's and Martyr's lists of the (for them) most important authorities among the Fathers revealed a remarkable coincidence.[59]

d. Martyr's Recommendations for a New Ecclesiastical Law

Based on his studies Anderson has ascertained that direct influences of Vermigli are to be attributed to the new ecclesiastical laws after the repeal of the Codex Iuris Canonici.[60]

A recapitulation of Martyr's theology in a few sentences will follow the treatment of Bucer and Hooper.

B. FUNDAMENTALS OF BUCER'S THEOLOGY AS REVEALED IN PARTICULAR BY EXAMPLES FROM HIS *CENSURA*

INTRODUCTORY REMARKS

Cranmer invited the great Strasbourg reformer Bucer (1491-1551)[61] to England in a letter dated October 2, 1548, to participate in bringing about the Reformation there. Bucer had maintained contact with the island by letter long before he emigrated to England. Bucer was known among Anglo-Saxon theologians through his translation into English of "Hermann's Consultation."[62] To be sure, it was Bucer's *Censura* which was of particular importance to Cranmer. This is an appraisal of The Book of Common Prayer of 1549. Bucer received the commission for writing this piece from Goodrich, Bishop of Ely.[63]

The impulses generated by the *Censura* led, in an important degree, to the revised edition of the BCP in 1552. You are reminded that the BCP of 1662 has remained in general the same as that of 1552. Today's form of the BCP would be unthinkable without the *Censura*. We want now, with the help of the *Censura,* to point out some important Reformation concepts which furnish a further contribution to the understanding of the revivalistic elements in the BCP. The quotations are taken from the English translation of the *Censura*.[64] Bucer wrote the *Censura* between 1549 and 1551, during his two-year residence in Cambridge. He completed it two months before his death.

Holy Scripture plays a central role with Bucer. With him it passes judgment on everything. The goal in Bucer's critical exposition on the BCP of 1549 is the awakening of faith.

1. MEASURES TO BE TAKEN FOR AWAKENING AND PROMOTING FAITH

a. General Understanding Reference Divine Services

Just for the very reason that a divine service exists for the spread of the faith, just so must the service activities be understandable for each one.

b. What Is Based on Holy Scripture Is God's Doctrine

Evidently Bucer means here that the exposition of Scripture in the sermon be accepted as divine instruction.

> This requires that whatever is taught from holy scripture is received as the teaching of God.[65]

29

c. What Is Spoken in Prayers or Thanksgiving Must Proceed from a Heartfelt Faith

The churchgoer must thus be made aware that a routine running off of prayers in the form of requests and thanksgiving which are made without taking any interest therein has no power to kindle faith:

> This requires that whatever is said in the prayers and thanksgivings is said from the faith and the heart of everyone present as in the sight of God.[66]

d. The Conduct of the Appointed Minister during the Divine Service Requires a Devotional Attitude

Bucer encourages the priests to recite the prayers, psalms, and lessons with greater solemnity and devotion and indeed with clearer and more expressive voices. This becomes clear in the following text:

> Clearly therefore it is a matter of absolute necessity that the ministers of churches should recite these prayers and psalms and lessons with the greatest solemnity and devotion, in a clear and expressive voice. . . . By these means faith will be effectively renewed.[67]

Of particular interest is Bucer's concern that liturgical prayers themselves should be the expression of a personal faith which must become noticeable in the vocal expression of the celebrant. The concepts of "solemnity" and "devotion" which come to the surface in the text above point to sacral[68] dignity and reverence, while the expression "clear and expressive voice" relates more to the restrained inner faith of the celebrant.

e. Church Discipline

Bucer appraised the opening rubrics of the communion liturgy of 1549[69] very positively since these required of the communicant that he, in the event of a wicked life-style or irreconcilable attitude because of involvement in disputes, first bring the awkward situation into order through repentance and reconciliation. These measures of church discipline are beneficial for the edifying of faith:

> These directions will certainly promote the building up of faith in the people of God. . . . The spirit of Christianity is lacking in people who, having of-

30

fended the Church of Christ by their open wickedness, refuse to declare to the churches their true repentance, or decline either to make amends to brethren they have harmed, or to show themselves forgiving to those who have harmed them. These . . . directions are of the greatest value to the health of the Church.[70]

These rubrics were first admitted in an abbreviated way in the BCP of 1552 and from there found their way into the canonical BCP of 1662.

In a like way Bucer ascribed special importance to a service of repentance on Ash Wednesday. In the BCP of 1549 this service is called "The first daie of Lente, commonly called Ashe-Wednesdaye."[71]

This service of repentance has indeed been preserved in The Book of Common Prayer of 1552 upon the urgent recommendation of Bucer, and thus it has then reached the BCP of 1662. There it is now called "A Commination or denouncing of God's Anger and Judgment against Sinners."[72] This service has the character of a collective church discipline in which the church members admonish and also reprove one another in a brotherly responsibility for each other's salvation. In Bucer's remarks about this service of repentance the following important aspect of faith comes to light: namely, the force of the community in a mutual responsibility in the sense of being a protector of one's brothers in the faith:

> This is a particularly wholesome ceremony, but I do not see why it should be used only on one day and not more often, at least four times a year. . . . But if it is our desire that the Lord Jesus should truly reign over us, it will be necessary that the whole discipline of penance and of the correction of sinners should be restored in the churches so that, to be sure, as the Lord and the Holy Spirit commanded, each man when he sees his brother secretely engaged in sin shall secretely admonish him and endeavour to gain him in the Lord.[73]

2. PRACTICES OBSTRUCTING FAITH

Bucer is critically opposed to ritual practices, though in a discriminating way. The criterion in his evaluation of ceremonials is simply whether they serve faith or not. In the appendix to the communion service of 1549[74] there are seven rubrics which Bucer submits to a withering criticism.

a. Unnecessary Ceremonial

In the first rubric an order is given that on Wednesdays and Fridays an abbreviated communion liturgy without the taking of communion by the congregation should occur. After the offertory verses the priest can then dismiss the congregation after a few supplementary prayers. Even though this does not constitute a proper eucharistic service the priest has to wear the robes.

Bucer sees in this interrupted termination of a church service, with its accompanying ceremonial of the vestments, a waste of energy because the purpose of building up faith cannot be accomplished in this way:

> What reason can be found in the word of God . . . , that this half Mass should be said at the Lord's Table in full array of Mass vestments? This evil must be shunned. . . . Our concern should be with things which can be depended on to build up faith in Christ, and not with a part imitation of things which we do not intend to complete.[75]

b. Representation in Matters of Faith

The fifth rubric required that at least one person besides the priest should be present at a communion service. If the person in question could not be present then any substitute was to take care of it. For Bucer a substitution in matters of faith is an impossibility.

> And when permission is given that a man may put in a substitute for himself at the holy Communion, for a cash consideration richer men persuade some pauper to communicate for them at the Lord's Table. How far is this different from buying Masses? . . . I could wish for the removal of the passage in this fifth paragraph.[76]

Bucer makes the same criticism in an even more biting way in reference to the baptism of infants[77] where the sponsors acting as proxy for the suckling answer questions of faith. The priest though addresses the question directly to the suckling. Bucer has the following to say about this in his *Censura*:

> At this point the godfathers and godmothers are required to renounce the devil and make a confession of faith on behalf of the infants, in such a way that when the infants are asked whether they renounce the devil and his works . . . , and whether they believe in God . . . , the godparents reply in place of the infants. But this practice, however ancient it may be, is not the

teaching of the scripture, and there is no other reason existing in its own right why you should question one who does not understand what you say and an other should answer for him from his own understanding, or why you should act like this in matters of the greatest importance which in all cases depend on the individual faith of each person. . . . But how is this to be applied to infants, who cannot yet understand or say anything.[78]

In this objection of the Strasbourg reformer the question is ultimately one of taking faith seriously, which must be a personal decision. Between the lines one can deduce from his criticism that Bucer entertains doubts about ascribing a rebirth to baptized sucklings. Rebirth of sucklings based on an effective baptism is taught in all three editions of the BCP. Thus after the spoken formula it reads:

Almighty God the father of our lorde Jesus Christ, who hath regenerate thee by water and the holy gost.[79]

In addition the same passage should be compared with its somewhat altered form in the canonical prayer book of 1662:

Seeing now, dearly beloved brethren, that this child is regenerate, and grafted into the body of Christ's Church.[80]

According to Bucer the act of baptism plants no seed of faith in the child which has only then to bloom. The godparents and parents have the duty to explain to the growing child God's will for salvation which has been proclaimed upon the occasion of baptism and the parents and godparents have to win the child over to a positive decision about faith. Bucer offers the following alternative to the godparents with reference to their giving the answers of a catechism in place of the child:

My hope is that all the questions of this catechism might be put to the godfathers and godmothers like this: Will you for your part give assurance that this infant, when he is old enough shall learn the catechism of our religion, and when he has fully learned it shall renounce Satan and profess that he believes in God the Father, the Son. . . . We must see to it that we undertake and perform only these things which are taught us in the law of God, things which are true and weighty and which build up faith in Christ.[81]

If the baptism of little children in fact imparts new birth by a ritual or substitutional faith, does this not then lead easily to the concept of a character indelebilis regarding faith? Does such an understanding of baptism not lead quickly to the proposition that personal faith and a conscious decision for Jesus are of little or no importance since the child has already procured his salvation by virtue of a second birth through inoculation?

Bucer intends also with his criticism of this form of baptism to meet the anabaptists something like halfway. Anabaptists, despite partially exaggerated notions, had done a service to the structure of established churches because they had called attention to a weak point.

Unfortunately neither of the two revisions of the BCP took Bucer's ideas on the meaning of baptism sufficiently into consideration. Nevertheless we want to establish that Bucer never dealt with it as an alternative between infant or adult baptism, but instead as a correction of the question of the effectiveness of a rebirth pronounced over the sucklings. If Bucer though does not speak in his critique on the formula for baptism in express words about the problem of rebirth of an infant, nevertheless inferences may be drawn from his commentary on the catechism and confirmation formulas.[82]

c. Chattering Talk in Declarations of Faith

The prayer books of 1549, 1552, and 1662 provide that prior to the confirmation service there is a catechism in which the half-grown children must give to the bishop answers about the essentials of the Christian faith. Included therein, among other things, is the requirement that they say by rote the Ten Commandments, the Creed, and the Lord's Prayer. Bucer then warns how great is the danger that such an examination might descend to chatter as pure lip service. To him it is important that a canonical court investigate the candidate for confirmation as to his style of living over an extended period of time prior to the examination into his faith. Only after a testing period should the candidate receive permission for confirmation. In this connexion Bucer requires testimony of a new birth from the candidate:

> A confession of faith should be required of such a kind as might be judged not to originate in the mouth. . . . It should be accompanied by signs in the conduct and manner of life of the candidate which the churches might accept as proceeding from the heart which truly believes the gospel and from the teaching of the Holy Spirit. . . . In no way should the opportunity be given to anyone to mock God and the churches by professing in words a faith . . . which the heart does not feel.[83]

The last sentence in the above quotation alludes rather clearly to the case of a man being changed through a rebirth. Bucer expresses his ideas even more clearly in the following sentences:

I do not know how it can be possible with a clear conscience to receive a confession of faith, especially a solemn and public confession in church, when it is made by people in whom these necessary signs of a new man and of true faith in Christ do not appear. . . . If only those are admitted in whom some vigour of new birth has become manifest: then the slower ones, if they indeed are born of God, will be the more excited by the example of those who deservedly were considered before them, to make a serious effort to learn the things which belong to Christ.[84]

In this quotation the talk about a rebirth is now in expressis verbis.

If the Strasbourg reformer had really had the idea that baptized infants are born again then he would have spared himself the problem of seeking with such earnestness in the confirmation candidate for some sign of a rebirth, and of demanding a verification period of his manner of life.

A rebirth which might adhere to one as a consequence of a spoken form having a character indelebilis would support an understanding which would hamstring the awakening of faith.

In this criticism by Bucer we see to what an extent revivalistic ideas are involved which are in turn passed on to the BCP of 1662.

d. Rubrics Which Encourage Minimalism

As we return to the rubric at the close of the communion service of 1549 we want to investigate Bucer's opinion of the sixth rubric. This requires that church members take communion at least once a year.[85]

Bucer vehemently opposed this once-a-year minimum rate of communion. The reformer remarks thereon:

How can a man communicate other than unworthily at the Lord's Table if he will do so only once a year and not then unless complied by law? For a man can not be worthy of the Communion at the Lord's Table if he does not understand the prize of this food and does not therefore seek it with his whole heart.[86]

Since faith constitutes an enduring lifetime bond with the Lord the result ought to be that holy communion is taken as often as possible:

There should be a weighty exhortation to pastors that they should teach and exhort their people that just as they should always live in Christ the Lord so particularly in the sacrament of the divine supper they should take this life from the Lord as often as it is celebrated in the holy assembly.[87]

Bucer wants to counteract that false conception of faith which permits membership in the congregation of Jesus on the basis of a calculated observation of some particular paragraphs which do no speak to the inner attitude of man.

This criticism by Bucer had the modest result that, in the closing rubric of the prayer books of 1552 and 1662, three communions per year are required as a minimum.[88]

e. The Prayer for the Dead

The reformer argues ingeniously in his criticism of the prayer for the dead. He rejects this prayer practice chiefly because Holy Scripture offers no support for it:

> Now there is no part of scripture which teaches us to pray for the dead, either by word or example. And it is forbidden to add or take away anything from scripture.[89]

Bucer plays it straight with reference to taking faith seriously, even to the ultimate consequences thereof. If a faithful person dies, then God takes care of him and forgiveness with the peace associated with it is the reality. The prayer for the dead is thus something of a downgrading of the power to carry one through which the believer has received by faith during his earthly period of life. Faith must lead to the certainty of salvation.[90] The prayer for the dead amounts to a contradictory attitude toward the certainty of salvation. Bucer expresses himself further thereon:

> But when prayer is offered for the dead that the Lord may grant them his mercy and everlasting peace, the common man supposes that this implies that the departed still feel the want of that peace and therefore of the full mercy of God by which He pardons their sins, and that the primary purpose of our prayers is to gain these things for them. No occasion must be given for this error.[91]

Moreover the prayer for those gone to their rest does not take seriously the decision which the deceased has taken during his earthly existence. Bucer's alternative solution is to remember those who have died in the faith and to give thanks for their faith and to take them as an example for oneself:

> For these reasons my own preference would be to omit the commendation of the dead and the prayer for their eternal peace. In place of this commendation and prayer, the following passage should be added . . . in which we

ask that we may follow the example of the saints and their steadfastness in the faith and their keeping of the commandments of God.[92]

In the BCP of 1662 this proposal of Bucer was taken to heart in the prayer for Christ's church militant here on earth, which is in the communion liturgy:

And we also bless thy holy Name for all thy servants departed this life in thy faith and fear, beseeching thee to give us grace so to follow their good examples, that with them we may be partakers of thy heavenly kingdom.[93]

f. Ritual Practices in Connexion with Consecration

Bucer alined himself against the transformation thinking in the long consecration prayer in the communion liturgy of 1549 which requires at the point of the epiclesis[94] the making of the sign of the cross over the elements of bread and wine. In the theology of the first Edwardian prayer book this transformation did not necessarily mean a transubstantiation. Nevertheless one understands by the transformation by virtue of an epiclesis made manifest through the outward signing of the cross, a specially produced presence of Jesus. This can easily lead to a calculated attitude on the part of the churchgoer by which his concentration on Jesus in the course of the liturgy is important only at brief, defined points in the course of the liturgy, in which the attention-awakening factor can be a gesture like the making of the sign of the cross over the elements. An attitude is often produced by this thinking[95] that the churchgoer supposes, based on some particularly executed form with its associated gesture, that special blessings have been freely conferred upon him completely unconnected with any faithlike attitude upon his part. Bucer perceives this danger and also sees in it a peril to faith. He makes the following criticism thereon:

We must reach exactly the same conclusion about the signs of the cross which are made over the bread and wine and about the way in which they are taken into the hands of the minister. . . . The same attitude is indicated by a number of people, . . . who recite the words over the bread and wine with such gestures that they seem more concerned in these words with an intention to change the bread and wine into the body and blood of the Lord than to arouse the people present to deny their own flesh and blood, which cannot inherit the kingdom of God, to desire to receive a fuller measure of the body and blood of Christ, and so live more completely in Him and have Him living in them.[96]

According to Bucer a proper understanding reference the taking of communion should aim at promoting the indwelling of Jesus in the hearts of men. The clause "to desire to receive a fuller measure of the body and blood of Christ, and so live more completely in him" shows clearly how profoundly a concern for the rebirth lies in the heart of this reformer.

At other times Bucer employs a very interesting expression: "mechanism of this world" or "process of this world." Bucer means thereby that Jesus does not become present in holy communion through any form. Things done without the impetus of an inner faith, as for example the pronouncing of formulas or the adoption of certain gestures, are in spite of their sacred appearance a part or a mechanism of this world. Some further quotations from the *Censura* may illuminate this:

> Moreover we receive all these things, the body and blood of the Lord, the whole Lord, God and man, and the confirmation of a new and eternal covenant with God, not by the natural senses of body and soul, not by any operation or process of our human nature or of this world, . . . but by faith alone, faith simple and unquestioning. . . . And again, since faith does not receive Christ by any mechanism of this world or by circumscribing Him in some specific place . . . , this reception of Him . . . does not call Him back to this world or in any way diminish His celestial glory.[97]

This criticism by Bucer of the prayer of consecration with epiclesis and the making of the sign of the cross over the elements has been taken into account in both revisions of the BCP. The consecration prayer is now also restored in the edition of 1662 in a purified form.

3. FAITH AS AN ASPECT OF AN EDIFYING FELLOWSHIP

a. Importance of Distinguishing between the Faithful and the Unfaithful

For Bucer this distinction is important since its rejection amounts to an enormous watering down of the substance of faith. If each is upright in faith in his own way then the church must relinquish its true comprehension of itself, which is to win men for the Redeemer. Bucer well knew that one creates enemies for himself with such a distinction. He heard the remonstrance that this attitude destroys the good terms among citizens with an unnecessary rift. Bucer counters this objection by pointing to Scripture which likewise distinguishes between the faithful and the unfaithful.

Whoever remains obedient to Holy Scripture lives best and happiest. Between the lines Bucer is perhaps saying the following: the faithful who stick together give the others a convincing example of a harmonious community bound together by love. Let Bucer speak for himself:

> There is no reason to suppose that any damage will come to the state or to the harmony of society if we distinguish between the undoubted people of God and those who in effect declare that they are not yet of his people. For first of all, this distinction is commanded by God, who cannot command anything which is not beneficial, and whose often repeated promise cannot deceive men, the promise that in the end those people will live in the best and most happy way, who order every aspect of their lives in accordance with his word.[98]

b. Responses and Those Texts Spoken by All

Bucer values the responses in the BCP of 1549 and thus he also pleads for their retention. The congregation should participate actively in the liturgy and the fellowship should be furthered in that direction, in which the responses can be of service. The more portions which the BCP contains which the congregation can speak or sing, the more will the prayer book become their own.

> And while the sacred prayers are being said in the name of the whole people, they should not only listen to the prayers with the greatest attention but they should also reply to the ministers: And not only Amen but also those other things which are customarily said in reply to ministers. . . . For these responses are not the concern of the clergy only . . . , but of the whole people.[99]

In the prayer book of 1549 responses were well provided for, though the congregation made too little use of the opportunity. Structurally there is much present in the BCP which the congregation can either speak or sing even if the rubric does not expressly provide for it. Perhaps Bucer's suggestions about activating the congregation's awareness of its own participation in the liturgy has led to the fact that the rubric is not followed slavishly. What Bucer in the continuation of the last-quoted text proposes is today practiced by most congregations loyal to the BCP.

> It would therefore be suitable if the people were to recite, together with the minister, both the confession of sins and that prayer[100] before the reception of the sacraments.[101]

c. Segregation of Choir from Congregation

Bucer objected to the separation of the choir from the congregation. A chasm is produced through too great a distance between the priest in the choir and the rest of the congregation. The result of this is that the congregation cannot follow the symbolic activities carried out by the priest. The reformer suggests that the service of worship belongs to the entire congregation, and not just to the priest. This idea of Bucer again reveals his characteristic feeling for the significance of fellowship.

> The separation of the choir at some distance from the rest of the Church, and the fact that holy rites are performed there which nevertheless concern all the people, are both contrary to the spirit of Christianity.[102]

d. Fellowship in the Sense of a Personal Exchange of Faith

We find an informative passage in the *Loci Communes* by Bucer where he speaks of the need for a Christian assembly in which an air of intimacy should prevail. Bucer maintains that at the profane level it happens that people who are sympathetic one to another also have pleasure with one another. In this connexion Bucer introduces the idea of "company." When Bucer on the contrary speaks of "intimacy" he probably means thereby the mutual exchange of personal experiences of faith which confirm the brothers and sisters in the Lord and may intensify the responsibility for a mutual salvation.[103]

In the Anglo-Saxon world they use for that association which mutually strengthens one another by a personal exchange of experiences of faith, the expression "fellowship." This type of association today is fostered chiefly by home Bible circles. Let the reformer speak to us on this:

> People who have a strong liking for each other, and even those who follow similar interests, are accustomed to meet together frequently and to delight in one another's company. But Christian love is a much more powerful bond, and therefore Christians ought to gather together more frequently ... therefore we must assemble together with greater frequency and intimacy. .... We are to be solicitous for each other's salvation.[104]

The revivalistic concepts of a Bucerian theology are particularly visible in the above quotation.

4. THE CHURCH AS THE FORM OF ORGANIZATION FOR BEARING WITNESS TO THE FAITH

a. A Fellowship of the Faithful

Bucer's ideas about the church in its various aspects are to a large degree ascertainable in his *Loci Communes.* For this reformer the church is the Bible engendered association of all the born again. This church has a universal distribution and hence an ecumenical breadth. The universal church lives by the same faith.

> We possess in the Scriptures the sole record for determining the consensus and mind of the Church. It is called moreover, the universal Church, the Church of all who have been born again by true faith. . . . For it is never gathered in one place. . . . It does indeed live by the same faith, it is nourished by the same gospel.[105]

b. Tests of a True Church

The hallmark of the true church has nothing to do with questions about any particular denomination. Bucer enumerated the following points by which one may recognize the true church: the true guardian of the congregation, Jesus, is offered its attention. The congregation concerns itself with doctrine and is anxious to provide apt servants of the Word. Besides the proper administration of the sacraments, the congregation must be concerned in the ordered mode of life of its members in righteousness and holiness. This factor of sanctification carries great weight and clearly this has always, again and again, been an important element of revivalistic circles.

> But the marks without which there cannot be a Church are as follows: Heed is paid to the voice of the Shepherd, to the ministry of teaching. . . . The third distinguishing . . . mark of the true Church . . . is the possession of suitable ministers and teachers of the word. . . . The fourth mark is the lawful dispensation of the sacraments. . . . The fifth distinguishing mark is righteousness and holiness of life, whereby God is glorified.[106]

c. Oneness of the True Church

To Bucer it is important that the unity of the church should not be dependent upon external ceremonies. Rather, true unity must prove itself to be woven into one by the Holy Ghost, which should be expressed in love as well as in agreement with references to God's Word and the sacraments. In matters in which Holy Scripture takes no position, freedom can reign. Bucer's understanding of unity is very important in view of the fact that members of the congregation should serve one another with their gifts. In the context thereof it appears that Bucer means by "gifts" the talents of each member, which then each of the faithful has to apply to the building of the body of Christ. The unity of the church thus exists in a living cooperation of its members, in order to maintain and express the single faith.

> Now in what does the unity of the Church consist? Not in ceremonies or in dress. . . . It consists therefore in the unity of the Spirit, of love, the word of God, Christ, the Sacraments, and the sharing of gifts, that we may aspire together to the same goal, and hold and express the same beliefs. . . . But unity is not necessary in anything not set forth in the word.[107]

d. Concerning the "Infallible Church"

Infallibility in reference to the church does not mean a special quality adhering to the members of the congregation such perhaps as perfection or errorlessness. Infallibility subsists in the faithfulness of God who does not refuse his faithful the support of the Holy Ghost regardless of where these faithful may be found. If even so few as two or three be gathered together to seek in worship the countenance of the Lord, then the satanic power cannot affect the faithful so bound together in fellowship. Bucer intends by "infallibility" that the true members of the body of Christ in the last analysis remain safe through God's preserving grace and do not fall into apostasy.

> If in referring us to the authority of the Church in the claim that it does not err, they had in mind the true members separated from the false . . . a particular true Church in a congregation of a few as two or three who truly worship God. . . . For because we are sons, He has sent the Holy Spirit into our hearts, whereby we cry Abba, and the gates of hell will not prevail against any of his true members.[108]

We are dealing here with an individualistic church concept which reminds one strongly of the ecclesiological ideas of pietistic-revivalistic circles. We are not dealing in this kind of ecclesiology of Bucer with a relativistic attitude since the reformer again and again praises the bond with Holy Scripture and the Holy Spirit. This ecclesiological tendency is individualistic only in so far as the individual does not exist for the collective, but rather that the fellowship has the welfare of the individual person in view. This means then also that each one finally is answerable for himself before God. When Christians concern themselves with salvation then it is a question of the deliverance of others as separate individuals. A surprising harmony with Bucer's "pietistic" church concept is found in the following passage in the communion liturgy of all three principal editions of the BCP:

> And that we are very members incorporate in the mystical body of thy Son, which is the blessed company of all faithful people, and are also heirs through hope of thy everlasting kingdom.[109]

e. Overcoming the Discrepancy between the Clerical and Lay Church

Especially worthy of mention, it seems to me, is Bucer's suggestion that the Bible should be read during church services completely within one year. Bucer also even forsees that a layman could undertake the interpretation of Scripture texts provided he has a special gift of interpretation.

> it is also established from the canons, that . . . the reading of the Bible should be systematically pursued in gatherings for worship, so that the whole Bible is completed during the year. The ministers used to expound all or part of the readings. . . . Those who adhere to this purpose will appoint to interpret the Scripture in the Church the person on whom the gift of interpretation has been bestowed, irrespective in the end of the position he occupies.[110]

Since Holy Scripture belongs to all, the congregation should be served in this by whoever has been given the gift of interpretation. One's professional position should play no role in this. The BCP follows a Bible reading plan which covers the whole of Holy Scripture at least once a year.[111] The BCP of 1549 already included a Bible reading plan before Bucer's *Censura* appeared. Nevertheless we should accept the fact that an influence proceeded from this reformer which allowed the people to become ever more aware of how important it is to take the Bible reading plan available in the BCP to one's heart. Here we have a further explanation of why the BCP was able to evolve into a handbook for home usage. The fact that the daily reading of the Psalms is a concern may be traced to Bucer. Constantine Hopf points out that the English translation of the Psalms from the Vulgate leans heavily upon Bucer's translation made in the year 1530. So thus the translation of the Psalms in the BCP bears the stamp of Bucer.[112] Plausibly, this translation which is associated with Bucer has been selected because of its melodiously fluid style which rather encourages one to one's daily reading.

5. FAITH IN ITS IMPACT IN THE SOCIAL FIELD

A few further examples from Bucer's most celebrated work, *De Regno Christi,* which he dedicated to King Edward VI, may now follow. Bucer's revivalistic theology has taken the question of the civic community seriously. The kingdom of God must, in its form for the time being symbolically materialized here on earth, exercise its influence on the civic community and the state.

a. The Responsibility of the Born Again vis-à-vis Their Fellow Citizens

Moreover, if we are born again through Christ and are made true citizens of his kingdom, then we should be so inflamed with charity and the desire to be a benefit to everybody, that nobody causes displeasure to his fellow-man.[113]

To begin with, Bucer in the above quotation formulates in a negative way the obligations of the born again who are citizens of the kingdom of God. A citizen of the kingdom of God must be zealous not to cause a fellow citizen any unpleasantness through annoyance. In the following quotation Bucer stresses emphatically the obligation of the faithful with respect to his fellow citizen who is an outsider:

But everybody should according to his ability as much as possible be profitable to the others in regards to salvation and welfare.[114]

Each one of the faithful is summoned to use all of his powers for the welfare and benefit of his fellow citizens.

44

b. Identification of the Chosen Congregation with the Political Inhabitants and the Consequences Arising Therefrom

Patrick Collinson reduces Bucer's religio-political thinking to the following denominator:

> Bucer came to identify the elect, loving community with the entire multitudinous society of the city.[115]

How is Collinson's analytical statement to be understood with reference to Bucer's Christian-social thinking? The mutual concern in the Christian congregation must spill over onto the political fellow citizens, to the others, since the call also goes out to these to let themselves be chosen by God. What Bucer means can perhaps be expressed in this way: Those who have already let themselves be chosen and are thereby helping to build the true congregation should stir up those still standing apart to a realization of their election.

(1) The Bringing to a Realization of One's Election through the Distribution of Spiritual Qualities

Whoever is already matured in the faith has the duty to enlist the person standing outside as a disciple and to encourage him in the knowledge of God. The invitation to make progress along the path of life intended by God is to be addressed to one's fellow citizen by the faithful. This discipline in one's spiritual responsibility is not simply a matter for the publicly acknowledged priest but is the duty of every Christian. Bucer expresses it in the following way:

> The discipline of life and morals consists of this that not only the official ministers of the church, but every single Christian has the duty to strengthen and encourage their fellowman with all possible means, in order that he may more and more progress in a Godly conduct of life and this should happen under the authority and guidance of our Lord Jesus Christ as it is fitting for His disciples who have faith and knowledge.[116]

When Christians concern themselves with the spiritual welfare of their fellow citizens, then perhaps those standing outside notice the Almighty God troubles himself with them and awaits the taking up of their election.

(2) The Bringing to a Realization of One's Election through the Distribution of Material Goods

The final quotation stems from the fourteenth chapter of the First Book of *De Regno Christi*. Therein it becomes clear that the earthly goods of the congregation belong actually to Jesus. That he really is Lord must become obvious therein, in that He himself may give from the abundance. The abundance of the riches of God obliges the congregation to a consciously responsible husbandry which should be revealed in a solicitude for the needy. Thus this social responsibility, in a material sense, produces the effect that needy men become aware of the outstretched hand of God through the experience of the alleviation of their need by interested Christians. Christians should let the Lord become credible for those not yet in the faith, by the performance of social service.

> After your sovereign majesty has refunded and given back the goods in a sufficient and reasonable way, the goods which have for a long time been dedicated and consecrated to the Lord Jesus, and after you have consecrated and sanctified the treasure of its finances and heritage in such an abundance as we should like it and believe it that it is our only Saviour who gives us abundance of all goods, your sovereign majesty has made a sixth law, in order to reinstate in Christ's Church within your kingdom this holy welfare service and solicitude for the poor needy, which the Holy Spirit has prescribed and without this solicitude no communion of saints is possible.[117]

Bucer's piety does not remain an inner spiritual and private matter. It is his great concern to operate in a missionary way within society. The Bucer mentality, though revealing a pietism, is never content to retreat into an unspoiled sphere without a social commitment. One does not forget those great works of charity of an August Francke, Georg Mueller, or Pastor Fliedner. To this type of piety questioning of the social structure is foreign. Nevertheless the social concern is there, but rather in the direction that the born again individuals might change the power structure in an organic way by virtue of the strength which proceeds from the faith of the individual.

GENERAL CLOSING COMMENTS ABOUT BUCER

Some few authors such as Gerard Itti,[118] Ernst Troeltsch,[119] and August Lang[120] have uncovered the trail of the revivalistic side of Bucer. That

Bucer came to terms also with the anabaptists in the sense of becoming reconciled, and sought to understand their arguments for the baptism of adults, indicates to some degree a revivalistic direction. D. F. Wright says in his introduction to a selection of Bucer's works:

> Bucer too was not without theological affinity to the Anabaptists. . . . He even acknowledged in 1524 that the Scriptures did not require the baptism of infants, and allowed, that baptism might be postponed until years of discretion.[121]

Martin Bucer's influence on the BCP reference its importance as a church and home manual is noteworthy. Surely it was through his participation that the BCP developed into a book useful both to a congregation and for faith awakening. The revised BCP of 1552 is scarcely imaginable without the proposals of Bucer. He did not want to question the traditions inherited from the early catholic church. Bucer encouraged the English church to retain the special traditions of the worldwide church, though taken into a new context, that is, in a context of Reformation thinking. With this attitude Bucer succeeded in building from what was on hand and in preserving the elements valued by the congregation. These are the prerequisites which are responsible for the fact that the congregations could accept the BCP, and for the fact that it did not seem alien to them. Constantine Hopf expresses with precision what has just been said in the following:

> His suggestion for improvements do not intend to overthrow tradition, and his constant reference to the Church Fathers and to ancient practices are evidence how much he valued that inheritance, and to which the Church of the Reformation was so indebted.[122]

In closing we only want to put the question as to whether there are perhaps traces present in the BCP of Bucer's masterpiece *De Regno Christi*, not only with reference to the title "Common Prayer Book," but also as they relate to the subject matter, which have led to the fact that the prayer book belongs to the general public. Indeed the BCP belongs not only to faithful and committed Christians, but also it is in the possession of most citizens. It is remarkable how the BCP comprises within itself the most important areas of life, whether it be of the individual, of the congregation, or of the government. Is there perhaps reflected in the BCP to a certain degree that theocracy which is revealed in Bucer's *De Regno Christi*?

C. JOHN HOOPER AS THE FATHER OF PURITANISM AND THE MAIN FEATURES OF HIS THEOLOGY

1. INTRODUCTORY REMARKS

John Hooper (1495-1555) is one of those important personalities with whom Thomas Cranmer had to deal intensively and separately. Hooper is credited with being the father of puritanism. This section will briefly cover when his interest in puritanism[123] arose and what was the appearance of its theology. Finally there follows a short exposition to illuminate a little of Hooper's influence on Cranmer and the essential circumstances connected therewith. It is worthy of note that the sources of puritanism, that spiritual attitude with its consequent preoccupation with the awakening of faith, are to be found in the aspirations within the English church which wanted to help the Reformation which had started on the mainland to attain its fulfillment.

Hooper even before his discovery of Reformation theology had received valuable impulses as a Cistercian in Cleeve Abbey, England. As is well known, the Cistercian Order attaches great value to sobriety and frugality in the decoration of their monastery churches. A genuine Cistercian church knows no decoration in images or statues. "Austeritas" and "simplicitas" belong to typical Cistercian thinking. Hence it isn't surprising that Hooper even as a monk acquired a love for the plain, simple, and essential, for that is what is meant by the word "purus." This is one of the roots from which developed the clearly defined puritanism of Hooper.

2. HIS EDUCATIONAL TOUR IN ZURICH AND HIS DIGESTION OF BULLINGER'S COVENANT THEOLOGY

The other and at the same time the most powerful roots for the growth of his puritanical theology developed in Zurich where Hooper, in the years 1547-1549, studied under Heinrich Bullinger, the successor to Zwingli. The rules promulgated by Zwingli and carried on by Bullinger for the minimum of decoration in church halls as well as church liturgies[124] cleansed of pagan elements left a lasting impression on Hooper.

W. M. S. West emphasizes one of the most important aspects of Hooper's experiences pertinent to the Zurich church when he writes:

In Zurich Hooper saw a church devoid of all ceremonies. . . . He saw churches emptied of all images and statues and retaining only such furniture as was absolutely necessary. . . . He saw ministers in the churches who even when preaching and administering the sacraments wore no distinctive dress, but the respectable clothes of the ordinary citizens.[125]

Three Biblical pillars bound one to another carry the load of the theological work of Hooper: (a) The furtherance of a church in accord with the practices of the churches of the time of the apostles;[126] (b) a heavy emphasis on a theology of the covenant between God and man with an accentuation of the Decalogue; (c) the untiring assertion of what Sola Scriptura implies in (a) and (b).

(a) The first important pillar in Hooper's theology reveals itself in nearly all of his writings, but comes to light in a concentrated way in the sermon on the prophet Jonah preached before Edward VI during Lent in the year 1550:

These things be spoken of me, most gracious and virtuous king, to commend your majesty's and your most honourable council's doings, that seek the glory of God and the restitution of his holy and apostolic church. . . . Help ye therefore, O ye bishops and priests, the king's majesty and his noble council's proceedings, that all things may be brought to a perfect and apostolical reformation. . . . If they will not be desirous and glad to have and help the ministry of the church to the primitive and perfect state again, the Lord doth cry vengence towards them.[127]

The profound impression which Hooper received from the great simplicity of the Zurich church is obviously reflected in the above text.

The purus cultus of the apostolic congregation without altar or liturgical vestments, which Hooper had learned about in the church at Zurich, that English reformer took as his norm.

The Zurich-puritanical party line with its rejection of altars was clearly expressed in a further sermon on Jonah on March 5, 1550:

It were well then, that it might please the magistrates to turn the altars into tables, according to the first institution of Christ, to take away the false persuasion of the people they have of sacrifices to be done upon the altars. . . . Therefore were it best that the magistrates removed all the monuments and tokens of idolatry and superstition; then should the true religion of God the sooner take place.[128]

In this connexion it is helpful to point out Hooper's doctrine reference ecclesiastical office in regard to Christ. Hooper particularly stressed the priestly ministry of Jesus which consists of his sacrifice made once for all time.[129] Rejection of altars has a direct connexion with this powerful stress upon the priestly office of Jesus.

There are no adiaphora for Hooper. The Bible is not only the standard for doctrine but also for questions in reference to church equipment and liturgy.[130] Hooper placed himself strongly against the use of liturgical vestments. As Hooper was about to be consecrated Bishop of Gloucester he refused in a letter addressed to the palace on October 3, 1550, the obligation that he must wear episcopal vestments:

> There is nothing to be had in use in the church which has not either its authority from the expressed word of God, or else is of itself, a thing indifferent. . . . The particular vestments in the ministry do not have the word of God unless they are ordained. . . . Therefore they ought not to be in use.[131]

This conception of the necessity for a church structure in accordance with a Biblical-apostolic model is a result of Hooper's understanding of Scripture which is to a large extent dependent upon Bullinger's masterpiece on hermeneutics.[132] This work was already circulating in England prior to Hooper's going to Zurich and in all probability Hooper must have read it before his tour of study in that city.[133] For Hooper there is something resembling a "canon of the canon" in the Bible and this is simply the "pura ecclesia" of the apostolic time.[134] This "pura ecclesia" arises then of course from an understanding of Scripture which is based as a hermeneutical principle on the most important creeds as well as on the Ten Commandments. Istvan Tökés, in an investigation into Bullinger's hermeneutical doctrine, comes to the conclusion: (translated)

> The genuine interpretation should agree first—with the rule of faith. . . . This rule is in fact identical with the apostolic symbol, but not only therewith, but also with the rest of the symbols of the Old Church.[135]

Hooper's connexion with Bullinger's hermeneutics on this point seems obvious. Let Hooper himself address us:

> those creeds are in such wise taken out of the word of God, that they do contain in them the sum of all christian doctrine.[136]

It is not only the regula fidei or the classical creeds which marked Hooper's understanding of Scripture in subjection to Bullinger. Ernest Koch's observation with reference to Bullinger's basic hermeneutical principles gives us an important supplement which allows Hooper's position to become more comprehensible:

Bullinger cites together with the Apostolic Creed the Lord's Prayer and the Decalogue, thus the whole catechism must be understood as the hermeneutic guide. (translated)[137]

(b) The second important pillar supporting Hooper's theology, which at the same time occupies the most important position as a principle of interpretation, is the Decalogue, as an expression of the covenant relationship between God and man. Decalogue and covenant have a pronounced soteriological meaning. The covenant relationship implies that the partner in the covenant holds himself bound by the conditions of the covenant. The fulfillment of these conditions, that is to say, of the Ten Commandments, guarantees salvation as well as eternal bliss for God's partners in the covenant. God's commitment to his partners in the covenant is suspended when these latter do not adhere to the conditions. Hooper writes in his foreword to his exegesis on the Ten Commandments:

> But forasmuch as there can be no contract, peace, alliance, or confoederacy between two persons or more, except first the persons that will contract agree within themselves upon such things as shall be contracted . . . also, seeing these ten commandments are nothing else but the tables or writings that contain the conditions of the peace between God and man. . . . The contents whereof bind God to aid and succour, keep and preserve, warrant and defend man from all ill . . . and at the last to give him eternal bliss.[138]

God sent Christ in confirmation of this covenant. Man through repentance and faith in Jesus and his promises becomes a member of the new covenant affirmed in Christ. The absolute requirement for remaining now in the relationship is the keeping of the Ten Commandments, or, to say it in other words, sanctification in one's daily life.

W. M. S. West comments pertinently on Hooper's understanding of the covenant:

> The way into the covenant is that of repentance and of faith and the way to remain within it is to live the Christian life.[139]

Whoever does not conform to the conditions of the new covenant confirmed in Christ, thus to the Ten Commandments, excludes himself from the covenant and the blessings attached thereto. Hooper writes thereon:

> Thus the Scripture answereth, that the promise of grace appertaineth unto every sort of men in the world . . . howbeit within certain limits and bounds,[140] the which if men neglect or pass over, they exclude themselves from the promise of Christ.[141]

W. M. S. West points out further that Hooper has extensively appropriated to himself the salient features of the covenant theology of Bullinger while Bullinger's federal theology is based on Zwingli.[142] Bullinger had further systematically advanced Zwingli's rudimentary covenant theology and pointedly articulated its connexion with the Decalogue.

Hooper then in his "Decalogue-theology" clearly emphasized how the Ten Commandments convict men of their sins. The special thing about Hooper is just this that he places a heavy stress on repentance in which the individual aspect of conversion is accentuated in a new way. We let Hooper have the floor:

> Generally, the word of God[143] rebuketh sin, and calleth sinners to repentance. . . . But to us those sorrows and repentance do no good, except we every man singularly repent and be sorrowful for his sins . . . no more is any man's repentance my repentance, or any other man's faith my faith; but I must repent, and I must believe myself to feel sorrowfulness for sin by the law, and remission thereof by faith in Christ: so that every private man must be in repentance sorry with the true repentant worry, and faithful with the true faithful.[144]

Thus through the Commandments must come a personal decision and experience.

Sanctification in conduct stands in the closest connexion with the proclamation of the Ten Commandments. This requires that men act in accordance with God's Commandments and seek to win others to the faith. Hooper combines the missionary task with sanctification:

> Thus by Christ we are sanctified only; and as Peter saith, "A people chosen, a princely priesthood, a holy people, and peculiar nation, to declare the power of him that hath called us from the darkness of error and sin into his wonderful light." These words declare the manner how we are sanctified, and what our office is after we be sanctified: to preach the power of him that hath called us from the darkness of sin.[145]

Every Christian bears the responsibility for the salvation of the next:

> Yet is every disciple of Christ bound to search the glory of God and the salvation of his neighbour, and commit the success unto God.[146]

The missionary task must above all find its realization in the family where the father has a catechistic assignment:

> For as God commandeth his word to be preached and heard, so he hath appointed a certain time, the sabbath, when people should hear it. And not only this order to be observed in the church but also in every family and

household. Of what degree soever he (the father) be, he should cause his family and children to read some part of the Bible for their erudition, to know God. Likewise he should constrain them to pray unto God for the promotion of his holy word.[147]

This missionary task of each Christian should continue to be voiced by a testimony of faith to everyone wherever the opportunity is presented:

> Our office is to communicate the knowledge of God with him, so to move a communication, that one might know the other's faith. . . . God take out of the hearts of men all fear and shame, that we freely confess him, as occasion shall be given.[148]

What has been said about the Ten Commandments and that connected therewith illuminates also the strongly soteriological accent on conduct of life. Ethics and soteriology are closely bound to one another. Hooper himself experienced the frailty of life with all its great menace at the time of the persecution under Bloody Mary. Under that heavy pressure of political-religious disorders Hooper learned in a singularly clear way to understand life as an arduous pilgrimage to the heavenly fatherland. To reach this goal the observance of the Ten Commandments, i.e., of God's Word, is imperative. This view of life is clearly expressed in a letter to Ann Warcop:[149]

> Sister, take heed: you shall in your journey towards heaven meet with many a monstrous beast: have salve of God's word therefore ready. . . . You shall meet with slander and contempt of the world . . . you shall hear and meet with cruel tyranny to do you all extremities . . . but pray to God and follow the star of the word and you shall arrive at the port of eternal salvation, by the merits only of Jesus Christ.[150]

We have already mentioned that in Hooper's conception the church has to exhibit the simplicity of the apostolic times. Still a further aspect of fundamental importance is the church as a community of such as adhere to the covenant, that is, the Decalogue. There is no invisible church. The church is the visible community of the faithful.[151] While the priesthood of all believers is of particular importance to Hooper, the apostolic succession does not make sense to him. To him the succession of the true faith is of primary importance. Pastors should see evangelizing sermons as their main work. To this belongs the proclamation of the Ten Commandments which play an almost substitutionary role for the whole of Scripture:

> Only the commandments of God contain such a copious and profound doctrine, that it can never be known sufficiently, nor never with sufficient di-

ligence declared unto the people. It is the abridgement and epitome of the whole Bible, compendiously containing the whole law and the gospel. . . . He that understandeth not them can be no christian man.[152]

Although Hooper had no small esteem for the order of consecrated pastors, the church did not stand or fall with the occupancy of a pastorate. Hooper knew the emergency situation where Christians had corrupt pastors and had to forgo a healthful preaching of the Gospel as well as an administration of the sacraments in accordance with Scripture. For these cases Hooper suggested the following solution:

> Where as the common ministry is corrupted, and the sacrament used contrary unto the institution of Christ: here every man may in his private chamber, with his christian and faithful brothers, communicate according unto the order of the Scripture.[153]

The congregation is thus a living organism of converts who share the faith with one another. These members of the true congregation examine by means of Scripture as to whether the doctrine in circulation is sound or not. The congregation of Jesus has thus something to do with coming of age:

> There is no better way to be used in this troublesome time for your consolation than many times to have assemblies together of such men and women as be of your religion in Christ, and there to talk and renew among yourselves the truth of your religion; to see what ye be by the word of God, and to remember what ye were before you came to the knowledge thereof, to weigh and confer the dreams and false lies of preachers that now preach, with the word of God that retaineth all truth.[154]

This brief sketch of Hooper's theology reveals chiefly the beginning of puritanism. Hooper is the first outstanding puritan. In this connexion it is of importance to us that the theology of the reformed Zurich, represented by Zwingli and Bullinger, performed a decisively important service in the development of puritanical spirituality. Hooper belongs among the most significant mediators of those ideas for the Anglo-Saxon world. This may be justified by the following historical analysis: The chief source of the puritanical ideas of Zurich at the time of Edward VI was Hooper. During the period of the exile under Bloody Mary important contacts with Geneva occurred among the theologians who had fled to the continent so that puritanism among the exiles also received strongly Calvinistic ideas. That the contact with Zurich found its continuation because of the "Marian exiles" long after the death of Hooper and until the time of Queen Elizabeth is emphasized in the two lists[155] provided by W. M. S. West on this and the next page.

**Bullinger's Contact with England and Englishmen
in the Reign of Mary 1553-1558
The Time of the Marian Exile**

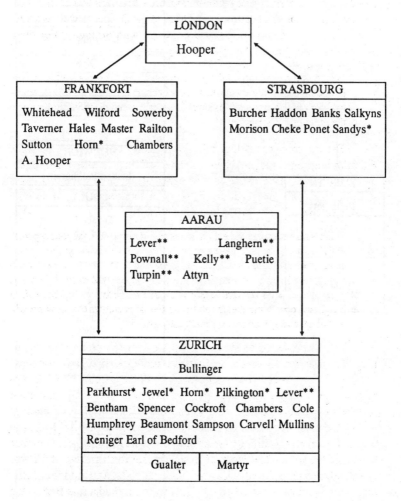

*These men became bishops in the Elizabethan church
**These men became ministers in the Elizabethan church

Bullinger's Contact with England and Englishmen
in the reign of Elizabeth I 1558-1575
(The latter being the year of Bullinger's death)

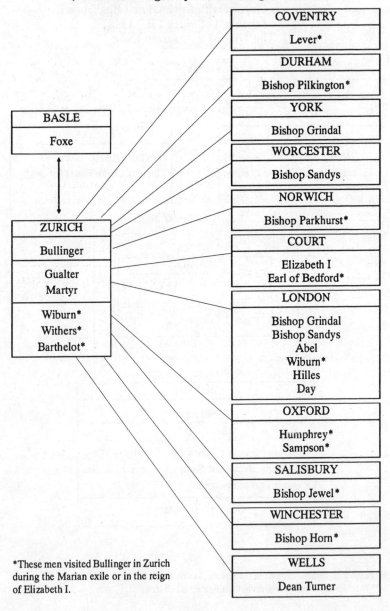

BASLE
Foxe

ZURICH
Bullinger
Gualter
Martyr
Wiburn*
Withers*
Barthelot*

COVENTRY
Lever*

DURHAM
Bishop Pilkington*

YORK
Bishop Grindal

WORCESTER
Bishop Sandys

NORWICH
Bishop Parkhurst*

COURT
Elizabeth I
Earl of Bedford*

LONDON
Bishop Grindal
Bishop Sandys
Abel
Wiburn*
Hilles
Day

OXFORD
Humphrey*
Sampson*

SALISBURY
Bishop Jewel*

WINCHESTER
Bishop Horn*

WELLS
Dean Turner

*These men visited Bullinger in Zurich
during the Marian exile or in the reign
of Elizabeth I.

We have sought to sketch puritanism and its source mainly for the reason that within its spirituality is the kernel of much of that related to the revivalistic spirit. It is especially interesting that the roots of puritanism in great part extend back to the Zwingli-Bullinger covenant theology of which Hooper became one of the most important representatives in England. W. M. S. West writes pertinently:

> As Hooper turned his face toward England it was with the conviction that he had found the church which in practice and in doctrine was the right one—the church of Zurich. . . . Hooper felt it his mission to make the church in England as like the church in Zurich as possible.[156]

In summary we want to establish:

Of the three pillars mentioned at the outset,[157] the second occupies a particularly important place. Out of the covenant and Decalogue theology taken over from Zwingli and more importantly from Bullinger, Hooper developed a puritanical ethic the observance of which is decisive toward an affiliation with the true congregation of Jesus. This is attained through a personal decision after the usus elenchticus of the Decalogue has been applied.[158] A member of the community of Jesus lives in sanctification;[159] one is conscious of the frailty of earthly life and understands existence in this world as a pilgrimage to a goal in the other world, to eternal bliss.[160]

Whoever takes good heed of the obligations of the covenant and hence belongs to the true church exists within a living community where an interchange of faith is encouraged[161] and the inner mission pursued. By this we wish to point out an important root for understanding revivalistic spirituality in the example of Hooper's theology.

Graphical Representation of the Three Pillars in Hooper's Theology upon Which Stands the Congregation, i.e., the Church

The church is the true fellowship of those who adhere to the Decalogue

True fellowship produces fruit through sanctification

Bible	Bible	Bible
The church as a place for the gathering of the believers where the service is held in a New Testament way and where the furnishings conform to Apostolic simplicity.	The Ten Commandments are to be understood as a pars pro toto in reference to Holy Scripture, and the Apostles' Creed is to be understood as the regula fidei.	The whole of Scripture is the test of all doctrine.

3. REFERENCE TO HOOPER'S ENCOURAGING AND PRODUCTIVE CONTACT WITH KING AND ARCHBISHOP

John Hooper exercised a great influence on Edward VI as well as on Archbishop Cranmer, as we learn from innumerable letters of theologians dealing with the English Reformation.

When Hooper returned home in early 1549 from his two years' study sojourn in Zurich he obtained the opportunity from Cranmer himself to preach and teach in various places in London. Hooper attracted a great multitude of men with his friendly and very faith-awakening sermons. Cranmer who himself resided in London had ample opportunity to confer with him. Hooper also said very troublesome things which must have directly challenged the archbishop to answer. Some evidence follows which should cast light upon Hooper's activities in London. Most of this evidence stems from disciples at Zurich of Heinrich Bullinger, Zwingli's successor. Since Hooper was now the principal representative in England of Bullinger theology, he also enjoyed for that reason great prestige among the friends of that Zurich theologian.

In a letter of Martin Micronius[162] to Heinrich Bullinger on September 30, 1549, it says:

> I think it my duty to send you a brief statement of our present condition. In the first place, Hooper is imposing himself a severe and constant labour in instructing the people who are more numerous and attentive. He lectures at least once every day, more frequently two or three times. The archbishop of Canterbury has become somewhat more favourably disposed to him.[163]

Very revealing is a letter of John Butler,[164] which he addressed on February 16, 1550, to Thomas Blaurer:[165]

> Our friend Hooper is lecturing in theology at London twice a day, (for he is a public professor there . . .) with the entire approbation of all good men. Besides this he frequently preaches both at court and in other places all over London. He has for some time been lecturing upon the psalms at the king's palace. Very many of the aldermen of London, who were veteran papists have embraced Christ. In a word, the truth is especially flourishing in London beyond all other parts of the kingdom.[166]

John Burcher wrote to Bullinger in his letter of April 20, 1550:

> The name of Hooper is celebrated throughout all England. He is appointed a royal preacher. . . . His praise is universally proclaimed both on account of his innocency of life and strictness of discipline.[167]

Peter Martyr was able to exercise his influence from Oxford, Bucer from Cambridge, but Hooper had the privilege to work out of the capital, from London, where the king and the archbishop resided. It was Cranmer who enabled Hooper to preach at the royal court before the monarch Edward VI. The Lenten sermons on the prophet Jonah[168] in the presence of the king and the archbishop produced important developments. Edward VI was deeply impressed by Hooper's message. As an expression of appreciation the king offered Hooper the bishopric of Gloucester. But Hooper immediately put forth conditions. He did not wish to be ordained in the conventional liturgical robes. Likewise he had to complain about the form of the episcopal oath, where the saints are called in as witnesses. Martin Micronius had something to say about this in his letter of May 20, 1550, to Bullinger:

> His Lent sermons before the king were preached with the greatest freedom, and attended with great advantage. Only he stirred up some lazy noblemen and bishops against himself, especially because he exhorted the king and council to a more complete reformation of the church. But the king took everything most kindly, as he showed afterwards; for he offered him by the chancellor on the 7th of April the bishopric of Gloucester. Hooper however refused to accept it, unless the bishopric were granted him without any superstitious ceremonies. He had some difficulty in obtaining this, owing to the great opposition of the bishops. . . . But contrary to all expectations, on the 15th of May he gained the victory.[169]

Cranmer had to give heed to the king. He had no right simply to ignore his decrees. By this time Cranmer and Edward VI had a very intimate relationship one to another because of official duties. As a matter of practice decrees of a theological import had to be acceptable after a thorough joint deliberation.

John ab Ulmis gives us an idea of what kind of thinking had flowed from Hooper to Edward VI. John ab Ulmis wrote Bullinger on August 22, 1550, in connexion with the forthcoming installation of Hooper as Bishop of Gloucester:

> Last week, when he confirmed Hooper in his bishopric, and demanded from him the oath, he chanced to notice that the saints were mentioned by the bishops in such sort, as though they were to swear and be confirmed by them. His majesty became much excited, and said: "What wickedness is here, Hooper? Are these offices ordained in the name of saints, or of God?" As soon as Hooper had declared his opinion, the king immediately erased with his own hand the error of the bishops.[170]

Hooper tried to use his influence with the help of Bullinger, while he at the same time encouraged the latter to dedicate his theological writings to the king or archbishop. Thus in December 1549 Hooper wrote his best friend Bullinger the following:

> Moreover, if you have anything which you purpose to send to the press, you should dedicate it to our most excellent sovereign, King Edward the sixth.[171]

In his letter of May 20, 1550, Martin Micronius shared with Bullinger what an impression the dedication of Decades had upon Edward VI. Thus Bullinger complied with Hooper's suggestion and Hooper himself presented this important work to the king with great satisfaction.

> He (Hooper) received your letter and Decades . . . on the 22nd of April. He presented to the king your book splendidly bound on the 25th of April: how acceptable it was to his majesty, you will learn better from Hooper himself at some future time. As far as I can understand your name is beginning to be in favour with the Archbishop of Canterbury.[172]

Hooper testified in one of his letters addressed to Bullinger in the year 1551 what a high opinion Cranmer had for him (Bullinger):

> My Lord of Canterbury, who is in truth a great admirer of you, when I received your last letter in his palace, and acquainted him with its contents, could hardly refrain from tears, when he understood your feelings in regard to the king and to the kingdom, and also the perseverance of your church in these most lamentable times. He made most honourable mention both of yourself and your profound erudition. You have no one, I am sure, among all your dearest friends, who is more interested about you, and who loves you in Christ more ardently than he does.[173]

Sympathy for Bullinger generally implied support for Hooper also. Hooper by the end of 1549 could even say:

> The archbishop of Canterbury entertains right views as to the nature of Christ's presence in the supper, and is now very friendly towards myself. He has some articles of religion, to which all preachers and lecturers in divinity are required to subscribe, or else a license for teaching is not granted them; and in these his sentiments respecting the eucharist are pure, and religious, and similar to yours in Switzerland.[174]

In a letter dated February 5, 1550, Hooper informed his friend Bullinger:

But now, as I hope, master Bullinger and Canterbury entertain the same opinions.[175]

The very influential Peter Martyr had emphatically interceded on behalf of Hooper who created a sensation in particular over the controversial questions about the wearing of liturgical vestments at the consecration of bishops and in doing so brought Cranmer into a difficult situation. Subsequent to these turbulent times Martyr wrote Bullinger the following on the subject of vestments:

> But the probity of this bishop, and his zeal for religion, together with the long intimacy that has existed between us, and lastly your special commendation of him, render him an object of my particular regard: wherefore you need no doubt but that I shall exert myself in his favour to the utmost of my power.[176]

Cranmer himself must have observed that his best theological advisers fought for Hooper. Thus for diplomatic reasons as well, it was out of the question for Cranmer to allow Hooper to fall. Hooper was anything but a conciliatory theologian. However, an archbishop was too much in danger from the expectations of the people to let himself be forced into the role of mediator. Cranmer demonstrated the necessary backbone and did not shame himself over the uncompromising theology of Hooper. Cranmer had struggled through to this uncompromising state, to give preference to a consequent Reformation. Cranmer himself gives, in a very important letter to Bullinger, valuable information about his relations with Hooper. In the letter written March 20, 1552, Cranmer says:

> The private affair upon which you wrote to me, was, that I should put an end to the controversy between the bishop of London and Hooper, bishop of Gloucester, respecting which it is now too late to reply. For I am aware that you have been informed long since, that this controversy has been entirely settled. And master Hooper is in such great esteem among us, that he is now appointed bishop of Worcester, and is at this time living in my house upon the most intimate terms, during the sitting of parliament.[177]

Cranmer's close friendship with Hooper clarifies for us also why this student of Bullinger could exercise an ever-growing influence in the English church. The archbishop must have recommended Hooper to the king for the appointment to the group of scholars who had to prepare a new church law. Peter Martyr wrote Bullinger about it in March 1552:

> the king has appointed two and thirty persons to frame ecclesiastical laws for this realm, namely eight bishops, eight divines, eight civil lawyers, and

eight common lawyers . . . and we also, I mean Hooper, a Lasco, and my-self, are enrolled among them.[178]

It was just at the time when Hooper was enjoying for a lengthy pe-riod Cranmer's hospitality[179] at Lambeth Palace that Micronius reported to Bullinger from London about Edward VI and Hooper. Hooper's influ-ence with the king can be readily seen in this remark in Micronius's letter:

> For the king is most anxious for purity, and is urgent for a serious reforma-tion.[180]

The term "purity" is typical of Hooper's theology; indeed it is noth-ing short of the "cantus firmus" of the Hooper way of thinking and it is not by chance that Edward VI is, in the opinion of Micronius, "most anxious for purity."

In concurring with that view Micronius says in the same letter of March 1552:

> The authority of master Hooper in the council is daily increasing, whence the greatest benefit, I hope, will accrue to the church.[181]

These statements should make it easier to understand the impor-tance of Hooper to Cranmer and hence also his influence on the BCP of 1552, of which more will be said in Chapter III.

4. AN ANALYSIS OF THE IMPORTANT ELEMENTS IN HOOPER'S PREACHING AND WRITING WITH REFERENCE TO CONTENT

a. Depravity of Man and His Frailty

Hooper emphasized the wickedness and depravity of man with ever-grow-ing intensity. In his "Homily in time of pestilence" addressed to his dioceses of Gloucester and Worcester in the year 1552 he designated sin as the source of all other evils:

> For indeed the chiefest causes of all plagues and sickness is sin, which re-maining within all men, worketh destruction not only of the body, but also of the soul, if remedy be not found.[182]

Exposure of sin runs like a red thread through the Lenten sermons which Hooper preached on the prophet Jonah before Edward VI in the year 1550. In the fourth sermon on Jonah Hooper cited the text from Luke 19:10, and went on with the following question:

> Who is it among us all that would not joyfully at the hearing of so amiable and sweet a saying rejoice, seeing we be all miserable and cursed sinners by nature; and yet would, as full of misery and blindness as we be, be saved, wish ever to be out of pain?[183]

In his "Homily in time of pestilence," an epidemic becomes plainly a symbol for sin, which is seen there as incurable within the realm of human potentialities. Cleverly, Hooper grasps the psychological leadership over the hearers of his homily while at the same time he points out the impotence of worldly medicine:

> For I see all the remedies that ever was devised by man is not able to remove assuredly the pestilence from him that is infected therewithal, although they be never so excellent and good.[184]

This pestilence has effects not only in the physical but also in the spiritual field, since it brings damnation with it:

> Notwithstanding, these effects of pestilence, sickness, death, and everlasting damnation cannot be removed, except first the causes of them be eschewed.[185]

In order to make the reader familiar with the medicine for treating this pestilence, Hooper has to identify its precise cause, namely sin:

> The original cause of all evil was Satan, and the ungodly consent of our forefather Adam in paradise, in crediting more the devil's sophistry and gloss than the plain and manifest word of God.[186]

The original sin is the mistrust of and the disobedience to God's Word. Time and again in the course of his sermons Hooper makes mention of this original sin. Hooper frequently supports his assertions with quotations from Holy Scripture.

b. The Way to Personal Awareness of Sin and Repentance

Hooper sees the misconception with respect to the source of the pestilence in the fact that the great mass of men understand the cause of epidemics to be external things such as contaminated water or polluted air. Hooper however wishes to lead the reader of his sermons to find the true source of pestilence within himself, in his heart:

And the infection taketh his original and beginning from such beasts, carrion, and other loathsome bodies that rot upon the face of the earth not buried, or else from moorish, standing, and dampish waters, sinks, or other such unwholesome moistures ... these causes are to be considered as natural and consonant to reason; yet there be reasons and causes of pestilence of more weight, and more worthy of deep and advised considerations and advertisements than these be: and the more, because they lie within man, and be marked but of very few, and hide themselves secretely, till they have poisoned the whole man, both body and soul. For indeed physicians that write, meddle with no causes that hurt man, but such as come unto man from without.[187]

The author brings the reader of the "Homily in time of pestilence" to that person, who casts light upon the heart as the root cause:

Whereupon Christ most mercifully pitieth the poor man, and with contrary knowledge both of sickness and the remedy thereof sheweth, that the disease man is infected with goeth further than reason and the outer action of the body, and occupieth the soul of man with concupiscence, rebellion, frowardness, and contumacy against God.[188]

Hooper does not just let it rest with the explanation of sin as the cause of pestilence nor with just an analysis of a man's heart as the original cause of sin. He makes the reader familiar with the true medicine which can heal the pestilence. What is said in the preceding quotation constitutes a background against which the urgency of the true medicine can become more evident.

c. Appropriation of Salvation through Penance and Rebirth

The psychological prerequisites are met by Hooper in persuading the reader of the need for the true medicine, for Jesus. Hooper writes with pictorial clarity:

in case to remove sin, the cause of sickness, this medicine of Christ is used, as the other is used to remove the effect of sin, which is sickness.[189]

The taking of this true medicine occurs through repentance:

and the means to come by the remedy was to repent, as ye shall know further hereafter, when you know what repentance is.[190]

Repentance is a fresh start upon a new life in Jesus through a renunciation of the old life. The sequel to repentance is a renewal or rebirth of the human soul or of the spirit, effected through the Holy Spirit:

65

Repentance, that God requireth, is the return of the sinner from sin into a new life in Christ; which return is an innovation and renovation[191] of the mind of man by God's Spirit in Christ, with denial of the former life, to begin a new and better life.[192]

Hooper presents the way to salvation as a method to be followed. This method is to be seen in the sequence of those elements, according to Hooper, which belong to penance. He speaks of the medicine of penitence which consists of the following elements:

This medicine of repentance, which consisteth of these parts: first in knowledge of sin; then in hatred of sin; thirdly, in forsaking of sin; fourthly, in believing the forgiveness of sins for Christ's sake; fifthly, to live in virtuous and godly life, to honour God, and to shew his obedience to God's law, that by sin is transgressed. And these parts of penance, which be the very true and only medicines against sickness and sin, be known only by God's laws.[193]

Faith is the instrument by which one receives salvation. However, this faith is an offering of the Gospel also, and thus a gift, and not something otherwise obtainable:

Faith also, that believeth remission of sin, is shewed, opened, and offered by the gospel, wherein be contained God's merciful promises towards sinners. . . . Faith doth credit and receive forgiveness of sins by the operation of God's Holy Spirit in the poor sinner.[194]

Those elements mentioned in sections a. through c. appear frequently in Hooper's sermons and writings. They belong to those factors which are in general typical of puritanism. William Haller who was concerned specially with the typical elements of puritanism in the late sixteenth and seventeenth centuries makes the following statement about a representative puritan named William Perkins:

He set forth in his Golden Chaine, in other weighty volumes, and in numerous shorter treatises what may best be called the descriptive psychology of sin and regeneration. In lucid and eminently readable prose he set forth the process by which, as anyone might observe, God converts the sinful soul into a state of grace, the technique by which man comes to be born again.[195]

With John Hooper we already have on hand the nucleus of a puritanical conversion theology.

d. Importance of the Ten Commandments and God's Word

As previously mentioned,[196] the Ten Commandments form in Hooper's theology one of the most important pillars. In an exhortative way Hooper proclaims the Decalogue and this untiring stress on the Ten Commandments is one of the typical elements in the sermons and writings of this important bishop. This element involving the emphasis on the Decalogue has become a genuine factor in the puritan way of thinking. From among his many exhortations to keep the Commandments we want to select just one quotation from his sermon "In the time of pestilence":

> The justices and gentlemen must look how they keep themselves and the king's majesty's people in the true knowledge and obedience of God's laws.[197]

God's Word as a whole, and not only as a pars pro toto in the Decalogue, is placed on a pedestal with ever-growing vehemence. One reads in the Lenten sermon on Jonah:

> For it is God's word and his law, that turneth the hearts of people to repentance. Ps. xix.cxix. For the word of God written is as perfect as God himself.[198]

Hooper's sermons and writings are permeated with citations from Scripture, for the purpose of authoritative quotations, which reveal his great respect for the Word of God. Hooper draws his knowledge of what is true and false from the Word of God:

"That is unlawful that fighteth and repugneth with the word of God"[199] said he to Edward VI in his sermon on Jonah, and he also testified to the following:

> And that this be done, it is the office of the king's majesty, his council, and all his magistrates, to see the true book of God, the holy Bible, to be taught and received of his majesty's subjects.[200]

The strong emphasis on the Commandments of God and His Word lead with Hooper to points of departure which have become important elements of puritan spirituality, namely, "pura vita," "pura doctrina," and "purus cultus."

(1) "Pura Vita" or Sanctification

Hooper in his work "A Declaration of Christ and His Office" reveals a clearly Biblical conception of sanctification:

> This sanctification is none other but a true knowledge of God in Christ by the gospel, that teacheth us how unclean we are by the sin of Adam, and that we are cleansed by Christ.[201]

Hooper sees the Word of God, meaning the Bible, as the way to sanctification,[202] which needs to be received in faith through the working of the Holy Spirit:

> The means to sanctify is the word of God, the Holy Ghost and faith, that receiveth the word of our redemption.[203]

The strong accent on the Decalogue as a "pars pro toto" for the entire Holy Scripture brings the ethical components into an understanding of sanctification, that is to say, the way of life that is pleasing to God. A sanctified way of life to the honour of God, a "pura vita," is a conspicuous factor in Hooper's sermons and writings. The term "virtuous life" or "godly life" emerges frequently.

> The sinner studieth and liveth a virtuous life, being led by the Holy Ghost, and worketh to serve God with such works as God's holy commandment commandeth every true christian man to work and do.[204]

Hooper in his sermons on Jonah charged Edward VI with the duty to take the identical measures the sailors took in that storm. They searched diligently to determine whether or not Jonah was in any way the cause of the storm. Thus the king was to examine carefully whether or not there be found in his kingdom or in his palace some Jonah who was preparing mischiefs. Such a Jonah had to be thrown overboard. The king had to search diligently also to determine what was the state of faith and the way of life of his own family. With reference to the palace it had to be noted that God dwelt therein. We let Hooper speak:

> When there cometh poverty, pestilence, war, hunger, and such like, he must diligently search whether there be any Jonas within his house, that is to say, any idle and unoccupied men, any thieves, adulterers, swearers, and such like; and the same to be amended and cast out of the house. Hereof your majesty must also take heed, that ye know the faith and conversation of your family; that whosoever of wit and knowledge enter your grace's court, may see the majesty of a godly house, and perceive by the order of your family that God dwelleth in the court and realm.[205]

This sanctification in connexion with a deep searching of the conscience leads to a certain punctiliousness which consists of the following, that a converted person withdraws from worldly things like dancing, theatre-going, cards, and dice games, or the visiting of taverns. Hooper tells Edward VI what shouldn't have a right to exist:

> Likewise, whereas God's laws forbiddeth dice and cards, and also the common statutes of this realm, it is used daily and hourly in the king's majesty's house; whereas not only the majesty of god is offended, but many an honest man undone in the year. That dicehouse must be cast into the sea: if it be not, God will cast the maintainers thereof at length into hell.[206]

The strong emphasis on ethics by way of emphasizing the Ten Commandments as the way of life is very typical of puritanism in all its phases. William Haller makes the following statement in regard to an examination of puritanism in reference to the Commandments of God:

> But of even more practical application was the Hebrew code of conduct, interpreted and reinforced by the trenchant epitomizing zeal of Paul. The preachers consequently, recast for their own age Paul's digest of the laws of Moses.[207]

Sanctification as we find it in Hooper strongly joined to an emphasis on the Ten Commandments is also a typical element of puritan spirituality. Haller writes in connexion with the representative work, "A Plaine and Familiar Exposition of the Ten Commandments" by the puritan John Dod:

> The puritan code of godly behaviour[208] in all the relations of family, household, business, church and state was never more exactly stated or carefully worked out.[209]

This nascent punctiliousness of Hooper developed particularly in later puritanism. Punctiliousness means precise statements about what is forbidden, and that became characteristic of the thinking of puritanism. What can be ethically defended and what cannot, is formulated in a very precise manner, and through this the Christian receives orientation in his life-style. This has particular consequences in regard to sexual ethics which in accordance with puritanical concepts could only be realized in marriage. In this respect puritanism is in direct contrast to the medieval conception of the troubadours. What has just been stated is important because it has a unique significance in social implications for family and community. Sanctification finds its special radius of activity within marriage and through this the family receives a new and unique value. We let Haller speak to us:

Like all other activities to which men might be called, marriage was an opportunity for spiritual effort, something to be sanctified by the spirit. The Puritan exaltation of the family could serve only to make the godly hold to that conception the more earnestly. . . . Romantic love, however, as presented in medieval literature, was characteristically associated with extramarital relations. . . . In Spenser[210] the woman idealized by the lover is the woman he is to marry. Any other love is evil.[211]

It is precisely for this that puritanism rejects worldly pleasures because in view of the possibilities the godly order of sexuality is particularly menaced and marriage and the family could be easily harmed.

In Hooper's "Injunctions"[212] we find clear instruction that the clergy should not tolerate illegitimate marriages:

Item, that every minister within this diocese do diligently exhort and teach the parisheners that all privy and secret contracts be forbidden by God's laws, and not to be used among christian people, not only because it dishonoureth the means and entrance into marriage, offendeth the parents . . . ; but also for the most part causeth much unhonest and unchaste life.[213]

Hooper thinks highly of marriage, which also leads him to a great respect for the family.

(2) "Pura Doctrina"

Hooper's love of true doctrine occupies the very highest position. Whatever cannot measure up to the Bible is not "pura doctrina." There is no justification for arbitrary interpretation of the Bible because the Bible interprets itself. Therefore God's Word cannot be submitted to human opinion. Hooper has the following to say about this:

It appertaineth unto no man, in what authority soever he be, to judge who preacheth false, or what true; but unto the word of God only, which interpreteth itself, when it is with judgment conferred.[214]

This conception of Hooper underlies the basic assumptions in his idea of the "pura doctrina" which predominates so strongly in his writings. Hooper expresses his concept of the "pura doctrina" very clearly in his "Sermons upon Jonas":

Christ instituted neither singers nor massers, but preachers and testimonies of his true doctrine. Mark xvi. Matt. xxviii. Luke xxiv. Acts i. He that leaveth this doctrine untaught in the church, or teacheth a contrary doctrine, flieth from the face of God, and do incur the danger of damnation that is written. Ezech. xxxiii.iii.[215]

For Hooper, God's Word and true doctrine are identical. The Word should not only be preached, but it should also above all be taught in a correct way. We read in the same series of sermons:

> Let us examine the bishops and priests, whether those that know the will of God by his holy word, diligently teach and preach the same unto other. Then whether any man of that vocation teach false doctrine in the church of Christ.[216]

Hooper summarizes just what this "pura doctrina" implies in the following manner:

> Item, that, forasmuch as both God and the king commandeth that the word of God be taught, that teacheth knowledge, the law, the gospel, faith, charity, love, hope, fear, obedience, heaven, hell, salvation, damnation, sin, virtue, and all other duties of a christian man, as well how to behave himself towards God as towards man; and the same is very godly, richly, virtuously, and compendiously appointed and set forth in the king's majesty's book of common prayer.[217]

The Bible offers the true doctrine as an absolute minimum essential and this precise "pura doctrina" of Holy Scripture is offered by The Book of Common Prayer in full accord with the statement above of Hooper. Hooper stands up, with reference to "pura doctrina," for an independent puritanism which propagates uniformity in doctrine and liturgy, which in the seventeenth century was not typical of puritanism.[218] The latter does indeed stand up for the proclamation of Biblical doctrine and for Biblical action but there is a skeptical attitude toward obligatory formulation of the dogma.

(3) "Purus Cultus"

In Hooper's sermons and writings "purus cultus" comes across, so to speak, step by step. "Purus cultus" is seen by Hooper as being in the closest connexion with Holy Scripture and we have already spoken of that in our work.[219]

A few examples from the "Sermons upon Jonas" may clarify this:

> And so I doubt not, most gracious king, but your highness will, according to your title and style, purge this church of England to the purity and sincerity of God's word.[220]

Hooper is concerned with the liturgy of the apostolic time, with its *simplicitas*; because, for Hooper, the form of worship of the apostolic time is free from pagan and superstitious elements. This becomes evident when Hooper in his "Sermons upon Jonas" says:

> Into the church we wish to be put such ministers as can and would teach the doctrine of the apostles . . . : then such as would minister the sacraments gravely, religiously and simply, as Christ and his apostles did; in baptism nothing to be used but the word, and the simple and bare water; in the supper of the Lord to use the ceremonies and rites of Christ and his apostles, and all occasions of superstition to be avoided.[221]

For Hooper, liturgical vestments, candles, crosses, and altars do not belong to the adiaphora (that is to say, to those things which are indifferent, so long as they do not become the objects of cultic or ceremonial adoration). Thus Hooper makes this point in the same sermons:

> And great shame it is for a noble king, emperor, or magistrate, contrary unto God's word to detain and keep from the devil or his minister any of their goods or treasure, as the candles, vestments, crosses, altars! For if they be kept in the church as things indifferent, at length they will be maintained as things necessary.[222]

As to gestures, Hooper had second thoughts in regard to kneeling:

> Wherefore, seeing kneeling is a shew and external sign of honouring and worshipping, and heretofore hath grievous and damnable idolatry been committed by the honouring of the sacrament, I would wish it were commanded by the magistrates, that the communicaters and receivers should do it standing or sitting. . . . Christ with his apostles used this sacrament, at the first, sitting.[223]

According to Hooper's belief, Holy Scripture also sets obligatory standards for the room where worship is held and for the carrying out of the liturgical actions, which is typical for puritanism generally. Puritanical thinking is particularly concerned that adoration be in the spirit and in truth.

Hooper recognizes another important aspect of "purus cultus." In his "Sermons upon Jonas" he points out in connexion with Holy Communion that one should collect alms for the poor:

> They should help the poor with their alms. This form, me thinketh, is most like unto the form of Christ and the apostles.[224]

Hooper's entire method of argumentation shows us an attitude towards Holy Scripture which has subsequently become famous as "Biblicism" or "fundamentalism."

e. The Importance of the Soul

The soul as the center of one's personality, as contrasted with the body, plays a very important role in Hooper's sermons and writings. In his "Homily in time of pestilence" Hooper is concerned with the following: the source of bodily ailments arises within the soul or the heart. Hooper would like to take over the function of a physician of the soul, with the help of God's Word:

> I will briefly, as by the way, somewhat speak of this disease, as they do: but as a preacher of God's word, and as a physician for the soul rather than for the body, entreat of the sickness and the remedy thereof after the advice and counsel of God's word.[225]

Hooper also preaches about the question of what happens to departed souls. He warns about the unbiblical doctrine of purgatory and he refers to Holy Scripture as the only source of the revelation of God:

> Is there any certainty that putteth all out of doubt our friends' souls to depart from the earth straight unto eternal life? Truly, after the flesh there is no such knowledge. . . . Only therefore the certainty is known by the scripture of God.[226]

When as previously said the emphasis is on confession of sin, penance, and rebirth[227]—then one is dealing primarily with the soul. William Haller writes that in puritanism the soul is of the utmost importance:

> The puritan faith invested the individual soul, the most trivial circumstances of the most commonplace existence, with the utmost significance.[228]

f. Warning and Threat of Judgment

The element of warning and threat of judgment is prevalent in Hooper's sermons and writings. Prevalent is the warning against losing divine blessing as well as eternal life through condemnation. Thus Hooper preaches in his "Sermons upon Jonas" before Edward VI in the following way:

> Seeing now that God hath sent his word, his king, his magistrates, and his preachers into England, and it is a very token that the sins of England is as-

cended up into his sight, and that out of hand we amend, or suddenly to look for the most severe and cruel punishment of God.[229]

Hooper again and again uses God's Word in his menacing preaching in order to verify what he wants to say:

> Noble Esay, the prophet, saith . . . : "woe is me, ye sinful people, people laden with iniquity, a seed malicious, lost children! . . ." Let every man look upon himself, knowledge his sin, and study to amend it from the highest to the lowest, for the Lord is ready to smite.[230]

Hooper challenges the king to throw the false "Jonasses" out of the ship of the commonwealth before it is too late and before they come to eternal damnation and spoil the nation:

> Doubtless it were pleasure to me to speak nothing at all, in case the necessity of my vocation, the danger of these Jonasses, and the salvation of this ship of our commonwealth forced me not thereunto. . . . The salvation of these wicked Jonasses moveth also to speak in this matter, and with the trump of God's word to wake them out of their sleep, lest they slumber and rest so long in their wickedness, that they go sleeping to eternal damnation.[231]

These menaces become more and more frequent in his sermons and they constitute an important factor for Hooper in order that a conversion of the English population might be brought about by means of the king. Accordingly, Hooper continues:

> But this I say to every man . . . : the less they feel the danger of eternal damnation, the nearer they be unto eternal pain and have already one foot in hell, which shall never come again, but the whole body and soul shall follow, except they repent: for no man is farther from heaven then he that feareth not hell.[232]

g. Contrast between a Transitory World and Everlasting Treasures[233]

In Hooper's sermons are found allusions to the transitoriness of the world and of life with all the misery connected with it. Indeed this aspect is to be found in a concentrated form in Hooper's letters, such as may be discovered in one of those letters called "An exhortation to patience, sent to his godly wife Anne Hooper: whereby all the true members of Christ may take comfort and courage to suffer trouble and affliction for the profession of his holy gospel." It is apparently a circular letter addressed to his wife to which Hooper attached great significance because he hoped to reach and comfort many believers through it.

> In the first part St. Paul commandeth us to think or set our affections on things that are above. When he biddeth us seek the things that are above, he requireth that our minds never cease from prayer and study in God's word, until we see, know and understand the vanities of this world, the shortness and misery of this life, and the treasures of the life to come, the immortality thereof, and the joys of that life.[234]

The contrast between the transitory and the eternal is expressed especially well in this letter. So long as one has the eternal treasures before his eyes it becomes possible to bear the iniquities of this earthly life:

> Therefore St. Paul giveth a very Godly and necessary lesson to all men in this short and transitory life, and therein showeth how a man may best bear the iniquity and troubles of this world: "If ye be risen again with Christ, seek the things which are above, where Christ sitteth at the right hand of God the Father.[235]

h. Earthly Life as a Pilgrimage[236]

The idea of this earthly life as a pilgrimage, which plays such a big part in puritanism, is present in Hooper and finds expression in a particularly apt way in a letter to Ann Warcop in which he writes:

> But, my loving sister, as you be travelling this perilous journey, take this lesson with you, practised by wise men; whereof ye may read in the second of St. Matthew's gospel.[237]

The story of the wise men from the east becomes for Hooper a symbol of the true life's journey. Thus Hooper continues:

> Such as travelled to find Christ followed only the star; and as long as they saw it, they were assured they were in the right way, and had great mirth in their journey. . . . Whereof we learn, in any case whiles we be going in this life to seek Christ that is above, to beware we lose not the star of God's word, that only is the mark that showeth us where Christ is, and which way we may come unto him.[238]

What Hooper is saying as one of the chief initiators of early puritanism about the pilgrimage of a Christian becomes a central theme at the peak of puritanism. W. Haller cogently remarks in his analysis of puritanism:

The Christian, knowing that he is only a stranger and eager to be at home, takes no delight in his journey. He enjoys the world only as a passer-by, having other and better business of his own elsewhere.[239]

i. Proclamation of the True Church with Its Various Aspects[240]

(1) The True Church Based on the Word and Not on External Aspects

The true church occupies an extraordinarily important place in the sermons and writings of Hooper. Whether it be a true church depends upon its attitude in regard to God's Word. Thus the structure, the hierarchical offices, as well as the apostolic succession are not relevant to the true church. Hooper writes in his work "Christ and His Office":

> And seeing the church is bound unto this infallible truth, the only word of God, it is a false and usurped authority that men attribute unto the clergy, and bind the word of God and Christ's Church to the succession of bishops or any college of cardinals, schools, ministers, or cathedral churches.[241]

(2) The True Church Is That Fellowship Which Adheres to the Word of God

> They only be the church, that embrace this holy book, the bible, heareth it, learneth it, and followeth the judgment of it.[242]

As mentioned earlier[243] the church does not stand or fall with the functioning of formal clergy. First of all the church is a loving fellowship of believers who come together to hear God's Word and to receive the sacrament of holy communion. Thus Hooper says in his work "A Brief and clear confession of the christian faith":

> I believe and confess one only catholic and universal church, which is a holy congregation and assembly of all faithful believers.[244]

(3) The True Church Possesses a Unity Effected through the Holy Spirit

The characteristics of this unity are concord, brotherly love, as well as a mutual readiness to help one another:

> I believe herewith that the unity of the Spirit, peace, concord, and charity,

that is to say, true amity and brotherly love, the sweet and friendly helping and supporting of one another, is also one of the works and signs of the true catholic church.[245]

(4) Safety and Life Also Belong to Hooper's Concept of the True Church

I believe that this church is like unto the ark of Noah, within the which is safety and life, without the same is death, decay and destruction.[246]

(5) This Church Is Also at War with the World and the Satanic Powers Which Is Why Hooper Calls It the "Church Militant"[247]

That church shall always have enemies, and shall still be tormented in the sea of this world with the thunderings of Anti-christ. . . . But in these waves she shall not be drowned, but shall abide for ever, because she has a good defence and foundation, which is Jesus Christ the righteous. And for this cause I call her the church militant.[248]

(6) The True Church Propagates No Heresies

I believe in the Holy Ghost, equally God with the Father and the Son, and proceeding from them both: by whose virtue, strength, and operation the catholic church is preserved from all errors and false doctrine, and teacheth the communion of saints in all truth and verity.[249]

The single believer indeed can err, but not the true church which is ruled by the Holy Spirit.

Thus, where the doctrine is sound and there is no idolatry, there you find the church that belongs to God, which is to say, the true church:

But where as the doctrine is sound, and no idolatry defended, that church is of God, as far as mortal man can judge.[250]

Hooper understands under the term "true church" not only the place where true doctrine prevails but also where the Word is correctly preached, i.e., in accordance with the Bible, and where the sacraments are administered in the proper way:

And these two marks, the true preaching of God's word and right use of the sacraments declare what and where the true church is.[251]

(7) Hooper Sees the True Church as a Fellowship for the Purpose of Edification and That Is an Important Aspect. We Repeat a Part of a Quotation Already Given on Page 54 of This Work

There is no better way to be used in this troublesome time for your consolation than many times to have assemblies together of such men and women as be of your religion in Christ, and there to talk and renew among yourselves the truth of your religion.

(8) The True Church Can Assuredly Have an External Organization with Established Structures and Historically Developed Forms

It would be false to think that Hooper sees the church merely as a community of believers who cannot be identified. For Hooper the main thing is to show what is essential, and that which endures in the church, that which is unshakeable in times of spiritual, political, and economic turbulence. If there is not an extreme persecution the church may have an organizational structure with a very special discipline. Thus Hooper, among other, speaks out for church discipline:

It is yet the custom of the old church to excommunicate such as were common adulterers, covetous persons . . . blasphemers, slanderers, drunkards . . . ; except they did open penitence. . . . But ye must understand, that this act and discipline of the church is but an act politic and civil to such as hath professed to live in the commonwealth of Christ's church. . . . There is no church than can be governed without this discipline.[252]

Hooper also definitely accepts liturgy as a help for an ordered church service. He uses for this the expression "ceremonies":

The ceremonies ordained for a good order to be observed in the church, should not be neglected.[253]

The church has an external organizational frame which is worthy of respect because of the royal authority. This framework is established by The Book of Common Prayer through intercessions, petitions, lessons, sermon, creed, and many other things. Within this frame people should become acquainted with faith and they should come with a respectful attitude:

Item, that every of them read and use the common prayers, lessons, homilies, and such other service as is appointed for the people in king's majesty's book, plainly, distinctly, openly, treatably, solemnly, honourably, and devoutly, and in such sort, and such place of the church, as the people may best understand, hear, and learn, bear away, and follow the godly knowledge, learning, and prayers there appointed.[254]

The true church is not an external juridically tangible organization, but that does not mean that organization and rules are not important. These are to be compared with the temple of brick and mortar which should emphasize the need for the spiritual temple of the true congregation.

Some of the most important ecclesiological conceptions of Hooper became sharply defined in the course of puritan spiritual history. This is particularly valid with reference to the concept that the true church consists of a fellowship of the sanctified and elected, and is universal. William Haller writes thereon:

First of all, it (the puritan sect) identified the true church not with society nor with the nation but with an exclusive congregation of saints, unanimous in belief and uniform in practice, admitting to its communion only those who would give satisfactory proof of their divine election.[255]

Hooper's idea that a congregation should celebrate the simple services of the primitive apostolic church became characteristic of puritanism.

What Hooper says about strengthening or edifying through a spiritual give and take is found to a large degree in a puritanical congregation:

The immediate outlet of their activity was the religious congregation, the band of devoted disciples drawing inspiration from their leader and strength from one another in their struggle with the powers of this world.[256]

Haller expresses this in an even clearer way when he writes:

The people were brought together. They learned to read, to use a book, to exchange ideas and experiences, to confer intellectually . . . , to partake of the exhilaration of discussion and self-expression.[257]

When Hooper compares the church with Noah's ark[258] we have in the picture a certain sense of domestic safety and a family atmosphere. Puritanical religious thinking sees the church at home among the family. William Haller mentions in this connexion the following with regard to the puritan John Carter:

The "House was a little Church." Thrice a day the scriptures were read and the children and servants catechized and instructed.[259]

Haller makes a general statement in regard to the puritan life-style at home:

Business done, he (the puritan) goes home and concludes the day by gathering his household once more about him. He reads to them from Scripture, catechizes them, sings psalms and prays with them.[260]

j. The Testifying to Faith as a Missionary Function[261]

Hooper writes in his important work "A declaration of the Ten Commandments" how vital it is to witness the faith to others and to win them in this way for the Lord:

The stranger likewise within thy port, though he be of another religion, thou shouldest assay to win him unto the knowledge and rites of thy religion.[262]

In the continuation of the text Hooper expresses his astonishment over the fact that people can be so very hesitant about sharing one's knowledge of God with a stranger in order to bear witness to him. A stranger or neighbor receives with far greater ease the ordinary necessities, but the most needed he receives not. Hooper means the witness of faith:

Likewise in this commandment is condemned our uncharitable behaviour toward our neighbor, and likewise the ungodly and carnal fear that we have to teach a stranger the knowledge of God. We give him the thing we owe him not . . . , a supper or dinner for his money . . . and never make mention of the thing we owe him.[263]

The witness of one's own faith belongs by all means to the puritanical mentality which Haller manages time and again to analyse in a subtle way:

Every Puritan saint in believing himself chosen by God to be saved knew that he must give witness to the grace that had befallen him by living a saintly life.[264]

5. THE MOST IMPORTANT ELEMENTS IN HOOPER'S SERMONS IN REGARD TO FORM

We only want to mention the most important features.

a. The Direct Appeal by Speaking in an Energetic and Exhortative Way

In the sequence of sermons called "Sermons upon Jonas" one encounters the exhortative way of speaking and of appealing to the conscience, which constitutes a typical element in Hooper's sermons. By this exhortative manner of speaking the obligatory character of the message becomes expressly emphasized. Hooper addresses those who seek to carry out intrigues behind the back of the king:

> And I do here appeal and burden every subject's conscience of this realm of England. First those that have the doings, receivings, occupyings and custody, oversight, rule and office of the king's majesty's goods or lands.[265]

Hooper now becomes, in the course of his sermon, very direct when he says:

> But I will feign thee, thou thief and robber of the king and of the commonwealth, to be king, and the king thy officer and receiver: wouldest thou thy officer should deceive thee? . . . Amend therefore, every man, and be true and faithful unto the realm, to the king, and laws of him and his realm.[266]

The energetic and even obtrusive way of speaking is intended principally the better to gain the attention of the hearer. This is clearly revealed when Hooper tells the king:

> At this day, gracious king, the ship of the commonwealth is sore moved with winds and tempests. Here your majesty and your most honourable council may not cease, if ye would the ship to come to rest, but take the pain to find out the authors of these troubles.[267]

Often there is a transition from this exhortative way of speaking into reproaches:

> Farther the love I bear unto the king's majesty and to this commonwealth of England compelleth me to speak; seeing I see the angry hand of God already stretched forth to punish us, if we awake not out of sin . . . : whosoever, of whatever degree he be, that is, or sheweth himself to be, offended

> with this my free and indifferent speaking of God's word, he or they, be they what they may, are the very Jonases and troublers of this common-wealth.[268]

The exhortative way of speaking was developed at an early stage of puritanism, which W. Haller has analysed:

> In Greenham and his pupils, Browne and Smith, we see the Puritan mind at the early stage of its development turned outward in exhortation and agitation.[269]

b. A Manner of Speaking Which Appeals to the Heart

A manner of speaking appealing to the heart consists in this, that the nouns are modified in such manner and style by adjectives that the nouns summon men much more to be earnest and sincere. This way of appealing to the heart is chiefly directed against a dead faith in letters without an inner commitment or against a formalistic confession of sin which is nothing but lip service.

Many examples of this are found in "Sermons upon Jonas." Thus Hooper says the following with reference to the "Jonases" who threaten the ship of the commonwealth:

> If they take the admonitions and the admonitors gently, and rail not against them . . . but with a true repentance of the heart follow this our prophet Jonas, who confessed his fault, and humbly asked remission and pardon for the same.[270]

One notes particularly that substantive connected to an adjective, "true repentance of the heart." Also adverbs can fulfill the same function, as revealed in the text above. The clause "humbly asked remission" is noteworthy. At the beginning of this series of sermons about Jonah, Hooper does not just speak of a "religion of the eternal God," but he discusses the "pure and sincere religion," in which these adjectives "pure" and "sincere" appeal to the heart:

> Among all other most noble and famous deeds of kings and princes, none is more godly, commendable, nor profitable to the commonwealth, than to promote and set forth unto their subjects the pure and sincere religion of the eternal God.[271]

In his explanation of what faith is Hooper uses adjectives which gainsay a formalistic understanding as if faith were only an intellectual matter:

> As touching faith, it is not an opinion and knowledge only, but a vehement, earnest, and certain persuasion of God's promises in Christ.[272]

Again, one should note the adjectives "vehement" and "earnest" which appeal so much to the heart.

Hooper qualifies the members of Christ as "true and living members":

> And in your majesty's so doing, ye bind not only the true and living members of Christ to give God thanks in his behalf, but also declare yourself to be the very favourer, nurse, and helper of the word of God.[273]

When the hearer of Hooper's sermon hearkens to those qualifying expressions "true" and "living" in reference to the membership of Jesus he feels compelled to search his conscience as to whether or not he is really a true member or a true disciple of Jesus. If you omit these qualifying adjectives then the element which appeals to the heart is lacking.

c. Graphic Illustrations

Hooper generally uses a very graphic way of speaking in his sermons. In his "Sermons upon Jonas" he compares the commonwealth to a ship in which many Jonahs are sailing and for various reasons these Jonahs imperil the ship.

> Then thought I, it is not without cause that wise men compare a commonwealth to a ship; for one thing loseth and saveth them both. For in case the master's officer in the ship obey not his law, the ship will of force drown.[274]

Hooper appeals directly to the king with this picture of a ship when he says:

> At this day, gracious king, the ship of the commonwealth is sore moved with winds and tempests. Here your majesty and your most honourable council may not cease, if ye would the ship to come to rest, but take the pain to find out the authors of these troubles.[275]

There are many more examples to illustrate Hooper's graphic manner of preaching.

William Haller makes the following observation about the preaching technique of the puritan:

His sermons were sown thick with imagery, but his images were drawn from sources which people felt they knew, and they bore directly upon the theme of redemption.[276]

d. Utilization of the Bible

The sermons of Hooper are rich in Bible texts used as authority in support. Hooper wants to give every important statement additional weight through the quotation of appropriate Bible citations. It is not necessary to offer further examples because these Bible quotations are so frequent.

e. Repetition

In his "Sermons upon Jonas" Hooper repeats time and again the theme of the ship of the commonwealth which is threatened by false Jonahs. Who are these false Jonahs? is said many times. One can even observe in this repetition a kind of crescendo which rises to a high point toward the end of the sermon. In the last sentences of the Jonah sermon Hooper admonishes the king with the greatest urgency to save the ship of the commonwealth.

With this completion of the elements in Hooper's sermons and writings we have merely sought to mention the most important under points 4 and 5. There are still other elements to be enumerated but we forgo doing so.

D. COMMENTS SUMMARIZING THE CONTRIBUTIONS OF MARTYR, BUCER, AND HOOPER

1. PETER MARTYR

This summary will be brief and will call up only the specific ways in which Martyr differs from Bucer and Hooper.

With Martyr we are dealing with a theologian who, in contrast to Bucer and Hooper, handles revivalistic theology on an intellectual basis. As a thinker belonging to the Augustinian tradition the theology of the "verbum visibile" is very important to him. Martyr takes from Aristotelian ethics the idea of analogy and the relation of proportions. Martyr closely connects this Aristotelian way of thinking with the Augustinian theology of the "verbum visibile." Through this conception Martyr establishes important assumptions in the typical Reformed thinking in which two different areas are maintained: namely, the created material realm and the uncreated spiritual realm. This adheres rather strictly to the maxim: "Finitum non capax infiniti." This doctrine of analogy and the relation of proportions in the service of awakening faith is the specific contribution of Martyr to Cranmer and hence to The Book of Common Prayer.

Thus Martyr justifies the "purus cultus" primarily through an intellectual-ideal approach through his emphasis on "finitum non capax infiniti."

For Martyr, sacramental symbols in the service of analogy are agencies for awakening faith, as S. Corda thus aptly says:

> In Vermigli's system the spiritual eating begins with the work of the Holy Spirit, who uses sacramental symbols as an instrument to stir up man's faith.[277]

With Martyr, theology is chiefly centred on holy communion as a means to awaken faith, while on the other hand questions of ethics and the exact development of the liturgy play only a subordinate role.

For Martyr the question of the wearing of liturgical vestments also lies in the area of the adiaphora.

With Martyr we are dealing with a theology which is more intellectually oriented and which displays a revivalistic character; however, it should not be classified as puritanical.

2. MARTIN BUCER

In Martyr we were dealing with a typical Reformation theologian, but Bucer presents himself to us as a mediator of theology. He belongs in the ranks of the Upper German Reformation theologians and he has his own place which lies between that of Luther and Zwingli. Bucer mediates in the doctrine of holy communion between the Zwinglian "finitum non capax infiniti" and the Lutheran "finitum capax infiniti."

Bucer's theology is certainly of a revivalistic nature. He brings his suggestions for a liturgical reform of the BCP of 1549 in a very practically oriented way while his main concern is the awakening of a living faith.

His main emphasis is on ecclesiology, on the question of the true church. This must illuminate and have an effect upon society, which is expressed in particular in his work dedicated to Edward VI, "De Regno Christi."

Bucer's special merit is that he presents the proof with his mediating theology that the awakening of faith is not dependent on an adjustment to theological distinctions such as the "finitum non capax infiniti" or the "finitum capax infiniti." Therefore Bucer introduced into The Book of Common Prayer by way of Cranmer, without any watering down, a viewpoint of ecumenical breadth and at the same time he put forward in *De Regno Christi* his concern that faith must have the ability to work a change in society. Because of this attitude Bucer is probably not innocent of the fact that the BCP became a book for the people and not just a book of the "Ecclesiola."

Bucer also had understanding for the so called "adiaphora." Ethics in the form of sanctification is with him substantially more in focus than with Martyr.

Bucer is a strongly oriented revivalistic theologian in whom however the puritanical elements are lacking.

3. JOHN HOOPER

John Hooper is as much concerned with the revival of a living faith as are Martyr and Bucer. Hooper maintained an active contact with Martyr as well as with Bucer. A cross-fertilization must certainly have existed.

What however particularly differentiates Hooper from the other two theologians are those elements which marked him in a very evident way which we classify as "puritanical": "pura doctrina," "pura vita," and "purus cultus." Certainly that which Martyr and Bucer teach is also "pura doctrina" but they do not emphasize again and again the necessity for the true doctrine as an element which is to be particularly esteemed. With Martyr and Bucer sound doctrine is present as a matter of course. Hooper repeatedly recalls that it is necessary to take sound doctrine into account.

The "pura vita" is treated similarly by Martyr and Bucer. This may be taken for granted and is not a subject for special inquiry although for Bucer sanctification stands in intimate association with it. However, with

Hooper the so called "punctiliousness" (the precise definition of what is ethically permitted) is found in intimate association with the "pura vita," which is hardly ever found in Martyr or Bucer.

A strong aversion to the pagan, to the godless, manifests itself very markedly in Hooper in his emphasis on "purus cultus."

Were we to analyse the revivalistic elements in Martyr, Bucer, and Hooper through their sermons there would be present a broad harmony. On the other hand we would have difficulty in finding a puritanical element with its particular emphasis in Martyr and Bucer. Hooper reveals himself sharply as a revivalistic and puritanical theologian. Indeed we can observe in Hooper that his puritanical ideas of "pura doctrina," "pura vita," and "purus cultus" are intended to promote the furtherance of revivalism.

In any case much of what is in The Book of Common Prayer would be unthinkable without Hooper's impact, with its revivalistic-puritanical ideas, upon Edward VI and Cranmer.

Next, in Chapter III, Cranmer's theology should become understood to be the result of his discussions with Martyr, Bucer, and above all, with Hooper. The BCP of 1552, a liturgical fruit of Cranmer's theology which was ripened in this interplay, should occupy us in particular.

III. Cranmer's Drafting of The Book of Common Prayer of 1552 as the Fruit of His Discussions with Martyr, Bucer, and Hooper

A. MAIN FEATURES OF CRANMER'S THEOLOGY

At the outset it should be said that Cranmer (1489-1556) is the most important compiler of The Book of Common Prayer for the editions of 1549 and 1552. Only a few direct allusions to The Book of Common Prayer are to be found in Cranmer's writings.[1] It is certainly true, though, that there is present in Cranmer's work a great deal of material which reveals his inner conception and intention for the BCP as a church and home manual as well as a dogmatic confessional document and an Instrumentum Reformationis. In Cranmer's works one can peer into the theological workshop where the English reformer prepared the building blocks for the BCP of 1552.

In this inquiry one should not forget what a powerful influence Martyr, Bucer, and most importantly, John Hooper had upon Cranmer.

Holy Scripture occupies for Cranmer a very special place. That Holy Scripture is the standard for all doctrine is found also in Martyr and Bucer. However in John Hooper we find an untiring emphasis that God's Word and the commandments contained therein must stand at the center of life and doctrine.[2]

It is obvious that Cranmer has primarily evolved his theology of the Word from his discussions with Hooper. We should not be misled by the fact that much which appears to us in Cranmer's writings as clear and uncompromising was penned prior to 1549. Martyr was already at work in England by 1547;, Bucer first commenced his activity there in 1549.[3] Hooper was certainly influential in England through his works and letters written from Zurich in the years 1547-1549.[4]

The question then is why does Cranmer in 1540 advance so clear a theology of the Word in his foreword to "The Great Bible" and this not enter in the expected way into the BCP of 1549? In my opinion Cranmer needed the indicated time to screw up the courage which would allow him to introduce without dubious concessions into a second edition, namely the BCP of 1552, a theology confirmed on the one hand as well as fertilized too by Martyr, Bucer, and Hooper.

1. CRANMER'S UNDERSTANDING OF HOLY SCRIPTURE

a. *Holy Scripture Is the Ultimate Authority in Reference to Questions Seeking Truth*

Holy Scripture must above all be intelligible to uneducated people. These thoughts are clearly expressed in the foreword composed by Cranmer to the revised Matthew Bible which is also known under the name of "Great Bible"[5] or "Cranmer's Bible." A translation in good English is important to him.

> Let us here discuss, what availeth scripture to be had and read of the lay and vulgar people. And to this question I intend here to say nothing but that was spoken and written by the noble doctor and moral divine, St. John Chrysostom, in his third sermon "De Lazaro." . . . He exhorteth there his audience, that every man should read by himself at home in the mean days and time . . . Holy Scripture.[6]

b. *Holy Scripture Is the Instrument for Our Salvation*

Just as the laborer understands how to use his tools, just so should Christians understand and employ the instrument of the Bible.

> Dost thou not mark and consider how the smith, mason, or carpenter or any other handy-craftsman, what need soever he be in, . . . he will not sell nor lay to pledge the tools of his occupation, . . . for then how should he get a living thereby? Of like mind and affection ought we to be towards holy scripture. For as mallets, hammers, saws, chisels, axes and hatchets be the tools of their occupation, so been the books of the prophets and apostles, and all holy writ inspired by the Holy Ghost, the instrument of our salvation.[7]

c. Holy Scripture Can Edify People However Learned

For the Holy Ghost has so ordered and attempered the Scriptures, that in them as well publicans, fishers and sheperds may find their edification.[8]

d. Cranmer Understands Holy Scripture as the Guide to Mastering a Practical Life Work as Well as for Orientation in the Proper Understanding of Divine Truths of Salvation. Pragmatism Which Is So Typical of English Mentality Becomes at Least Apparent Here in the Statement of Cranmer

Wherefore, in few words to comprehend the largeness and utility of the Scripture, how it containeth fruitful instruction and erudition for every man, if any things be necessary to be learned, of the Holy Scripture we may learn it. . . . Here may all manner of persons . . . in this book learn all things what they ought to believe, what they ought to do, and what they should not do.[9]

e. Cranmer's Understanding of Holy Scripture Discloses a Fundamentalistic[10] Approach Which Should Become Obvious in the Following:

(1) The Bible Is Nourishment without Unwholesome Impurities or Indeed Any Toxic Elements

In the Scriptures be the fat pastures of the soul. Therein is no venomous meat, no unwholesome thing. They are the very dainty and pure feeding.[11]

(2) There Are No Truths Which Do Not Require Confirmation through Scripture

If there be truths also outside of the Bible, these have yet been included in Scripture in some way, in the course of which God's Word gives sanction thereto. The Bible does not need supplementation from outside. Cranmer lets this perception become particularly clear in his treatise "A Confutation of unwritten Verities" (1547):

For this is most true, that no unwritten verity is or can be necessary for our salvation, for then should the sacred and holy scriptures, written by the apostles in the Spirit of God and sealed with their bloods, seem to be insufficient and not able to bring us unto salvation.[12]

(3) Holy Scripture Neither Lies Nor Deceives

If thou therefore be desirous to know, whether thou be in the right faith or no, seek it not at man's mouth, . . . but at God's own mouth, which is his holy word written, which can neither lie, deceive nor be deceived.[13]

(4) Cranmer Goes So Far as to Employ the Idea of Infallibility in His Understanding of Scripture

But cleave ye fast to the sound and certain doctrine of God's infallible word, written in the canonical books of the New and Old Testament.[14]

(5) The Bible Is Not Subject to Any Council and Consequently Not to the Church as an Outside Organization

On the contrary, the Bible prevails over a general council and not the reverse.

More credit is to be given to a man that is singularly learned in scripture, bringing forth catholic authority, than to the general council.

A simple layman, bringing forth the scriptures, is to be believed rather than a whole council.[15]

f. Revelations by Means of Occult Phenomena Are to Be Shunned

Only in Holy Scripture is the true revelation to be found, in contrast to all pseudo-revelations.

But God, from whom nothing is hid, hath stopped his way to those snares, and he favouring us hath not suffered that any soul at any time should come from thence hither, to tell what is there done to any man living, teaching us that we should rather believe the scriptures than all other things.

If you doubt of any thing know that it is written, that those nations, which the Lord shall scatter before thy face, shall hearken to dreams and soothsayers. But the Lord, thy God, hath commanded thee not to do so. But if you will know things that be doubtful, give yourselves to the testimonies of the law and the scriptures.[16]

g. Cranmer Argues for the Self-Sufficiency of the Word

This implies something like an objective healing power which becomes effective when the thoughts, will, and feelings of men are greatly reduced in their functioning as a result of sorrow and troubles.

Now therefore, in this common sorrow, I know nothing that is more able to suage our griefs, and to comfort our heaviness, than is the word of God. For as the sun many times with his beams driveth away great thick and dark clouds, and stayeth great storms of winds, so doth the light of God's word stay men's minds, bringing them from trouble to quietness.[17]

h. God's Word Is Also Even for Children

With this observation Cranmer displays an understanding that the Bible seems to affect not simply the reflective intellect but also other organs. According to Cranmer if a person is subjected to the substance of Holy Scripture from childhood on, behind it stands the wisdom of that old saying: "Repeated drops of water cut stone."

Surely there can be no greater hope . . . other to be brought to all honest conversation of living or to be more apt to set forth and maintain all godliness . . . than of such as have been from childhood nourished and fed with the sweet milk, and as it were the pap, of God's holy word.[18]

i. The Word Exercises a Missionary Influence upon Adults through Their Children Who Are Instructed in Holy Scripture

For . . . not only the youth of your Grace's realm may learn to know God, . . . but many of the older sort, such as love God . . . and yet in their youth, through negligence were brought up in ignorance, may, by hearing of their children, learn in their age that which past them in their youth.[19]

j. God's Word Operates to Promote Maturity in People

Education toward maturity should take place during divine worship so that the congregation, thanks to comprehensible language in the priest's sermon, can take a position and give their approval.

> Therefore God's will and commandment is, that when the people be gathered together, ministers should use such language as the people may understand and profit thereby . . . that then all the people, understanding what the priests say, might give their minds and voices with them, and say Amen.[20]

2. THE BASIC PRINCIPLES IN CRANMER'S HERMENEUTICS REVEAL THEMSELVES IN FOUR DIFFERENT WAYS

a. Dark Passages in Scripture

Dark passages in Scripture can never serve as excuses for not having to read the Bible. The better understood explain the obscure passages. Cranmer here rests upon Augustine.

> But when scriptures be hard and doubtful, and seem to be contrary one to another, by mistaking and wrong understanding whereof divers heresies do arise, how shall a man know the truth in such diversity of opinions . . . ? Dark places are to be expounded by more plain places, for that is the surest way of declaring the scriptures.[21]

b. Dark Passages in the Bible Reveal Themselves

Dark passages in the Bible reveal themselves to those who allow themselves to be illuminated in their hearts by the Holy Spirit. Here Cranmer relies upon Chrysostom who anticipates the "testimonium internum Spiritus Sancti" of a Calvin:

> Yet the Lord himself, entering our hearts from above, shall give light into our minds, and pour his bright beams into our reason and understanding, and open the things that be hid and teach us those whereof we are ignorant.[22]

c. Cranmer Is Thereby Convinced
That the Bible Interprets Itself

Thus the English reformer compiles selected Bible passages which should give an indication as to what the Bible thinks of itself. The brief table of hermeneutic principles contained in the Bible is revealed by the following collection of quotations from Scripture reference the Word:

> Ye shall put nothing to the Word which I command you. (Deut. 4)

> The prophet which shall presume to speak a word in my name, which I have not commanded him to speak, or that speaketh in the name of strange gods, that prophet shall die. (Deut. 18)

> All the words of God are pure and clean, for he is a shield unto all them that put their trust in him. Put thou nothing into his words, lest he reprove thee and thou be found a liar." (Prov. 30)

> "Search the scriptures, for in them ye think ye have eternal life, and they are they which testify of me. (John 5)

> For all scripture, given by the inspiration of God, is profitable to teach, to improve, to amend, to instruct in righteousness, that the man of God may be perfect and prepared to all good works. (2 Tim. 3)[23]

In these examples we see clearly how Cranmer lets the Bible explain itself as a trustworthy book whose content permits of no human deletions or additions.

d. The Soundness of the Interpretation of Scripture Passages

The soundness of the interpretation of Scripture passages may also according to Cranmer be determined by examining as many Church Fathers as possible as to their interpretation of the meaning of a Bible text.

> When all the fathers agreed in the exposition of any place of Scripture, he looked on that as flowing from the Spirit of God.[24]

Based on these points we wish to allude somewhat more searchingly to those elements which stamp the BCP as a home and church manual.

UNDER POINT 1.A.

That which claims the highest authority in reference to truth, even Holy Scripture, should be introduced in a suitable form among the people. How could this be accomplished better than by means of the BCP in which Holy Scripture is in large part integrated through the scheduling of pericopes of the Epistle and Gospel texts written out in full, in contrast to mere citations?

The Bible reading plan[25] in the BCP is of decided importance since it takes a congregation's members through the Old Testament within a year, and through the New Testament even more often.

Indeed, since Cranmer attributed so much importance to Holy Scripture, he wanted to smuggle the Bible via the BCP into homes (at that time Holy Scripture was still a big expense for simple townspeople). Its Bible reading plan let The Book of Common Prayer become a home and worship book.

UNDER POINT B.

Since Scripture is an instrument for our salvation, Cranmer was thus suggesting that people by means of a general prayer book make use of the Bible as a tool for instruction in mastering life's problems. J. I. Packer aptly expresses this idea of Cranmer when he says:

> Nothing, he held, matters more for the christian than to read, mark, learn, and inwardly digest, the Bible.[26]

UNDER POINT C.

The conviction that the Bible offers spiritual nourishment for the simple as well as learned people must have caused Cranmer for that reason to fashion The Book of Common Prayer into a home manual in order in that way to guarantee one's daily supplement of divine food.

UNDER POINT D.

Where, above all, must guidance in the mastering of life's practical problems be found if not in the everyday surroundings of the home environment? Thus there is again revealed here a reference to the BCP as a home manual.

UNDER POINT E.

Cranmer's fundamentalistic view with reference to Holy Scripture obviously calls for making the Bible accessible to the public by offering it as church and home manuals. One could only combine God's Word with a prayer book for the general public based upon the conviction that Holy Scripture gives no cause for confusion, but instead unites the various beliefs of men under a single standard. There should be no difference of opinion over the interpretation of the directions for the operation of household utensils. What is meant must be made clear to any normal man. It is the same with Cranmer's understanding of Scripture. The Bible must pragmatically give its instructions or recipe for a positive mastery of life.[27]

UNDER POINT H.

Indeed, since the Word is comprehensible also to children it should have its regular place in the family, which makes clear a further reason for Cranmer's drafting of the BCP as a manual for the home.

UNDER POINT J.

If God's Word accelerates the maturity of people it is clear why Cranmer wanted the BCP also as a home manual. It is indeed the house, the family, which is the basic unit of people.

UNDER POINTS 2.A.-D.

That Cranmer wants to make the Bible into a home manual through the medium of the BCP is due to his conception that obscure passages are of no significance in the untutored man's comprehension of Scripture. Indeed, the better understood passages furnish the key to any obscure texts. Cranmer relies moreover on the "Testimonium Internum Spiritus Sancti," which is no respecter of persons.

The principle of "Scriptura Sui Ipsius Interpres" is a compelling basis upon which to free Scripture from the hands of clerical power and to open God's Word to all, for which the BCP as a manual for the home is a suitable instrument. In the BCP Cranmer clearly extols the principle of "Scriptura Interpres Sui Ipsius" through the joining together of the self-interpreting passages from Scripture in the various worship service formulas.[28] It is characteristic of Cranmer that he will not stand alone in his fundamentalistic outlook. For that reason Cranmer cites many quotations from the Church Fathers to let his convictions be confirmed by them. Indeed, for Cranmer the Church Fathers are the representatives of the true catholic[29] church so their understanding of Scripture must be that of the one universal holy church.

The BCP is also, above all, a church manual inasmuch as it to a greater extent unites the congregation through its most important worship formulas. The BCP is a home manual in the sense that it likewise can bring the congregation together on the small family scale for devotional reading.

3. THE THREE PRINCIPAL LITURGIES IN THE BCP OF 1552 AS REFLECTIONS OF CRANMER'S COMPILATORY THEOLOGY

That which we have established in the preceding sections 1. and 2. with reference to the Bible in the works of this great English reformer has been integrated by Cranmer into the BCP as a dogmatic confession of faith. His Bible theology is also dogmatic and could have been treated in this section as well. It nevertheless seems to me proper that we have discussed Cranmer's scriptural theology beforehand, since God's Word truly forms the presupposition for the derivation of the remaining dogmatic principles.

We select the most important dogmatic concepts from the BCP of 1552.

In this we confine ourselves first to setting forth the central dogmatic elements of Morning and Evening Prayer, and second, those of the eucharistic service. Subsequently we want to investigate in Cranmer's theological writings those dogmatic conceptions that the reformer has worked up as the building blocks for the creation of The Book of Common Prayer. For Cranmer's specific view in connexion with Reformation principles, referred to in an abbreviated form as sin-grace-faith, in which faith occupies a special place, we refer you to the discussion at pages 113-20 of our work.

a. The Most Important Dogmatic Elements in Morning as Well as in Evening Prayer with Reference to Sin-Grace-Faith

The triple beat of sin-grace-faith which resounds throughout the entire BCPs of 1552 and 1662, particularly noticeable in the principal liturgies, distinctly supports the Biblical-Reformation doctrine of justification. Gregory Dix reduces this statement to a brief and convincing quotation when he writes:

> As a piece of liturgical craftsmanship it is in the first rank—once its intention is understood. It is not a disordered attempt at a Catholic rite, but the only effective attempt ever made to give liturgical expression to the doctrine of justification alone.[30]

Thus we see sin-grace-faith as an abbreviation for the basic elements of Reformation theology. In accordance with Reformation thinking, sin is well understood Biblically in a qualitative sense as the utter depravity of man. Sin is primarily understood in a personal way as designating the situation of man in the sense of his separation from God. The Catholic concept of sin at that time was determined more by a quantitative thinking in which guilt carries more of a moralistic accent. Particular offences are emphasized rather than the incorrigibility of man before God. Grace is, in the Reformation view, the wholly gift-like turning of God to man in Jesus Christ through the forgiveness of sins. In accordance with the Catholic view of that time the sacramental event of a Gratia Infusa is emphasized, which is expressed particularly in the concept of baptism.

In the Reformation the perception broke through that faith is above all a personal relationship to God through the revealed Word of Scripture. The Catholic attitude toward faith reveals itself generally in obedience to the church as an institution, which expresses itself through worship and doctrine.

To generalize, one could put it this way: Reformation theology resists any magical understanding of sin-grace-faith.

(1) Sin-Grace-Faith in the Twelve Introductory Quotations from Scripture[31] in Morning Prayer[32]

By the arrangement of the twelve opening quotations from Scripture the Bible expounds itself with reference to the sinful condition of man and with regard to the offered grace of God. This refers to the following quotations: Ezekiel 18:27; Psalm 51:3; Psalm 51:9; Psalm 51:17; Joel 2:13; Daniel 9:9 and 10; Jeremiah 10:24; Psalm 6:1; Matthew 3:2; Luke 15:18 and 19; Psalm 143:2; 1 John 1:8 and 9.[33]

Exactly what The Book of Common Prayer understands sin to be may be determined from the above-mentioned passages. Ezekiel 18:27 speaks of the wicked man. He may only save his soul when he does that which is lawful and right. Thus the man who contravenes the promulgations of God is sinful. In accordance with Daniel 9:9 and 10, man's rebellion against God and his contravention of the laws of God is sin:

> To thee, O Lord God belongeth mercy and forgeueness: for we have gone away from thee, and have not harkened to thy voyce, whereby we might walke in thy lawes, which thou hast appoynted for us.

The idea of grace may also be deduced from these texts. In Luke 15:18 and 19 the subject is the prodigal son who may return to his father. Grace thus means the kindness of God, which grants the repentant opportunity for conversion. What is meant by grace comes out with particular clarity in the text of 1 John 1:8 and 9:

> Yf we saye that we have no synne, we deceyve ourselves, and there is no trueth in us.

Grace is not only the opportunity for conversion, grace is forgiveness in the sense of becoming accepted by God and a reconditioning of a depraved man through a cleansing process.

The twelve scriptural passages say only indirectly what faith is. Faith is revealed in them chiefly by what men do with sin and grace. To faith belongs the acknowledgment of sin, and at the same time the confidence that God can take away the guilt. Psalm 51:3 and 9 expresses this:

> I do know mine owne wickednes, and my synne is alway against me.

(2) Sin-Grace-Faith in the Exhortations, Confession, and Absolution

We assemble the important concepts of the exhortations:[34] sin, wickedness, humble, lowly, penitent, obedient heart, forgiveness, goodness, mercy, benefits, heavenly grace, thanks, praise.

We add the following concepts from the confession and absolution,[35] thus producing the supplement: devices, desires of our own hearts, no health in us, faults, absolution, remission, repent, believe, eternal joy.

We can group the collected concepts around the three core words sin-grace-faith:

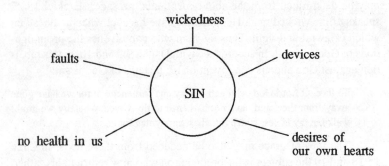

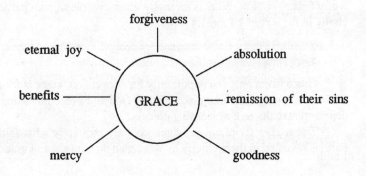

100

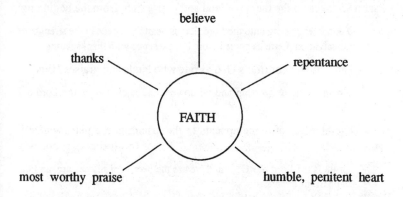

The exhortations, confession, and absolution are elements which tend to animate the act of faith. Thus the exhortations should lead the congregation to draw the consequences from the message of the twelve opening Biblical texts: namely through the faith offered by grace, to make repentance and accept forgiveness. In the confession occurs the realization as to where the Scriptural texts and the exhortation may lead: an admission of guilt arises and an explicit desire for forgiveness.

(3) Sin-Grace-Faith in the Lord's Prayer, Opening Sentences, and Psalm 95

The Lord's Prayer,[36] following the absolution, clearly points to the theme of sin-grace-faith, just as do the following opening sentences[37] which begin with the words: "O Lord, open thou our lips . . ." etc. The opening sentences declare the principal functions of faith, namely laud and praise. Also, the Lord's Prayer ends with laud and praise.

The opening sentences indeed do not neglect to emphasize the calling of men upon divine help as a consequence of their frailty and sin:

> O God, make spede to save us.
> O Lord, make haste to help us.

Psalm 95[38] is especially informative in regard to the understanding of faith.

If we define faith as the positive attitude of men toward God's plan of salvation, then we see in Psalm 95 some important aspects of faith. Psalm 95 takes up the theme of laud and praise right from the beginning:

> O come let us syng unto the Lord: Let us heartely rejoice in the strength of our salvation. Lette us come before hys presence with thanksgeuing.

The believer confronts God as one who lauds and praises Him.

> O come, lette us worship and fal downe, and knele before the Lord our maker.

The element of grace appears in this psalm at the place where it says:

> For he is the Lord our God: and we are the people of his pasture, and the shepe of his hands.

This psalm likewise calls attention to the sins of men which exist in their stubbornness toward God:

> Forty yeres long was I grieved with this generation, and said: It is a people that do erre in their harts, for they have not known my wayes.

The elements of sin-grace-faith are clearly present in Psalm 95, even if not in this exact order. Faith in this psalm is expressed in the attitude of the psalmist who gives God the glory in worship at the same time that he recognizes God as the lord of creation and he perceives the place given by grace to sinful man as one belonging to the flock of the divine shepherd.

In accordance with the rubric the appropriate psalms for the day follow after Psalm 95 which ends with the minor doxology.[39] These all then terminate with the minor doxology which denotes faith as an act of worship.

(4) Old Testament Lesson

The lesson in itself calls for faith under the aspect of listening to a message from God's Word.

(5) In the Te Deum Laudamus[40] Faith Again Is Expressed as Praise, in the Course of Which Sin and Grace Also Resound

> When thou tookest upon thee to deliver man: thou dyddest not abhor the virgin's womb. When thou hadst overcomed the sharpness of death: thou diddest open the kingdom of heaven to all beleeuers.

(6) New Testament Lesson

Just as in the Old Testament lesson faith is understood as the obedient listening to the Word of God, here is demanded the taking seriously of the Old Testament promises which came to fulfillment in the New Covenant.

(7) Benedictus (Luke 1:68ff.)[41]

In the Benedictus the three beats of sin-grace-faith may be detected in the course of which that grace which kindles faith is particularly emphasized. Verses 68-73 of Luke 1 reveal God's gracious dealings with his chosen people through a realization of the prophetic promises. Faith ignited by grace desires holiness and righteousness as the fruits of faith, in accordance with verses 74 and 75:

> That we beyng deliuered out of the handes of oure enemies: might serue hym wythoute feare.

We find a clear reference to sin in verses 77 and 79 where at the same time it speaks of grace:

> To geue knowledge of salvacion unto hys people: for the remission of theyr sinnes, through the tender mercye of oure God: whereby the daye-spring from on hyghe hath vysited us.[42]

The Benedictus may also be replaced with Psalm 100.

(8) Apostles' Creed[43]

In the Apostles' Creed we encounter the center of the liturgical concerns in Morning Prayer. This creed brings forward for believers in a concentrated way as the hard core of faith the facts of salvation as the gracious acts of God. Here is the understanding of faith as a conscious and trusting acceptance of the events of salvation which became events for each one by grace.

In the triple beat of sin-grace-faith, faith is the central element which is expressed in the Creed in one voice by expressis verbis. The acts of salvation mentioned in the Creed extol the element of grace on which faith should be founded. When reference is made in the Creed to the crucifixion, sin is of necessity envisioned thereby. It is worthy of note that the Creed begins in the first-person singular. Neither an institution nor a collective can believe in a substitutional way for an individual. Each must answer for his faith himself.

(9) Miserere[44]

> Lord, have mercy upon us. Christ, have mercy upon us.
> Lord, have mercy upon us.

Here occurs a reference to sin and grace simultaneously.

(10) Lord's Prayer[45]

This second Lord's Prayer serves the function of closing the parentheses. That which precedes[46] the first Lord's Prayer has the purpose of an introduction and prelude to the worship service and supplies the dogmatic theme in advance. That which stands within the parentheses themselves[47] is the presentation and especially the development of the sin-grace-faith theme. That which stands then beyond the closed parenthesis after the second Lord's Prayer is a phasing out of the worship service by means of the closing sentences[48] and some prayers spoken for the appointed occasion.

(11) Closing Sentences

These take up the theme of sin-grace-faith, though in a milder form. Grace is clearly expressed where it says:

> O Lord, shewe thy mercy upon us. And graunt us thy saluacion.
> O Lord, saue thy people. And blesse thine enheritaunce.

The text strikes up the theme of sinfulness where it says:

O God, make clean our heartes within us.

Faith then exists in this that one places sin and grace with respect to one another in the proper relation.

We do not have to go specially into Evening Prayer since the same dogmatic architecture is present.

b. The Most Important Dogmatic Elements in the Eucharistic Liturgy[49] with Reference to Sin-Grace-Faith

In the eucharistic liturgy of the BCP of 1552 we find the triple beat of sin-grace-faith in even stronger measure than in Morning and Evening Prayer.

(1) Opening Collect

The opening collect[50] follows immediately after the Lord's Prayer. It is especially important.

Almightie God, unto whom all heartes be open, all desyres knowen, and from whom no secretes are hyd: clense the thoughtes of our heartes by the inspiracion of thy holy spirit, that we maye perfectlye loue thee, and worthely magnify thy holy name: through Christ our Lorde.

This collect sees the heart of man as that area which should be cleansed by the Holy Spirit. The opening collect perceives man as rotten to the core. It designates that program which must be the reality for men purified by the Holy Spirit: faith, in the sense of love of God and praise of God.

(2) Decalogue[51]

Those who are faithful at heart adhere to the Ten Commandments of God as long as they live. Thus Cranmer permits the Decalogue to follow immediately after the opening collect, with a responsive interruption in which the congregation prays to keep the law in their hearts.

Lord, haue mercye upon us, and encline our heartes to kepe this lawe.

The congregation responds in this fashion after each previously read Commandment. This liturgical treatment of the Decalogue reveals an attitude which sees the faith within as operative even in the outer sphere of activity. The author of the liturgy guards against any misunderstanding as to whether a purely outer compliance with the law can be true faith. There can be no genuine faith without the heart's commitment. The Lord must stir the heart into producing the real fruit in an obedience to the Commandments.[52]

The "Lord, have mercy upon us," the response made by the congregation to each declaration of a Commandment, again expresses faith as an aspect of recognizing one's own sinfulness.[53]

(3) Twenty Offertory Sentences[54]

After the Decalogue follows the prayer for the royal family, to which is attached the collect for the day, and then right after the Epistle and Gospel comes the Creed, followed by the twenty offertory sentences taken from Holy Scripture. These encourage a practical charity and take up in the nature of a reprise what the Ten Commandments as a whole wished to express about faith, namely: faith shows it is sincere in works. Thus these Biblical quotations at the beginning of the offertory stress the sacrificial character of faith.

(4) Prayer for the Church Militant[55]
(Christ's Church Militant Here on Earth)

The twenty offertory sentences are developed in this prayer of the Ecclesia Militans. The concept of offering[56] is worthy of consideration. The object of the contributions are prayers to God for the universal church in the course of which the petition for the church consists of the following requests: inspiration of the church with a spirit of truth, unity, and concord. Truth is to be seen to be in intimate connexion with grace, and clearly to the extent that the truth of God is a merciful verbal revelation.

Since God's truth is of an exclusive type, all must submit themselves to it, which is expressed in the concept of unity. This grace-given manifestation of truth is revealed by Holy Scripture:

> We humbly beseche thee, most mercifullye to accepte our almose and to receiue these our prayers, which we offer unto thy diuine Majestie, besech-

106

ing thee to inspire continually the uniuersall churche with the spirite of trueth, unitie, and concorde: and graunt that all they that dooe confesse thy holye name, may agree in the trueth of thy holy woord.[57]

Man would know absolutely nothing of sin-grace-faith without the Word of God. Grace and faith are stressed especially in this prayer for the Ecclesia Militans, sin somewhat less. One doesn't find a direct definition of faith. An understanding of faith is crystallized out of the concerns expressed in the prayer. In the following passage we find an understanding of faith in accordance with which the clerical officials must set forth the Word of God in their life and teaching:

> Geue grace (O heauenly father) to all Bisshops, Pastours, and Curates, that they maye bothe by their lyfe and doctrine sette foorth thy true and lyuely woord.[58]

The way in which grace-faith and the Word of Scripture mutually affect each other is clearly revealed where it says:

> And to all thy people geue thy heauenly grace and especiallye to thys congregacion here present that, with meke hearte and due reuerence they may heare and receiue thy holy woord, truely seruing thee in holynesse and ryghteousnesse all the dayes of theyr lyfe.[59]

In this prayer for the church militant faith is understood as a kind of act of offering which comes forth so clearly in that passage at the outset that we bring it to your attention once again:

> We humbly besche thee to accepte our almose and to receiue these our prayers, which we offer unto thy diuine Majestie.

The petition for the acceptance of the material gift stands in a situation parallel to the petition for the acceptance of the offered prayer.

(5) Sin-Grace-Faith in the Three Exhortations[60]

In the three exhortations we find the reasoned basis for a true comprehension of holy communion presented in a sermon-like style. The first exhortation[61] chiefly emphasizes grace under the aspect of God inviting the lost sinner. The picture of the banquet to which all are invited plays a great role therein. But this exhortation particularly warns against rejecting the grace offered by the Redeemer host inasmuch as the expected consequences would be serious:

I bidde you all that be here present, and beseche you for the Lord Jesus Christes sake, that ye will not refuse to come thereto, being so louingly called and bidden of god hymselfe.[62]

The first exhortation points out clearly that the grace is not inexpensive. Whoever scorns it bears the consequences:

Wherefore, most derely beloued in Christ, take ye good hede, lest ye with drawyng yourselues from this holy supper, prouoke god's indignacion against you.[63]

The second exhortation[64] takes particular aim at the sinful depravity of man and speaks of the conditions which lead to forgiveness. Whoever wishes to bring himself to God must submit himself to a searching exploration of his conscience and come to a repentance with respect to his recognized sins. Recognition of sins therefore becomes advantageous since then one can be granted a gracious forgiveness.

Thus in the second exhortation there exists the weight of the acknowledged sin as well as the receiving of pardon:

First to examine your liues and conuersacion by the rule of goddes commaundements, and whereinsoeuer ye shall perceiue your selues to have offended, either by will, word, or dede, there beewaile your owne sinful liues, confess your selfes to almightie god with ful purpose of amendment of life.[65]

At the end of the second exhortation it says:

And that by the ministery of God's word he may receiue coumfort and the benefite of absolucion.[66]

In the third exhortation[67] faith is the subject in express words. Faith is here the taking of Jesus in a spiritual sense by means of the sacramental symbols:

For as the benefite is great, if with a truly penitent heart and liuely fayth, we receiue that holy Sacrament (for then we spirituallye eate the fleshe of Christ, and drynke hys bloud, then we dwel in Christ and Christ in us, we be one with Christ, and Christ with us).

The theme of sin-grace-faith is implicit in all of the three exhortations, in which an increase in faith is built up in the first two exhortations which achieves its high point in the third exhortation.

(6) Invitation to Confession, Confession, and Absolution

In the invitation to confession faith is associated with the condition that one repent and hold the intention of leading a new life in accordance with the commandments:

> You that doe truly and earnestly repente of your synnes, . . . and entende to leade a newe lyfe, folowyng the commaundments of God. . . . Drawe nere and take this holy Sacramente to your comfort.[68]

In the confession itself the churchgoers themselves declare their rejection and repudiation of sin. In the absolution[69] grace is evident in the consolation of the forgiveness.

(7) The Four Comfortable Words from the New Testament[70]

The four comfortable words from Matthew 11:28; John 3:16; 1 Timothy 1:15; and 1 John 2:1 make reference to the depravity of man and his need for redemption. These quotations from Scripture call attention chiefly to the comforting features of the offer of grace.

(8) Preface with Sanctus[71]

Man, to whom forgiveness is granted due to the confession of sins and absolution, is now free to give thanks and praise, which is clearly existent in the little hymn-like passages of the Preface and Sanctus.

> Lyfte up your heartes.
> We lyfte them up unto the Lorde.
> Let us geue thankes unto our Lorde God.
> It is mete and right so to doe.
> It is very mete, ryght, and oure bounden duetie, that we should at al times, and in al places, geue thankes unto thee, O Lord holy father, almightie euerlastyng God.
> Therefore with Angelles and Archangelles, and with al the companye of heauen, we laude and magnifye thy glorious name, euermore praysing thee, and saying: Holye, holye, Holye, Lorde God of hostes: heauen and yearthe are full of thy glory.

Faith is recognized here under the aspect of thanksgiving, laud, and worship.

If we wanted to portray graphically the development of the eucharistic service up to the present point we would have a picture of a spiral staircase in which three steps would continuously rise in unison. In this single ascending spiral are entwined the three steps of sin, grace, and faith.

(9) Prayer of Humble Access[72]

Faith is also prominent in this prayer of humble access in which one can well perceive the two preceding steps of sin and grace:

> We doe not presume to come to this thy table (O mercyfull Lorde) trustinge in our owne righteousnesse, but in thy manifolde and greate mercies: we bee not worthye, so much as to gather up the crommes under thy table: but thou art the same Lorde whose propertie is alwayes to haue mercye: graunt us therefore (gracious lord) so to eate the fleshe of thy dere sonne Jesus Christ, and to drinke his bloud, . . . that we may euermore dwel in him, and he in us.

Faith reveals itself to us in this prayer in the form of a personal living fellowship with Jesus in the sense of John 15:4ff.

(10) Consecration Prayer[73]

The consecration prayer has to do with a participation in Jesus' sacrificial death based on the remembrance of the actual act of salvation:

> Heare us O mercyefull father wee beeseche thee: and graunt that wee, receyuing these thy creatures of bread and wyne, accordinge to thy sonne our Sauioure Jesus Christ's holy institucion, in remembraunce of his death and passion, maye be partakers of his most blcssed body and bloud.

In the Roman canon the consecration, with its subsequent transubstantiation, conceals the danger of a certain immanentism so that the simple churchgoer seeks Jesus too strongly in the horizontal at the cost of the vertical. A magical understanding linked to objects related to the presence of Jesus can easily restrict us to the limits of the here and now. The consecration prayer reveals the ascending spiral clearly with its three steps of sin-grace-faith.

The text of the consecration prayer puts its brand on our sin when it says:

> Almighty God oure heauenly father, whiche of thy tender mercye dyddest geue thine onely sonne Jesus Christ, to suffre death upon the crosse for our redempcion, who made there a full, perfecte and sufficiente sacrifice, oblacion, and satisfaccion for the synnes of the whole worlde.[74]

Sin is strongly accented in the text because it suggests what God has let it cost him in the redemption of men. At the same time grace also receives a powerful emphasis. The high point is met in the words of distribution which invite those taking part in the service to take the consequences of the forgiveness granted through the power of grace. This consequence is a seizing of the salvation offered by grace in the sacrament of bread and wine, or as otherwise expressed: faith.

> Take and eate this, in remembraunce that Christ dyed for thee and feede on him in thy hearte by faythe, with thankesgeuing.[75]

(11) Closing Prayers after the Lord's Prayer[76]

In the first closing prayer, praise and thanks made by faith are understood as acts of sacrifice in which the entire man with body and soul is the subject of the sacrificial gift:

> O Lorde . . . , we thy humble seruaunts entierly desire thy fatherly goodnes, mercifully to accept this our Sacrifice of prayse and thanks geuing: . . . and here we offre and presente unto thee, O lord, our selfes, our soules, and bodies, to be a reasonable, holy, and liuely Sacrifice unto thee.

The second closing prayer stresses once more the goodness and grace of God.

(12) Gloria[77]

This great hymn at the close of the service is intended just by its placement to indicate in connexion with all of the liturgy that the most noble activity and indeed the acme of faith consists of laud and praise.

4. CITATIONS FROM CRANMER'S WORKS FOR THE UNDERSTANDING OF THE PRINCIPAL DOGMATIC ELEMENTS OF SIN-GRACE-FAITH

The fourth point consists chiefly in searching out from among his writings the dogmatic building blocks of sin-grace-faith which Cranmer knew how to use in a masterful way in the construction of this liturgy. It should be necessary to mention only a few citations which are in this connexion instructive. Very useful for this are Cranmer's "Homilies of salvation, faith, and good works" from the year 1547.[78]

We have seen under Morning Prayer that Cranmer held the dogmatic conception that justification only arises from faith, whereby this justification arises out of faith drawing proper conclusions from sin and grace. The same is also valid for the holy communion liturgy.

a. Justification according to Cranmer

In his "Homily of Salvation" Cranmer writes:

> But our justification doth come freely by the mere mercy of God, and of so great and free mercy, that whereas all the world was not able of themselves to pay any part towards their ransom, it pleased our heavenly Father, of his infinite mercy, without any our desert . . . , to prepare for us the most precious jewels of Christ's body and blood, whereby our ransom might be fully paid, the law fulfilled, and his justice fully satisfied. So that Christ is now the righteousness of all them that truly believe in Him.[79]

The pronounced stress on grace in the foregoing quotation reminds one of the beginning of the consecration prayer in the communion service where it says:

> Almighty God . . . , whiche of thy tender mercye dyddest geue thine onely sonne Jesus Christ, to suffre death upon the crosse for our redempcion, who made there a full, perfecte and sufficiente sacrifice, oblacion, and satisfaccion for the synnes of the whole worlde.[80]

Justification is a pure act of giving and receiving. Nor is the act of faith in any way meritorious behaviour. Cranmer gives expression to this idea when he says:

> Justification is not the office of man, but of God: for man can not justify himself by his own works neither in part, nor in the whole. . . . But justifi-

cation ... is not a thing which we render unto Him, but which we receive of Him ... by His free mercy.[81]

One finds an echo of this conviction of Cranmer in the first closing prayer of the communion service where we read:

> And although we bee unworthy throughe oure manifolde sinnes to offre unto thee any Sacrifice: yet we beseche thee to accept this our bounden duetie and seruice not weighing our merites, but pardoning our offences, through Jesus Christ our Lord.[82]

B. ASPECTS OF CRANMER'S CONCEPT OF FAITH

The proper interplay of sin-grace-faith in the lives of men is realized in justification. Of the three central ideas, Cranmer considered faith as the most prominent.

As we shall now devote our attention chiefly to Cranmer's ideas on faith we then will be seeking also on occasion to find places in the BCP where Cranmer's conception of faith is reflected.

Citations from the BCP will be generally confined to the communion liturgy, and in so doing no sequence in reference to the liturgical unity will be observed.

(1) Faith as the Acceptance of the Promise and the Forgiveness of Sins

In the third part of the "Homily of Salvation" we find an important aspect of Cranmer's concept of faith:

> Nevertheless, faith doth directly send us to Christ for remission of our sins, and that by faith given us of God we embrace the promise of God's mercy and of the remission of our sins.[83]

Promises play an important role in the psalms and hymns of Morning and Evening Prayer. Faith exists in the acceptance of these divine promises. As one example among many others one is reminded of the promise-filled Benedictus from Luke 1:68-79 in Morning Prayer. One should embrace the promises, as well as the exhortation mentioning forgiveness. What Cranmer says in the above quotation coincides with the concept in Morning and Evening Prayer in which the opening portion seeks to lead the churchgoer by the exhortation, confession, and absolution to become so much aware thereby of this consolation consisting of the forgiveness that he embraces this[84] almost with avidity.

In the words of distribution[85] in the communion service the spiritual act of receiving Jesus is accompanied in a symbolic sense by a gesture at the time of receiving which expresses itself in kneeling and with outstretched open hands. The communicant embraces in faith the grace of forgiveness offered to him in the symbols of bread and wine.

Cranmer speaks somewhat less powerfully when he speaks simply of faith as a firm trust in forgiving grace. One can understand the confession as an exercise in faith. This interpretation is obvious when one considers the following passage from Cranmer's "Homily of the true, lively and christian faith . . .":

> And this faith is also a sure trust and confidence of the mercy of God through our Lord Jesus Christ, . . . and although we through infirmity or temptation of our ghostly enemy, do fall from him by sin, yet if we return again unto him by true repentance, that he will forgive and forget our offences for His Son's sake.[86]

(2) Faith as a Matter of the Heart

> This is the true, lively and unfeigned christian faith, and is not in the mouth and outward profession only, but it liveth and stirreth inwardly in the heart. And this faith is not without hope and trust in God, nor without the love of God and our neighbors . . . nor without the desire to hear God's word and to follow the same . . . in doing gladly all good works.[87]

Heartfelt faith is far-reaching. It reveals itself in hope and trust in God as well as in love of the Lord. Therein is included the hearing and the taking to heart of Holy Scripture. Thus heartfelt faith is not simply lip service, but it produces fruit at the same time that it engages the thinking, feeling, and the will of men.

(3) Faith as a Consequence in Good Works

In the same writings of Cranmer we find passages which serve as commentaries on the Ten Commandments[88] and on the twenty-four offertory texts[89] of the communion liturgy:

> A true faith cannot be kept secret, but when occasion is offered, it will break out, and show itself by good works.[90]

(4) Faith as a Spiritual Sacramental Eating

Cranmer's understanding of holy communion is of particular importance in this connexion. In his masterpiece "A Defence of the True and Catholic Doctrine of the Sacrament of the Body and Blood of our Saviour Christ" he stresses that a spiritual eating and drinking is referred to in the eucharist. The strong emphasis on the communion's character as a memorial is clarified by this conception. For Cranmer there is a close connexion between faith and the spiritual-sacramental eating and drinking. To begin with, the following text may indicate how far Cranmer is removed from the doctrine of transubstantiation:

> The scripture is plain, and you confess also that it was bread that Christ spake of when he said, This is my Body. And what need we any other scripture to encounter with these words, seeing that all men know that bread is not Christ's body . . . ? Wherefore in that speech must needs be sought another sense and meaning, than the words of themselves do give, which is that the bread is a figure and sacrament of Christ's Body.[91]

Behind this quotation is set Cranmer's conviction that the conception of an "Ex Opere Operato," a self-acting effect of the sacrament independent of the attitude of the recipients, is dangerous. How easily then can holy communion be misunderstood as an inoculation given orally. The concept of a spiritual food is found in the second of the communion liturgy's selection of closing prayers:

> Almightie and euerliuing God, we most heartely thank thee, for that thou dooest vouchsafe to fede us, whiche haue duely receyued these holye misteries, with the spirituall foode of the most precious body and bloud of thy sonne our sauiour Jesus Christ.[92]

This is expressed even more clearly in the next quotation from Cranmer. Communion should, through the act of receiving it, be a particular realization of faith and also an exercise in faith. An understanding of communion which addresses itself to the spiritual eating and drinking has a decidedly more faith-awakening force. The "Ex Opere Operato" conception works against the faith-awakening intention of the Biblical concept of communion. Cranmer's following statements which may persuade us of the truth of the spiritual communication with Jesus in holy communion, are rather humorous:

> And whosoever hath this godly hunger, is blessed of God. . . . But this hunger and thirst is not easely perceived of the carnal man. For when he heareth the Holy Ghost speak of meat and drink, his mind is by and by in the kitchen and buttery, and he thinketh upon his dishes and pots, his mouth and his belly. . . . But the Scripture in sundry places useth special words, whereby to draw our gross minds from phantasying of our teeth and belly. . . . And also when our Saviour Christ said: "He that cometh to me shall not hunger and he that believeth on me shall never be thirsty," he gave them a plane watchword that there was another kind of meat and drink. . . . The meat, drink, food and refreshing of the soul is our Saviour Christ.[93]

Cranmer has the objective in the above text, through the analogy[94] made, to stress the importance of holy communion. Cranmer elucidates from the bodily eating and drinking the need for taking a spiritual nourishment. Now Cranmer's meaning is that the sacrament, in its ritual-liturgical employment, should release a process in the spiritual sphere of the soul based on the efficacy which lies in the analogy. A very interesting remark of Cranmer provides instruction in connexion with the revival of a living faith. The analogy plays an important role therein also. Cranmer establishes that our physical living should not begin with material nourishment but by begetting by the parents. Preservation then of the physical body occurs through material food and liquids. In the spiritual-sacred realm our entry also occurs through a procreation, namely, through that of Jesus. He himself is the spiritual food which sustains us in a genuine existence. The very strongly emphasized doctrine of the new birth among revivalistic circles is clearly advocated in its essence by Cranmer. The being born again is indeed the door to the true faith:

> For as there is a carnal generation, and a carnal feeding . . . , so is there also a spiritual generation, and a spiritual feeding. And as every man by carnal generation of father and mother, is carnally begotten and born unto this mortal life: so is every good christian spiritually born by Christ unto eternal life. . . . But our Saviour Christ is both the first beginner of our spiritual life and also afterward he is our lively food. . . . And the believing and feeling of these things, is the believing and feeling of Christ in our hearts.[95]

To believe is at the same time a spiritual eating or a spiritual act of letting oneself be nourished. Faith apprehends Jesus as án affair of the heart in a grateful attitude and perceives or experiences him in the soul. The latter part of the quotation above finds a clear echo in the words of distribution in the eucharistic liturgy:

> Take and eate this, in remembraunce that Christ dyed for thee, and feede on him in thy hearte by faythe, with thanksgeuing.[96]

God wishes, having regard to the psychophysical structure of men, graciously to underwrite legally, as it were, the objective state of affairs of a spiritual occurrence. This thinking of Cranmer becomes very obvious in the continuation of the previously quoted text:

> And for this consideration our Saviour . . . hath not only set forth these things most plainly in his holy word, that we may hear them with our ears, but he hath also ordained . . . one visible sacrament of spiritual nourishment in bread and wine, to the intent, that as much as it is possible for man, we may see Christ with our eyes, smell him at our nose, taste him with our mouths, grope him with our hands, and perceive him with all our senses. . . . Thus our Saviour . . . knowing us to be in this world, as it were, but babes and weaklings in faith hath ordained sensible signs and tokens whereby to allure and to draw us to more strength and more constant faith in him.[97]

Cranmer understands the sensible domain as the sphere of manifestation of God's activity.

Of greater significance is Cranmer's persuasion that not every agreeable churchgoer receives Jesus in communion, but only the born again, the faithful:

> And that Christ doth indeed feed such as be regenerated in him, . . . this I confess also. But that he feedeth . . . infidels, if they receive the sacrament . . . this neither I confess, nor any ancient scripture or ancient writer ever taught, but they teach, that he is eaten spiritually in our hearts and by faith.[98]

In the third exhortation in the eucharistic liturgy one finds a plain result of that which Cranmer has just told us. Satan takes possession of the unfaithful or of them living in sin by the unworthy taking of communion.

> Therefore, yf any of you be a blasphemer of God, an hynderer or slaunderer of his worde, an adulterer, or be in malice or enuie, or in any other greuous cryme, bewayle your sinnes, and come not to thys holy Table, . . . lest the Deuill entre into you.[99]

Behind the formulation and exposition as we have now perceived it from Cranmer's pen, there lies as its source an unmistakable puritanical-revivalistic influence.[100] The association of faith and heart points in the direction of a revivalistic spirituality as we wish to point out more particularly later on in the details of the text of the BCP.

For Cranmer, the more one avoids any misunderstanding about a mechanically operating force the more the sacrament receives earnestness and dignity. Cranmer places faith so very much in the foreground that the need for taking communion for salvation comes to naught:

> And as He is spiritually present, so is He spiritually eaten of all christian faithful men, not only when they receive the sacrament, but continually so long as they be members spiritual of Christ's mystical body.... And as the Holy Ghost doth not come only to us in baptism, and Christ doth there clothe us, but they do the same to us continually, so long as we dwell in Christ, so likewise doth Christ feed us so long as we dwell in Him and He in us.[101]

Faith receives a very high valuation since it occasions the sacrament, and not the contrary. The sacraments are a very helpful area for the activity and confirmation of faith. One can also understand the sacrament as a seal. Still, it is never an absolute necessity. In this connexion Cranmer quotes Augustine's well-known sentence from the 25th Discourse on St. John's Gospel:

> Prepare not your mouth or your jaws, but your heart. Why dost thou prepare thy belly and teeth? Believe and thou hast eaten.[102]

(5) Faith as Consecration[103]

Of greater significance in reference to Cranmer's understanding of faith is his opinion in connexion with the question of conversion or transformation in the communion liturgy, about which something additional should be said.

Cranmer wants to divert the attention from an outer transformation. This means nothing to him. Of much greater importance to him is the transformation of the hearts of men through faith. Such a transformation is guaranteed much more now through participation in the effect of the sacrificial death of Jesus by a memorial as an act of realization of that which has occurred for our salvation:[104]

> Take and eate this, in remembraunce that Christ dyed for thee, and feede on him in thy hearte by faythe, with thankesgeuing.[105]

On questions concerning the consecration Cranmer followed the range of ideas of the Church Father Eusebius Emissenus (295-359), as well as the mutually supporting opinions of Theodoret of Cyrrus (395-460), Saint John Chrysostom (354-407), and Saint Augustine (354-430).[106] In interpreting Eusebius Emissenus, and thereby revealing his own views, Cranmer writes:

> And yet he meant not, that the water of baptism in itself is really turned into the substance of Christ, nor likewise bread and wine in the Lord's supper, but that in the action water, wine and bread as sacraments, be sacramentally converted, unto him that duly receiveth them. . . . So that the sacramental conversion is in the sacraments, and the real conversion is in him that receiveth the sacraments, which real conversion is inward, invisible, spiritual.[107]

To be sure, Cranmer speaks also of a sacramental conversion.

But thereby he means no more than the occurrence of a demarcation through a change of meaning, during which the ordinary bread by its use in holy communion becomes of course a symbol and seal for the therein given Jesus. The same occurs to the wine.

(6) Faith as an Uplifting of the Heart[108]

An important key to the eucharistic understanding of the BCP is Cranmer's conception of the "lifting up of the heart," which begins the introductory formula of the Preface as follows:

> Lyfte up your heartes. We lyfte them up unto the Lorde.[109]

Christ is found with his glorified body in the place of heavenly splendour.[110] This fact should cause the faithful to orient themselves heavenward. Thus faith leads to an active spiritual attitude in accordance with which one watches for everlasting happiness through an assured expectation, and rejoices in the anticipation. Cranmer takes up the ideas of Theodoret of Cyrrhus and interprets these in connexion with the "lift up your hearts" as follows:

> Theodoretus sheweth us that the cause thereof was this, that we should not have so much respect to the bread and wine as we should have to Christ himself, in whom we believe with out hearts, and feel and taste Him by our faith. . . . These things we ought to remember and revolve in our minds, and to lift up our hearts from the bread and wine unto Christ that sitteth above.[111]

Cranmer's conception of faith as encountered in his writings above, with the theological comprehension of sin and grace there assimilated, is principally reflected in the eucharistic liturgy of the BCP. It is interesting that the roots of these ideas about faith, with their related revivalistic spirituality, extend back to the patristic period.

B. PRINCIPAL DIFFERENCES IN THE PRAYER BOOK OF 1552 AND THE TRACES OF MARTYR, BUCER, AND HOOPER

GENERAL COMMENTS

a. Elimination or Rearrangement of Certain Liturgical Elements

Most of the matter offensive to Reformation thinking which has already been mentioned in Chapter I is found no more in the BCP of 1552. Pursuant though to this process of elimination such liturgical pearls as the Introitus[112] and the Agnus Dei[113] vanish from the communion liturgy. The major Gloria[114] remains as the only sung text. In the above-mentioned process of elimination the canon[115] also happened to lose its identity. A comparison of the two communion liturgies of 1549 and 1552 may facilitate the summarizing and permit the differences to emerge clearly:

1549	1552
1 Introit	1 Lord's Prayer
2 Lord's Prayer	2 Opening collect
3 Opening collect	3 Decalogue
4 Kyrie	4 Collect for the king
5 Major Gloria	5 Collect for the day
6 Collect for the king	6 Epistle
7 Collect for the day[116]	7 Gospel
8 Epistle	8 Creed
9 Gospel	9 Notices
10 Creed	10 Sermon
11 Sermon	11 Offertory verse (A ceremonial preparation of the elements is lacking)

1549 (cont.)	**1552 (cont.)**
12 Exhortations (two)[117]	12 Intercessory prayer for the church militant and its living members**
13 Offertory verse (At the same time *a ceremonial preparation of the communion elements*)	13 Exhortations (three)
14 Sursum Corda*	14 Words of invitation
15 Preface*	15 Confession (with absolution)
16 Sanctus*	16 Comfortable words
17 Intercessory prayer for the church militant, living or dead*	17 Sursum Corda**
18 Consecration *with Epiclesis**[118]	18 Preface**
19 Prayer of thanks *with Anamnesis**[119]	19 Sanctus**
20 Lord's Prayer	20 Prayer of humble access**
21 Versicle	21 Consecration without epiclesis**
22 Agnus Dei (not sung)	22 Words of distribution
23 Words of invitation	23 Lord's Prayer
24 Confession with absolution	24 Two of the selection of prayers of thanks without anamnesis
25 Comfortable words	25 Gloria
26 Prayer of humble access	26 Benediction
27 Words of distribution	
28 Agnus Dei (sung)	
29 Bible text in the sense of an *invitation to sanctification*	
30 Versicle	
31 Prayer of thanks	
32 Benediction	

*Canon. See G. Cuming, *The Godly Order, Texts and Studies Relating to The Book of Common Prayer*, London 1983. Cf. chiefly chap. 5, "The Canon of 1549," pp. 91-107.
**Part of the canon.

The italicized portions in the left column indicate those elements which are no longer present in the edition of 1552.

Does this mean an impoverishment of the BCP of 1552? The following elucidation may supply the answer.

Despite the Reformation elements introduced into the BCP of 1549 there are nevertheless some places particularly evident within the canon which to a certain degree contain a tendency to superstition: thus in the Middle Ages as it still is in Southern Catholicism the Ecclesia Triumphans had been made an operation through the saints with nothing short of a soteriological significance unrelated to Christ. In this connexion one thinks of the doctrine of the surplus wealth of the grace of saints.

The prayer for the dead (to be strictly distinguished from a commemoration of the dead) stands in contradiction to the Biblical doctrine of justification. There remains therein the idea that man may still through the practice of sacrifice in the sense of prayer have an influence over the dead. Do we not here in intercessions made for the dead have to deal with an anthropocentric tendency? Theological analysis should reveal that the approval of such intercessions implies a Bible-repugnant legalistic understanding of soteriology. In accordance with the Roman Catholic conception as it prevailed generally prior to the Second Vatican, salvation of the soul is bound in a calculable way to the fulfillment of a minimum legally understood ecclesiastical requirement. That means confessing and communing at least once a year.[120]

Behind this stands, doubtlessly, the idea of the Gratia Infusa which stamps the recipient forever with the character of perpetual grace. From such assumptions as this any personal communication with God has no decisive soteriological value, which in addition fosters the purgatory doctrine. The epiclesis is omitted from the consecration in order to stress that it is not any formula but instead the Word of God understood by faith which sanctifies the elements. Thus, the reference to the angel who bears the prayers of the faithful to the presence of God[121] no longer finds a place, for the congregation should avoid the danger of entrusting themselves to intermediaries.

Cranmer above all took seriously the criticism[122] of Bucer with reference to the elimination of the prayers for the dead and the epiclesis as well as the passages where the angel bears the prayers of the faithful up to God.

The twenty quotations from the Bible used as offertory verses[123] are placed at a great distance from the so-called "canon." It isn't by chance that the Bible verses used in making the offertory follow immediately after the sermon. Cranmer wishes to emphasize thereby that a true sacrifice doesn't consist of the offering of bread and wine, but rather in the fact that the preached Word should bring forth fruit in the life of every individual.

These changes in the BCP of 1552 have no other purpose than to return to the pure Word of God.

b. Elimination of Symbols and Gestures

Cranmer accepted Bucer's suggestion to do away with the making of the sign of the cross over the elements in connexion with the consecration formula. Thus then Cranmer on the whole included in the so-called consecration prayer in the communion liturgy of 1552 no consecration formula.

Cranmer did not abolish the gesture of kneeling, although this gesture had been strongly questioned by the puritanical side, especially by Hooper.[124] There was a hard fight to retain the gesture of kneeling. Thanks to Hooper's and John Knox's statements thereon, Cranmer introduced the so-called "black rubric" as an appendix to the holy communion service. This "black rubric" explains the gesture of kneeling and invalidates any connexion with the worship and veneration of the host. The black rubric reads:

> Whereas it is ordeyned in the booke of common prayer, in the administracion of the Lord's Supper, that the Communicants knelyng shoulde receyue the holye Communion: whiche thynge beyng well mente, for a sygnificacion of the humble and gratefull acknowledgyng of the benefites of Chryst, geuen unto the woorthye receyuer, and to auoyde the prophanacion and dysordre. . . . Leste yet the same kneelyng myght be thought or taken otherwyse, we dooe declare that it is not ment thereby, that any adoracion is doone, or oughte to bee doone, eyther unto the Sacramentall bread or wyne there bodily receyued, or unto anye reall and essencial presence there beeyng of Christ's naturall fleshe and bloude. For as concernynge the Sacramentall bread and wyne, they remayne styll in theyr verye naturall substaunces, and therefore may not be adored, for that were Idolatrye to be abhorred of all faythfull christians. And as concernynge the naturall body and blood of our sauiour Christ, they are in heauen and not here. For it is agaynst the trueth of Christes true natural bodye, to be in moe places then in one, at one tyme.[125]

Here the influence of Hooper, with his Zwinglian-Bullingerian theology, comes very clearly to light.

c. Additions and Innovations

Morning and Evening Prayer in the BCP of 1552 contain twelve Biblical opening quotations which set forth with special force the sinful depravity of man, but also the offer of grace for the repentant.[126] These opening sentences from Holy Scripture are a crucial innovation. The exhortation in Morning and Evening Prayer is also an important addition. It was chiefly Martyr who laid particular emphasis on the exhortative element.[127] The first exhortation in the holy communion liturgy of 1552, and possibly also the third,[128] stems from Peter Martyr.

The introduction of the Decalogue[129] in the communion liturgy, and in particular its placement at the outset of the Holy Communion Service, is due to John Hooper,[130] for whom holy communion was to a special degree a seal to the divine covenant with man. This positioning of the Decalogue almost at the start of a communion liturgy is unique.[131]

d. Modifications with Reference to Altar and Vestments

The BCP of 1552 no longer uses the term "altar," but rather, "table." Thus in the opening rubric to the communion service it reads:

> The Table hauyng at the Communiontyme a fayre white lynnen clothe upon it. . . . And the Priest standing at the north syde of the Table.[132]

The difference from the opening rubric in the BCP of 1549 should be noted, where the word "altar" is used, where in respect to it the priest should stand in the middle in front of the altar:

> The priest standing humbly afore the middes of the Altar.[133]

Hooper devoted himself particularly to the matter of the "altar" in order to replace it with a table.[134] In order to nullify any association with an altar, the BCP of 1552 prescribes the position of the priest at the north end of the table.

Cranmer emphasizes the table character too, but he sees the altar character on the basis that every divine service, not only holy communion, should constitute a sacrifice of praise and thanksgiving:

> First, the form of a table shall more move the simple from the superstitious opinions of the Popish mass unto the right use of the Lord's Supper. For the use of an altar is to make sacrifice upon it: the use of a table is to serve for men to eat upon.[135]

Cranmer also pleads for the term "altar" which appears in the prayer book of 1549. Thus Cranmer urges the following:

> The Book of Common Prayer[136] calleth the thing whereupon the Lord's Supper is ministered indifferently a table, an altar, or the Lord's board. . . . For as it calleth the table where the holy Communion is distributed, with lauds and thanksgiving unto the Lord, an altar.[137]

The vestments are reduced in the BCP of 1552 to the black cassock and the white surplice[138] whereas the BCP of 1549 directs the wearing of eucharistic vestments at holy communion.[139] That Cranmer reduced the vestments to a minimum has to be attributed principally to the vehement opposition against the wearing of vestments expressed by Hooper[140] which reflects his conception of the church as an ecclesia simplicitatis.

e. Brief Summary and Conclusion

The summary will concentrate on the communion liturgy while mentioning again the rearrangement in the order, as well as the elimination, of certain liturgical elements:

1. The Ten Commandments stand conspicuously right at the beginning. This demonstrates the priority of God's Word in the development of the whole liturgy and emphasizes here an attitude of repentance in the sense of a usus elenchticus.[141]
2. The offertory verses come immediately after the sermon and do not serve as an introduction to the canon as was the case in the BCP of 1549. Attention is directed to what was said on pages 122-23 of this work.
3. The prayer for the church militant is deleted from the canon whereas in the BCP of 1549 it is an important component of the canon and is placed near the consecration formula.
4. The exhortations are longer. In contrast to that of 1549 reference to God's Word is much more explicit. The obligatory character of the taking of holy communion is stressed much more strongly.
5. The confession with absolution comes much earlier in the course of the liturgy than in the edition of 1549, hence long before the words of institution. In the 1549 formula the confession is located near the words of distribution. This change in location reflects another theological point of view. Whereas the confession of 1549 is located

near the words of distribution and hence implies the idea that the consciousness of guilt arises from awe for the Sanctissimum,[142] the confession of 1552 with its position following the exhortations implies more the Reformation perception of a radical depravity. If the confession turns up right in the immediate neighborhood of the Sanctissimum, in my opinion it reflects a quantitative understanding of sin.

6. The canon in the eucharistic liturgy is dissolved in contrast to that of 1549. We have to be aware that this dissolution represents something of a shibboleth for the Reformation.[143]

7. The altar is replaced by a table and the eucharistic vestments are reduced to the minimum "cassock" and "surplice."

Should it not then perhaps have been better to leave the most important parts belonging to the canon and only omit those points which might create some misunderstanding? Pure theological thinking should not be opposed to a purged canon. But indeed there in this complex of prayers closely crowded together are included some passages sensitive to Reformation thinking so that only a disassembled canon would do for a Protestantism grounded on Scripture. Instinctively the reformers probably perceived that the canon is very suited to be a connecting link for the reunion of the various denominations with the Ecclesia Romana. Did they want to prevent such a dénouement? One's ears prick up when one hears that today's church reformers have striven in their communion liturgy to restore the shattered canon or to introduce it anew.[144]

Do such measures perhaps arise out of a determined ecumenical understanding with the possibility of a worldwide organized federation of the various denominations, and which also welcomes this?

Cranmer had let himself be stimulated by the fruitful theology of a Martyr, Bucer, and Hooper. He had assimilated this important impulse in such a way that he made the Biblical distillation of sin-grace-faith, upon which revivalistic elements retain such a strong position, the theological basis for the BCP.

Indeed this Biblical distillate of sin-grace-faith is Cranmer's own great theological achievement. Cranmer is to be compared with a tapestry weaver who has woven the views of Martyr, Bucer, Hooper, and important Church Fathers like threads into the practical tapestry of the BCP of 1552.

For the puritanical contributions to the BCP of 1552 Cranmer has chiefly to thank his discussions with John Hooper for the fact that the Reformation and revivalistic substance did not become obscured by elements akin to the pagan.

Thus The Book of Common Prayer of 1552, stimulated by the Refformation, was able to become a church and home manual.

In the next chapter the origins of the prayer book of 1662 is the subject of investigation in which we intend in particular to deal with the revivalistic thinking of that edition, the presently "canonical" BCP.

IV. The Book of Common Prayer of 1662

A. THE ROAD TO AND THE FIGHT FOR THE INTEGRATION OF THE PRAYER BOOK OF 1552 INTO THE EDITION OF 1662

1. FORCES DIRECTLY AND INDIRECTLY INVOLVED IN THE FIGHT

a. The Elizabethan Puritanism of Edmund Grindal and the BCP of 1559

After the death of Edward VI the Catholic Mary Tudor succeeded to the royal power. During her reign in the years 1553-1558 unnumbered Protestants had to pay for their faith with their death. The famous reformers Hooper (died 1555), N. Ridley (died 1555), H. Latimer (died 1555), and Cranmer (died 1556) suffered martyrdom.[1] Peter Martyr had to flee from England. Every person in England who revealed the slightest potential for a later carrying out of the Reformation in England met either a violent death or had to flee. Mary Tudor annulled the Book of Common Prayer of 1552. Yet a Biblical law had to prevail. Men with whom we have already become acquainted in Chapters II and III place Holy Scripture in the liturgy of the prayer book of 1552 upon a pedestal in such a beautiful way that Isaiah 55:11 had to take effect: "So shall my word be that goeth forth out of my mouth: it shall not return unto me void, but it shall accomplish that which I please, and it shall prosper in the thing whereto I sent it."

The Protestant Elizabeth I took the royal throne after the death of Bloody Mary Tudor. Still, Elizabeth did not want to lose the Catholics who had grown strong under Mary Tudor and accordingly did not speak up for a thoroughgoing Protestantism bearing a puritanical stamp. Her sympathies were with The Book of Common Prayer of 1549 which had taken a middle stand. In the Act of Uniformity issued by the queen in 1559 Elizabeth wished to put through a standardized liturgy binding upon all inhabitants. It first was necessary to compile a new liturgy before the monarch could give Archbishop Parker a mandate to supervise the enforcement of the Act of Uniformity.[2] Hence a committee was needed which was to draw up the liturgy desired by the queen. It was now of great importance that the two factions, one with Roman sympathies and the other with Reformation thinking, constitute a numerical balance upon the commission which was to deal with the liturgy.

Edmund Grindal (1519-1583) was especially prominent as a theologian on the Reformation side. He had a very remarkable influence in the years 1559-1570 as Bishop of London. Grindal stood theologically in the tradition of John Hooper. His ideas[3] should be mentioned briefly in order to be able to understand better the phenomenon of the common prayer book of 1559. Grindal was an ardent supporter of the Edwardian reform as it is expressed above all in the BCP of 1552. Essentially he advocated those ideas which Hooper had defended with vehemence in his sermons and discussions in the presence of Edward VI. "Sola Scriptura" is of supreme importance to Grindal. He had in mind the lively congregations which existed among Protestants who fled to the Continent under Mary Tudor.

Grindal who himself lived in Germany during the time of persecution in England learned to know those lively English refugee congregations which had to function without an established denominational structure. Grindal then was able to find out on the Continent how the revivalistic-puritanical theology[4] of a Martyr, Bucer, or Hooper, which was so very beloved by him, appeared in a practical setting. In Strasbourg Grindal had had a lively contact with Martyr and those theologians who during the reign of Edward VI carried on a busy Reformation operation under the influence of Henry Bullinger acting through Hooper.[5] To those theologians belonged people like John Jewel, Sandys, John Cheke, and many others. These all had a very high opinion of the Reformation as carried out under Edward VI. As with John Hooper, one finds in Grindal a sympathetic ecclesiological conception. On the one hand Grindal wants lively revivalistic congregations which govern themselves purely by the Word. On the other hand the congregations should have a rigid obligatory external order in their church life.

This order in the form of a prayer book binding upon all must be so structured that it constitutes as it were a vessel which indicates and insists upon the correct Biblical content. The king should be the guarantor of this ecclesiastical order.[6] Grindal rightly knew that so called "free congregations" which are answerable to no government can split up a nation.

A sound Biblically oriented government is thus the most desirable for a nation. If as in the time of Edward VI the church structure as an external framework is then in a Biblical sense sound and the puritanical concepts in the main respected, no "free congregation" should want to be set up because of prevailing unity and order. This attitude of Grindal is nicely expressed in minutes recording a conference of Bishop Grindal in London with some puritans inclining towards independence. The puritans participating in the conference had to justify themselves before Grindal, at that time Bishop of London, because of unauthorized meetings in homes with the celebration of holy communion without priests and because of seditious talk against the royal household.[7]

In the following quotation we clearly see Grindal's sympathy for the ecclesiastical order bearing the stamp of Edward VI:

> But to the matter. In this severing yourselves from the society of other Christians, you condemn not only us, but also the whole state of the church reformed in King Edward's days, which was well reformed according to the word of God, yea, and many good men have shed their blood for the same, which your doings condemn.[8]

Grindal knew whom England had basically to thank for the Edwardian Reformation, namely in large part to the reformed tradition as it was developed in the Upper German and Swiss regions. In a letter of thanks to the magistrates of Frankfort in the year 1561 Grindal expresses his appreciation for the hospitality of the government to the English refugees who were permitted to establish a congregation in Frankfort, in which he distinctly referred to the origin of the theological help in weaponry for carrying out the Reformation in England:

> I indeed, most illustrious and worshipful sirs, have willingly seized this opportunity of writing, not only for the sake of gratifying them, but also in my own name, and the name of all English exiles, I might return thanks to your honours for your great kindness and piety towards us in the time of our greatest affliction. No time will ever remove this your benefit from the minds of Englishmen. England owes it to Strasburg, Zurich, Basle, Worms, but above all to your renowned republic, that she has so many bishops, and other ministers of God's Word, who at this day are preaching the pure doctrines of the gospel.[9]

Grindal had the privilege to be permitted to occupy the position of a royal chaplain and preacher[10] at the court of Edward VI prior to the Marian persecution. It seems likely that there he must have encountered some traces of John Hooper. Indeed Hooper had exercised a great influence at the same court only a year and a half before with his Lenten sermons. Grindal thus played a big role in connexion with the BCP of 1559, as already mentioned.[11]

The following personalities were members of the commission for the revision of the liturgy on the Reformation side: first, Grindal himself, then Jewel, Horne, Whitehead, Cox, Guest, Aelmer, and Scory. Most of these eight members of the commission for liturgical reform had spent many years as refugees on the Continent and maintained an active contact with Bullinger, which was true of Grindal, Jewel, Horne, Cox, and Whitehead.[12] Grindal, as the most prominent among these theologians, was the spokesman for that theology of Bullinger which created to a large degree the basic requirements for the development of a puritanical spirituality.[13]

Those eight theologians on the Reformation side were able to exercise their influence chiefly because of Grindal's impact on the eight other theologians on the Catholic side. Those eight theologians home from exile, who set themselves so doggedly toward the eventual carrying out of the Reformation, are to be thanked for the fact that the prayer book of 1549 was not restored, but instead a new validity was acquired by the BCP of 1552.

It is however true that the queen insisted on a few changes. These changes applied chiefly to the rubrics. Thus that rubric from the BCP of 1549 which prescribed eucharistic vestments was reintroduced. That passage in the seventh rubric in the annex to the Holy Communion Service of the BCP of 1552 which was intended to combat any misunderstanding of kneeling as a worship of the elements of the holy communion was deleted: that is to say, the so-called "Black Rubric."[14] By this deletion of the "Black Rubric" Queen Elizabeth I hoped to provide the Catholics with more room to manoeuvre in the direction of a real bodily presence.

This prayer book authorized in 1559, The Book of Common Prayer of 1559, is essentially the genuine Reformation BCP of 1552 with the addition of that rubric of the BCP of 1549 which prescribed the communion vestments, and with the elimination of the "Black Rubric."[15] Still, one wonders what would have been the consequences if the queen had succeeded with her desire for the restoration of the first Edwardian prayer book. Patrick Collinson speaks directly to the point:

> Elizabeth may well have favoured something more conservative than the second Edwardian Prayer Book: 1549, perhaps, with its superficial affinities to a Lutheranism which was both diplomatically advantageous and to her own taste.[16]

The consequences in any case are of modest import since the revision was limited in the main to a few rubrics and let stand practically all of the text of the liturgy of 1552.[17] Grindal and the members of the commission on liturgical reform who were on his side indicated they were unhappy with the previously mentioned changes. In particular the obligation imposed on the clergy based on the Act of Uniformity to wear the communion vestments during the Holy Communion Service became more and more of a vexation to the puritanically minded priests and laity.

Grindal showed a great deal of understanding for these puritans, which is expressed in the previously mentioned discussion "The Examination of certain Londoners before the Commissioners": One of the critically minded puritans named Ireland let fall a remark in Grindal's presence:

> But you go like one of the mass-priests still.

To which Grindal replied as follows:

> You see me wear a cope or a surplice in St. Paul's. I had rather minister without these things, but for order's sake and obedience to the prince.[18]

Grindal of course knew that it is not worthwhile to provoke a split among the faithful just because of vestments. It was very clear to Grindal that eucharistic vestments are to be perceived in connexion with the Roman doctrine of the repeated sacrifice at the altar and therefore do not belong simply to the adiaphora. It would have been wise, in the view of Grindal, especially for the sake of the puritanically minded, to make the wearing of eucharistic vestments and kneeling optional.

Grindal did whatever lay within his power to strengthen the puritanical spirit. Specifically, he selected pastors from the clergy of the various congregations of exiles in Switzerland who had been active in Geneva and Aarau and who declared themselves ready to introduce a thoroughgoing Reformation in their homeland. Thus Grindal ordained many such puritanically oriented clergy in his own diocese of London.[19] He likewise ordained clergy from the refugee congregation at Frankfort. These ministers with their strong Biblically oriented attitude became a hardy seed in the Church of England, destined to blossom later.

Those pastors who had been at one time active in a refugee congregation well knew what is needed for the survival of a true congregation. They therefore didn't emphasize the externals, the formal and juridical matters of the church, but rather the spiritual and what really belongs to true life. Grindal became the most significant supporter of the puritans within the English church, but he fought independentism[20] with all his might.

Grindal as superintendent of the foreign congregations in England had adopted what was for that day a truly ecumenical attitude, when he acknowledged their liturgical identity, which consisted of the Geneva liturgy.[21] In the year 1570 Grindal moved up to a higher position when he was allowed to assume the office of Archbishop of York.

One of his greatest contributions during his six-year term as archbishop was the thorough distribution of admonitory letters for clergy and laity on the subject of the Christian life, the so-called "injunctions." In his "Injunctions to the dean and chapter of York" Grindal required the inauguration of regular Bible seminars at which the clergy of his diocese had to attend lectures on Holy Scripture and undergo examinations on their knowledge of the Bible.[22] It was intended by this to raise the standards among the clergy and thereby to give a guarantee for the effective propagation of Biblical-Reformation doctrine among the people.

Such conferences of the clergy which were intended to further their knowledge of Scripture were called "prophesyings"[23] although the conferences had nothing whatsoever to do with the true function of a prophet. Grindal's precedent was imitated as other dioceses followed his example.

"Prophesyings" had become an established institution in Zurich under Zwingli. He had initiated the convening of these seminars for clergy with doctrinal lectures for the deepening of their knowledge of Scripture.[24] Heinrich Bullinger preserved and expanded this Zwinglian bequest of "prophesyings." English refugees from Bloody Mary learned about "prophesyings" during their period of exile in Zurich and were deeply impressed thereby. It is obvious that Grindal was won over to the "prophesyings" of Bullinger and was persuaded by those returning home from exile to implement them.[25]

In these gatherings called "prophesyings" the participants not only worked painstakingly upon their studies of Scripture but they also applied themselves to prayer. Through this the "prophesyings" became something like a pattern for puritanical services because of the thoroughly unliturgical form and the emphasis on Holy Scripture. Thus Patrick Collinson can also say:

> Yorkshire puritanism was embryonic in the 1570s, but it must be reckoned the most considerable long term consequence of the policies of Grindal.[26]

Puritans interested in the Church of England greatly admired Grindal because of the "prophesyings."

As soon as Grindal obtained the hierarchical rank of Archbishop of Canterbury in the year 1576 he was able as the highest officeholder in the

Ecclesia Anglicana to exercise substantially more influence. Grindal succeeded in winning over innumerable of the puritanically oriented into an active participation in the church. In 1576 the "prophesyings" device spread into the south and east of England also.[27]

Queen Elizabeth I revealed a considerable distrust for "prophesyings" which supported a puritanical priesthood. Elizabeth feared that a strengthening of the puritans would encourage nonconformity and independency. The queen had pointedly assailed Grindal because of the "prophesyings." Elizabeth demanded of Grindal that he reduce the number of preaching clergy.

Grindal answered the Queen with reference to her attacks in a courageous letter dated December 20, 1576. Grindal shows in this letter that he was no "manpleaser." He sought to show his sovereign that the "prophesyings" (also called "exercises") were to the advantage of the church. He gave the Queen an explanation of exactly what happened in the "prophesyings" and how very necessary they were. Grindal called his monarch's attention to the fact that he owed more obedience to God than to her.

Some passages from this important letter to the queen may show us Grindal's clarity and his consciousness of responsibility as the Archbishop of Canterbury:

> It may please the same to be advertised, that the speeches which it hath pleased you to deliver unto me, when I last attended on Your Highness, concerning abridging the number of preachers, and the utter suppression of all learned exercises and conferences among the ministers of the church, allowed by their bishops and ordinaries, have exceedingly dismayed and discomforted me. Not so much for that the said speeches sounded very hardly against my own person ... but most of all for that the same might both tend to the public harm of God's church, whereof your Highness ought to be nutricia, and also to the heavy burdening of your own conscience before God, if they should be put in strict execution.[28]

Grindal expresses to the queen quite clearly the principle that "One must be more obedient to God than to men" when he says:

> Neither do I ever intend to offend your Majesty in any thing, unless, in the cause of God or of his church, by necessity of office, and burden of conscience, I shall thereunto be enforced.[29]

In response to Elizabeth's command to reduce the number of clergy who take seriously the service of preaching he writes:

> Alas, Madam! is the scripture more plain in any one thing, than that the

134

gospel of Christ should be plentifully preached; and that plenty of labourers should be sent into the Lord's harvest; which, being great and large, standeth in need, not of a few, but many workmen?[30]

Grindal tells the queen in plain speech what God's Word can accomplish:

> By preaching of God's Word the glory of God is enlarged, faith is nourished, and charity increased. By it the ignorant is instructed, the negligent exhorted and incited, the stubborn rebuked, the weak conscience comforted. . . . By preaching also due obedience to Christian princes and magistrates is planted in the hearts of subjects.[31]

Grindal appeals to the fruit which the "prophesyings" have produced and thus he writes in the same letter:

> Howsoever report hath been made to your Majesty concerning these exercises, yet I and others of your bishops . . . , as they have testified unto me by their letters, having found by experience, that these profits and commodities following have ensued of them: 1. The ministers of the church are more skilful and ready in the scriptures, and apter to teach their flocks. 2. It withdraweth them from idleness, wandering, gaming, &c. 3. Some, afore suspected in doctrine, are brought hereby to open confession of the truth. 4. Ignorant ministers are driven to study. . . . 5. The opinion of laymen, touching the idleness of the clergy, is hereby removed. 6. Nothing by experience beateth down popery more than that ministers grow to such good knowledge, by means of these exercises, that where afore were not three able preachers, now are thirty.[32]

Toward the close of the letter Grindal writes that he doesn't intend to submit to the will of the queen, while he appeals to the sound judgment of the monarch:

> I trust, when your Majesty hath considered and well weighed the premises, you will rest satisfied, and judge that no such inconvenience can grow of these exercises, as you have been informed, but rather the clean contrary. And for my part, because I am very well assured, both by reasons and arguments taken out of the holy scriptures and by experience, I am forced, with all humility, and yet plainly, to profess, that I cannot with safe conscience, and without the offence of the majesty of God, give my assent to the suppressing of the said exercises: much less can I send out any injunction for the utter and universal subversion of the same.[33]

This courageous and uncompromising attitude persuaded many puritans to remain in the church and to fight further for a thorough Reformation.

The substance offered in the BCP of 1559[34] caused the puritans difficulties in only a few points. These few points were however of great importance. These dealt with the wearing of eucharistic vestments during holy communion and the gesture of kneeling as well as a few points in the baptism and confirmation rituals. Grindal managed to give the puritans hope for a more complete Reformation within the English church. He cited a sentence from Bullinger which the latter had written specially with reference to the situation of the English church on the wearing of vestments:

> And though we use them (the vestments) not here (in Zurich) in our ministry, yet we may lawfully use them as things that have not yet been removed away.[35]

In view of Bullinger's dictum the hope arose among many puritans that the eucharistic vestments might be something only temporary and in the near future would in that form be surmounted.

Grindal as one representing so-called Elizabethan puritanism[36] stood up for loyalty to church and state subject to the proviso that obedience to the crown should not turn out to be in conflict with divine commandments.

Grindal supported the proposition that the puritanically minded at least should be under no compulsion to conform with the gesture of kneeling and that eucharistic vestments not be obligatory. Had such concessions as proposed by Grindal been supported, the Civil War in the opinion of the well-known Grindal disciple Richard Baxter might have been avoided.[37] This heritage of Hooper which was carried forward by Grindal bore fruit long after his death. The "prophesyings" introduced into England by Grindal produced effects therein well into the seventeenth century, lacking which the genesis of The Book of Common Prayer of 1662 would be inexplicable. Therefore Patrick Collinson can with justice say:

> But what would surely have pleased Grindal most was that the prophesyings which he had defended in his letter to the queen were alive and well and remained one of the most distinctive institutions of the reformed Church of England in what was, in some sense, its Jacobean heyday.[38]

Grindal marked off the momentous course which was partially responsible for the surmounting of the questionable rubrics in the BCP of 1559. However from other sides came distinct contributions which constituted factors in the BCP of 1662. Hence for the next point we will briefly examine independency and presbyterianism as well as the militant puritanism of Oliver Cromwell against a background of episcopalianism and royalism.

b. Independency, Presbyterianism, and Militant Puritanism against a Background of Royalism and Episcopalianism

Hooper like Grindal had a positive understanding of the crown and state. Both saw in the great competence of the royal household as well as of the government an enormous opportunity for an evangelization of the nation on the presupposition that the monarch was a believer, i.e., that God's Word is submitted to as the highest authority. The reign of Edward VI came up to just such an expectation. Why could not the following monarchs also be witnesses to the nation through their attitudes toward a Biblical faith, and thus encourage their people in that direction?

But instead, many puritanically inclined Christians were witnesses to Mary Tudor who carried out a terror of faith bearing a Roman Catholic stamp. Queen Elizabeth stood well within the ranks of Protestantism but she showed an inclination toward compromise which manifested itself in the rubric demanded by her in the BCP of 1559. Such puritans as Robert Browne (1550-1633), John Greenwood (died 1593), Henry Barrow (1550-1593), and many others noted that the Oath of Supremacy and the Act of Uniformity of 1559 would, in the event of a godless and unscrupulous monarch, lead the church into an abyss since the sovereign is head not only of the state but also of the church. In case a monarch hostile to the Word of God were crowned, the existence of the congregation of Jesus within the state church would be especially menaced, particularly where bishops and archbishops no longer dared to address the conscience of king or queen. It was recognized that Archbishop Grindal constituted something of an exception. Accordingly puritans of the above-mentioned type began to prepare for that emergency by demanding with reference to the church structure the independence of crown and state church.

Richard Fytz pointed out in his work "The true marks of Christ's Church," penned about 1570, that the marks of the true church exist not in canonical law or juridically comprehended definitions but rather in the freedom to proclaim the gospel independently of episcopal license. Robert Browne emphasized the spiritual priesthood of every believer as well as the brotherly interchange of spiritual experiences. Robert Browne formulated his concept of the church in the following way:

> A church of Christ planted in truth and properly nurtured is: a fellowship of faithful people, separated from the unfaithful, gathered in the name of Christ, whom they worship with sincerity and they obey him eagerly. They

137

are a brotherhood, a congregation of the saints in which each individual stands free in Christ and is responsible for Christian freedom—in practice to accomplish that which God has always ordered and has revealed in his holy Word.[39]

Under the influence of the puritans mentioned above, independent congregations maintaining their own autonomy came into existence.

Grindal's successor as Archbishop of Canterbury, John Whitgift, straightway persecuted the puritans. Whitgift became a representative of an episcopalianism which justified the earlier fears of the puritans. In the year 1593 John Whitgift let several of these puritans be put to death in connexion with the founding of free congregations; even Henry Barrow was among the victims.

Of vital importance to the supporters of independency was the question as to whether a truly Biblical congregation could exist in a time of distress in which the state and the official church had opened the door to secularization. Unfortunately puritanism of the independency stamp gave the official church and the state no further chance, and precipitated a showdown in this critical situation. Independency was mistaken in its doctrine of the "pure congregation," by which was meant that one must separate the wheat from the chaff.

It should not be forgotten that royalism as represented by Elizabeth's successor James I (1603-1625) must have discouraged puritans of all shades. James I indulged in a much stronger absolutism than was the case with his predecessor. The crown was for James of divine origin and required unlimited power. His saying "No bishop, no king" betrayed an attitude which interpreted a denial of the episcopal structure as treason to the monarch. Evidently it appeared thus to James I because as a bishop is a spiritual monarch he must support as well a secular monarch. James I constituted a provocation to puritans of all orientations. The clerically committed puritans had misgivings about such a strong connexion between royalism and episcopalianism. One of those clerically committed puritans, Dr. Reynolds, spoke of an alternative ecclesiastical governmental structure, namely the presbyterian system.

Sympathizers of Dr. Reynolds submitted a petition to the king with eight hundred signatures, the so-called "Millenary Petition" (called that because the signatures amounted to almost one thousand).[40] As a consequence to the submission of this petition James I in January 1604 summoned a three-day meeting, the Hampton Court Conference. Nine bishops and nine other dignitaries represented the establishment of the

Anglican church while only four representatives of puritanism were admitted, among whom was the well-known Dr. Reynolds.

This petition didn't propose any revolutionary changes. Reynolds had not made a bit of propaganda in his "Millenary Petition" for a presbyterian system although his sympathies lay with presbyterianism. The signatories in this petition advocated that the wearing of the liturgical white vestment of the priest in a church service, the "surplice," the gesture of kneeling in the communion liturgy, as well as the making of a sign of the cross on the foreheads of infants being baptized should not be obligatory.

The puritans gave further voice to their opinions which were critical of several points in The Order of Confirmation and of the ceremony of the ring exchange in The Form of Solemnization of Matrimony. Also objectionable to them was the reading of texts from the Apocrypha which would thereby be declared to be Holy Scripture. In addition to this criticism of The Book of Common Prayer of 1559 the signers pleaded for a thorough sanctification of Sundays. In the above we have referred only to the most important points of the puritans.

It appears from the minutes of the three-day Hampton Court Conference[41] that James I and the bishops present dealt unfairly and harshly with the puritans. The bishops assumed an attitude toward the monarch verging on the idolatrous in their reverence. Thus C. S. Carter writes in reference to this conference:

> We cannot but be struck, in reading the various accounts of this conference, at the extremely partial attitude of James, and at the abjectly cringing conduct of the bishops and dignitaries. Even after making allowance for the almost superstitious spirit of reverence for the sovereign . . . , their fulsome adulation almost surpassed the bounds of truth and propriety. . . . On the other hand, the bishops seem to have treated their opponents in an unnecessary bitter and intolerant spirit.[42]

It is of great importance to note that the puritans standing behind the "Millenary Petition" were not independents but rather were Anglicans committed to the church who as such were not denying any connexion of altar and crown yet who stood up for a certain nonconformity in liturgical questions. In the address to the king at the beginning of the "Millenary Petition" respect and honour for the king as well as for the head of the church is clearly expressed:

> Most gracious and dread sovereign, seeing it hath pleased the Divine Majesty, to the great comfort of all good Christians, to advance your highness, according to your just title, to the peaceable government of this church and

commonwealth of England: We the ministers of the gospel in this land, neither as factious men, affecting a popular parity in the church, nor as schismatics, aiming at the dissolution of the state ecclesiastical, but as the faithful servants of Christ and loyal subjects to your majesty, desiring and longing for the redress of divers abuses of the church, could do no less, in our obedience to God, service to your majesty, and love to his church, than acquaint your princely majesty with our particular griefs.[43]

This friendly and reverent address which was intended to convey their loyalty to the king encountered a flat rejection. When the puritans participating there in the course of the Hampton Court Conference made the suggestion that a bishop in any diocesan synod should consult the opinion of the presbyters on important questions, James I became furious and said:

If this be all your party have to say I will make them conform, or I will harry them out of this land, or else worse.[44]

This attitude of James I discouraged many of the ecclesiastically committed puritans so that for understandable reasons more and more sympathy began to arise for a presbyterian system where one no longer would be turned over to bishops who collaborated with corrupt sovereigns. Quite a few of these ecclesiastical puritans such as Cartwright, Travers, Manton, Alleine, and many others turned toward the Calvinistic-Knoxian presbyterianism of a Scottish character. The following important elements pertained to this presbyterianism:

1. A disciplined structure in its church organization analogous to a democratic-republican organization of the state, but rejecting an episcopacy.
2. The ordering of the divine services could bear a thoroughly liturgical stamp, as revealed in the Scotch "Book of Common Order."
3. The love for fixed formulas of one's own theological persuasion is expressed in formal creeds, as for example in the Westminster Confession.
4. In order to carry out presbyterian ideas under certain circumstances use is made of the state or of governing classes such as the nobility.
5. Also typical is an emerging comprehension of discipline according to juridical categories.
6. The main purpose is to make the kingdom of God visible on earth.[45]

The following features are common to independent puritanism as well as to that bearing a presbyterian stamp: emphasis on the lay element, an unambiguous rejection of the papacy, accentuation of sanctification as a way of life, and the central significance of preaching as well as personal study of the Bible. Points 1 to 6 mentioned above refer principally to the Scottish church but they can also be applied to a marked degree to other presbyterian-oriented state churches.

In our context it is of note that both types of puritanism, the independent as well as state-connected presbyterian, were forces contributing to the final edition of The Book of Common Prayer of 1662.

The success of the Hampton Court Conference was seemingly for the ecclesiastically oriented puritans a very modest one which understandably constituted grist to the mill of the independents. A brief discussion follows of this seemingly very meagre success: Although those puritans were unable to succeed in abolishing the making of a sign of the cross, kneeling, and vestments, as well as the use of the ring in the marriage ceremony, several concessions were made at the Hampton Court Conference to the puritans:

First: The catechism[46] which precedes the confirmation service required an answer from the candidate in respect to the Creed, the Decalogue, and the Lord's Prayer when the candidate replied to the bishop's questions. Puritans regretted that in the prayer books of 1552 and 1559 no answers were required in regard to the sacraments of baptism and holy communion. Reynolds and his partisans therefore requested an addition in which the candidate for confirmation had to give an account of the significance and the prerequisites for receiving those sacraments. By the proposed addition it was intended to make it clear that a personal conviction is the determining factor for receiving the sacraments, and that permission should not simply follow based on a formal membership in the church. The puritans were accommodated.[47]

Second: The Hampton Court Conference took seriously the proposal of the puritan minded that the apocrypha be reduced to a minimum and that it not be declared to be Holy Scripture.[48]

Third: The puritans demanded a revision of the "English Bible" in order to make it accessible to a wider class of society. The Hampton Court Conference adopted the suggestion for this kind of revision and issued an order for the production of that translation which became famous under the name of the "King James Version."[49]

It first became obvious nearly six decades later how well the struggle of the puritans at the Hampton Court Conference had been rewarded, although there was at the moment but little fruit to be seen in the Anglican church. Many great battles had still to be contested in connexion with the provocations of James I and his successor Charles I. James I sought to impose the episcopacy on the presbyterians of the Scottish church. This was a tocsin for those English puritans who sympathized with presbyterianism, as well as for puritans of an independent view. Puritans considered as a particular affront the issuance in the year 1618 of a decree called "Book of Sports," a list of permitted Sunday pleasures, which was an offense to the observance of the Sabbath.

The marriage of the king's successor, Charles I, to a Catholic, Henrietta Marie of France, produced additional distrust in puritan circles. Charles I (1625-1649) continued the policies of his father to a more aggravated degree. Charles succeeded in gaining a High-Churchman as Archbishop of Canterbury, namely William Laud (1573-1645). Laud exerted himself seriously in the development of a liturgical-ceremonial prayer book and in favour of uniformity. For William Laud the essential thing was the principle of the absolute power of the bishops in ecclesiastical concerns under the auspices of the crown. Charles knew of no better man on the church side to have in support of his sway. Persecution of puritans of every shade reached its high point during the reign of Charles I. The well-known historian G. M. Trevelyan expresses himself thereon as follows:

> The ritual side of worship in the parish churches was increased by episcopal command and visitation, while evangelical practice, preaching and lecturing were effectively prohibited within the Church. At the same time nonconformist worship outside the Church was persecuted with increasing rigour. The emigration of the Puritans to America in these years was a measure of the degree to which Laud made life intolerable to them in England. Owing to his activities it became impossible for a Puritan to live in his native country and worship God freely.[50]

The attempt to Anglicize Scotland led in 1637 to a rebellion of the Scots. In order to quell the revolt Charles needed funds which he could only obtain in a constitutional way from Parliament. Parliament was more and more recruited from among puritans of an independency and presbyterian stamp who began to refuse to accept the absolutism of Charles I and to exert themselves in behalf of the rights of the people. By 1642 this had gone so far that the absolute royal power confronted an almost equally absolute parliamentary power. By parliamentary resolution bishops were excluded from the upper house. The king was no longer honoured. Parliament now began to organize a presbyterian-oriented church establishment for England. For this purpose Parliament named an advisory group, the so-called Westminster Synod (1643-1647), from which emerged the Westminster Confession. Presbyterians stood for religious freedom only in a collective sense, which means that a country decides for itself on this or that confession of faith. However the independency minority backed individual freedom of religion, for a full autonomy of any congregation, and for independence from the state. Into this situation strode Oliver Cromwell (1599-1658), an independent of the highest calibre. He became the true leader in the Civil War (1642-1658). He succeeded as a kind of charismatic leader, with the help of an army composed of independents, in bringing about the following:

First: He evicted the presbyterians from Parliament because these presbyterians as a matter of principle would not condemn the crown. He succeeded in this in 1648.

Second: He succeeded in driving the royalists from Parliament and in executing Charles I in the year 1649. The execution of Archbishop Laud had already been accomplished upon his instigation in 1645.

Third: As a result of these measures accomplished by the Rump Parliament Cromwell organized the Parliament of "saints." With this Parliament of Saints Cromwell aimed at something like a theocracy.

Fourth: With the idea that "the source of all legitimate power lies with the people" Cromwell established the principle of the sovereignty of the people.

Fifth: Cromwell established religious freedom except for Catholics and episcopalians[51] and stood up strongly for the oppressed Protestant minorities in other lands.

Sixth: Cromwell undertook iconoclastic actions with his militant troops in Anglican churches.[52] He intended thereby to proclaim the purity of the Christian services.

In all these six points just mentioned Cromwell was concerned principally with a religious revival of the people. Much is due him for his victory over a church which had become congealed in its forms of worship and which was unable even to awaken dead hearts to new life. Thus Cromwell contributed greatly thereby to laying the foundation for an important type of ecumenism, an ecumenism of true believers. The broadminded Anglican puritan Richard Baxter indirectly gives Cromwell a testimonial because he sent "triers" out into the towns and countryside:

> The truth is—which must be credited to them (the triers)—that they accomplished very much good for the church. They freed many a congregation from its ignorant, worldly, drunken preacher.[53]

Cromwell went so far as to have Parliament adopt a strict formula as to what type of pastor should be called to the service of a congregation:

> No one is to be called to a parish office if there is not some evidence of
> the working of God's grace in his life. One has to look for this evidence
> so far as it is possible to form an opinion from a Christian point of view.
> This forming of an opinion should never happen in a senseless or fool-
> ish way.[54]

These militant actions of Cromwell, despite many negative sides,
nevertheless caused as a consequence a wholesome shake-up of the Anglican church. The fact that in Cromwell's era the most recent attempt in
history was made to subject a nation's entire cultural life to the reign of
Christian principles had to bear its fruit.

c. The Restoration and The Book of Common Prayer of 1662

During the period of the Commonwealth (1649-1660) an ecclesiastical
anarchy existed, i.e., there was no established church present which might
provide the people with guidance. The vessel which should possess for
the nation a form which provides a container for the right spiritual content was lacking. Seeking persons and unbelievers very often do not find
a home within independent congregations where only the converted have
place. In the longer run Cromwell, the dictator and Lord Protector, had no
chance, although he had to fulfill a particular and important task. He had
created conditions for the freedom of faith and conscience.

The Restoration which occurred in 1660 through the resumption of
the throne by the House of Stuart through Charles II allowed the episcopal church to come to power again. Charles II owed his return to power
in large measure to those disposed toward presbyterianism who longed
for the restitution of an established church, naturally in the hope that the
church would be reformed more in accordance with the Scottish pattern.
As a diplomat who because of his marriage to a Catholic spouse (Catherine
of Braganza) developed a sympathy for the Roman faith, Charles sus-
tained High Church theologians to a marked degree, but at the same time
he supported the concerns of the presbyterians. Charles II hoped by these
tactics to camouflage better his sympathies for Roman Catholicism. The
king found himself compelled by the urging of presbyterian-oriented puritans and High-Churchmen to pave the way for a revision of The Book of
Common Prayer. Charles accordingly called a conference in 1661 at the
residence of the Bishop of London, Savoy Palace, for the preparation of
The Book of Common Prayer. Hence one speaks of the Savoy Confer-

ence.[55] There were twenty-one theologians on each side, the episcopalian and the presbyterian. Very prominent personalities of both parties had something to say. On the episcopal side the Bishop of Durham, John Cosin, and Bishop Sheldon of London were especially outstanding. The puritan party was distinguished particularly by Reynolds, Bishop of Norwich, and Richard Baxter.

Those puritans who were ecclesiastically minded presented to the king essentially the same ideas with a few additions as had the puritans at another time in their "Millenary Petition" which had led to the Hampton Court Conference. By their suggestions at the Savoy Conference the puritans intended that ineffective ceremonial elements which might be a stumbling block to brothers inclined to be weak and scrupulous be declared optional. In their first petition they stated that the ceremonial elements in The Book of Common Prayer to which they objected, dealt in their opinion with a trifling disagreement:

> And though we do most heartily acknowledge your majesty to be custos utriusque tabulae, and to be supream governour over all persons, and in all things and causes, as well ecclesiastical as civil, in these your majesty's dominions, yet we humbly crave leave to beseech your majesty to consider whether, as a Christian magistrate, you be not as well obliged by that doctrine of the apostle touching things indifferent, in not occasioning an offence to weak brethren, as the apostle himself judged himself to be obliged by; and whether the great work wherewith the Lord hath intrusted your majesty be not rather to provide by your sacred authority that the things which are necessary, by virtue of divine command, in his worship should be duly performed, than that things unnecessary should be made by humane command necessary and penal. And how greatly pleasing it will be to the Lord that your majesty's heart is so tenderly and religiously compassionate to such of his poor servants differing in some small matters.[56]

To the points[57] already raised at the Hampton Court Conference there were some more added of which we want to mention only a few:[58] The puritans criticized holy days for saints although these holy days for saints were introduced only as memorial days for New Testament personalities. There was a passage which caused criticism in the formula for baptism, where the baptised suckling is adjudged to be born again. There was also some opposition to that rubric which requires at the conclusion of the reading of the psalms in Morning and Evening Prayer the little doxology: "Glory be to the Father, and to the Son, and to the Holy Ghost. . . ." The many responses of the congregation were also criticized. For the puritans it was a bone of contention that in The Order for the Burial of the Dead it spoke in general of the "brother," even when referring to a life just concluded which was obviously that of an unbeliever and a mocker. The puritans did indeed strike some weak points in The Book of Common Prayer by their criticism of the baptismal and burial services. It was also for them a matter of concern that there should be not only formal prayers in the BCP but also that room should be allotted for prayers which addressed themselves to some momentarily concrete situation. In addition they desired some formula for the public baptism of adults.

On what points did the Savoy Conference show a willingness to oblige the puritanically minded?

First: The concessions decided upon at the Hampton Court Conference[59] were retained and a mandate issued to carry them out.

Second: That rubric in the BCP of 1559 which prescribed the use of eucharistic vestments was deleted and the rubric from the Common Prayer Book of 1552 prescribing the "surplice" and "cassock" was reintroduced, which solution had after all been adopted previously at the Hampton Court Conference.

Third: It was resolved to reintroduce the "Black Rubric" which had been deleted in the BCP of 1559.

Fourth: The Savoy Conference agreed to the desire for a baptismal formula for adults.

Fifth: Prayers of thanksgiving prepared by the puritans, which were applicable to concrete situations, were sanctioned for the new edition of The Book of Common Prayer. These include a "General Thanksgiving," "For Rain," "For Fair Weather," "For Plenty," "For Peace, and Deliverance from our Enemies," and "For Deliverance from the Plague, or other common Sickness."[60]

The High Church forces at the Savoy Conference succeeded in preserving the gesture of kneeling as well as the exchange of rings in the marriage service and the making of the sign of the cross on the forehead of infants at baptism.

Upon the occasion of the Savoy Conference John Cosin, Bishop of Durham (1594-1672),[61] defended very strongly the initiatives which originated with Archbishop William Laud (died 1645) who had been executed in the Civil War. The latter had at the command of Charles I for the purpose of Anglicanizing Scotland revised its prayer book along High Church lines in the so called Scottish Prayer Book of 1637. In it Laud's leitmotiv, "Worship the Lord in the beauty of holiness" from Psalm 29:2 finds a very special expression. Thus Laud demanded that all stand during the reading of the Gospel and also altar rails for holy communion in order to teach reverence. John Cosin was able to carry out these demands of Laud which he himself included in his own liturgical edition, the "Durham Prayer Book." Moreover, it is noteworthy there that in comparison with the BCP of 1552 an opportunity is provided not only for the speaking of the Creed but also for the singing thereof. In the prayer for Christ's church militant here on earth there has been added this passage by Martin Bucer in which those who have departed this life in the faith are remembered, although one doesn't pray for them:

> And we also bless thy holy Name for all thy servants departed this life in thy faith and fear, beseeching thee to give us grace so to follow their good examples, that with them we may be partakers of thy heavenly kingdom.[62]

During the distribution of the holy communion there are additions which were still lacking in the BCP of 1552:

> The Body of our Lord Jesus Christ, which was given for thee, preserve thy body and soul unto everlasting life.[63]

Here then we have mentioned the most important elements which in the form of earlier additions or retentions as well as through eliminations and modifications at the Savoy Conference have led to The Book of Common Prayer 1662.

Therefore you should understand the prayer book of 1662 as a product which came into existence through the manifold forces of puritanism and its militant manifestation in the Civil War on the one side and also through the pressure of the royalistic and episcopal wing on the other side.

Ideas for the edition of the BCP of 1662 have been planted, grown, and ripened in various individual "nurseries" in the form of liturgical designs and conference resolutions as well as in historical periods of exceptional spirituality.

The diagram on the following page may make this clear.

John Hooper, who borrowed the Zwinglian-
Bullinger theology of the Decalogue and
formed it in a puritan way.

Hampton Court Conference
of 1604

The Book of Common Order
brought to Scotland from Geneva
by John Knox

The spirituality
of the Civil War
as an impulse to
persona l piety
and sanctification

The Scottish Prayer Book of
1637, revised by Archbishop
William Laud

BCP
1662

John Cosin's
Durham
Prayer Book

BCP of 1549

The Savoy Conference
of 1661

BCP of 1552

B. EVALUATION AND DEDUCTIONS

Thanks to the interplay of forces between a puritan way of thinking on the one side and a royalistic-episcopalian High Church spirituality on the other there came into existence a well-balanced, in the best sense, Book of Common Prayer in which the legitimate concerns of both sides were respected without any betrayal of Reformation concerns.

How can one explain the fact that the BCP of 1552 has been in large part integrated into the prayer book of 1662? We recall the tremendous persecution of puritans both by the state as well as by the official church. Indeed this BCP of 1552 is largely the product of the much-despised puritans yet was nevertheless able to find its way into the version of 1662. The Biblical-revivalistic substance, as it had been incorporated from Peter Martyr, Martin Bucer, and Hooper, through Cranmer into the BCP has been maintained with great conscientiousness by ecclesiastically committed puritans such as the influential Grindal and many others under a good stewardship as an entrusted spiritual bequest. At a time when ecclesiastical offices and liturgical forms were being made absolute at the cost of a committed faith—and this even under the protection of the crown— Cromwell succeeded through the storm of Civil War in letting revivalistic concerns permeate the consciousness of ordinary folk.

In spite of its many culture-damaging encroachments the Civil War on the whole had intensified the proper and legitimate perceptions of puritanism in the people's consciousness so that the Restoration of the incoming Charles II with its Catholic tendencies was not able to efface the achievements of the puritans. Cromwell had been able to impart to the people a feeling for and a knowledge of what must be preserved and what is important.

It is also well that the legitimate concerns of the High Church people could be realized at least to a certain degree.

High-Churchmen living in the period of Charles I and Charles II are referred to as "Caroline Divines." They are to be thanked for the idea that a costly content should also have an appropriately dignified form. High-Churchmen possessed an exceptionally strong sense of the Ecclesia Triumphans which had to be included in the liturgy. Likewise the "mysterium" was for them a big concern. In the BCP of 1662 the term "Holy Mystery" appears more frequently than in the BCP of 1552. By "Holy Mystery" is meant the secretive character of God's act of salvation revealed through the sacramental symbols. The manner and way of the presence of Jesus in holy communion does not permit itself to be defined to

149

the smallest detail. Thus the term "Holy Mystery" is somewhat of an admonition that we shouldn't discuss the secret of His presence in holy communion, but very much to the contrary we should adopt an attitude of reverential awe.

It is well that High-Churchmen could give balance to a certain onesidedness on the part of puritans such as their outspoken and strong hostility to liturgy plus a dearth of appreciation for esthetic values.

Some well-known works on The Book of Common Prayer depict puritanism as a movement which could exercise but little influence on the general prayer book, since it was overcome by High-Churchism. Thus Martin Schmitt thinks that the BCP of 1662 has much more in common with the BCP of 1549 than with the second Edwardian prayer book of 1552.[64] This view however does not coincide with the facts. Several of the points already mentioned show us clearly that puritanism has carried off the victory:

1. The canon is also dissolved in the edition of 1662 and this fact expresses a clear commitment to the Reformation of the Reformed type.

2. Those questionable passages[65] which appear in the canon of the holy communion liturgy as well as in other services are also eliminated from the BCP of 1662.

3. The second Edwardian Prayer Book of 1552 being so strongly influenced by the fathers of early puritanism (John Hooper) has been almost entirely integrated in the version of 1662.

4. The measures introduced by the High-Churchmen to be understood as balancing additions are minimal when the prayer books of 1552 and 1662 are compared.

5. High-Churchmen speak of an altar while in the 1662 prayer book one finds only the expressions "holy table" or "the Lord's table."

6. High-Churchmen celebrate the communion while standing before the altar with their line of sight toward the east as was the case in the BCP of 1549. In the corresponding rubric in the BCP of 1662 the priest stands or kneels at the north side of the table of the Lord.

One could only speak of an approximation to the BCP of 1549 if the canon and its medieval ceremonial had been reintroduced.

In accordance with ordinary human calculation High-Churchmen should indeed have gained the victory when we reflect upon the following four successive monarchs and their attitudes:

Elizabeth I, James I, Charles I, and Charles II were decided opponents and even persecutors of the puritans. All four had an outspokenly strong affinity with episcopalianism and High-Churchism. One can speak here of a miracle of God in that the puritans have carried off the victory, and High Church influences were prevailed upon to be constrained by Biblical fences. We are indebted to these circumstances for one of the finest liturgical pearls: The Book of Common Prayer 1662.

C. ANALYSIS OF THE GENUINE REVIVALISTIC ELEMENTS IN THE THREE PRINCIPAL LITURGIES IN THE BCP OF 1662

OPENING REMARKS

In Chapters II and III we sought to show how the revivalistic spirit worked upon Cranmer through Martyr, Bucer, and Hooper and how the Archbishop of Canterbury assimilated this impulse in his second edition of The Book of Common Prayer. It should have become clear in the course of the presentation how directly the puritanical forces, including in particular John Hooper, advocated and placed upon a pedestal the revivalistic spirit to a very special degree through "pura doctrina," "purus cultus," and "pura vita." The beginning of this chapter under Section A has shown the fighting involvement of the ecclesiastically committed puritans for the preservation of its precious revivalistic substance. Now it is our task to make a detailed analysis of the revivalistic elements occurring in The Book of Common Prayer.

1. MORNING PRAYER

a. Introductory Sentences[66]

The twelve quotations from Scripture which portray the depravity of man sound a theme which still plays a central role in revivalistic circles.

We will use Hooper's[67] preaching which for substance and style are typical of the evangelistic or revivalistic when we need an example.

It should not be forgotten that the reformers have done the pioneering work without which revivalistic theology is inconceivable.

The text of our sentences are so compiled that they let one discern for himself the way to overcome sin through repentance. The following texts from among the twelve quotations occupy a particularly important position: Ezekiel 18:27; Psalm 51:3, 9, and 17; and Joel 2:13; etc.

The very first quotation from Ezekiel 18 shows the way to prevail over sin:

> When the wicked man turneth away from his wickedness that he hath committed, and doeth that which is lawful and right, he shall save his soul alive.[68]

b. Exhortation[69]

This is where the revivalistic style chiefly reveals itself.

The exhortation speaks to the congregation directly as to brothers and points out what kind of attitude of the heart should lie behind the confession which is to follow. The revivalistic impulse comes principally in the appeal to the inner man, to the heart. The text speaks to the churchgoer or to the reader of Morning Prayer in his own home so as to confront him in a convincing way with his sins before God, as well as with the forgiveness which is offered and the eternal salvation which is promised.

The exhortation in this church service makes it clear that forgiveness together with the preceding confession and repentance should be a preparation for the congregation so it will know better how to laud and praise the Lord and to listen attentively to His Word.

The conclusion of the exhortation contains an invitation to draw near the divine throne with a pure heart and a humble voice. The unique character of it is that the enormous weight of theological doctrine doesn't operate formally, but rather in a vital way which is also comprehensible to the common man.

Now we want to analyse the individual sentences of this exhortation for their revivalistic content. The text reads:

> [1] Dearly beloved brethren, [2] the Scripture moveth us in sundry places [3] to acknowledge and confess our manifold sins and wickedness, [4] and that we should not dissemble nor cloke them before the face of Almighty God our heavenly Father, [5] but confess them [6] with a humble, lowly, penitent and obedient heart [7] to the end that we may obtain forgiveness of the same [8] by his infinite goodness and mercy. [9] And although we ought at all times humbly to acknowledge our sins before God, [10] yet ought we most chiefly so to do, when we assemble and meet together [11] to

render thanks for the great benefits that we have received at his hands, [12] to set forth his most worthy praise, [13] to hear his most holy Word, [14] and to ask those things which are requisite and necessary, as well for the body as the soul. [15] Wherefore I pray and beseech you, as many as are here present, to accompany me with a pure heart and humble voice unto the throne of the heavenly grace.[70]

We might evaluate this exhortation as being to a certain degree "mini-evangelization."

In the salutation "Dearly beloved brethren" [1] an affectionate solicitation is expressed for a start of the march on the path to salvation. The direction of the march is not left to the option of men. The text citing an admonition of Holy Scripture indicates that the way leads through confession: "The Scripture moveth us in sundry places. . . ." [2] By its continuation[71] which establishes a confession and acknowledgment of guilt as necessary steps, we have reached the basic ingredients as we have already found them in Hooper's manner of preaching.[72]

The exhortation views man in a strictly evangelical-Reformation way as one who wishes to disguise his sinfulness and lives with a propensity for avoiding God.[73]

The following phrase deserves particular note:

[5] But confess them [6] with a humble, lowly, penitent and obedient heart.

The exhortation demands repentance, though in a way which makes its appeal to the inner sphere of men, to the heart.[74] The word repentance is not used there simply as a beautiful liturgical flourish but it is explained by pointing out the need for a humble, lowly, and obedient attitude. This massing of adjectives in the sense of attributes which modify a certain substantive, seems to me characteristic of a revivalistic style.[75] Parts [7] and [8] of our exhortation guard against any misunderstanding as to whether forgiveness is due to the merits of any man or even an obligation of God. The basis for forgiveness lies solely in his infinite goodness. A didactic element has been woven into the text in a discrete way.

The emphasis on the congregation and on fellowship assuredly belongs to the fundamental principles of revivalistic theology. We have devoted several pages in Hooper's sermon to this point.[76]

Parts [9] and [10] in the exhortation declare that an acknowledgment of sin should occur within the context of the congregation. In parts [11] and [12] it is made clearly manifest that men owe thanks and praise to their Lord for their forgiveness.[77] In the passage indicated by [13] we again encounter the emphasis on the Word of Scripture[78] and in [14] there emerges an anthropological conception of the dichotomy which is so crucial in revivalistic theology.[79] In sentence [15] the urging and encouragement implicit in the exhortation appears in expressis verbis:

> Wherefore I pray and beseech you, as many as are here present, to accompany me with a pure heart and humble voice unto the throne of the heavenly grace.

We have already considered briefly this type of urging and challenging address.[80]

c. Confession

Just as in a great evangelization the people clearly perceive a call to repentance, so in this miniature evangelization the exhortation requires a confession to be made by the congregation.

> [1] Almighty and most merciful Father, [2] we have erred and strayed from thy ways like lost sheep. [3] We have followed too much the devices and desires of our own hearts, [4] we have offended against thy holy laws, [5] we have left undone those things which we ought to have done; and we have done those things which we ought not to have done; [6] and there is no health in us: [7] But thou, O Lord, have mercy upon us miserable offenders. [8] Spare thou them, O God, which confess their faults. [9] Restore thou them that are penitent; [10] according to thy promises declared unto mankind in Christ Jesus our Lord. [11] And grant, O most merciful Father, for his sake, that we may hereafter live a godly, righteous, and sober life, [12] To the glory of thy holy Name. Amen.[81]

The Biblical concept of sin is clearly expressed in [2] and [3]. Man has abandoned God's paths. In [3] we see that the text comprehends sin as man's ceaseless declaration of independence vis-à-vis God, in that he trusts in his own schemes and obeys his own appetites. This attitude leads to a contempt for God's laws which [4] makes clear to us.

The clarity with which our text describes man's sinful condition belongs to revivalistic thinking. The metaphor of the lost sheep contains a starkly expressive message:

> We have erred and strayed from thy ways like lost sheep [2].[82]

One is reminded too of evangelistic spirituality in that style of speaking in which a thematic idea is carried forward to a climax by repetition—though in modified form. In our confession from clauses [2] to

[6], the theme of sin builds on an ascending line which reaches a climax in the Pauline quotation from Romans 7:18:

> and there is no health in us. [6]

We have sought to find the just-mentioned structural elements of revivalistic rhetoric in Hooper's sermons. In the "Sermons upon Jonas" sin is spoken of in the guise of the false Jonahs and specifically in such a way that by reiteration it rises to a high point approaching a crescendo.[83] Parts [7] to [12] appeal for the mercy of God with a clear emphasis on repentance. [11] and [12] are permeated through and through with the wholly anti-anthropocentric Soli Deo Gloria. Referring to lifestyle the confession thus pledges that it should redound to the benefit of God. Sanctification comes as a consequence of the forgiveness of sins, a concept which belongs to the basic concepts of evangelistic preaching.[84]

Whoever prays this confession heedfully cannot dismiss it as potentially non-committal. In this confession is revealed that special merit of the Reformation in having again brought into prominence the truth which illuminates the psyche of man with the acuteness of God.

d. Absolution[85]

[1] Almighty God, the Father of our Lord Jesus Christ, [2] who desireth not the death of a sinner, [3] but rather that he may turn from his wickedness and live; [4] hath given power and commandment to his Ministers, [5] to declare and pronounce to his people, being penitent, the Absolution and Remission of their sins: [6] He pardoneth and absolveth all them that truly repent and unfeignedly believe his holy Gospel. [7] Wherefore let us beseech him to grant us true repentance and his holy Spirit, [8] that those things may please him which we do at this present, [9] and that the rest of our life hereafter may be pure and holy, [10] so that at the last we may come to his eternal joy through Jesus Christ our Lord.[86]

In [1] we are informed in the didactical sense as to who the Almighty God is, namely the Father of our Lord Jesus Christ. One marks the personal note in the expression: "the Father of our Lord Jesus Christ." The personal pronoun in the first person plural (our) produces an intimate atmosphere which is typical of revivalistic thinking. In [2] we perceive dogmatically that God is he who does not wish the death of sinners but instead their return to a proper life. By death is meant here the spiritual state of sinners separated from God, which time and again is a favoured theme in revivalistic preaching.[87]

It is clear from [3] that conversion means life.[88] The text at [6] closely associates forgiveness with an unhypocritical faith in the Gospel:

> He pardoneth and absolveth all them that truly repent and unfeignedly believe his Holy Gospel.

The terms "truly" and "unfeignedly" are intended to show that repentance must be a matter of the heart and not simply a form of lip service. Here again we encounter the revivalistic spirit which invariably wants to reach the inner man.[89] [7] and [9] obviously state that forgiveness has to exercise its influence upon a consecrated life through the Holy Spirit. The essence of sanctification has already been mentioned in connexion with the confession. We often encounter repetitions.

The high point in the text is found at [10], at the goal to which every evangelization or revivalistic address has to bring its participants, namely to eternal joy and glory through Jesus Christ:

> So that at the last we may come to his eternal joy through Jesus Christ our Lord.

The text guards against any misunderstanding that such an association with Jesus already contains one's full salvation, so that whatever follows after the death of the earthly body is irrelevant. The phrase "so that at the last we may come . . ." undoubtedly bespeaks an eschatological as well as an individualistic-other world understanding of salvation. Revivalistic sermons are saturated with tempting promises which paint the eschatological pleasures of salvation right before one's eyes.[90]

The text of the absolution points out to us a dynamic unfolding of an eschatological consummation in expressions of time: "at this present time" [8], "hereafter" [9], and "at last" [10]. The consequences of a forgiveness received through the absolution should extend throughout the past, present, and into the future of the hereafter.

The following sections of Morning Prayer are based on both of the following divine offices of the Roman and, principally, of the Sarum breviary: matins and lauds.

e. Opening Sentences

After the Lord's Prayer there follows the responsively made opening sentences from Psalm 51:15, found also at the opening of matins[91] in the Roman as well as in the Sarum breviaries:

> O Lord, open thou our lips.
> And our mouth shall show forth thy praise.
> O God make speed to save us.
> O Lord make haste to help us.
> Glory be to the Father, and to the Son, and to the Holy Ghost;
> As it was in the beginning, is now, and ever shall be, world
> without end. Amen.[92]

A theological statement is expressed in the most concise form in these opening sentences: On the one hand man is for the Soli Deo Gloria, while on the other hand he has to recognize himself as lost.

f. Psalm 95[93]

After the opening sentences one finds in Psalm 95, which in a structural sense is again taken from matins in the Roman breviary, some statements illuminating mankind's existence in connexion with the wandering of God's people in the wilderness. The central declaration is in the second part of verse 10:

> It is a people that do err in their hearts, for they have not known my ways.

Following Psalm 95 comes the Psalm corresponding to the current day of the week.[94]

g. Old Testament Lesson

An interruption in the strictly liturgical portion occurs in the reading of a Bible text from the Old Testament in conformity with the sequence provided for in the Sarum matins which in turn was partially dependent on the Roman breviary.[95]

h. Te Deum Laudamus[96]

A discussion of this "Ambrosian Song of Praise" from the point of view of lauds and praises will follow later. The Te Deum following the reading of the Old Testament lesson[97] is still a part of the Roman as well as of the Sarum matins. It would be interesting to know why Cranmer made use of so many elements of the old church liturgies and from what point of view did he make his choice. It seems to me that he let himself be guided in matters of substance in accordance with revivalistic theological considerations and also in the choice of liturgical elements, although at this time the term "revivalistic" did not exist in theological history. That Psalm 95 suited our compiler is not difficult to understand when one considers the emphasis therein on the depravity and corruption of man. There are however other places also to be found in the Te Deum which agree with the evangelistic way of thinking, such as the suggestion that men have need of deliverance from slavery (perhaps of Satan):

> When thou tookest upon thee to deliver man: thou didst not abhor the Virgin's womb.[98]

Further along is that interesting passage where it says:

> When thou hadst overcome the sharpness of death: thou didst open the Kingdom of Heaven to all believers.[99]

Noteworthy in the above text is the statement about the sharpness of death, for in the later development of Roman Catholic theology death is seen more as something natural, perhaps in strong contrast to a Calvinistic understanding of death. Not to be overlooked in the same text is the suggestion about the faithful for whom, through the merits of Jesus, heaven stands open. Salvation is thus not something automatic but becomes operative through the faith of men. Revivalistic theology has much to say about this saving faith.

We want to quote still one final passage:

> We therefore pray thee, help thy servants: whom thou hast redeemed with thy precious blood.[100]

Accentuation of the huge ransom which Jesus paid in the form of his blood sacrifice is typical of revivalistic and evangelical thinking.

The rubric provides as an alternative to the Te Deum the "Benedicite Omnia Opera." This is a specialty of lauds in the Sarum breviary. This song of praise is the translation of a part of the third chapter in the book of Daniel in accordance with the Septuagint version. We go into this in more detail later on when the discussion concerns praise.[101]

i. Benedictus

After the New Testament lesson[102] comes the Benedictus.[103] Psalm 95 spoke of the depravity of men, then the Benedictus takes up the salvation line, particularly in verses 76 to 79 of Luke 1:

> And thou, child, shalt be called the prophet of the Highest: For thou shalt go before the face of the Lord to prepare his ways, to give knowledge of salvation unto his people: for the remission of their sins, through the tender mercy of our God: whereby the dayspring from on high hath visited us, to give light to them that sit in darkness, and in the shadow of death: and to guide our feet into the way of peace.

In accordance with verse 77 John the Baptist was to proclaim in a prefigurative way through the consolation of forgiveness in baptism the coming salvation in Jesus. According to verse 79 Jesus as the true light overcame the structure of death. As an alternative to the Benedictus the Jubilate Deo, which is Psalm 100, can be inserted, which however seldom happens.

j. Apostles' Creed[104]

We find the Creed already in the offices of the Roman breviary.[105] In the pre-Reformation services it followed the Lord's Prayer amongst the prayers of Prime. The old practice in the Sarum breviary was for the priest to recite the Creed alone and inaudibly. The location of the Creed in Morning Prayer is significant. The Apostles' Creed follows immediately after the Biblical Benedictus and thereby signifies that faith is grounded in Scripture. In addition, the litany-like sentences,[106] the Lord's Prayer, as well as the closing versicles and the prayer of dismissal have some reference to the Creed in that these components[107] following the Creed likewise call for faith. Charles Neil with reference to the placing of the Creed says the following:

> Its present position is much more appropriate. It follows upon the reading of Holy Scripture, the foundation of faith, and precedes prayer, which both needs and sustains faith.[108]

k. Responsive Closing Versicles[109]

Among the closing versicles[110] which follow the Lord's Prayer, of primary interest to us are the first, second, seventh, ninth, tenth, eleventh, and twelth:

Priest:	O Lord, shew thy mercy upon us.	[1]
Answer:	And grant us thy salvation.	[2]
Priest:	O Lord, save thy people.	[7]
Answer:	And bless thine inheritance.	
Priest:	Give peace in our time, O Lord.	[9]
Answer:	Because there is none other that fighteth for us, but only thou, O God.	[10]
Priest:	O God, make clean our hearts within us.	[11]
Answer:	And take not thy holy Spirit from us.	[12]

The first two versicles allude to the fundamental theme of Holy Scripture: they refer to the concept that God may bestow his mercy upon one. Versicle seven makes clear of what the mercy of God consists. One can experience the mercy of God in His willingness to save. It is made clear in versicles nine and ten that a real peace must find its basis in the Lord so that one does not lapse into the sleep of the just through false assurances such as the then current calculation of human merit, which had indeed a soteriological implication.

The last sentences from Psalm 51:10 and 11 reveal, like the preceding, a most important revivalistic substance. That "O God, make clean our hearts within us" points obviously to the need for an innocent heart[111] here, in contrast to simple religiosity which can exhaust itself so easily in outer appearances and form. It is apparent from this that a purified heart has to come through the working of the Holy Spirit: "And take not thy holy Spirit from us." The compiler has used these closing versicles[112] from the divine offices of lauds and prime in the Sarum breviary.[113]

l. Seven Closing Prayers

Right after the versicles Morning Prayer comes to an end with prayers for various concerns.

160

(1) First Collect

This is the collect appropriate to the current Sunday.

(2) Collect for Peace

The collect for peace corresponds to the preceding versicles [9] and [10] which in their brevity operate rather formally. However the collect for peace makes the previous sentences concrete and binding:

> O God, who art the author of peace and lover of concord, in knowledge of whom standeth our eternal life, whose service is perfect freedom: Defend us thy humble servants in all assaults of our enemies, that we surely trusting in thy defence, may not fear the power of any adversaries, through the might of Jesus Christ our Lord.[114]

Some reflection of a revivalistic spirituality may have played a part in the translation of this prayer from the Latin. This refers to that passage where it says "whose service is perfect freedom." Behind this clause which has already been interpreted may lie a hidden suggestion that the service of God should not be misunderstood in a mechanical-liturgical sense.

(3) Collect for Grace

The prayer books of 1549 and 1552 ended the morning service with this collect.[115] The prayer is an expansion of what was stated in versicle [11]: "O God, make clean our hearts within us."

The text of the prayer takes up the idea of sanctification which is present only in a preliminary way in versicle [11]. The most important part of this collect reads:

> And grant that this day we fall into no sin, neither run into any kind of danger; but that all our doings may be ordered by thy governance, to do always that is righteous in thy sight; through Jesus Christ our Lord. Amen.[116]

In our text sanctification is to be seen plainly as something that God must impart to men. Revivalistic theology concerns itself time and again with the theme of sanctification.[117]

(4) Prayer for the King or Queen

A submissive acknowledgment of national sovereignty is one of the features of the two forces which, among other things, helped to shape the nineteenth century: revivalism and romanticism. Our prayer expands upon the concern contained in the third versicle.[118] This humble attitude toward the throne could be symbolic and at the same time an exercise in the acknowledgment of the highest authority, namely the divine. J. Dowden makes a striking comment on this prayer when he says:

> We know from Holy Scripture (Rev. xix:16 and xvii:14) that it is He whose name is called "the Word of God, that has on His vesture written King of kings and Lord of Lords." Hence it is "the Lamb" who is the "Lord of Lords and King of kings."[119]

(5) Prayer for the Royal Family[120]

This petition is very similar to that for the crown. Both prayers are expressions of the Reformation loyalty with respect to the state. The latter prayer stems from Tudor times. The prayer here goes back probably to Archbishop Whitgift. It found its present place in the year 1662.

(6) Prayer for the Clergy and People[121]

This also has reference to the sentences, namely to versicles [5] and [6]. It is significant that the text names the priest and the congregation in one passage and implores for both in equal measure the "healthful Spirit of thy grace." Rivalry between clergy and congregation is to be avoided.

(7) Prayer of St. Chrysostom[122]

Cranmer selected this prayer from the Byzantine Chrysostom liturgy. It is the final prayer before the benediction. It is difficult to explain just why Cranmer selected this prayer. I surmise that he instinctively perceived how well this prayer was suited to express the objectives of revivalistic spirituality. The text reads:

Almighty God, who hast given us grace at this time with one accord to make our common supplications unto thee, and dost promise that when two or three are gathered together in thy Name thou wilt grant their requests: Fulfil now, O Lord, the desires and petitions of thy servants, as may be most expedient for them, granting us in this world knowledge of thy truth, and in the world to come life everlasting. Amen.

This prayer, taking its cue from Matthew 18:19, understands a divine service as one in which the worshippers are assembled in the name of Jesus. Evangelistic thinking has constantly before its eyes the goal of eternal salvation, which becomes evident at the close of the prayer. It seems to me the passage toward the end is worthy of note, where it says: "granting us in this world knowledge of thy truth." A feature of revivalistic thinking is to know about God's truth by means of a basic knowledge of his Word. Hence it is not by chance that revivalistic Christendom and Biblicism generally belong closely together.

(8) Closing Benediction

This well known Biblical benediction from 2 Corinthians 13:13 brings Morning Prayer to a close. In view of these liturgical formulas which are filled so completely with Biblical elements it seems as if the compiler wishes to say in this closing benediction: in a proper divine service the Word of Scripture must be opening, middle, and close.[123]

2. EVENING PRAYER

a. The Liturgical Building Blocks

These are vespers and compline, taken from the Sarum breviary.

b. Structure

The order of the individual liturgical elements is identical to that present in Morning Prayer. The opening sentences,[124] exhortation,[125] confession, absolution,[126] closing sentences, and the benediction are the same.

c. The Most Important Differences between the Liturgical Elements of Evening Prayer and Morning Prayer

(1) Magnificat[127] and Nunc Dimittis[128]

These hymns from Luke 1:46-55 and Luke 2:29-32 lend Evening Prayer a special distinction. The Nunc Dimittis, that song of praise of venerable Simeon, reminds one particularly of revivalistic ideas where it refers to the experiencing of salvation through a personal encounter with Jesus.

(2) Second and Third Collects

A petition for that peace which the world cannot give emerges from the second collect. One finds in revivalistic-evangelical theology a certain disparaging attitude toward the world. This prayer in addition asks for an obedient heart with respect to the Commandments, which testifies to the seriousness of the sanctification. The text of the second collect reads:

> O God, from whom all holy desires, all good counsels, and all just works do proceed: Give unto thy servants that peace which the world cannot give, that both our hearts may be set to obey thy commandments, and also that by thee we being defended from the fear of our enemies may pass our time in rest and quietness; through the merits of Jesus Christ our Saviour. Amen.[129]

The third collect[130] is very short. It uses the gathering darkness of evening as a symbol for sinful men who find themselves in darkness.

CLOSING REMARKS ABOUT MORNING AND EVENING PRAYER

Our question is: Where then lies the chief difference between these two divine services and the offices of the Roman breviary? Are not the Latin offices upon which our two services are largely based taken from the same Biblical material?

The answer to these questions is furnished by the four crucial elements brought in by the Reformation, namely, the twelve sentences quoted from Scripture which introduce Morning as well as Evening Prayer, the exhortation, the expanded confession, and absolution.[131] The four elements are to be understood like factors standing in front of a parenthesis in a mathematical equation which modifies everything within the parenthesis in the appropriate orientation. Morning and Evening Prayer bring to the surface the substance of God's Word in the opening sentences, but chiefly in the exhortation, confession, and absolution and present it (the substance of God's Word) in a propagandistic way to the churchgoer.

The offices of the Roman breviary lack a satisfactory confession and absolution.[132] Exhortations are missing altogether. Only a very weak expression is given to the idea that man is lost.

The closing prayers in Morning and Evening Prayer give the impression that they were spoken spontaneously. This also occurs with those prayers which are not a creation of the Reformation, but were taken from the Latin tradition. The Latin formulas of the Sarum tradition obviously include in their prayer material some substance which in the translation by Reformation theologians into English received a revivalistic impress.

3. HOLY COMMUNION LITURGY[133]

The Holy Communion Service deserves particular attention. The Anglican church in England has introduced for this church service three alternative formulas[134] which though do not as yet possess canonical legality. We intend to go into these formulas later on. The communion service is important for the reason that to a special degree it has to be a witness to the unity of Christians despite legitimate confessional variations.

We will confine ourselves in the current inquiry to those parts which abound with evidence of revivalistic thinking.

a. General Statements in the Opening Rubric[135]

The ethical aspect plays a major role in the context of the overall view of holy communion. The rubric requires that the priest allow no unrepentant sinner to commune. This means people who have harmed their neighbors by word or deed. Such sinners must, according to the rubric, acknowledge their repentance openly before the congregation, and better their style of living. Also, members of the congregation who are in conflict with one another should not take communion until both parties have been reconciled.

The injured party is called upon to forgive his enemy from the bottom of his heart. Some particularly important sentences from this rubric now follow:

> And if any of those be an open and notorious evil liver, or have done any wrong to his neighbours by word or deed, so that the congregation be thereby offended, the Curate, having knowledge thereof, shall call him and advertise him, that in any wise he presume not to come to the Lord's Table, until he have openly declared himself to have truly repented and amended his former life, that the Congregation therefore be satisfied, which before were offended. . . . The same order shall the Curate use with those betwixt whom he perceiveth malice and hatred to reign, not suffering them to be partakers of the Lord's Table, until he knew them to be reconciled. And if one of the parties so at variance be content to forgive from the bottom of his heart all that the other hath trespassed against him . . . the minister in that case ought to admit the penitent person to the Holy Communion.

The emphasis on a worthy receiving based on repentance and atonement points to a conception, especially developed in puritanism, that an examination of one's conscience is required before the taking of the sacraments. In this way a course is set for the development of piety in the direction of revivalism. In the above partially quoted rubric the individual is understood to be accountable to the congregation. Holy communion is thus an event wherein the individual members acknowledge themselves as a congregation of Jesus Christ, and for that reason the relation among them demands a settlement by forgiveness. Communion calls for a binding fellowship[136] in which sanctification[137] is assumed. The furthering of a settled relationship among men in the presence of the taking of communion pertains to sanctification.

(1) Comparison with the Pre-Second Vatican Council Missal

A comparison with the Roman missal[138] which was still in use in the 1960s indicates that the current Catholic communion liturgy recognizes no rubric appealing to the conscience of the churchgoer. The question of personal guilt which needs to be brought in order within the congregation as an expression of the realization of sanctification, is not in view. The opening of the mass occurs with the so called "Asperges Me," whereupon the priest with his acolytes strides from the portal to the altar and sprinkles the congregation with holy water. At the same time the choir sings verses 9 and 3 of the Fifty-first Psalm. Any appeal to the innermost core of depraved man is missing:

Asperges me, Domine, hyssopo, et mundabor: Lavabis me, et super nivem dealbabor. Miserere mei, Deus, secundam magnam misericordiam tuam.[139]

The ceremony with the holy water lies rather in the field of cultish cleansing in which the personal aspect is largely lacking.[140]

b. Opening Collect

The opening collect (collect of purity) is placed just after the Lord's Prayer, and shows a connexion with the opening rubric. This "collect of purity" reminds the churchgoer therein that he must take to heart what is said in the opening rubric. The following quotation should indicate this:

Almighty God, unto whom all hearts be open, all desires known, and from whom no secrets are hid; cleanse the thoughts of our hearts by the inspiration of thy Holy Spirit, that we may perfectly love thee, and worthily magnify thy holy Name; through Christ our Lord. Amen.[141]

No one taking communion should conceal his failures from God and ought to clear up any misunderstandings with his neighbours. In accordance with the opening rubric such a settlement should be a forgiveness from the bottom of the heart. The "collect of purity" speaks of God as he who sees into all hearts and who is aware of the most hidden wishes and secrets. How could one dare to go routinely to the table of the Lord without searching one's conscience?

This opening collect appeals to the innermost core of man, to his heart. The thoughts of the heart need to be cleansed by the power of the Holy Spirit. This force, thrusting in the opening collect to the core of man, to his soul, is evidence of the revivalistic spirit. The "collect of purity" contains in this condensed manner the program of the eucharistic service: Man is called therein to let the roots of his being (the thoughts of the heart) be cleansed by God, that is to say, by the Holy Spirit, in order thereafter to be properly prepared to praise the Almighty Lord.

c. Proclamation of the Ten Commandments[142]

The Ten Commandments establish a field of activity in which man, living by grace and forgiveness, can place in evidence his bond with God by his obedience. An inner logic exists here in connexion with the opening collect. In keeping the Commandments sanctification must be attained and

167

clearly within the context of the congregation. The New Testament often speaks of sanctification as a concern of the congregation. This is taken into consideration in our proclamation of the Commandments when the congregation in humility answers the priest's proclamation of each Commandment:

> Lord, have mercy upon us, and incline our hearts to keep this law.

We have already mentioned that the assignment of a special importance to the Commandments is a characteristic of revivalistic circles, particularly in connexion with sanctification.[143]

d. Two Collects for the Royal Government

In the intercessory prayer for the Queen[144] below, the following ideas are expressed: In it one prays that the queen might in all things seek God's honor and glory wherefore the people should submit themselves as ready to serve the sovereign. The queen is in a certain sense the representative of God. One element reminiscent of revivalism is the appeal to the heart of the queen:

> And so rule the heart of thy chosen Servant Elizabeth, our Queen and Governor, that she (knowing whose minister she is) may above all things seek thy honor and glory: and that we, and all her subjects (duly considering whose authority she hath) may faithfully serve, honor and obey her, in thee, and for thee, according to thy blessed Word and ordinance.

Toward the end of the prayer above, obedience to the monarch is based on Scripture. In the second of the optional intercessory prayers for the queen the thought is expressed that the representatives of the government are the pawns of God. Nor does the prayer neglect here again to lead Holy Scripture onto the field to support the validity of its message:

> Almighty and everlasting God, we are taught by thy holy Word, that the hearts of Kings are in thy rule and governance, and thou dost dispose and turn them as it seemeth best to thy godly wisdom: We humbly beseech thee so to dispose and govern the heart of ELIZABETH thy Servant, our queen and Governor,[145] that in all her thoughts, words, and works, she may ever seek thy honor.

Again it seems to me worthy of note that there is an inherent logic which exists in the connexion of the two prayers with the proclamation of the Commandments. These prayers point to the government as having been commissioned by God as the executrix of earthly justice. This conception of government bears the strong imprint of Hooper and Grindal. In this connexion I refer to the quotation from Hooper's works on page 78, middle, in our work.

An interesting parallel to this attitude with reference to the government as represented by the crown, as we have established it in the prayers cited above, is found in the restorations of the nineteenth century.[146] At that time loyalty to the throne played an important role in revivalism and romanticism.

e. Rubrics[147]

The rubric following mentions by name the next sections in the service such as the collect for the day, the Epistle, the Gospel, and the Creed. Following the Creed is an additional rubric which instructs the pastor to give any appropriate notices to the congregation, and thereafter to deliver his sermon.

f. Quotations from Scripture in the Introduction to the Offertory[148]

The quotations from Scripture[149] in the introduction to the offertory establish the primacy of the Word of Scripture. Here we are dealing with an emphasis on the readiness to sacrifice which occurs in a typically fundamentalistic way just as one finds it in the thinking of revivalistic circles.[150]

This collection of Scripture quotations reminds one of the thinking processes which time and again forcefully distinguish the evangelistically focused Christian. Thus there are present in these offertory verses some important structural elements of revivalistic theology: In Matthew 5:16 we find that element of the Christian witness in accordance with which one should win others for the Lord (first Scriptural quotation). Matthew 6:19 and 20 emphasize the importance of the imperishable heavenly treasures[151] for the gaining of which no sacrifice can be too great (second Scriptural quotation). In the sixth quotation from 1 Corinthians 9:7 the idea of compensation comes through, which is central to revivalistic thinking.

169

g. Prayer for the Church Militant[152]

(1) The Emphasis on the Divine Word

It is remarkable how the reference to Scripture shows up like a red thread throughout this magnificent prayer. Three times we encounter the idea of faithfulness to Scripture. In the first we read:

> And grant, that all they that do confess thy holy Name may agree in the truth of thy holy Word, and live in unity and godly love.[153]

The authenticity or truth of Holy Scripture belongs to the basic presuppositions of revivalistic theology. The divine Word constitutes the real unity among the faithful and not principally some human tradition. As the text continues, about two-thirds of the way through we encounter this significant sentence:

> Give grace, O heavenly Father, to all Bishops and Curates, that they may both by their life and doctrine set forth thy true and lively Word.[154]

The expression "true and lively Word" is interesting. Regardless of how much credit is due to orthodoxy with reference to an understanding of Scripture, nevertheless it has examined the Biblical Word too much from a static point of view, at the cost of a dynamic point of view. Revivalistic Christianity of a puritanical character has contributed much to a dynamic understanding of God's Word without abandoning the legitimate static side of Holy Scripture.[155]

Since God's Word is even true and lively, it must also affect one's manner of living. The ethical consequences of God's Word thus stand in full view in the above text. In this connexion it is not surprising that revivalistically committed congregations practice church discipline to emphasize the necessary connexion between doctrine and a practical lifestyle.

In the final third of our text we again encounter the Word in a similar connexion:

> And to all thy people give thy heavenly grace; and specially to this congregation here present, that with meek heart and due reverence, they may hear, and receive thy holy Word; truly serving thee in holiness and righteousness all the days of their life.[156]

The expressions "meek heart" and "due reverence" are conspicuous in the text above. The divine Word requires for its acceptance chiefly a heart properly prepared and appropriate respect. "Meek heart" signifies a submissive spiritual attitude in connexion with a consciousness of one's unworthiness. Revivalistic theology, which we do not want to differentiate greatly from pietistic thinking, speaks often of the heart and of its attitude in contrast to a cold intellectuality which considers the Word of God without any inner commitment.

In the text cited above the connexion of the Word with an ethical life-style is established, hence with sanctification:

Truly serving thee in holiness and righteousness all the days of their life.[157]

(2) Transitoriness of This Life, with Its Misery

In the last third of the prayer we find a quotation which expresses a solidarity with all the poor and miserable in this world:

And we most humbly beseech thee of thy goodness, O Lord, to comfort and succour all them, who in this transitory life are in trouble, sorrow, need, sickness, or any other adversity.[158]

We mentioned earlier how revivalistic circles strongly emphasize the transitoriness and misery of this life.[159] Earthly life is realistically seen for what it is in the normal case.

(3) Remembrance of the Faithful Dead

A downgrading of the world occurs in revivalistic circles as background to the emphasis on eternal glory, with its imperishable treasures of salvation. In connexion with the just-mentioned quotations in our text we find in logical relationship—logical at least in revivalistic understanding—an orientation towards life after death in relationship to the faithful dead.

And we also bless thy holy Name for all thy servants departed this life in thy faith and fear; beseeching thee to give us grace so to follow their good examples, that with them we may be partakers of thy heavenly kingdom: Grant this, O Father, for Jesus Christ's sake, our only Mediator and Advocate. Amen.[160]

We encounter here a clearly Biblically founded attitude toward the departed. Prayers for the dead can exert no influence over the fate of the dead. On the contrary one should and may give thanks as Christians for

171

those who have departed in the faith. Those dead who in life were faithful are, on the basis of the propitiatory death of Jesus, cleansed and therefore require no additional purification in purgatory. When it says almost at the end of this prayer

> We bless thy holy Name for all thy servants departed this life in thy faith and fear.

the verb bless is to be taken as meaning glorify or extoll. Since in revivalistic circles a firm belief in one's salvation[161] is often a reality there frequently prevails during the funeral obsequies an atmosphere more of thankfulness and repressed joy than any impression of grief.

Our prayer for the ecclesia militans sets forth in a strictly evangelical way the example of the deceased though in such a manner that we might be inspired by their faith, and not by some particular deeds of a heroic nature; otherwise there would exist a fatal misunderstanding about the achievement of righteousness by works.

h. Three Exhortations[162]

The three exhortations constitute a unity although as a rule only one of the exhortations is read in church use. We are dealing with the essence of revivalistic thinking in these exhortations. The revivalistic elements here are far more plentiful than in the exhortations in Morning and Evening Prayer. All three exhortations begin with a salutation which is stamped with the spirit of charity: "Dearly beloved . . ."[163]

(1) First Exhortation[164]

What we have said in reference to the exhortation in Morning Prayer[165] also applies to the first exhortation. The difference is only one of degree. In the exhortation in Morning Prayer there is a warning not to appear before God unworthily by taking part in a church service, but to examine one's conscience and to make known one's repentance and atonement. In the first exhortation of the communion liturgy it goes further than just to take part seriously in the service. Here it calls for the worthy receiving of God himself in a spiritual way in the sacrament. This presupposes a faith whose substance the exhortation expresses at the outset in the following way:

I purpose through God's assistance, to administer to all such as shall be religiously and devoutly disposed the most comfortable sacrament of the Body and Blood of Christ, to be by them received in remembrance of his meritorious Cross and Passion, whereby alone we obtain remission of our sins and are made partakers of the kingdom of heaven.[166]

Further on in the exhortation one perceives a more intensive urge to worthiness and purity and an allusion to the consequences of taking communion frivolously. As faith is a prerequisite to the taking of communion, a revivalistic admonition is likewise necessary since so-called faith (speaking formally) can easily become a cushion of repose. In the text we find the expressive picture of the wedding garment[167] from Matthew 22:12:

My duty is to exhort you in the mean season to consider the dignity of that holy mystery, and the great peril of the unworthy receiving thereof, and so to search and examine your own consciences, and that not lightly, and after the manner of dissemblers with God: But so that you may come holy and clean to such a heavenly feast, in the marriage garment required by God in holy Scripture, and be received as worthy partakers of that holy Table.[168]

At a marriage where a marriage garment is de rigueur it is binding in the strictest degree upon the person. Perhaps behind this picture of the wedding garment stands the idea that only those are worthy to come to the table of the Lord who, on the basis of a personal relationship with Jesus,[169] have a share in his righteousness and are therefore pure. One is reminded of the song written in 1638 in Leipzig which Nikolaus Ludwig von Zinzendorf (1700-1760) has expanded with seven additional verses:

The Blood and Righteousness of Christ:
My honored robe and ornament,
In which I may approach my God
When I am heaven sent.[170]

We encounter in this a theme which belongs to the essentials of revivalistic thinking. The summons to come to the feast in a marriage garment implies the possibility of getting lost. Our exhortation addresses this matter in its final quarter, after a repetition of that which the opening rubric sought to enjoin:

And if ye shall perceive your offences to be such as are not only against God, but also against your neighbours; then ye shall reconcile yourselves unto them; being ready to make restitution and satisfaction, according to the uttermost of your powers, for all injuries and wrongs done by you to any other; and being likewise ready to forgive others that have offended you . . . : For otherwise the receiving of the holy Communion doth nothing else but increase your damnation.[171]

The warning not to lay oneself open to the condemnation of God[172] reaches a crescendo such that one might suppose one were present at a fiery evangelization.

Therefore if any of you be a blasphemer of God, an hinderer or slanderer of his Word, an adulterer, or be in malice, or envy, or in any other grievous crime, repent you of your sins, or else come not to that holy Table, lest after the taking of that holy Sacrament, the devil enter into you, as he entered into Judas, and fill you full of all iniquities, and bring you to destruction both of body and soul.[173]

The counting off of the individual sins in this first exhortation in order to make one's guilt vivid is a practice frequently found in revivalistic church services. It is intended here to refer to events of practical life. Mention of the power of Satan which we also find here is met in almost every evangelization. The closing section of our exhortation speaks of a remarkable possibility:

Therefore if there be any of you, who by this means cannot quiet his own conscience herein, but requiereth further comfort or counsel, let him come to me, or to some other discreet and learned Minister of God's Word, and open his grief.[174]

In this passage just cited we are dealing with an important phenomenon which is parallel to the usual evangelization arrangement. In most evangelizations there is the possibility available for those who have been stirred up by the message and for spiritually convicted persons to come after the close of the service for a personal conversation with the evangelist or his team. The purpose is the same as that spoken in the closing sentences of the exhortation:

That by the ministry of God's holy Word he may receive the benefit of absolution, together with ghostly counsel and advice, to the quieting of his conscience, and avoiding of all scruple and doubtfulness.[175]

This refers to the overcoming of scruples and doubts which might hinder the working of the Holy Spirit.

(2) Second Exhortation

The second exhortation is to be used when the churchgoers adopt an indifferent attitude toward the taking of communion, and remain away from the taking of the sacrament.

It is not so much a matter here of making one aware that any person taking communion must have a worthy attitude. It is much more a matter of giving urgent notice of the great trouble to which God has put Himself in order to invite sinful men to his table.

> I bid you all that are here present, and beseech you, for the Lord Jesus Christ's sake, that you will not refuse to come thereto, being so lovingly called and bidden by God himself.[176]

The exhortation further on then sets forth the similarity here with that man in the Gospel who invited all available persons and even the unavailable to a banquet. But most had an excuse since worldly affairs were more important to them.

The exhortation threatens God's wrath against those who scorn the pleading-loving invitation. Neither worldly business nor a hypocritically disguised pretence of being a miserable sinner will serve as an excuse.

> If any man say, I am a grievous sinner, and therefore am afraid to come: wherefore then do ye not repent and amend?[177]

Then further along the summons and request that this invitation to holy communion not be undervalued becomes always more intense until in the last third of the text reasons are given which one won't find any better stated in an evangelization:

> And according to mine Office, I bid you in the Name of God, I call you in Christ's behalf, I exhort you, as ye love your own salvation, that ye will be partakers of this holy Communion.[178]

What a crescendo lies in the successive phrases: "I bid you in the Name of God," "I call you on Christ's behalf," "I exhort you, as ye love your own salvation"! So we encounter here again the previously mentioned crescendo.[179] Towards the close of the exhortation we also encounter threats:

> Consider with yourselves how great injury ye do unto God, and how sore punishment hangeth over your heads for the same; when ye wilfully abstain from the Lord's Table, and separate from your brethren.[180]

175

Primarily the pressure used here is intended theocentrically (how great injury ye do unto God), since it refers to the honour of God. Only secondarily is an anthropocentric idea expressed, in the sense of a warning of dreadful punishments. There is an implication in this text that man is not even mature and hence has need of warnings and threats.

(3) Third Exhortation[181]

We find repetitions in this exhortation of what has been said already. Repetitions in evangelizations are immediately noticeable to the critically minded person. These repetitions have their peculiarities. They spiral up toward a high point so that one absorbs something more than he started with, at least emotionally. The spiral staircase in the church tower may lead one in a circle. After a while you reach the goal and enjoy a lovely view all around.

Worthy of note in our text is the massing of attributive adjectives which modify in a revivalistic style the prepositional objects:

> For as the benefit is great, if with a true penitent heart and lively faith we receive that holy Sacrament; so is the danger great if we receive the same unworthily.[182]

This attention-catching manner[183] expressed in such phrases as "true penitent heart" and "lively faith," stirs up the conscience of men.

We run up against repetitions of the warnings which are moreover substantially stronger than those in the two preceding exhortations.[184] In the continuation of the text it says:

> For then we are guilty of the Body and Blood of Christ our Saviour; we eat and drink our own damnation . . . ; we kindle God's wrath against us; we provoke him to plague us with divers diseases, and sundry kinds of death.[185]

The strong warning tone in the text above borders on a scolding.[186]

An appeal to gratitude follows at the beginning of the second half of the exhortation. The expression "above all things" introduces a sentence which makes people aware of their total dependence on God's grace and that complete thanks are due him therefore. The text reviews what Jesus has done for us:

> And above all things ye must give most humble and hearty thanks to God, the Father, the Son, and the Holy Ghost, for the redemption of the world by the death and passion of our Saviour Christ, both God and man, who did

humble himself, even to the death upon the Cross, for us miserable sinners, who lay in darkness and the shadow of death, that he may make us the children of God.[187]

Worthy of note, above, is the expression "hearty thanks," which indicates that the thanks should not be formal but must flow from the innermost part of man.

The text confronts us with some important doctrinal statements. Thus the churchgoer perceives that Christ is both God and man. Sinners are dead, in a spiritual sense. The fruit of the sacrificial death of Jesus is that the churchgoer becomes a child of God.

Pietistic undertones are to be detected during the further course of the third exhortation:

And to the end that we should alway remember the exceeding great love of our Master and only Saviour Jesus Christ, thus dying for us, and the innumerable benefits which by his precious blood-shedding he hath obtained to us.[188]

This expression, "exceeding great love," betrays the spirituality of a profound faith and a personal commitment to Jesus. When it speaks of the shedding of his precious blood it fits in well with the revivalistic spirit as we know of it in a Zinzendorf-stamped pietism.

i. Invitation[189]

This follows immediately after the three exhortations and is chiefly an encouraging address by the priest to the congregation. The invitation, which may be understood as a fourth exhortation, summarizes the requested prerequisites for the taking of communion found in the three preceding exhortations and forms a transition to the confession. The most important sentence in this "invitation" contains then the important challenge to an act of faith:

Draw near with faith, and take this holy Sacrament to your comfort.

But this invitation can only be accepted properly by those who truly and earnestly repent.

There is therefore in this communion liturgy a very conscientious attempt to guard against those people who want to participate habitually and mechanically in the eucharistic service. The two adjectives "truly" and "earnestly" indicate again an appeal to the heart and conscience which is so typical of the revivalistic spirit.

Ye that do truly and earnestly repent you of your sins, and are in love and charity with your neighbours, and intend to lead a new life.

The "invitation" forms a transition with its last sentence to the confession.

j. Confession and Absolution[190]

Almighty God, Father of our Lord Jesus Christ, Maker of all things, Judge of all men; We acknowledge and bewail our manifold sins and wickedness, Which we, from time to time, most grievously have committed, By thought, word, and deed, Against thy Divine Majesty, Provoking most justly thy wrath and indignation against us.

Any congregation which speaks the confession immediately appreciates didactically the character of the God to Whom it prays. Thus He is the creator of all things and the judge of all mankind. It is important that in the course of the confession a particular conception of sin is revealed. It is implicit in the terms "manifold sins" and "wickedness" that sinning exists in one's individual actions as well as in the basic deportment of men. The text declares a central theological point when it portrays sin as the act of giving offence to the majesty of God.

Further along in the course of the confession we read:

We do earnestly repent, And are heartily sorry for these our misdoings; The remembrance of them is grievous unto us; The burden of them is intolerable.

Since man recognizes the consequences of this offense to His majesty, then the expressions "earnestly repent" and "heartily sorry," spoken to the heart and filled with revivalistic power, are also understandable. These expressions alone make it apparent that a confession should not be simply lip service.

The petition at the conclusion points to the need for a rebirth[191] at least according to the substance if indeed this idea be not found verbatim:

And grant that we may ever hereafter Serve and please thee In newness of life, To the honour and glory of thy Name; Through Jesus Christ our Lord. Amen.

The phrase "newness of life" means substantially the same as a conversion or rebirth of men.[192] The doctrine of rebirth has received special attention in pietism and revivalism.

It becomes clear in the subsequent absolution that only the truly faithful receive forgiveness. The operative words of a revivalistic character are "hearty repentance" and "true faith."

One should not underrate the significance of the fact that the Anglican communion liturgy prepares its churchgoers so carefully for the taking of the sacrament. The difference is revealed with special clarity when compared with the Roman mass, as it was still in use prior to the Second Vatican. Nothing like the exhortations existed in the mass liturgy which might warn the participants against an unworthy partaking. Lacking was any requirement that one's affairs with men be put in order first. Any allusion to the total depravity of man was lacking. The Confiteor came without anyone having to be reconciled.

The name of Jesus is to be sought in vain. The sacrificial act of Jesus on the cross plays the most important role in reference to the forgiveness of sin and hence the name of Jesus in a confession of sin is indispensable.

Here is the wording of the Catholic Confiteor as it was in use in the early 1960s:

> I confess to almighty God, to blessed Mary, ever virgin, to blessed Michael the archangel, to blessed John the Baptist, to the holy apostles Peter and Paul, to all the saints and to you, Father, that I have sinned exceedingly in thought, word, and deed, through my fault, through my fault, through my most grievous fault. Therefore I beseech blessed Mary, ever virgin, blessed Michael the archangel, . . . and all the saints, and you Father, to pray to the Lord our God for me.[193]

In the absolution a knowledge of salvation is not expressed as it is in the Anglican absolution. In the Roman absolution it says:

> May almighty God have mercy upon you, forgive you your sins, and bring you to life everlasting.

In the Anglican absolution a knowledge of the certainty of salvation is expressed since the text relies on the Biblical promise of the forgiveness of sins which is granted to all true believers:

> Almighty God, our heavenly Father, who of his great mercy hath promised forgiveness of sins to all them that with hearty repentance and true faith turn unto him.

In the 1975 book of the mass a certain improvement is noticeable as compared with the Roman missal which was in use prior to the close of the Second Vatican. The current Roman book of the mass[194] offers three variations for the confession. Still, all three are far different from the revivalistic spirit. An urgent searching of the conscience and a commitment to a living faith as well as a summons to a settlement of affairs among men is lacking. The most important name in connexion with the petition for forgiveness is not to be found, the name of Jesus. The first variation reads:

> I confess to almighty God, and to you, my brothers and sisters, that I have sinned through my own fault, in my thoughts and in my words, in what I have done, and in what I have failed to do; and I ask blessed Mary, ever virgin, all the angels and saints, and you my brothers and sisters, to pray for me to the Lord our God.

The quotation above is taken from the Ordinarium[195] for the celebration of mass.

k. The Four Comfortable Words[196]

These four comforting quotations of Holy Scripture, taken from Matthew 11:28; John 3:16; 1 Timothy 1:15; and 1 John 2:1, repeat the ideas of the three exhortations like an echo, for the purpose of corroboration. In our discussion of the liturgy we only wish to examine those parts which reveal a genuine revivalistic character.

l. Words of Distribution[197]

Subsequent to the great prayer of consecration the priest speaks these significant words during the distribution of the sacrament:

> Take and eat this in remembrance that Christ died for thee and feed on him in thy heart by faith with thanksgiving.

The expression that one be nourished in the heart through faith in Jesus clearly reflects the inner feelings of revivalistic spirituality.[198]

The presence of Jesus is not in the elements but chiefly in the hearts of the faithful. Here we are dealing with the essence of the personal encounter and fellowship with Jesus.[199]

m. First Prayer of Thanksgiving[200]

The first thanksgiving which is given optionally after the second Lord's Prayer has as its principal object a supplication for the acceptance of a genuine sacrifice. Revivalistic thinking is clearly revealed in the following passage at the end of the first half, taken from Romans 12:1:

> And here we offer and present unto thee, O Lord, ourselves, our souls and bodies, to be a reasonable, holy, and lively sacrifice unto thee.

The revivalistic concept is expressed in the conviction that God should have the whole man, including body and soul. Typical of this spirituality is again the accumulation of the attributive adjectives "reasonable, holy, lively."

In an obvious contradiction to Catholic thinking, our text turns with its request to God, not to weigh one's merits, but rather to forgive one's transgressions:

> And although we be unworthy, through our manifold sins, to offer unto thee any sacrifice, yet we beseech thee to accept this our bounden duty and service, not weighing our merits, but pardoning our offences, through Jesus Christ our Lord.

n. Second Alternative Prayer of Thanksgiving[201]

In the second thanksgiving we find further important revivalistic elements:

> Almighty and everliving God, we most heartily thank thee, for that thou dost vouchsafe to feed us, who have duly received these holy mysteries, with the spiritual food of the most precious Body and Blood of thy Son our Saviour Jesus Christ.

Worthy of note are the expressions "we most heartily thank thee" and "who have duly received." The little word "duly" guards against a cheap sacramentalism. This asserts that the effectiveness of the sacrament is not due to an Ex Opere Operato.[202] Also, the word "assure" further on in the text expresses matters of importance:

> And dost assure us thereby of thy favour and goodness towards us; and that we are very members incorporate in the mystical body of thy Son, which is the blessed company of all faithful people; and are also heirs through

> hope of thy everlasting kingdom, by the merits of the most precious death
> and passion of thy dear Son.

The term "assure" is best defined as lending certainty. In pietistic-Calvinistic circles they speak much about the certainty of faith. In our prayer above this certainty, in the revivalistic sense, proceeds in three directions:

First: the communicant has the certainty of the goodness and favour of God towards him:

> And dost assure us thereby of thy favour and goodness towards us.

Second, the communicant has the assurance of belonging to the fellowship of the faithful and the born again:

> And that we are very members incorporate in the mystical body of thy Son,
> which is the blessed company of all faithful people.

In revivalistic circles the fellowship, in the sense of an exchange of spiritual ideas and experiences,[203] as well as getting together for group praying, praising, and giving thanks, plays a central role. The text above anticipates the ideas of the pietists and revivalists, since it does not reduce the mystical body of Christ to an organized and, juridically speaking, strictly tangible entity. One is reminded a bit of Ph. J. Spener (1635-1705) with his conception of an Ecclesiola in Ecclesia.[204]

Toward the end of the prayer the significant term "fellowship" emerges, of which we have already spoken elsewhere:[205]

> And we most humbly beseech you, O Heavenly Father, so to assist us with
> thy grace, that we may continue in that holy fellowship.

We can characterize "fellowship" also as an intimate relationship among the born again or believers. There is thus an important concern in the prayer that God might assist in the continuity of this fellowship through his grace.

Third: the communion guest enjoys the conviction of being an heir to heavenly glory. Wherever necessary for the prevention of erroneous concepts definitions are nearly always present in a very natural way. With reference to being heirs to eternal glory, the text explains that this is a pure gift by virtue of the sacrificial death of Jesus:

> And are also heirs through hope of thy everlasting kingdom, by the merits
> of the most precious death and passion of thy dear Son.

The closing benediction which follows the Gloria,[206] in contrast to that in Morning and Evening Prayers, is taken from Philippians 4:7.[207]

o. Concluding Remarks

The task which we assigned ourselves in section C was to point out in detail the revivalistic elements taken over into their prayer book through Cranmer by Martyr, Bucer, and Hooper. For that reason I have again and again pointed out the parallels in Hooper's sermons wherever occur similar revivalistic or evangelistic elements either from the viewpoint of substance or form. In order to point out these elements it would have been equally possible to submit an analysis of a sermon of Martyr or Bucer. This section should have made it clear that we are dealing with a kind of mini-evangelization in the Morning and Evening Prayers as well as in the communion liturgy, which should make explicable the presence of such outspokenly strong revivalistic elements. The BCP of 1662 is thus something of a liturgical echo of the revivalistic theology and evangelistic preaching of Martyr, Bucer, and Hooper, for which Cranmer was the great and gifted compiler. Ecclesiastically committed puritans on the contrary distinguished themselves as the great defenders and advocates of its revivalistic-evangelical substance so that this did not become watered down despite all the bitter struggles.

Chapter II has pointed out for us the origin of revivalistic spirituality so it was the purpose of Chapter III to present Cranmer as the grand architect of revivalistic thinking in his matured liturgical work, the BCP of 1552. Chapter IV is intended to set before our eyes the great fight led by the puritans for the preservation of this inalienable inheritance,[208] which gained its victory in the BCP of 1662.

D. CONSEQUENCES OF "PURA DOCTRINA" AND "PURUS CULTUS" IN THE BOOK OF COMMON PRAYER OF 1662

1. ECCLESIOLOGICAL CHARACTERISTICS

a. Catholicity

It should be worthwhile simply to provide in broad strokes a few ecclesiastical definitions from the patristic and Reformation periods. There follow definitions by Ignatius of Antioch (died 117), Vincent of Lérins (died about 450), Cyril of Jerusalem (died 386), Thomas Cranmer, and John Calvin as a basis for the understanding of catholicity in the BCP of 1662.

(1) The Concept of "Catholic" of Ignatius (Died 117)

In the letter of Ignatius to the people of Smyrna the following definition is found in the 8th Chapter:

> Wheresoever the bishop shall appear, there let the people be; even as where Jesus may be, there is the universal church.[209]

(2) Vincent's Concept of "Catholic" (Died before 450)

Vincent sees "catholic" in the continuity of that which from the very first has been traditional in a universal way in respect to the treasures of faith:

> In the catholic church itself, every care should be taken to hold fast to what has been believed everywhere, always, and by all. This is truly and properly, catholic.[210]

(3) The Concept of "Catholic" of Cyril of Jerusalem (Died 386)

In his catechism for baptismal candidates, Cyril writes:

> But the word Ecclesia has several different applications. . . . If ever you sojourn in the cities, do not ask simply where the Lord's house is nor merely

184

where the church is, but where the catholic church is. For this is the distinctive name of His holy church, the mother of us all, and the spouse of our Lord Jesus Christ . . . and it is the figure and copy of the Jerusalem above, which is free and the mother of us all.[211]

With Cyril "catholic" has still the important sense of an association holding itself apart from heretics. The character of the church as an image in the sense of a representational portrayal of the heavenly Jerusalem is an important aspect of "catholic."

(4) Cranmer's Understanding of "Catholic" in the Reformation Era

Cranmer often replaces the adjective "catholic" with "universal." He also interprets it with expressions such as "old," "primitive," "ancient," "apostolic," and "pure."[212] He generally associates these adjectives with the nouns "church," "faith," or "practice."

Consequently "catholic" means the following: "catholic" is all that which conforms with the Biblical Spirit in the doctrine of faith and in a church service formula is confirmed by the apostles and has been handed down by the primitive church and the Church Fathers in a pure form. Cranmer can no longer credit as "catholic" that which Holy Scripture contradicts. Cranmer places in the second rank the Vox Patrum as a standard for the correctness of declarations of faith and liturgical practices. The Bible remains the absolute guide in all matters.

We let Cranmer speak to us from his work "A Defence of the true and Catholic Doctrine of the Sacrament."

In the following quotation "catholic" is to be understood in the sense of whatever is based on Scripture and Cranmer argues against his foe Stephen Gardiner in a convincing way:

> Wherefore by your own description and rule of a catholic faith, your doctrine and teaching in these four articles cannot be good and catholic, except you can find it in plain terms in the scripture and old catholic doctors.[213]

A further quotation should make it clear how the conception of "catholic" is connected with a fundamentalistic attitude:

> But the true catholic faith—grounded upon God's most infallible word, teaches us, that our Saviour Christ is gone up to heaven.[214]

The doctrine of the Bible and that of the church coincide:

185

This is the teaching of the true catholic church, as it is taught by God's Word.[215]

"Catholic" is also found as something universal and established as true. In Cranmer's concept of catholicity, that is conclusive which existed from the very beginning and bears a universal character.

And so the true confession and belief of the universal church, from the beginning, is not such as you many times affirmed, but never can prove.[216]

Cranmer considered the historically grown confessions of the old church as important ingredients of catholicity. These constitute in large measure that which has been proven for a long time:

This needeth no better nor stronger proof than that which the old authors bring for the same, that is to say, the general profession of all christian people in the common creed . . . this hath been ever the catholic faith of christian people.[217]

Interesting also is the conception of "catholic" as the pure and untainted in the liturgical-ceremonial field. Cranmer speaks of the "primitive church" as a pure and unspoiled entity:

All these foolish and devilish superstitions the papists, of their own idle brain, have devised of later years, which devices were never known in the old church. And yet they cry out against them that profess the gospel . . . and would have them follow the example of their church. And so would they gladly do, if the papists would follow the first church of the apostles, which was most pure and incorrupt. . . . The manner of the Holy Communion, which is now set forth within this realm, is agreeable with the institution of Christ, with St. Paul and the old primitive and apostolic church.[218]

One finds a further important aspect of "catholicity" in the sense of a fellowship guided by the Holy Spirit. This "catholic" church has from its inception been pure and has provided solace:

Whereas, on the other side, the very true doctrine of Christ and his pure church from the beginning is plain, certain, without wrinkles, . . . so cheerful and comfortable to all christian people, that it must needs come from the Spirit of God.[219]

(5) An Important Aspect of "Catholic" with Calvin

From his *Institutes* we single out the following important passages:

For no hope of future inheritance remains to us unless we have been united with all other members under Christ, our Head. The church is called "catholic," or "universal," because there could not be two or three churches unless Christ be torn asunder.... But all the elect are so united in Christ that as they are dependent on one Head, they also grow together into one body.... They are made truly one since they live together in one faith, hope, and love, and in the same Spirit of God.... Although the melancholy desolation ... may cry that no remnant of the Church is left, let us know that Christ's death is fruitful, and that God miraculously keeps his church as in hiding places.[220]

Unity is for Calvin an important element of catholicity. It does not appear from the above quotation that this unity is to be understood as fundamentally institutional. Those bound together in Christ as a result of the same faith and the same hope build a unity even though this may exist in dark obscurity. One has to think of the persecuted Christians behind the Iron Curtain who experience from their circumstances indeed a unity of the church in the darkest secrecy.

(6) A Few Points in the Understanding of Catholicity in the BCP

First: The Concept of "Catholic" in the Preface to the BCP

One reads in its preface that the English church has rejected all liturgical changes having dangerous consequences which might come into conflict with well-authenticated doctrine and established forms of divine service. Well-authenticated doctrine and established liturgical tradition are precisely characteristic of the genuine catholic church. The Church of England identifies itself with this church:

> And therefore of the sundry Alterations proposed unto us, we have rejected all such as were either of dangerous consequence (as secretely striking at some established Doctrine, or laudable Practice of the Church of England, or indeed of the whole Catholick Church of Christ).[221]

Second: The Catholicity in Morning and Evening Prayer

These two formulas of divine service are taken from the daily offices observed in the western monastery churches, above all from matins and lauds as to Morning Prayer and from vespers and compline as to Evening Prayer.[222]

Here "catholic" has more the meaning of a cultural and sacred history concern.

One finds in the Creed in Morning and Evening Prayer in the third paragraph the expression:

I believe in the Holy Ghost; the holy Catholick Church.

Here "catholic" has more the meaning of a worldwide association among the faithful.

Third: The Term "Catholic" in the Eucharistic Liturgy

There we find the expression also in the Creed, and specifically in the Nicene. "Catholic" is defined to some extent when it says:

And I believe one Catholick and Apostolick Church.[223]

Here catholic is understood in the sense of an association which considers itself to be united based on the doctrine and Gospel vouched for by the apostles.

In the closing prayer, immediately before the Gloria, the idea of "catholic" is found in a paraphrased form:

And dost assure us thereby of thy favour and goodness towards us and that we are very members incorporate in the mystical body of thy Son, which is the blessed company of all faithful people.[224]

This quotation understands "catholic" in the sense of the mystical body of Christ which is composed of all the sincerely faithful.[225] "Catholic" in this connexion has the true Biblical comprehensiveness of a spiritual ecumenicity.

One can also designate the eucharistic liturgy as such as "catholic" if we understand it here from the cultural and sacred history point of view.

Fourth: "Catholicity" in Reference to Organizational Doctrine

For church officers the BCP stands, with its three tiers of deacon, priest, and bishop, in the tradition of the old church. A service of consecration is provided for all three offices. In the formula for the ordering of deacons it says in the litany:

We sinners do beseech thee to hear us, O Lord God: and that it may please thee to rule and govern thy holy church universal in the right way.[226]

The "catholic" church is not subject to the disposal of men. It belongs to God. He must rule it. In the formula for the Ordering of the Priests it says:

Wherefore consider with yourselves the end of your ministry towards the children of God, towards the Spouse and Body of Christ.[227]

The text here understands the church as the bride of Christ. The "catholic" church is an association of the faithful standing in an intimate relationship with Jesus. The accent lies on the intimacy and the relationship of subordination.

Fifth: Catholicity in The Thirty-nine Articles

The definition in the Nineteenth Article completely expresses the principal dimensions of true catholicity when it says:

> The visible Church of Christ is a congregation of faithful men, in the which the pure Word of God is preached, and the Sacraments be duly ministered according to Christ's ordinance.[228]

(7) Comparison of the BCP with the Conceptions of the Earlier-Mentioned Catholicity of the Patristic and of the Reformation

The patristic and the Reformation elements with their contribution in regard to an understanding of catholicity are taken into account in the BCP. Thus an understanding of continuity which we find in Vincent of Lérins is very much present and fundamental to its catholicity. But the conception of the church as an image of the heavenly liturgy, in the sense of Cyril of Jerusalem, we also clearly find in the BCP. This is obvious in the Preface prayer with its Sanctus[229] annexed, where the congregation joins in with the heavenly hosts in the song of praise. The particularly solemn manner of divine service in the cathedrals points in the same direction. A further suggestion of catholicity in the sense just mentioned are the cited memorial days of the apostles and the evangelists in the BCP as well as the Biblical Lady Days[230] with their own collects and lessons.

In the BCP catholicity is apparent principally with reference to Cranmer's Reformation thinking as to the dependence upon Scripture which runs through the whole BCP like a red thread.[231]

We find very evident in the prayer for the church militant that concept of catholicity under the aspect of a unity such as we encountered in the quotation from Calvin:

> Beseeching thee to inspire continually the universal Church with the spirit of truth, unity, and concord: And grant, that all they that do confess thy holy Name may agree in the truth of thy holy Word, and live in unity and godly love.[232]

Just as Calvin speaks of a secret unity, the BCP also points to a conception of "catholic" which comprehends the true church as the blessed company of all faithful people. This association is not primarily a juristically organized tangible entity, but rather a federation of convinced Christians[233] which has an informal character. Here we are dealing with an element which in a special measure accords with revivalistic spirituality.

An understanding of catholicity which extols faithfulness to Scripture should likewise be in harmony with revivalistic thinking.

b. The Congregation

The BCP understands the congregation as the band of believers assembled round the Word, and specifically in two aspects:

First: The congregation whose nucleus is the family at home, and

Second: The congregation as a multi-family association for worship in a church.

First: The Congregation as the Nucleus in the Family at Home

The BCP has been so fashioned that household prayers are made possible:[234] Its plan for Bible readings with Psalms appropriately appointed for each day constitutes a direct connexion with this concept of the congregation. Horton Davies says in reference thereto:

> This concern for edification (a Pauline term for building up in the faith), combined with giving a greater responsibility to the laity because they were recognized as being an important part of the people of God and not merely those who were not the "religious," must also account for the expectation that the laity would model their devotions in their own homes and test their children.[235]

We can speak here of a microcosm of a congregation, since it concerns the intimate circle of the family in the community of the household, which utilizes the forms of Morning and Evening Prayer for its devotions.

Second: The Congregation as a Multi-Family Association

We are dealing here with the macrocosm of a congregation. It exists in the coming together of the faithful for the celebration of the liturgy unfolded in all its beauty in a church sanctuary. The significance of this lies in the fact that the same forms are used for the splendid display as for the family devotions at home. This means that the intimate segment of the congregation during the week must emerge from its household surroundings in order to become on Sunday a part of the festive congregation. If one follows through on this conception of the meaning of the BCP then the band of churchgoers collected together for the splendid liturgy is not a dead congregation.

Third: Generalities concerning Congregation and Catholicity

The congregation is a group of members who have something to do with each other. The opening rubric to the Holy Communion Service expresses this clearly when it summons the quarreling members to a reconciliation. The individual occupies a responsible relationship towards the others.

Responses occurring in almost all of the formulas of divine service make it evident that the congregation is God's partner in a conversation.

Although the concepts of "catholic church" and congregation often overflow into each other, they are not in fact identical. Under church is rather to be understood the vessel and the form thereof in which the individual faithful assemble. In connexion with catholicity there is involved the question of tradition and heritage which this vessel has passed on. With the term congregation the accent is placed more on the individual faithful and their mutual relations in life.

c. Ecumenicity

(1) The Abundance of Theological Streams in the BCP

It is the ecumenicity of the BCP which has something of the utmost importance to say in these very times. A special riches exists in this that in the BCP powerful theological streams have flowed together into a single large stream. The dominant theological prototype bears a Reformed stamp, though Lutheran undertones are not to be gainsaid. The Reformed stamp is obvious in the garb of a Zwinglian, Calvinistic, and puritan theology.

The old church of the Latin Rite has supplied the liturgical structure extensively, with modifications of the Sarum missal and the Sarum breviary which to some extent has found its way through the Lutheran liturgies into the BCP in an already purified form.

Ecumenical power is to a great degree present directly through these theological streams which are at the same time types of a particular spirituality.

191

(2) The Variety of Theological Streams in the Service of Unity

The BCP demonstrates unity in multiplicity. Its various principal theological streams which have been concentrated in differing denominations are not to be understood as contradictions but much more as complementary colours. Differing colours applied to the same substance do not alter that substance. It is similarly the case with the substance of Biblical truth, which has been preserved through the centuries in the various denominations. The BCP should not be misunderstood in this as to whether the principal types of theology represented therein might be the occasion for an organizational merger in the sense of a worldwide church.[236] The various denominations have the duty to correct one another. This function can be discharged much better in the situation of a division of the one "catholic" church into independent denominations. It is necessary to emphasize the true unity as a spiritual reality which is traceable and discernible across all the denominations. Could not a forced organizational union easily obscure the need for spiritual unity, so that one might consider the outer fusion to be the real unity? That such trains of thought are not simply snatched out of the air is indicated by the opinions of concerned and well-known theologians such as Oscar Cullman who in this connexion says the following:

> I conclude: an ecumenism which pursues as its goal the fusion of the church destroys not only the true unity in the Holy Spirit but will be for Christians of the various denominations even a temptation to surrender the foundations of faith and to seek for the principle of unity outside of them. Only an ecumenism based on a respect for the variety of the charismatic gifts can make us one in Christ and at the same time it leads the Christian church of all creeds to the source of Christian faith.[237]

The interpretations of the eucharistic service in the BCP can well be referred to as indicating the unity in its conjoined theological streams. There are, in the Anglican communion service, starting points for an interpretation of the eucharist in a Zwinglian,[238] Lutheran,[239] Calvinistic, as well as Roman Catholic[240] way. Since these diverse styles of interpretation can exist nicely side by side in the BCP, for that reason no single denomination can hold a monopoly on its own interpretation under its pretension to be the single correct interpretation of holy communion.

All these attempts at interpretation intend to do homage to Jesus. One can himself in obedience to Scripture come in all sincerity to the several interpretations of holy communion without the substance, the living Lord, suffering diminution.

192

I must however affirm that, based on our analysis, the Zwinglian-puritanical interpretation of holy communion in the BCP of 1662 is most probably correct.

In the BCP the concept of "mystery,"[241] originating probably in the Bucer influence, is a great help. Moreover this concept also plays a significant role in the Eastern Church doctrine about the sacrament.

The idea of mystery in addition furnishes a good reason not to beat to death the institution of the communion meal through Jesus, but rather to recognize him as the host who invites one across the legitimate barriers of the denominations to his banquet here. The existence of the different denominations could become the basis for letting a dynamic unity occur through the mutually granted hospitality at their holy communion.

G. W. Locher remarks in a worthwhile study thereon that Jesus is the host for all Christians. Hence the individual denominations should recognize a right to hospitality toward each other:

> It were indeed no serious conception of sin if we satisfied ourselves with separate tables until the end of time as if it were our inevitable tragic destiny. . . . Congregations experience today at the celebration of holy communion three things: 1) the special nearness of the Lord, 2) the duty and readiness to forgive, 3) the confessing gathering of committed Christians. . . . These points are Biblical and worthy of all consideration.[242]

We may be dealing with a true spiritual ecumenism here.

(3) The Mission of the Streams Present in the BCP

A history of the origin of the BCP clearly indicates how the three principal streams which are expressed in the Catholic, Lutheran, and Reformed[243] spirituality have made their contribution. The streams joined in the BCP in a special stream, the Anglican, exist now indeed in segregated ways also as confessional entities. What the streams mentioned in reference to the BCP have accomplished, that also the various denominations are also accomplishing with reference to the one universal apostolic church as we call it in Reformed circles.

We intend to make mention only in rough outline of the contribution of the above mentioned streams:

First: The Task of the Catholic Stream

The contribution of the Catholic element is to guarantee dignity and reverence as well the esthetic in the form in order to maintain an adequate setting for the substance of the faith.

Second: The Contribution of Lutheranism

We see the Lutheran contribution as a stress on a very important aspect, namely in the justification of sinners by faith alone. Lutherans have appropriated and preserved the old church traditions in a purified form in their liturgical style.

Third: The Importance of the Reformed Tradition Expressed in Presbyterianism and Puritanism

In presbyterianism it is demonstrated that a church can have an externally rigid organization even without an episcopacy. The more puritanically tinged Reformed tradition expresses in a special way that the congregation can live here by the naked Word without special compromises with the esthetic and emotional-psychological requirements of mankind. This is significant chiefly in regards to possible extreme situations where through war and catastrophe all which appeal to the senses of man can be taken from him. Toward the close of the Holy Communion Service in the BCP is found a passage which particularly meets puritan ecclesiology:

> And that we are very members incorporate in the mystical body of thy Son, which is the blessed company of all faithful people.

To the mystical body of Christ, that is to say to the one universal apostolic church, belong all those who come together as faithful Christians on the basis of a unified bond, the person of Jesus and His Word, in an edifying fellowship. Here we are dealing with a unifying bond which cuts across all denominations. After all, it is often the puritans who call attention to this reality of a genuine ecumenism of the faithful. That which in the BCP is not only a bequest of the important reformers, Cranmer, Bucer, and Peter Martyr, but equally well a legacy of the puritans, namely the protective concern for the revivalistic elements and the teaching thereof, exactly this must be present in all Christian denominations if these are not to deteriorate into paralysis. This revivalistic commitment which undertakes to bring men into a saving personal relationship with Jesus creates a natural ecumenical unity by a spiritual unity of which W. Künneth says:

> It (the church) is intrinsically at all times an ecumenical unity even when this reality of Christ remains in obscurity and experiences no visible form of organization. The promise of Jesus, "that all may be one," is not just the basis for a hope of some future realization but is now indeed reality. For

194

across all denominations exists the community of the disciples of Jesus in a "unity" of the faith and with it of the Holy Spirit.[244]

2. SACRAL ASPECTS

a. Definition of "Sacral" Based on the Biblical Conception

There is no intention to give here even a very short history of religion review of the phenomenon of "holiness." However some points in explanation of it which appear important to me may be mentioned briefly: an event not specifically referring to God and his kingdom which because it is closely bound up with immanency is characterized as an everyday occurrence we call "profane." The particular acts performed in worship stand out through their transcendent character. They refer particularly in the Old Testament to God's act of salvation wherein the areas set aside for worship play an important role. Thus those officiating and objects found in the worship tabernacle are, in a ceremonial sense, holy. The time devoted to holy affairs also has a sacral character.[245]

Our understanding of holiness is anchored more in the prophetic-ethical conception of sacrality than in the priestly ceremonial. The connexion between "holiness" and "salvation" plays therein a role in which God offers salvation as the Redeemer. We do not want to exclude the priestly ceremonial understanding of holiness, with its static ingredients, but rather to ascribe to it a value for the sake of its typological-symbolical as well as psychological meaning. In the New Testament and in particular in a Pauline sense we want to understand holiness as the concept of a personal relationship.

We take the elements to form our understanding of holiness from Ephesians 2:19-22, 5:18-20; Romans 12:1-2; as well as from Revelation 4:8-11. Many other Biblical passages can also be cited in this connexion.[246] From Ephesians 2:19-22 the following is fundamental to an understanding of holiness: it pertains to men standing in the faith who are bound together with Jesus Christ as master and thus form a holy temple as an association of the faithful in connexion with which the prophets and apostles form the dogmatic foundation. The text speaks also of "an habitation of God through the spirit." In accordance with Ephesians 5:18-20 this association of the faithful should not let itself be impaired by intoxication and consequently by ecstatic seizures. Therein would lie the opposite to holiness, namely wickedness. Temperance belongs to the true sacrality.

Of decisive importance is then the connexion of holiness with the Third Person of the Trinity. Each member belonging to this living temple has need of the Holy Ghost, which stimulates the faithful to hymns of praise. In Romans 12:1-2 we find the ethical dimensions of the sacral which concerns itself with sanctification and continues the prophetic-ethical conception of the Old Testament. Revelation 4:8-11 as well as other passages in this New Testament apocalypse put forward the sacral in the ceremonial act of worshipping God. Certain elements of Old Testament ceremonials are borrowed, such as the vestments, the gestures, the incense, and the altar.

We do not want to overlook a discussion of a holy time and a holy place. Of course what is meant thereby is not a holiness in the sense of an "Ex Opere Operato." The sacrality which we mean occurs in such a way that the objects, places, or times are taken as symbolic pronouncements for God and for that reason demand the respect of men and instruct in reverence.

The holiness meant by us therefore has a pedagogical function. Thus it is helpful to be aware of a structure whose room regularly serves the same purpose, even the preaching of God's Word and the special assemblage of the faithful for prayers of thanks and intercession as well as for worship. For this reason such a structure receives a special power to draw attention to the noble duty owed God through the assembled congregation. The holiness of a structure with its ecclesiastical fittings occurs not by force of consecration but rather on the grounds of its importance based on a history of salvation. The recognition of this holiness occurs not through a special gesture toward objects of worship as is the case in a Catholic room, but rather through the recognition of the meaning of salvation conveyed by the symbol. Thus the danger of idolatry is excluded. Holiness results from the fact that something of the heavenly glory becomes reflected in the worship sphere by material means.

The sacred may also be found there where no special worship phenomenology is present as perhaps through the, as regards liturgy, very prosaic Baptists or in an assembly of the Salvation Army. The reason for this is that the actual foundation for the sacred consists of the fellowship of the faithful oriented to the Biblical Word. In such circles holiness expresses itself in the atmospheric diffusion of security which does not give rise to an uncertainty of the faith.

b. Sacrality according to Harvey Cox

To define more closely our understanding of holiness we want now to enter briefly into the sacral understanding of Cox. Cox is important for the reason that he speaks in an extremely provocative manner of the sacred and of the profane with the result that the Biblical conception of the sacred becomes well contrasted. In his book *The Seduction of the Spirit* he describes an Easter celebration organized by him in a Boston discothèque[247] which exhibited byzantine elements, among other things. The following quoted excerpts from his portrayal give us a good insight into Cox's understanding of sacrality:

> By three-thirty A.M. the discothèque was already teeming with people, heavy on youth but spanning the alleged generation gap. We had placed a huge table in the middle of the dance floor as an altar. As people arrived they heaped it high with pumpernickel, cinnamon buns, doughnuts, twinkies, long French loaves, matzos, scones, heavy black bread and raisin tarts. People painted z's (for "He lives," from the movie that was popular at that time), peace signs, fishes, crosses, and assorted graffiti on one another's faces and bodies. Some fashioned tiaras out of silver foil and crowned one another.... By four there were nearly two thousand people present, creating their own cathedral and costuming one another for the rite.... Everyone grew serious as a multiscreen light-and-music collage transformed the Tea Party into a temporary Via Crucis, with scenes of war, death, cruelty, loneliness and racism.... Then an extraordinary group of freewheeling liturgical dancers dressed in black and white leotards began to move among the multitudes enticing them into sacred gesture and ritual motion. People who had never danced in their lives before stretched out arms and flexed legs and torsos. The lithe solemnity of the movements made me think we should get rid of pews in churches for ever. After the dancing, people came together in small groups to prepare for the ceremony of the Mass. Hands reached out and clots of people, from three to fifteen, formed. The human clusters swayed, hugged, moaned and clung together as people lifted each other and reached out toward the flickering pictures on the walls. In one group a teeny began humming "Jesus loves me," and soon her whole arm-and-leg-enmeshed group began to hum with her.... Again people clasped and unclasped in embraces; arms reached up and out.... Not only did they sing, they jumped, danced, applauded. As the last Amens of the chorus faded, the procession entered ... candles flickered, vestments glistened and clouds of incense wafted through the air.... A resurrection light collage leaped onto the walls.... Just as the collage was reaching its apex with the Beatles singing "Here comes the Sun," someone threw open the back door.[248]

197

With Cox, there is emphasized as a most important element of the sacral a dionysian intoxication which can intensify itself into an ecstasy. It is interesting that the author of *Secular City* notes a playful delight in the cultic display of pomp such as garments, candles, incense, and ceremonial gestures. The cultic display of pomp is an additional element which is fundamental to the comprehension of the sacrality of Cox. Where enthusiasm occurs, there the sacred prevails. In addition to the above-cited description of a liturgical night, bodily contact in the sense of a group intertwined among each other seems to play a role, since by this means security and the feeling of the mysterious arise.

Cox gives much elucidation on his theology of the sacral again in the description of his own experiences during a conference at the Esalen Institute in California. This refers to one of the greatest centers where sensitivity training and transcendental meditation are fostered. A speciality of these centers of religious syncretism are the "mystic baths" of which Cox speaks with enthusiasm. He tells us with his own words what he experienced there:

> We unzipped and unbuttoned fast. The water is just deep enough to reach to the armpits of a seated person of normal height. The sensation was delicious. At first we all looked at one another in a kind of ecstatic relief. We had broken taboo and we were not dead. That alone gave us all a little lift. Furthermore we were floating together in a kind of free zone where progressing from nakedness to intercourse was not required. So after the first splash-down and the subsequent quiet languor another mood usually sets in. It begins with chanting or with quiet conversation, then often escalates into group massaging or boisterous horseplay. The massaging is a complex affair. In fact after I'd enjoyed the sheer sensation of it for a while, I even began to have a vision. The candles[249] seemed to expand and I caught a glimpse of Teilhard de Chardin's Omega Point, a supra-personal future in which individuals become joyous corpuscles in a more inclusive organism. Was I a muscle cell, a brain nerve, a bit of stomach lining? . . . Now all the candles were one flame and all the fingers were on the great hand. The combination of water, chanting, body dissociation and massage was moving me beyond a pleasantly sensuous swoon into something closer to what I could only imagine was either a fanciful reverie or a mystical trance. . . . Now I felt something I had read about many times before but never understood, the underlying unity of Brahman and Atman, the oneness of self, other and All.[250]

Cox furthermore admits in connexion with this bathing experience: "For me the 'bath experience' was both sexy and spiritual, both voluptuous and innocent."[251]

One can draw further significant conclusions in connexion with Cox's understanding of sacrality from the description of his bathing outing at Esalen Institute. Thus, transgressing taboo boundaries relating to one's sense of shame is a part of the sacral. The "Fascinosum" and "Tremendum" occurs through reveling in sensuality. The erotic sphere beyond the bourgeois limits is here a further intrinsic element for Cox's concept of the sacral. Here appears the mystical element as it is found in the tradition of the Hindu identity mysticism. The sacred arises through a fusion process by which the clear separation between subject and object is neutralized.

Hence it follows from what has been said that with Cox the secular field is by its nature sacral. The world itself is holy.

Recapitulation of a. and Differentiation with Respect to Cox

Holiness in accordance with our Holy Scripture oriented conception can be understood under the following aspects:

1. Under the aspect of a concept of a personal relationship.
2. Under the aspect of members bound by faith in Jesus to the community.
3. Under the aspect of one obedient to doctrine handed down by the prophets and the apostles. With Cox the factor of obedience to a fixed doctrine is lacking. Instead, unlimited openness is decisive for him, which immediately reveals itself in the cultic sphere in the pleasure of experimentation. The community of the faithful which makes the sacred visible within the meaning of apostolic doctrine is for Cox untenable. For Cox, the sacred is sufficiently present in the adventure of the various human encounters without any Biblical criteria of any ethical or theological type being required.
4. Under the aspect of the temple function where the faithful prepare themselves as living quarters for the Holy Spirit. The aspect of sanctification with all that which is also demanded in an ethical sense of a "living temple" does not fall within the field of vision of Cox.
5. Under the aspect of sobriety, which must be exhibited in doctrine and the church service. For Cox, frenzy, ecstasy, and mystery are of significance.
6. Under the aspect of laud and praise.

7. Under the aspect of sanctification in the precise ethical sense.[252]
8. Under the aspect of worshipping God.
9. Under the aspects of preaching or liturgical symbols devoted to God which also have a pedagogical function. In accordance with Cox the liturgical-worship symbols are subjects for esthetic enjoyment rather than instruction or as proclamations announcing the Good News.
10. Under the aspect of a mirror of the heavenly Glory through material things devoted to the service of God such as altar cloths, robes, incense, festive songs, processions, candlelight, etc.

The sacral as a consequence of "pura doctrina" and "purus cultus," as it is found in the puritanically refined BCP of 1662, is in large measure achieved by its expression in worship.

c. Adoration

(1) In Morning Prayer

Adoration is a very important element in the BCP. It runs through the three principal services. Adoration is never placed at the beginning of a service since the believer needs first a conviction of his sinful downfall, then repentance, and confession.[253] Only after receiving absolution is the way cleared for adoration. Then we find the first element of adoration in the Lord's Prayer.

First: The Lord's Prayer[254]

Verses 9 and 13 of Matthew 6 chiefly exhibit adoration, thus at the start and the end of the prayer:

> Our Father which art in heaven, Hallowed be thy name. . . . For thine is the kingdom, and the power, and the glory, for ever. Amen.

The rubric requires kneeling as an accompanying gesture.

Second: The Opening Sentences and the Responses Thereto[255]

These originate in Psalm 51:15:

> O Lord, open thou our lips.
> And our mouth shall shew forth thy praise. [responsively]

The opening sentences declare the solemn theme of the service, namely laud and praise. Upon answering these opening sentences the congregation arises as an expression of reverence:

> Glory be to the Father, and to the Son; and to the Holy Ghost;
> As it was in the beginning, is now, and ever shall be. [respon.]

Prior to the reading of the first Psalm the priest calls to the congregation in unmistakable terms:

> Praise ye the Lord.[256]

The congregation answers:

> The Lord's name be praised.

Third: Psalm 95[257]

Now one proceeds with action in regard to laud and praise and joins in Psalm 95 which itself includes the theme of adoration. Here is presented an interesting psychological impulse. The congregation cannot permit itself to become entirely lost in laud and praise. It should not let slip the impulse to reflect upon what it is doing at any particular moment. In our thinking, reflection is a safety-valve against formalism. Thus Psalm 95 in verses 1 to 6 which is encountered by the congregation during the process of praising, reminds it not to forget that its function is and must remain adoration. This Psalm is intended to assure that the whole process of the church service is devoted to praise. Right at the first verse it says:

> O come, let us sing unto the Lord: let us heartily rejoice in the strength of our salvation.

Rejoicing and singing are thus a part of adoration. In the second verse thanksgiving is added:

> Let us come before his presence with thanksgiving: and shew ourselves glad in him with Psalms.

The second verse wishes to give a key to an understanding of the remaining Psalms:

> And shew ourselves glad in him with Psalms.

The Psalter spoken or sung in Morning and Evening Prayer is an expression of adoration, although the theme of laud and praise does not appear in each individual Psalm. In verses 3 to 6 the psalmist comprehends adoration as humbling oneself before God as the creator.

201

Fourth: The Minor Doxology[258]

A further indication that this liturgy perceives the Psalms as adoration is the doxology following each Psalm:

> Glory be to the Father, and to the Son: and to the Holy Ghost; as it was in the beginning, is now, and ever shall be; world without end. Amen.

Fifth: The Te Deum[259]

After the Old Testament lesson the congregation sings or says the Te Deum Laudamus. In this outspoken song of laud and praise there appears something like a joining in the hymns of adoration of the hierarchy of the angels, of the apostles, of the prophets, and of the martyrs. The liturgy here takes up in a particularly clear way the connexion with the church triumphant. As an alternative to the Te Deum the liturgy offers the apocryphal "Benedicite Omnia Opera." This song of praise draws the natural phenomena and the elements of water, fire, air, as well as plants and animals into the adoration. The hymn gives a voice to the subjects of nature and its creatures which themselves show forth the praise of God.

This lending of voices occurs on behalf of voiceless creation as man reflects with a more profound respect upon creation with its glorious variety and gives God the credit therefore. Something similar is found in Psalm 148.

It is noteworthy that in the Benedicite Omnia Opera the various stages of creation from Genesis 1 are employed for laud and praise, such as water, fire, air, and earth, as well as the stars also as the representatives of the Quinta Essentia:

> O ye waters that be above the firmament, bless ye the Lord, praise him and magnify him for ever, o ye winds of God, . . . O ye fire and heat, . . . O ye stars of heaven, . . . O ye mountains and hills.

The lesson from the New Testament is closed with the Benedictus[260] or Psalm 100 as an alternative thereto.

Sixth: Psalm 100[261]

This Psalm is an outspoken hymn of praise. The principal themes of this Psalm are joy in the presence of God in the sanctuary and gratitude in the face of his goodness. Strictly speaking, adoration comes to a close after the Creed and the second Lord's Prayer.

(2) In Evening Prayer

Evening Prayer is organized like Morning Prayer. The difference lies solely in the differing hymns, Psalms, and closing prayers.

First: The Magnificat

This is a hymn taken from Luke 1:46-55. Verses 46 and 47 have a distinct character as adoration:[262]

> My soul doth magnify the Lord: and my spirit hath rejoiced in God my Saviour.

In High Church circles the priest gives the Magnificat a special touch by the use of incense which underlines further its character as adoration.

Second: The Alternatively Proposed Psalm 98 is Essentially a Hymn of Laud and Praise

Verses 1 as well as 4-6 stress in particular the importance of laud and praise. In verse 5 is found something similar to that in the second verse of the Ninety-fifth Psalm:[263]

> Praise the Lord upon the harp: sing to the harp with a psalm of thanksgiving.

The text here calls attention to a further aspect of adoration which a Psalm should contain: namely an aspect of thanksgiving.

Third: The Apostles' Creed

A particularly solemn act of adoration is seen in Evensong when the congregation arises to recite the Apostles' Creed and turns toward the altar. This custom was adopted in the English church in the seventeenth century. This facing toward the east constitutes an obeisance in adoration of the real son which has arisen in the form of Jesus Christ in the Near East.[264]

Fourth: Thoughts on the Magnificently Fashioned Evening Prayer (Evensong)

Boys' choirs trained to the uttermost sing an Evensong in the best cathedrals at the close of every day during the school year. This type of divine service again and again provokes sharp criticism for the reason that the congregation is involved much too little. However there is also another point of view here, which can no longer be ignored: it is sometimes a part of adoration for a member of the congregation to be able to dwell upon the astonishing beauty of a divine service as though from the outside, and thus to participate therein more in the contemplative sense. Adoration would then consist of giving back to the Lord that magnificent esthetic experience as an offering of praise and thanksgiving. In a normal service there is much that is heavy in its outer expression. The singing of some choirs, with members in widely differing stages of life, often leaves much to be desired. The reading may be inferior in its expression and the sermon boorish in its style.

When though a trained boys' choir sings the Psalms and anthems and a trained speaker reads the lesson, then it borders closely on the perfect, so far as earthly conditions allow. A churchgoer possessing artistic interests will be able to use the esthetically perfect presentation of the sacred liturgy as a medium so that what he himself could never express at this level to the King of Kings, he can nevertheless impart to his Lord. In other words, only the best is good enough for God, but even if one's own talents be lacking for the display of such a splendid service one can equally so to speak engage a fine choir and a magnificent ceremony in order at any event to proffer a sacred offering unto the Lord.

A divine service should not be understood only as an active involvement of the congregation, but it can be as well a holy performance in which the congregation delights in the sacred production in a contemplative way, in the sense of a spiritual and emotional edification. In this way the congregation receives a special foretaste of the heavenly liturgy.

Such services radiate peace and create an atmosphere of objectivity through their static character. These characteristics of a divine service which have just been mentioned create a good prerequisite for adoration.

Divine services of this nature gain in significance if we understand them as incitements and stimuli for adoration.

(3) In the Holy Communion Service[265]

First: The Lord's Prayer[266]

Adoration is in evidence at the outset of the eucharistic liturgy in the first and last parts of the Lord's Prayer.[267]

Second: The Opening Collect (Collect for Purity)[268]

The opening collect includes a petition to worthily praise His Name, based on a cleansing of the heart by the Holy Spirit. In this collect it says:

> Cleanse the thoughts of our hearts by the inspiration of thy Holy Spirit, . . .
> that we may worthily magnify thy holy name.

Third: The Ten Commandments[269]

The inclusion of the Ten Commandments in the adjacent section implies that true adoration must include the doing of God's will.

Fourth: The Twenty Biblical Offertory Verses[270]

After the Creed, the twenty Bible quotations follow as offertory verses, in which the liturgy sees adoration, among other things, from the aspect of sacrifice and a mutual responsibility even, indeed, extending into the social sphere.

Fifth: The Exhortations[271]

The exhortations following the prayer for the church militant give a new dimension to adoration. The exhortations declare the dignity and sanctity of what the sacraments signify. The first exhortation uses for this the expression "mystery." In accordance with the explanations, warnings, and summonses in the exhortations the churchgoer should reach the point of a speculative contemplation of the mysteries embedded in this sacred act.

> My duty is to exhort you in the mean season to consider the dignity of that holy mystery.[272]

The third exhortation uses the expression "mystery" twice:

> Amend your lives, and be in perfect charity with all men, so shall ye be meet partakers of these holy mysteries . . . he hath instituted and ordained holy mysteries, as pledges of his love, and for a continual remembrance of his death.

The adoration of God is connected with a contemplation of these mysteries under the aspect of his love which accepts sinners in a wondrous way.

Ultimately the mystery of his love and grace cannot be clothed in words and hence the term "mystery" serves as a code word for the God who must be adored in awe and who acts through the eucharistic sacrament.

Sixth: The Comfortable Words[273]

After the confession and absolution follow the comfortable words from Matthew 11:28; John 3:16; 1 Timothy 1:15; and 1 John 2:1. These quotations from Scripture bring to the eyes of the churchgoer the unfathomable saving love of God and point out something of the content of the mysteries which invite one to adoration.

Seventh: Preface with Sanctus[274]

The Preface is concerned with the exaltation of the heart with a heaven-directed attitude, by virtue of which the faithful unite with the heavenly host in adoration:

> Therefore with Angels and Archangels, and with all the company of heaven, we laud and magnify thy glorious Name, evermore praising thee, and saying: Holy, holy, holy, Lord God of Hosts.

Eighth: Prayer of Humble Access[275]

We find adoration in this prayer as an expression of submissiveness and unworthiness.

Ninth: Words of Institution in the Prayer of Consecration[276]

The celebrant in the consecration prayer speaks the words of institution in a solemn tone by which he inter.ds to express an attitude of adora.ion.

Tenth: Words of Distribution[277]

During the words of distribution the faithful receive the holy communion in a kneeling posture by which they intend to express their attitude of adoration.

Eleventh: Gloria[278]

The final culminating point in adoration is the Gloria in which the reason why God is worthy of adoration is voiced. This great doxology summarizes the meaning of the liturgy and brings it to a crowning close.

d. Romantic Peculiarities

Here we can only touch upon this complex of questions. It would merit the writing of a book just on it.

The questions about the romantic elements in the BCP are based on the fact that the very important English romanticist, William Wordsworth (1770-1850), has written poems about the BCP in his "Ecclesiastical Sonnets."

One can actually have a romantic experience with the BCP. Why should that be?

It is hard to give a clear definition of just what "romantic" means. But still we want to enumerate some few points:

(1) An important element in the romantic is the experience of that which overwhelms one with beauty. This, as an example, proves true in the sublime and wild landscapes in the pictures of Caspar David Friedrich (1774-1840).

(2) A further element also is the transfigured security in middle class living which is experienced as a power that orders life.

Carl Spitzweg (1808-1885) as a romantic painter chiefly expresses this feature in his representation of the early Victorian period. The church should not be forgotten as a place of security.

(3) Experiencing historical relevancy plays a big role and with it is a love for that which has grown organically and historically. It may refer to a nation or to a church which has its roots in the Middle Ages. Poets like Novalis and the brothers Schlegel saw in Catholicism the ideal dimensions for creative moulding of the further development of history. For Novalis the solution for the salvation of Western culture lies in a return to the Mother Church, i.e., to Ecclesia Romana.

This love for organized growth is often connected with an attitude of political conservatism which seeks to maintain the status quo.

(4) An inclination toward the religious, in the sense of the sacred, plays a large role in the feeling and thinking of romanticists. Thus the romanticist likes to let himself be transported by the fascinosum and tremendum. He might forget himself in that reverential wonder which the word "awe" may most aptly express.

(5) A further peculiarity of the romantic is its cross connexion with the revivalistic movement

The elements mentioned above emerge to some degree in the BCP. The splendour of the liturgy's beauty can indeed overpower one so that it leads to a wondering reverence, even to this "awe." The point of view of security is beautifully expressed in the experiencing of the Church as a mother's womb.

The Thirty-nine Articles[279] give the Anglican in a dogmatic reference thereto an inner security as to what the official church teaches. This is what, among other things, we mean by the idea of security. The household feature bears a close connexion with this security as we encounter it in the genre paintings of a Spitzweg or Ludwig Richter (1803-1884). The BCP offers something analogous when one uses for family prayers within the family circle the forms for Morning and Evening Prayer as well as the Bible plan for meditation on Holy Scripture. The snug and the domestic manifest themselves just as they may very well be portrayed in romantic genre paintings. The liturgies of the BCP let the participant in a divine service share in a natural way in a continuity with the early Catholic Church and in the fascinosum and tremendum of the Middle Ages. The political conservatism of the BCP proceeds in obvious loyalty to the crown as a divinely ordained government of the day.

We regard this curiosity of a true evangelical spirituality, connected with the beauty of the early Catholic and Middle Ages structure as well as with the puritanical revivalistic elements, as a kind of romantic phenomenon.

Wordsworth wrote the "Ecclesiastical Sonnets." We want to take a look at some of these poems:

The poet seeks in the sonnet "Pastoral Character" to reproduce the serenity-filled atmosphere of the interior of an Anglical rectory:

> A genial hearth, a hospitable board,
> And a refined rusticity, belong
> To the neat mansion, where, his flock among,
> The learned pastor dwells, their watchful Lord.
> Though meek and patient as a sheathed sword . . .
> He from the pulpit lifts his awful hand.[280]

In his poem "The Liturgy" Wordsworth depicts the atmosphere of mystery which also is expressed in the liturgical process with regard to the church year:

> Yes, if the intensities of hope and fear
> Attract us still, and passionate exercise
> Of lofty thoughts, the way before us lies
> Distinct with signs, through which in set career,
> As though a zodiac, moves the ritual year
> Of England's Church, stupendous mysteries!
> Which whoso travels in her bosom eyes,
> As he approaches them, with solemn cheer.
> Upon that circle traced from sacred story
> We only dare to cast a transient glance,
> Trusting in hope that Others may advance
> With mind intent upon the King of Glory,
> From his mild advent till his countenance
> Shall dissipate the seas and mountains hoary.[281]

Wordsworth wrote poems to the following divine service formulas in the BCP: to baptism, confirmation, visitation of the sick, the commina-

tion service, funeral service, catechizing, the marriage ceremony, thanksgiving after childbirth, etc.

The sonnet "The Marriage Ceremony" says to us:

> The Vested Priest before the Altar stands.
> Approach, come gladly, ye prepared, in sight
> Of God and chosen friends, your troth to plight
> With the symbolic ring and willing hands
> Solemnly joined. Now sanctify the bands
> O Father!—to the Espoused thy blessing give,
> That mutually assisted they may live
> Obedient, as here taught, to thy commands.
> So prays the Church, to consecrate a Vow
> "The which would endless matrimony make."
> Union that shadows forth and doth partake
> A mystery potent human love to endow
> With heavenly, each more prized for the other's sake.
> Weep not, meek Bride! uplift thy timid brow.[282]

These sonnets are an illustration of how one can experience the BCP
in a romantic way. That Wordsworth, unlike Novalis, indeed thinks with
a Reformation mentality and yet does not have to abandon his identity as
a romanticist is revealed in his poem "Cathedrals," which was probably
suggested by the BCP, and which gives evidence of a rather spiritual conception of the church:

> Open your gates, ye everlasting Piles!
> Types of the spiritual Church which God hath reared.
> Not loth we quit the newly-hallowed sward
> And humble altar, 'mid your sumptuous aisles
> To kneel, or thread your intricate defiles,
> Or down the nave to pace in motion slow,
> Watching, with upward eye, the tall tower grow
> And mount, at every step, with living wiles
> Instinct—to rouse the heart and lead the will
> By a bright ladder to the world above.
> Open your gates, ye Monuments of love
> Divine! thou Lincoln, on thy sovereign hill!
> Thou, stately York! And Ye, whose splendours cheer
> Isis and Cam, to patient Science dear![283]

e. What Serves for Adoration

(1) The Speech Used in the BCP in Morning and Evening Prayer[284]

In Morning and Evening Prayer the responsive passages produce a particularly esthetic luster. The opening sentences "O Lord, open thou our lips" and the answer thereto "and our mouth shall shew forth thy praise"[285] give right at the start of the service a worshipping accent. In the solemn evensong which is sung daily in the cathedrals[286] these sentences set the splendid tone which is intended for the further course of the service. The reverend forms of address "thou" and "thee" introduce a spirit of nobility into the liturgy.

The doxologies are a very beautiful device which supply the liturgy with conciseness and accentuate it at the same time. After each Psalm sung or spoken in the Morning or Evening Prayer as well as after each hymnic text this dignified doxology follows:

> Glory be to the Father and to the Son and to the Holy Ghost; as it was in the beginning, is now and ever shall be: world without end, Amen.[287]

The responsive structure requires that there be unchanging parts. In that way the churchgoer becomes accustomed to a fixed rhythm. He is conscious in advance of what follows and of how many syllables the next word is composed.

For that reason Morning and Evening Prayer lend themselves to singing since the speech and style are sonorous and beautifully proportioned. Individual sections are distinguished as to length or brevity through their balance. Units which arrange themselves harmoniously in succession are clearly delineated and accordingly produce the esthetic. The separate units are composed of the monologue-like exhortation[288] of the priest, the confession of the congregation uttered in melancholy tones,[289] again the absolution[290] of the priest, spoken as a monologue which he delivers in an apodictical tone of voice. The Lord's Prayer, initiated by the priest is then taken up and prayed by the congregation. This produces a prayer which is meditated upon within. The following concisely expressed versicles[291] or opening sentences provide additional embellishment. The following minor doxology,[292] which as already stated comes after each psalm, has a splendidly solemn coloration.

The psalms[293] introduce a poetic style. The responsive element is very much present there. If Morning and Evening Prayer are sung, the interruption for the Bible lesson operates as a pleasing contrast.

Thus the liturgy of Morning and Evening Prayer provides a poetic element in the Psalm which alternates with the prose of the Scripture lesson. In the further course of the liturgy under consideration the alternation continues when after the lesson there follows a hymn.[294] In Morning Prayer are the great hymns, the Te Deum and the Benedictus,[295] in Evening Prayer the Magnificat and the Nunc Dimittis.[296] The Creed,[297] spoken in unison, follows the last hymn selected which in turn followed the reading of the New Testament.

One can appreciate how well the immensely powerful Creed is balanced by the subsequent brief but decorative single sentences: "The Lord be with you," followed by the answer: "And with thy Spirit." Again the melancholy element appears in the short ornamental prayer:

> Let us pray. Lord have mercy upon us. Christ have mercy upon us. Lord have mercy upon us.[298]

These graceful sentences serve again as a counterpoise to the following Lord's Prayer which is spoken in unison.

The responsive sentences[299] initiating the close of the service again contain the ornamental.

(2) Gestures[300]

(a) Kneeling in the Three Principal Liturgies[301]

Rubrics in Morning and Evening Prayer as well as in the holy communion liturgy give important instructions in reference to the gesture of kneeling.

First: Kneeling during Morning Prayer

The congregation kneels during the confession, absolution, and the Lord's Prayer.[302] After the Creed the congregation again kneels during the Kyrie and Lord's Prayer as well as during the responsive closing sentences and the following collects.[303]

Second: Kneeling during Evening Prayer

One kneels during Evening Prayer at the same liturgical places as in Morning Prayer.[304]

211

Third: Kneeling during the Holy Communion Service

The congregation kneels during the Lord's Prayer, during the opening collect as well as during the proclamation of the Ten Commandments, and during the intercessory prayer for the royal sovereign.[305]

The congregation kneels down again on the occasion of the confession and the absolution.[306] This posture is interrupted only while going to the communion rail where the faithful kneel down again to receive the bread and wine. Churchgoers, after returning to their pews from taking communion, remain in a kneeling position until the close of the service.

(b) Standing during the Three Principal Liturgies

First: Standing during Morning Prayer

After the opening sentence, "O Lord, open thou our lips," etc., the congregation arises for the Little Gloria.[307]

The congregation stands during the recitation of the psalm although this does not issue clearly from the rubric. One assumes a standing position again during the reciting of the Creed.[308]

Second: Standing during Evening Prayer

One stands during Evening Prayer at the same liturgical places as in Morning Prayer.[309]

Third: Standing during the Communion Service

The congregation stands during the reading of the Gospel. The congregation also again takes a standing position during the Creed.[310] Although no rubric pronounces upon it expressly, the congregation again takes a standing posture during the greater Gloria.

(c) Sitting in the Three Liturgies

In Morning and Evening Prayer as well as in the communion service one sits only during the reading of the Old Testament as well as the Epistle and during the sermon.

(d) Processing in the Three Principal Liturgies

In the three services processing is assigned a great importance. The beginning of a service occurs at the time when the choir processes solemnly

212

through the principal aisle of the church's nave to the choir stalls, led by a crucifer, followed by the priest. No rubric provides for the procession at the beginning nor at the end of the service either. One may speak here of an unwritten liturgical law which originated in the High Church movement of the thirties of the last century.[311] E. Pusey played a special role therein.[312]

Closing remarks about Point (2)

The various gestures have the intent to express a certain inner attitude as a reaction to the holy. The standing posture should above all indicate respect for God as the majestic. The gesture of kneeling indicates more of a humble attitude of the man who is constantly the beneficiary of God. By sitting the churchgoer makes it clear that he is listening to God's Word and pondering what is said.

(3) Liturgical Vestments and Cloths

We do not intend to enter into historical origins here. Mention should merely be made of the garments in use during the three principal services.

Of particular importance is the rubric located immediately before Morning Prayer, where it says:

> And here is to be noted, that such ornaments of the Church, and of the Ministers thereof, at all Times of their Ministration, shall be retained, and be in use, as were in this Church of England, by the Authority of Parliament, in the Second Year of the Reign of King Edward the Sixth.[313]

It was to this directive that the High-Churchmen appealed in the nineteenth century to reintroduce the attire used in the Middle Ages. In accordance with the above rubric one could urge that usage which was valid in the BCP of 1549, which is to say in the second year of the reign of Edward VI. In the rubric to the communion service of the BCP of 1549 we read:

> Upon the daie and at the time appoincted for the ministracion of the holy Communion, the Priest that shal execute the holy ministery, shall put upon hym the vesture appoincted for that ministracion, that is to saye: a white Albe plain, with a vestement or Cope.[314]

There was great altercation with reference to the interpretation of this rubric.[315]

What is now of extraordinary importance can be determined from the historical facts: The so-called "Ornaments Rubric,"[316] on which the High-Churchmen rely, is also to be found in the Elizabethan prayer book of 1559 and this had been inserted by the queen herself without receiving the sanction of Parliament.

This "Ornaments Rubric" was improperly interpreted at the beginning of the Anglo-Catholic movement because the binding declarations of the Hampton Court Conference of 1604 were not respected. One of the most important co-contributors to the BCP of 1662, John Cosin, Bishop of Durham, published so-called visitation questions and he gave these visitation questions to the clergy whom he wanted to visit. It is made clear in these visitation questions that the wearing of vestments as prescribed in the BCP of 1552 and at the Hampton Court Conference would be respected as binding:

> Have you a large and decent surplice for the minister to wear at all times of his public ministration in the Church?[317]

A further quotation of Cosin from the "Visitation Inquiries" reads:

> Doth he always at the reading or celebrating any Divine office in your church or chapel constantly wear the surplice . . . ? And doth he never omit it?[318]

The false interpretation with respect to the "Ornaments Rubric" by the Anglo-Catholic movement in the nineteenth century with the consequence of the reintroduction of the late Medieval ceremonials could only happen because the declarations of the Hampton Court and Savoy Conferences were overlooked. Elizabeth would have liked to understand this rubric in the sense of a reintroduction of vestments, but Parliament enacted a clause to the Act of Uniformity which interprets the "Ornament Rubric" in a very definite direction:

> Provided always, and be it enacted, That such Ornaments of the Church and of the Ministers thereof, shall be retained and be in use, as was in this Church of England by authority of parliament, in the second year of the reign of King Edward the Sixth, until other order shall therein be taken by the Authority of the Queen's Majesty, with the advice of her commissioners appointed and authorised under the great Seal of England for Causes Ecclesiastical.[319]

Griffith Thomas points out that the expression "shall be retained and be in use" used in the above quotation could equally well mean "shall be retained and be in trust." That would mean that the vestments prescribed in the BCP of 1549 should not be released for private sale inasmuch as such are still on hand in large quantities from earlier times. These vestments should instead be preserved until an order be given by the government to sell them. Thus Griffith Thomas writes in an illuminating way:

> The above clause[320] . . . was intended as a safeguard against the embezzlement of the property of the Church before the administrative Officers of the Crown could give the instructions for the disposal of it. There is contemporary evidence that the meaning of "be in use" was "be in trust," i.e., not appropriated to private benefit.[321]

Even if Elizabeth herself wished this "Ornaments Rubric" to be understood otherwise for the BCP of 1559 we cannot ignore that the compilers of the BCP of 1662 interpreted this clause of the Act of Uniformity for the "Ornaments Rubric" found just before Morning Prayer in this suggested sense.

We let Griffith Thomas again address us who confirms unequivocally what has been the interpretation of the rubric for centuries:

> From 1662 onwards for at least two hundred years the uniform practice of the Church was according to the Prayer Book of 1552. In 1689 Commissioners were appointed to revise the Prayer Book, and their view of the law can be seen by their own words, "Whereas the surplice is appointed to be used by all ministers in performing Divine Offices." Thenceforward the practice continued uniform and consistent through the Church until the rise of the Tractarian Movement, when the question was raised, and an interpretation put upon the Ornaments Rubric which is opposed to everything known and observed in the Church of England for nearly three centuries.[322]

(a) Vestments for Morning and Evening Prayer[323]

For the Anglican church the typical vestments are the "cassock" and the "surplice." By "cassock" is meant a robe-like black garment with long sleeves which is buttoned with many buttons from the neck almost to the feet. For liturgical usage one requires a "cassock" with over it a "surplice," a white choir-like top garment with open arms which reaches down to the knees. For Morning and Evening Prayer the priest still today makes use of these traditional vestments. The sacristan wears the "cassock" without the "surplice" during the service. A choir participating in Morning and Evening Prayer is also clad in the "cassock" and "surplice." Only in High Church circles does the priest utilize during the solemn Evensong (Evening Prayer) the pluvial,[324] an overcoat-like cope with cowl and tassel thereon.

(b) Vestments for Holy Communion

Before the High Church movement one tended even in the celebration of the eucharistic service to wear just the "cassock" with the "surplice." An exception existed only in the cathedrals where the priest was permitted the wearing of the pluvial during the communion liturgy.

The vestments of the mass such as the alb, chasuble, and stole first found entry into the Anglican communion service with the Oxford Movement of the last century.[325] The alb[326] is a white linen tunic having closed sleeves and reaching to the feet. Generally the alb is provided with a cord. The priest celebrating the eucharist service wears the chasuble (the little house) over the alb.[327] The chasuble confers upon the sacral vestments of the priest a certain completeness. The chasuble bears a color appropriate to the church year and often exhibits beautiful embroidery with ornamental or Christian-symbolical themes. The chasuble is an over-the-head semicircular and armless jacket-like vestment which covers the priest to the knees. There are very many different styles.[328]

Priests of the Anglican Church wear the stole[329] directly over the alb during the communion service. The stole is like a scarf in breadth but is substantially longer. Frequently the priest wears the stole in such a way that it is suspended about the neck and hangs in two halves over both shoulders.

(c) Vestments for Special Occasions Such as Baptisms, Marriages, and Funerals

As a rule the priest wears simply the alb and stole.

(d) Symbolism of Vestments in East and West Churches

There were reports of the use of liturgical vestments even in late Christian antiquity.[330] To be sure, explanations by the Church Fathers as to the symbolism of the vestments for worship are lacking. A proper symbolism of the vestments was evolved first through the introduction of the canons of colour in the Western tradition in the thirteenth century. Since vestments and their symbolism represent a significant aspect of the sacral, some thoughts on the meaning of the liturgical vestments by the important worship theologian, Germanos of Constantinople (died 733), should find mention.[331] Although the vestments of the Eastern-Orthodox tradition differ from those of the Latin church, certain correspondences nevertheless exist, which affords us to some degree an understanding of the symbolism of the Western Church.

While pulling on the liturgical vestments the priest always utters a prayer for the particular piece of ceremonial clothing. These prayers exhibit some influence of Germanos. While the priest puts on the alb, designated the sticharion,[332] he speaks the following prayer:

> My soul rejoices in the Lord, for he has clothed me with the garb of salvation and enveloped me with the raiment of joy. He has bedecked me like a bridegroom and crowned me with costly objects like a bride.[333]

If we understand the prayer about the alb as taken from Holy Scripture at the suggestion of Germanos, then this particular piece of clothing is a symbol of the partially arrived new order of salvation in Jesus by which those believing stand spotless before God. The white color of the alb refers to cleanliness in the sense of the new righteousness valid before God.

In putting on the epitrachelion corresponding to the stole the priest makes use of the following prayer:

> Blessed be our God who pours grace upon his priest like ointment upon the head, which flows down to the beard, the beard of Aaron; which flows down to the hem of his garment.[334]

This prayer, which is also applicable to the stole, would have the motion of grace perceived as a downward flow.

The most important and beautiful garment, the phelonion which corresponds to the chasuble, likewise has its own prayer. This reads:

> Thy priests, Lord, garb themselves in righteousness, and thy saints exult in joy; forever, now and always and in all eternity. Amen.[335]

This prayer applicable to the phelonion, and hence to the appropriate chasuble, points by its closing "forever, now and always and in all eternity. Amen" also to the coming glory. Consequently this vestment is a symbol for that perfection where, unlike here on earth, it is not just the soul which shares the experience in the new order through a new birth, but also the body, in the sense of a body transfigured and incorruptible. Thus the vestments have a function in the sacral as a reflection and representation of the new order of salvation.

In the great edition of the Roman missal in use for altar service[336] before the Second Vatican there were also prayers for the putting on of vestments.[337] We may cite the prayers for the alb, stole, and chasuble. The prayer for the alb reads:

> Dealba me, Domine, et munda cor meum; ut, in Sanguine Agni dealbatus, gaudiis perfruar sempiternis.[338]

This bears, in its essentials, an affinity with the Eastern Church prayer on the sticharion. Nevertheless the Latin tradition lays a much sharper stress on the atoning component through the mention of the blood of Jesus. The sinner in his dependency on purification comes more distinctly into focus. The prayer in respect to the stole presents a different symbolism from that which is expressed in the hymnic words for the epitrachelion:

> Redde mihi, Domine, stolam immortalitatis, quam perdidi in praevaricatione primi parentis: et, quamvis indignus accedo ad tuum sacrum mysterium, meream tamen gaudium sempiterum.[339]

Here again is present a reference to being snared by sin, where the text alludes to original sin in connexion with the first parents. The stole in the prayer above becomes a symbol of immortality which man has lost precisely because of original sin.

The symbolism of the chasuble is unusual:

> Domine, qui dixisti: Jugum meum suave est et onus meum leve: fac, ut istud portare sic valeam, quod consequar tuam gratiam. Amen.[340]

The chasuble is hence a symbol for the burden laid upon man which he must bear. Here the symbolism diverges substantially from that of the phelonion. It speaks somewhat of the Roman consciousness of duty with its practical orientation.

It is interesting that these prayers in the Roman tradition are petitions; in the eastern liturgy the prayers for the vestments deal exclusively with a Biblical-hymnal text.

Symbols characteristically are not one hundred percent unequivocal. I see a possibility of establishing a connexion between 2 Corinthians 5:1-3 and the chasuble. In this connexion the chasuble would then be the symbol for the new dwelling place of the soul in the body risen from the grave. The black "cassock" in the Anglican church is worn by the priest during the eucharist service underneath all other vestments. The black colour could be a symbol of the earthly mortal body; the alb put on over it might allude to the purified soul due to the power of forgiveness. The chasuble—as just said—becomes the token for men restored to perfection, who now in a bodily sense participate in immortality.

Because of the emphasis on the glory in connexion with its symbolism we connect the interpretation of the eucharistic vestments in the Anglican church service more with the Orthodox tradition.[341]

Definitive Remarks on (3)

This digression among the vestments used by the High Church wing has shown us that apparently there is present more profusion in the Anglo-Catholic tradition than in the settled rubrics of the BCP of 1662.

We must however make it clear that the iron rations of symbolism are assured with the "cassock" and "surplice."

The "cassock" as a black toga-like gown alludes to the frailty of the earthly body. The "surplice" as a white coat-like wrap[342] may exhibit clearly the new righteousness for the believers imparted in Jesus. The absence of the chasuble is of a great significance. This cloak is to be seen in close connexion with the conception of the priest as one of those presenting the bloodless sacrifice of Jesus at the altar, as W. H. Griffith Thomas so trenchantly expresses it:

> And this vestment (the chasuble), together with the Alb has long been inextricably associated with Roman Catholic and Medieval sacerdotal teaching on the Holy Communion.[343]

Since the chasuble or the "eucharistic vestment"—as it is rather adroitly called today—implies this Roman Catholic concept of the priest as sacrificer, the BCP of 1662 rejected such liturgical vestments. The BCP of 1662 wishes to express an additional central truth by the elimination of the chasuble:

By this elimination it is also intended to proclaim that in the Service of Holy Communion the faithful receive in the elements nothing more valuable than the Word. This then is the reason why in all types of divine services the same kind of vestments are used based on what is prescribed in the BCP of 1662. The danger is great that especially conspicuous raiment on the occasion of holy communion, such as the chasuble, might lure one into the idea that more is received in the Holy Communion Service than the Word, i.e., that the reading of Scripture and the sermon amount to less than the communion.

(e) The Liturgical Vested Choir as a Genuine Anglican Heritage

The BCP of 1662 includes no rubric which provides a liturgical dress for the choir. It is remarkable also that the strongly evangelical Anglicans holding true to the BCP of 1662 have liturgically vested choirs in their churches for all three principal services. Anglicans strongly oriented towards the Bible and committed to the BCP of 1662 have accepted this custom introduced by the Oxford Movement of 1839, since Biblical roots are present therein. In the Old Testament mention is made of the temple choir[344] clad in white robes. The genuine Anglican takes the position in accordance with Calvin's thinking that the choir serves the function of animating the churchgoer at the Sunday service to join in the singing. However the daily evensongs in the cathedrals with vested choirs is a tradition found only in the Anglican church.

(f) Liturgical Linen

The BCP of 1662 prescribes simply a linen cloth for the communion table and a small linen cloth in order to cover the bread remaining after the distribution.

The BCP of 1662 recognizes no colour canon. Despite this even those congregations loyal to the BCP of 1662 have introduced antependiums[345] in the colour of the appropriate time of the church year. The colour canon had been first enunciated as binding in the church of the Middle Ages by Innocent III in the thirteenth century. The antependium became something genuinely Anglican in the seventeenth century and the liturgical colour according to the church year was first suggested by the High Church movement of the nineteenth century. By the use of the liturgical colour of the antependium even the evangelical Anglicans loyal to the BCP of 1662 wished to accentuate the progress through the church year based on Holy Scripture.

(4) The Sacral Place and Its Appurtenances[346]

(a) The Altar-Like Communion Table and Its Accessories

In the easterly oriented choir stands the communion table which is usually made of wood. This is covered with an antependium[347] which bears a colour appropriate to the church year and which is decorated with very

220

beautiful ornamentation. Candles are always located on the north and south surfaces of the table. This usage is based on a decree of Edward VI in the year 1547 where it says:

> Two lights upon the high altar, before the sacrament, which for the signification that Christ is the very true light of the world, they shall suffer to remain still.

Although there is no rubric in the BCP of 1662 providing for candles this custom of placing them on the communion table became common during the Restoration under Charles II. In the middle of the communion table stands a metal cross without any figure of Christ thereon which is another indication that the Anglican church forms a part of the Reformed tradition. Nor is this custom prescribed in the BCP of 1662. The communion table is separated from the rest of the choir area by altar rails[348] where kneelers are placed for the communicants. The altar-like communion table occupies a very important position in the Anglican church room. The altar rails in front of the communion table are intended in a special way to promote reverence. When Archbishop Laud succeeded in the year 1634 with this tradition of the altar rails stemming from the late Middle Ages he was seeking a specific attitude of reverence: this refers to a reverence for the Verbum Visibile which finds expression in this altar-like communion table. The altar-like element of the communion table reveals itself in an often present reredos,[349] a partition-like structure at the back of the table with a niche where central events of salvation history are depicted by incised figures, particularly the sacrificial scene on Golgotha,[350] while other representations of the resurrection, ascension, and Pentecost are not lacking. The antependia sometimes—though not often—provide the same depiction in embroidery.

We can see that this altar-like communion table with its generally elevated location expresses the Verbum Visibile in the clearest way when the Ten Commandments and the Apostles' Creed and the Lord's Prayer are written on the reredos. We are dealing here with the very important influence of John Hooper[351] who understood the Decalogue chiefly as a pars pro toto for the whole of Scripture. Such a reredos has no pictorial representations but places the naked Word upon a pedestal. We have to take note of the fact that in the collection of regulations concerning the decoration of the interiors of churches in Whitehead's *Church Law*[352] the writing of the Ten Commandments, the Apostles' Creed, and the Lord's Prayer fall under the "articles legally required" in contrast to "articles legal, but not compulsory."

The altar-like liturgical table is not an object of liturgical devotion in the Roman Catholic sense, but rather a means for giving validity to the concept of Sola Scriptura by means of representations appealing to the senses. In this function we understand the elevated position as well as the prominent placement of the communion table as a device to catch the eye to focus attention on it as the center of faith. In my opinion it is quite legitimate to emphasize not only its aspect as a table but also as an altar. This does not mean a repeated bloodless sacrifice in the Roman Catholic sense—that is to be totally rejected—but it means bringing to mind time and again what God has let it cost himself to bring about salvation for us through the sacrificial death of Jesus. It is a matter of bringing to mind in the sense of a "Recordatio" which is that type of recollection which brings some long ago event into the present.[353] The challenge to reflect upon the atoning sacrifice of Jesus should proceed from the communion table and clearly from the fact that one is reminded of more than just a table. The carvings or the enameled Apostles' Creed on the reredos are a reminder of all the central facts of the story of salvation[354] shared with us through the Biblical Word, especially of the sacrificial death of Jesus on the wooden altar of the cross without which there would be no salvation.

Cranmer advocated in reference to the communion table the opinion that it be also justly called an altar[355] since the congregation brings, as it were, a sacrifice of praise and thanksgiving.

The aspect of the table should not become blurred, since the character of the table should point to the need for fellowship of the faithful, one to another.

There is also found in Anglican churches—and not just in those with an Anglo-Catholic tradition—a baldachin stretched over the communion table.[356] This represents symbolically the heavenly sphere. Finally the altar-like communion table also has the function to represent the throne in the sense of Revelation 7:11ff. Thus the congregation should practice in the here and now the worship of the Lamb in order to be able to do that sometime in a perfect way at the consummation.[357]

In summary we want to establish the following with reference to the altar-like communion table: As a "Verbum Visibile" the altar-like communion table is an eye catcher for the Word of God and to bring before the eyes of the churchgoer the most vital facts of the story of salvation in the representations on the reredos together with Christmas, the passion, crucifixion, ascension, and Pentecost, in connexion with which the pictureless reredos with Decalogue, Creed, and Lord's Prayer comes closest to the Reformation thinking of the BCP of 1662.

(b) Choir Stall

In the choir on the north and south sides in front of the altar one finds a choir stall which as a rule provides fourteen to twenty places for singers.

(c) Pulpit

This as a rule is located on the north side immediately in front of the choir stall. Generally the pulpit stands almost at the same height as the pews of the members of the congregation. Higher pulpits which require many steps to reach are seldom found in Anglican churches. Possibly this is connected with the popularity of the reading of the Bible in Anglican regions. The people's intimate association with God's Word forbids any great distance to the place from whence the priest expounds the Scriptures.

(d) Lectern

On the south side in front of the choir stall is found a representation of an eagle on a lectern for the Epistles. The Holy Scriptures are always found upon this reading desk.

(e) Seating Facilities for the Congregation

The churchgoers have no kneelers at their disposal, but only cushions which are mounted on the backs of the pews. Chairs are much more common than benches.

(f) Church Windows

The church windows are often provided with stained glass decorations.

(g) The Sanctuary Light

In ecclesiastical structures of the High Church tradition a sanctuary light hangs from the ceiling between the choir stall and the altar. Sometimes a hanging lamp is also mounted on the wall near the container holding the sacraments. There are many other lamps which bear no connexion with the tabernacle.

(h) Baptismal Font

The baptismal font often stands in the back part of the church and not in the choir or near the communion table, as is customary in Reformed churches.

3. EFFECTS OF THE LITURGY

a. Spirituality

This splendid synthesis of a Catholic church service structure with evangelical-Biblical thinking gives rise to a reality in which the sacral, and what is more, the fascinosum and tremendum occur in a purified way.

The noble manner of speech, gestures, and other symbols combine in an ideal harmony.

To this effect of the sacral belongs the fact that one encounters the total other worldliness of the divine world. The polished forms, the magnificent choir music, ceremonial dress, solemn gestures, and incense[358] discernible by the outer senses, affect the souls of men positively.

b. The Form as Support for the Word

The liturgical forms are designed so that they will lay stress upon and lift on high the divine Word. Morning and Evening Prayer, apart from the exhortations, the confession, and the prayers, are made indeed almost solely of artistically compiled Biblical quotations.

When the choir boys, led by the crucifer, march in procession[359] into the church for Evensong they bow in a restrained manner in front of the altar before they take their places in the choir stall. When the choir boys make the Biblical text ring out with the singing of a Psalm they bow for the doxology[360] at the end of each Psalm. The gesture of bowing is to be understood as a magnification of the doxology. The doxology itself is a praising and acknowledging response to the foregoing Psalm.

The style of worshipping by a responsive participation in the Psalms and other Biblical texts is to be understood as an expression of emphasis on the importance of the Word of Scripture, which is offered through the experience of a dialogue. The responsive form allows the basic intention of the Biblical Word to become apparent, namely to lead to a discourse

between God and man. The congregation is able by its interest in participating in an esthetic dialogue to comprehend better the monological truth
of God in the Bible. Since the Word of God is presented in an exemplary
way in an artistically fashioned combination of various styles, it results
in something artistic and rich in variety. The artistic and sacral elements
are to that extent related to one another, since both can contain something
of the fascinosum and tremendum.

c. The Holy Communion Liturgy as a Dramatic
Presentation of Salvation

The communion liturgy is celebrated in a particularly fine way chiefly in
cathedrals and college churches.

The communion liturgy doesn't present the salvation doctrine set
forth in Scripture merely to the sense of hearing and thus to the intellect.
The liturgy tries to appeal to all five senses. The psychic-physical nature
of man is taken seriously in this.

The churchgoer witnesses the solemn entrance of the choir in its
red, white, or purple robes. The crucifer marches in front. The symbol of
the cross points immediately in an unverbal way to the basic theme of the
salvation drama: The atoning death of Jesus and his resurrection. Indeed,
since the cross in an Anglican church is not a crucifix, it becomes for that
reason a symbol of victory over death.

The choir is to a certain degree representative of the congregation.
The congregation can see itself in an anticipatory way as what in some
future time it will be in its redeemed condition: A celebrating fellowship
approaching Jesus with glorified bodies. The colorful robes with white
surplices[361] may refer to one's resurrection body.

The congregation is nevertheless not simply spectator but also to a
certain extent participant in this drama of salvation. The congregation after
all, thanks to the responsive structure of the service, at least gives answers
in verbal form as well as by gestures too. The congregation stands up during
the reading of the Gospel, and now it observes how the priest makes his
way to the Gospel side of the altar, escorted on his right and left by candle-
bearers and sometimes by a censer who goes in front. The candles raised
on both sides of the opened Bible proclaim the Gospel to be the true light
of the world. During the reading an acolyte swings the censer.

This "Light of the World" reveals itself in the ritual development of the mystery of salvation which exists in the sacrificial death and resurrection. In the Creed the congregation affirms this resurrection story.

Of great importance is the intercessory prayer for the Ecclesia Militans in which a connexion exists with the Ecclesia Triumphans in memory of those who have died in the faith. In the following exhortation we find an important concept, namely the word "mystery." The elements of the bread and the wine are "mysteries." In the first exhortation[362] it says:

> My duty is to exhort you in the mean season to consider the dignity of that holy mystery.

A mystery is something concealed by God, which God in his grace reveals to men.

During the offertory[363] the priest removes the chalice veil, the covering napkin, from the chalice. The congregation can follow it all visually in a devotional way. It is a matter of making salvation apparent through a step-by-step process of a symbolic unveiling. At the moment when the priest enters upon the Preface,[364] he reveals in a special way that now the connexion with the heavenly world is established. In the Preface the congregation participates in a song of praise of the heavenly host. This prayer is visibly supported through the raising of the celebrant's hands. During the prayer of consecration itself the priest at the time of the words of institution lifts up the host and the cup, whereupon an acolyte sounds a small bell. Soon after the words of institution are spoken the churchgoers receive holy communion and experience therein the high point of the mystery. Jesus meets them in a spiritual way as the bread of heaven. Thus Jesus has revealed himself progressively during the course of the liturgy and has reasserted the culmination of his immolation in the distribution of the sacrament. In the carrying out of the communion the faithful experience a drama of the story of salvation expressed in the form of worship. Although Jesus reveals himself as the mystery, the secret character nevertheless remains. The altar rail indeed calls attention to the holy awe with which one should receive Jesus. After the taking of communion the priest carefully covers over the remaining unconsumed elements. After the closing benediction the choir processes out of the church with the crucifer in front and the clergy behind.

d. Daily Morning and Evening Prayer as a Proclamation of the Self-Interpretation of Holy Scripture

There is a fascinating effect arising out of the daily-sung Evening Prayer

(Evensong).[365] The church celebrates this vespers service with an enchanting beauty. Choir boys trained in the cathedral schools of England sing each day to the glory of God at a concert level.[366] In doing so a liturgical display of magnificence in the vestments and gestures is furnished in full measure. The really noteworthy thing about it is that this type of service is celebrated at great expense without regard for an audience. It can well happen that no one outside of choir and clergy is present. Behind this practice probably stands the idea of the self-effectuation of the divine Word which should be openly acknowledged according to the sense it has in Isaiah 55:11. The effect resulting from such a service reveals itself in an atmosphere of security which becomes something like a refuge independent of the demands of men.

e. The True Reasons Underlying the Sacrality of the BCP of 1662

The title of Section D of this chapter has already clearly indicated the answer herein.

Since the Bible supplies not only the historic theme of salvation for a divine service but equally well the liturgical building blocks, something blessed must result. This exists in the proclamation of the Good News and equally in the worthy and exalted form thereof.

Holy Scripture operates as a useful boundary which acts as a restraint on possible excrescences. Negative consequences with reference to the esthetics of the liturgy result wherever the Word of God is not the ultimate court of appeal. The communion liturgy of the BCP demands a celebration style which accords with that circumspection and propriety that is expected in the reading of the Bible. An automatic unrolling of the service in the BCP is exposed as a breach of style by the formulas included therein. The fact that the text of the BCP insists upon liturgies being understood with the heart also has a connexion.

At first glance it does not seem evident that the puritans have had anything to do with the sacrality of the BCP. However one should not forget that their participation in the revision of the BCP[367] had especially in mind a sanctity which comes into existence through convinced Bible-believing Christians and which prevents the evaporation of the sacred simply into visible forms. For puritans holiness is defined more in terms of behaviour in the sense of a sanctification which must occur by faith in the inner man. The theological content hence had to be thoroughly tested through the pressures exerted by the puritans so that the substance of the prayer book was more and more refined until the contents finally created also a cleansed external form. The puritans vigorously pointed out that the sacral occurs not through pomp but through Biblical doctrine lived.

The sacral—and this is the proof of its genuineness—may also prevail without external esthetic forms. We have this precise case in the puritans. Since these vehemently adhere to Scripture and based on this have staunchly held the eternal salvation of man in view, for that reason one finds with them an obvious sense of security. Their living style clearly is to be contrasted with the phenomenology of a fallen world. The Soli Deo Gloria motive must, in the Calvinistic sense, be the driving force of all men's doings, rather than respect for vogue and trend.

A meeting place in which puritanical prayer meetings and Bible lessons are offered with a childlike faith produces a peculiar solemnity which no "Coxlike liturgy" producing its own Fascinosum and Tremendum can match. The puritans thus have acted a little like one's liver for the final edition of the BCP of 1662. The liver has the function among all the organs of the body of acting as a filter. This is a significant reason why the BCP has so much substance and in addition of such a sort that when it provides a form for itself it does it in a glorious way.

The BCP of 1662 deserves our special attention because in this book of liturgy the Reformation principle of "scriptura sui ipsius interpres" and the self-effectuating power of the Bible in a revivalistic form builds the cantus firmus. Thus The Book of Common Prayer stands within a tradition which considering the disastrous consequences of the historical-critical method has once again been exalted through today's theologians like E. W. Kohls,[368] Wilhelm Maurer, Samuel Külling, Francis Schaeffer, and the many theologians who signed the far-reaching nineteen-article "Chicago Declaration"[369] on the occasion of the "International Council on Biblical Inerrancy" in 1978 in Chicago. The BCP of 1662 is thus very timely in its understanding of Scripture and it has even more power because of the integration of the Word of the Bible therein to accomplish what Wilhelm Maurer says so pertinently of Holy Scripture:

> All that really matters is that dependent on the insight of Luther, that the self acting Word of God in which Christ is effective on earth in a real sense accomplishes missionary work. The Word has an impact on the individual, on the congregation, and on the church and makes them the instruments of the divine mission for the world and in the world. . . . We live by this Word, while we serve it.[370]

V. The Oxford Movement (Tractarian Movement) as an Expression of Dissatisfaction with the Principle of Sola Scriptura and Its Consequences

A. THE ANGLO-CATHOLIC MOVEMENT (OXFORD OR TRACTARIAN MOVEMENT) CONSTITUTES THE ANTITHESIS TO THE BOOK OF COMMON PRAYER OF 1662

1. INTRODUCTORY REMARKS

There is no intention in the course of Chapter V to give a summary of the historical and theological development of Anglo-Catholicism.[1] We intend only to show in a cursory way some important features of the theological thinking of Anglo-Catholicism and from this to make comprehensible by a brief outline the genesis of the new liturgy, *The Alternative Service Book 1980*.

2. ITS PRELUDE IN "THE TRACTS FOR THE TIMES"

The Oxford Movement could be traced back to predecessors, as for instance, at least in some respects, to the "Caroline Divines" of the seventeenth century.[2] The Anglo-Catholic Movement as such had its origin in the Hadleigh Conference in the year 1833. Some High-Churchmen, discontented with the condition of the English church, gathered together in Hadleigh, a village near Oxford, in the local rectory. Among them were such important theologians as H. J. Rose, W. Palmer, A. P. Perceval, and R. H. Froude. A close contact was maintained with the theologians of the Hadleigh Conference by J. H. Newman and John Keble as well as by E. B. Pusey.

The reasons leading to The Oxford Movement are complex. But a few points should be mentioned: "The Test Act"[3] of the year 1673 provided that only Anglicans had access to positions in the government, thus no Catholics nor dissenters. When this Test Act was repealed and the "Catholic Emancipation Act"[4] was pass in 1829, there was alarm among High Church people. As a result of this "Catholic Emancipation Act" it was not only the Catholics who gained access to political office, but also dissenters, i.e., puritans. To see puritans in high political position was naturally for High-Churchmen a very special thorn in the flesh. The state intruded into the economic affairs of the Anglican church in Ireland with its "Irish Church Reform Bill" of 1833, which was cause for concern for the High-Churchmen.

But the most important reason was very likely the strongly marked rationalistic theology mixed with liberal concepts emanating from the Continent, which put in question the supernatural character of Holy Scripture.

These few points should suffice to sketch the background of Anglo-Catholicism.

The theologians of the Hadleigh Conference and their sympathizers created an organ in which they could express their ideas reference the renewal of the Anglican church: "The Tracts for the Times," which grew to ninety articles. Among the authors of the tracts were Newman, Keble, Pusey, Froude, and others, although Newman composed more than a quarter of the tracts. There existed among these Anglo-Catholic theologians a great unity, but also a profound difference: On the one hand were the "Caroline Divines," the High Church adherents of the seventeenth century. On the other side a Roman Catholic tendency was strongly exhibited, which became responsible for the second important phase within The Oxford Movement, that is to say, the rise of ritualism.

"The Tracts for the Times" with its brand of theology took a turn which has been very influential in the Anglican church even to the present.

3. SOME OF THE SALIENT FEATURES OF THE OXFORD MOVEMENT

We want to sketch only a few of the most important basic concepts of The Oxford Movement.

a. The Oxford Movement's Understanding of Scripture

Newman as well as Pusey were very concerned because of the liberal and rationalistic spirit which did not spare even the English church. Pusey had become acquainted with rationalistic theology at its source during his periods of study in Germany. He was therefore especially sensitive.

Newman and Pusey had an understanding of Scripture which today would be identified with "fundamentalism." For them every word of Holy Scripture was inspired by the Holy Spirit. In a letter to his friend R. H. Froude dated August 23, 1835, he writes "Every word of Scripture is inspired." Similar passages by Pusey and Keble and many others in The Oxford Movement may be found. Pusey together with a friend issued a typical document[5] addressed to the archbishops and bishops of the churches of England and Ireland, and there one reads:

> We . . . hold it to be our bounden duty to the Church and to the soul of men to declare our firm belief that the Church of England and Ireland, in common with the whole Catholic Church, maintains without reserve or qualification the Inspiration and Divine Authority of the whole Canonical Scriptures as not only containing but being the Word of God.[6]

It is of great consequence that Newman stood up for a conception of the divine mystical character[7] of Holy Scripture, which became the cause of contradictions and various interpretations of the Bible. Thus Newman can say despite his doctrine of inspiration: "Intimations of doctrine . . . are . . . faintly given in Scripture."[8]

If one adopts the point of view of that conception it is certain that the Reformation idea of "scriptura sui ipsius interpres" must be denied. Holy Scripture would then be lacking the vitally important "perspicuitas." From the point of view of this presupposition it is a necessity for Tractarians (the authors of "The Tracts for the Times") to hold that tradition has to become the principle of interpretation. The church as the guardian of tradition undertakes this duty.

In Tract XC Newman asserts the following with reference to Article VI of the Thirty-nine Articles, "Of the Sufficiency of the holy Scriptures for Salvation":

> In the sense in which it is commonly understood at this day, Scripture, it is plain, is not, on Anglican principles, the Rule of Faith.[9]

On this point M. Keller-Hüschemenger says in his analysis of Tractarian theology:

> The mystery-like arcane character of Holy Scripture which is based on the divine dignity of inspiration within the revealed truths makes an immediate and general human understanding impossible, therefore requiring for the scriptural messages an interpretative and annotative supplement.[10]

For the Tractarians it is a matter of course that the fundamental truths of salvation are substantially present in Holy Scripture.[11] But the isolated individual is not able to understand these truths of salvation unless the church makes the interpretation through its traditional material. This conception is articulated by Newman in most of his writings. A quotation from his "Lectures of the Prophetical Office of the Church" reveals to us this typical Tractarian idea:

> I repeat it; while Scripture is written by inspired men, with one and one only view of doctrine in their hearts and thoughts, even the Truth which was from the beginning, yet being written not to instruct in doctrine, . . . not with direct announcements but with intimations and implications of the faith, the qualifications for rightly apprehending it are so rare and high, that a prudent man . . . will not risk his salvation on the chance of his having them; but will read it with the aid of those subsidiary guides which ever have been supplied as if to meet our need. I would not deny as an abstract proposition that a Christian may gain the whole truth from the Scriptures, but would maintain that the chances are very seriously against a given individual. . . . The Catholic Church may be truly said almost infallibly to interpret Scripture aright, though from the possession of past tradition.[12]

Since in accordance with Anglo-Catholic conceptions the Word of Holy Scripture cannot be interpreted[13] through the Bible itself, therefore tradition takes precedence over Holy Scripture.[14]

The "unwritten verities," against which Cranmer inveighed so stoutly, existed according to the conception of the Tractarians as an oral tradition before the New Testament was reduced to writing.

Thus John Keble can express himself in the following way:

> Because it is affirmed that the full tradition of Christianity existed before Christian Scriptures, and so far independent of them, we are charged with alleging two distinct systems or words of God, the one written, the other unwritten, running as it were parallel to each other quite down to our own time.[15]

The consequence of a tradition which is put above Holy Scripture leads to the affirmation which W. G. Ward has made in *The British Critic,* a leading Anglo-Catholic periodical:

> Without reading Scripture or knowing a word of it, men may be good Christians.[16]

Another important element in the understanding of Scripture among theologians of The Oxford Movement is the concept of the potential for development within Holy Scripture and the furthering of doctrine through tradition. Thus oral tradition is so structured as to lead to development.[17]

In his composition "An Essay on the Development of Christian Doctrine" Newman expresses this idea of the potential for development of the Biblical Word in unmistakable language:

> But the whole Bible, not its prophetical portion only, is written on the principle of development.[18]

The changing circumstances in the course of time which have occurred since the writing of Holy Scripture, especially that of the New Testament, demand an application differing from that necessary in the early Christian period. This change in application is termed development by Newman:

> But outward circumstances have changed, and with the change, a different application of the revealed word has of necessity been demanded, that is, a development.[19]

For instance, in some period of time a special interest in the fate of the departed can arise. Because the Bible has very little to say about this, a doctrine then which is produced by a certain development process has to give the information rather than Holy Scripture itself. This is what Newman means when he writes in the same essay:

> There is another subject . . . on which Scripture does not . . . keep silence, but says so little as to require, and so much as to suggest, information beyond its letter, the intermediate state between death and the Resurrection.[20]

The idea of assimilation plays an important role for Newman with reference to the development of the dogma which grew out of Scripture and out of oral and written tradition. Under assimilation Newman understands the incorporation of new elements into dogma but in such a way that unity and harmony prevail. Thus Newman makes the following affirmation which carries with it substantial consequences:

> An eclectic, conservative, assimilating, healing, moulding process, a unitive power, is of the essence, . . . of a faithful development.[21]

This conception of Holy Scripture is practically identical with the Roman Catholic conception. When this conception is carried through in a consequent way, then one must arrive at the following conception which the famous Roman Catholic dogmatist Karl Adam has expressed in his classical work *Das Wesen des Katholizismus (The Essence of Catholicism)* as follows:

> We Catholics confirm without blushing, yes we confirm it with pride: Catholicism is not to be absolutely and in every respect identified with early Christendom or even with the message of Christ any more than we can identify a mature oak tree with a little acorn. There is no mechanical identity, but there is organic identity. A historian of religion in the 5th millennium after Christ will without difficulty discover in Catholicism imaginations, forms, and structures whose place of origin is India, Japan, and China, and he should discover a far more developed complexio oppositorum.[22]

Newman with his conception of Holy Scripture and dogma has set a course which has not only had consequences for the Anglo-Catholic movement but has also provided very important points of departure for the development of modernistic theology.

For Newman and the leading theologians of The Oxford Movement Holy Scripture has to be submitted to and ordered by the church.

Although Newman, John Keble, and E. B. Pusey were convinced of the full inspiration of Holy Scripture, they did not teach "Sola Scriptura." To stand up for verbal inspiration does not mean that you propagate "Sola Scriptura" at all. The classical Roman Catholic doctrine of inspiration can be called verbal inspiration when you read the utterances of Pope Pius X in his syllabus of July 3, 1907, under the title "Errores modernistarum de Ecclesia, revelatione, Christo, sacramentis." There you read:

> Inspiratio divina non ita ad totam Scripturam sacram extenditur, ut omnes et singulas eius partes ab omni errore praemuniat.[23]

It is of great consequence too that in Newman's understanding of Scripture, and generally in that of the theologians of The Oxford Movement, there is lacking, in a way analogous to Roman Catholic doctrine, any insight into the need for a "Testimonium Interni Spiritus Sancti."

b. Its Understanding with Reference to Reason

We don't intend here to go into detail, but only to establish the principles. When one examines briefly the concept of reason among the Tractarian theologians one is apt to be sympathetic with the way that they stood up against the tendencies in rationalism to dissolve the substance of the Bible. Tractarians were against an intellectualism which denied the supernatural dimension.[24] Reason though was accorded a very high value among the Tractarians. One only has to fight reason when it behaves in a usurpatory way, and that means: the use of secular and nonreligious premises in the judging of matters of faith.[25] Otherwise reason is to be highly valued because reason has not been corrupted basically by the fall of man. Newman even goes so far that he speaks of reason as "the judge of the faith."[26]

From this conception's point of view regarding reason it becomes understandable why the development of dogma to the point of special doctrines (meaning unbiblical doctrines) can be judged in such a positive way. For Newman, reason has in itself to support a continuous process of development. Newman speaks of a so-called "progress process" which is essentially inherent in reason. Max Keller-Hüschemenger says the following in regard to that:

> This progress process can also be going on within Christianity, that is to say, in the area of the church itself this progress process is going on through a process of doctrine and the unfolding of hidden "inspired statements," "inward impressions," or the "Catholic idea," to clarify and itemize "Catholic doctrines" of the church with the help of "reason."[27]

To a large degree it is this concept of reason which has marked The Oxford Movement's understanding of the church.

c. Ecclesiological Features of The Oxford Movement

(1) The True Church as a Historical, Territorial, Juridical, and Ritualistic Entity

The Tractarians of that time relied upon a principle that was very important to them. This refers to the principle of the "Consensus Quinquesaecularis."[28] We have to understand the following: the true church presented itself at a certain time within a certain historical period, namely in the first five centuries, as a unity in organizational, doctrinal, and ceremonial respects, which however doesn't imply that the same liturgical formulas have been used in the Latin and Greek portions of the one true church.

Everything which has been determined upon in the great councils of the first five centuries is to be considered "catholic" and is binding. One of the essential factors which documents this unity is apostolic succession. Since this is maintained in the Greek, Roman, and Anglican churches, these three named ecclesiastical corporations therefore belong to the sole and true "catholic" church.

In the theology of The Oxford Movement the continental churches like the Lutheran, Calvinist, Zwinglian, and those bearing the free church stamp have no right to be designated as the true church. Why? Because the apostolic succession is lacking, and also, except in Lutheranism, the doctrine of the bodily presence of Jesus in holy communion is also lacking.

The unity of the church which existed in its first five hundred years thereby indicates that its doctrine was sound.

In accordance with the High Church conception, the rise of different autonomous Eastern churches and of other ecclesiastical corporations having apostolic succession is, on the one hand, something of a tragedy, but on the other hand the autonomy of different catholic churches which are independent of each other should also help to strengthen their national consciousness.

Whatever can be found in the first five centuries among the Church Fathers concerning doctrine together with whatever developed further in the course of the traditional process is valid to the extent that it bears the truth of "antiquity." The principle of antiquity is hence normative and this implies that everything in regard to doctrine and liturgical custom can claim legitimacy only if it has been already verified through the centuries by those churches which stand up for apostolic succession.

Certain liturgical customs receive an emphasis to such an extent that they amount to credentials proving one's unity with the one true "catholic" church. M. Keller-Hüschemenger formulated clearly what place liturgy takes in accordance with Tractarian standards.

> Also "worship" and "liturgy" have to prove a right to their claim to the theological and ecclesiological legitimacy of their organization and authority through their apostolic-catholic origin and character, i.e., to their harmony with reference to a compatibility with Scripture and the tradition of the undivided old patristic church/Christian antiquity.[29]

A further term which the Tractarian liked to use in reference to doctrine and liturgy is the word "fulness." This term means that that doctrine and those liturgical forms which came into existence in the first five centuries reached in the course of time in the three great ecclesiastical corporations of the Greek, Roman, and English churches a fulness which is of a normative character.[30] Those churches which do not display this "fulness" are in a true sense sects.

236

(2) Doctrine with Respect to Sacraments

Tractarians placed an extraordinarily great emphasis on sacraments, especially holy communion, as well as on the truly sacramental character of the apostolic succession. In the sense of a kind of chain reaction the supernatural power of the Holy Spirit is passed on to the priest being consecrated through the laying on of hands by the bishop, and he thereby receives full power to carry out his duties. The chain of succession reaches back to the apostles and to Jesus. Theologians of The Oxford Movement tried to have it established that anyone converted to the Anglican from Reformed continental churches had to be ordained anew. Only clergymen standing in the apostolic succession can handle sacraments properly.

Baptism is the instrument for justification. It makes a person a Christian. Baptism causes first of all the rebirth. In contradiction to Luther we see here the predominance of baptism vis-à-vis faith.[31] Among Tractarians sacraments are not limited to baptism and holy communion and are to be understood as channels for divine material powers. For Luther justification as used in Holy Scripture is confined entirely to "Sola fide," where man thankfully accepts the salvation offered in Jesus and receives this gift through an act of faith without any merit.

M. Keller-Hüschemenger presents the sacramental concept of the Tractarians lucidly when he says in reference to justification:

> For the tractarian theologians justification is an ontologically effective quality of being which comes to man primarily through an "infusion" of the grace of the Holy Spirit in the sacrament of baptism and which also gives an ontologically effective "sacramental" communion with Christ.[32]

The doctrine of the Tractarians concerning sacraments differs in principle from that of the English reformers.[33]

Jesus is present in the sacrament of holy communion in greater measure than in other types of services.[34] This means that the churchgoer receives more from holy communion than can be provided by the Word.

(3) Doctrine with Respect to Incarnation

The doctrine of incarnation is a part of the ecclesiological conception of the Tractarians. These see in the incarnation the center of Holy Scripture. In this there does not stand "in the foreground any Biblical-Reformation redemptive motif of the justification of sinners before God through the

237

cross of Jesus Christ, but rather an ontological motif of the deification of man's nature as the fruit of the incarnation of God in His Son."[35]

It is not sin separating man from God which moved God to send his Son down to Earth there to suffer the atoning death on the cross. Even if mankind had not sinned God would have become man in Jesus in order to bring men into touch with his divine nature. Pusey as an important spokesman for The Oxford Movement defended this conception.[36] Max Keller-Hüschemenger remarks in this respect:

> With such a conception the two ventricles of the Biblical Gospel, i.e., God's love for the sinner and the cross of Christ, are so emptied of content that they become a mere accidental result of the condescension of God for us in his incarnation in Jesus Christ.[37]

Tractarians maintained the idea that the church is the continued incarnation of Christ on earth in which the sacraments constitute the effective means.[38] In connexion with this incarnation doctrine, which views the church as the effective and lengthened arm of Jesus in the world, one finds in part a sharp criticism of society, culture, and social problems.[39] This lengthened arm has to act in accordance with the requirements of the situation of this world.

d. Consequences of These Ecclesiological Conceptions

If it be conceded that the Eastern and Latin churches receive the credit for having the true catholicity due to a "Consensus Quinquesaecularis" and due to the dogmas developed to the full in the course of the centuries, then it becomes obvious that one should strive after a reunion of these three churches. Newman, Pusey, and Keble hold to this opinion. The church reunited as one because of this accomplished unity could no longer err.[40]

Indeed in the later phases of the Anglo-Catholic Movement there is to be observed a special inclination towards Roman Catholicism. This has to be explained by the idea that the stream of tradition is the clearest and the least interrupted within the Roman Church. R. H. Froude in a letter to Keble dated January 9, 1834, offered the suggestion that the Anglican church should in cases of doubt adapt to the Roman since its tradition is uninterrupted.[41] This suggestion of Froude is followed faithfully in today's ecumenical process.

This Anglo-Catholic ecclesiological conception demands an exact definition as to who really belongs to the true "catholic" church. The true catholic church is a "super-natural, spirit led sociological organism equipped with infallibility whose criterion of catholicity is the membership of those who submit to this organism with obedience."[42]

From the point of view of this conception it is clear that all those who have fellowship with each other through the Word of God who however do not belong to the Greek,[43] Latin, or Anglican church are sectarians. The puritans and above all the churches of the Continent of a Calvinistic and Lutheran stamp do not belong to the true church.[44] What constitutes the church in a true sense is the "Consensus Quinquesaecularis" and the tradition derived therefrom while the apostolic succession and the use of the sacraments in the sense of an "Ex Opere Operato" are of decisive significance. The consequence of such an ecclesiology is of course that the church cannot be primarily defined as the congregation of Jesus. One does not enter the church through a personal decision.

Of a not unimportant consequence is the Anglo-Catholic ecclesiological conception with its emphasis on the episcopal monarchical power and on the sacrament as basing its efficacy on an "Ex Opere Operato": lacking to a large degree is any challenge to one's personal faith as well as a serious concern with the individual. The puritanical forces however have strongly emphasized the responsibility of the individual before God, a responsibility in which no organized ecclesiastical corporation functions as mediator between God and man. Thus the Reformation-puritanical mentality furthered a free market of a capitalistic stamp thanks to its strong emphasis on the independence and self-responsibility of man.

Tractarians of a later phase who sympathized chiefly with Roman Catholicism had to be concerned about the social state of the population in Catholic countries, while those countries which adhered to the Reformation could demonstrate a certain social well-being among its population. Their hostility towards the continental Reformation did not allow Tractarians of a later phase[45] to see this fact in a positive way; on the contrary, they condemned continental Protestantism and accused it as regards its economic social impact with having caused the dominion of the rich over the poor. In short, continental Protestantism was to be blamed for the origin of a proletariat.[46]

e. Remarks in Summary

We have tried to sketch the most important features of The Oxford Movement, although there might be much more to be said. These elements of the Tractarian Movement should help us to understand better the further development of Anglo-Catholicism and its significance in regards to efforts to change The Book of Common Prayer.

For the next point we want in particular to take up the Anglo-Catholic antithesis to The Book of Common Prayer.

4. NEWMAN'S TRACT XC AND THE BOOK OF COMMON PRAYER OF 1662

Tractarians of the first phase prior to 1850 exerted themselves strongly in behalf of the preservation of the BCP of 1662. For them the perception was very important that the liturgy should not be just a factor of order in the documentation of the unity of the church but also a kind of mirror in which is reflected the church's doctrine. In the storm of time with its liberal and latitudinarian tendencies the English liturgy should be a stable rock. Thus F. Oakeley could say the following in his article "The Church Service," published in *The British Critic:*

> Its fixedness has been truly wonderful, in contrast not merely with the political changes which it has outlived, but with the fluctuations of English theology, in the midst of which it has stood as a rock.[47]

Newman even warns in his Tract III against slight changes in the BCP. Keble went so far as to say that God himself has given The Book of Common Prayer to the English Church.[48] The Tractarians were able to bring it about that The Book of Common Prayer which was so appreciated by the common people could be exalted and in addition their antithesis with reference to its Biblical-Reformation substance could also be exalted through nothing less than a magnificent change of interpretation.

This couldn't have been done in a better way. In his Tract XC J. H. Newman took his position concerning the theology of the BCP by using the Thirty-nine Articles. What are welcomed by Tractarians such as Newman are the formal liturgical structures of the BCP from the time of the first five centuries of the "Apostolic Church." Although the BCP of 1662 adopted only what was legitimate from the standpoint of Holy Scripture, Newman in a matter-of-course way held the opinion that he could rely on all those doctrines which are peculiar to the "Consensus Quinquesaecularis" despite the fact that they are not expressly mentioned in the BCP. Among the Church Fathers of the first five centuries, the time of the "pure and inerrant apostolic church," one can indeed find the starting point or nucleus of all such things as developed later on into unbiblical doctrine in the Roman Church. We have already mentioned the interpretation of Article VI[49] among the Thirty-nine Articles. This is of great consequence because here we have a genuine anti-Reformation interpretation contradicting the intention of Article VI which puts Holy Scripture on a pedestal as the "Rule of Faith."

Newman explains with reference to Article XXII of the Thirty-nine Articles that the article doesn't say anything against the doctrine of purgatory as such and that it doesn't say anything against the doctrine of indulgences and against the doctrine of the veneration of pictures as such. The article is only directed against the genuine Roman Catholic interpretation of that time. The same is true with respect to the invocation of the saints. Newman strongly emphasizes the word "Romish" in Article XXII which reads as follows:

> The *Romish* Doctrine concerning Purgatory, Pardons, Worshipping and Adoration, as well of Images as of Reliques, and also invocation of Saints, is a fond thing vainly invented, and grounded upon no warranty of Scripture, but rather repugnant to the Word of God.[50]

Newman can thus say:

> None of these doctrines does the Article condemn; any of them may be held by the Anglo-Catholic as a matter of private belief.[51]

In the course of his explanations Newman refers to the great Church Fathers Augustine and Cyprian strictly in accordance with the "Consensus Quinquesaecularis" conception:

> On the other hand, the Council of Trent, and Augustine and Cyprian, so far as they express or imply any opinion approximating to that of the Council, held Purgatory to be a place for believers, not unbelievers, . . . may gain pardon, but where those who have already been pardoned in this life, may be cleansed and purified for beholding the face of God.[52]

With respect to the veneration of pictures and relics Newman holds to the opinion that this deals only with the prohibition of the improper use of those practices such as perhaps flourish in vulgar Catholicism. The Article never forbids the veneration of pictures and relics as such. He bases his authority upon a citation from the work of the Church Father Ambrosius.[53]

Invocation of saints is legitimate. Newman refers to the Psalms where angels too are apparently invoked:

> By "invocation" here is not meant the mere circumstance of addressing beings out of sight, because we use the Psalms in our daily service, which are frequent in invocations of Angels to praise and bless God.[54]

Article XXII thus is only opposed to an abuse which would consist in adoration of saints. Newman also quotes Bellarmine, a well-known Jesuit, in order to demonstrate the legitimate conception of the invocation of saints right down the line of article XXII. Bellarmine bases his opinion on Gregory of Nazianzen. The text of Bellarmine cited by Newman may be quoted in part:

> However, it must be observed, when we say, that nothing should be asked of saints but their prayers for us, the question is not about the words, but the sense of the words. For, as far as words go, it is lawful to say: "St. Peter, pity me, save me, open for me the gate of heaven . . . also grant me this or that by thy prayers and merits." For so speaks Gregory Nazianzen, and many others of the ancients.[55]

In his opinion on Article XXXVII,[56] where it says, among other things: "The Bishop of Rome hath no jurisdiction in this realm of England," Newman makes the assertion by way of interpretation that the Bishop of Rome, the Pope, isn't the center of ecclesiastical unity but that he is at least a primus inter pares:

> Bishop is superior to bishop only in rank, not in real power; and the Bishop of Rome, the head of the Catholic world, is not the centre of unity, except as having a primacy of order.[57]

Newman implies in this statement that the Roman bishop has a position of preeminence within the Catholic world to which in accordance with Tractarian concepts the Ecclesia Anglicana also belongs. In his attitude toward Article XXXVII Newman also expresses an important point in his understanding of the church which never harmonizes with the ecclesiology advocated in Article XIX:

> Each diocese is a perfect independent Church, sufficient for itself; and the communion of Christians one with another, and the unity of them altogether, lie, not in a mutual understanding, intercourse, and combination, but in what they are and have in common, in their possession of the Succession, their Episcopal form, their Apostolical faith, and the use of the Sacraments.[58]

According to the ecclesiology of Article XIX it is clearly stated that the visible church of Christ consists in the fellowship of believers, in which the pure Word of God is preached and the sacraments distributed according to the instruction of Jesus:

> The visible Church of Christ is a congregation of faithful men, in the which

the pure Word of God is preached, and the sacraments be duly ministered according to Christ's ordinance.[59]

In his "Conclusion" to Tract XC Newman says in an unequivocal way what he wants to get at with his interpretation:

> In the first place, it is a duty which we owe both to the Catholic Church and to our own, to take our reformed confessions in the most Catholic sense they will admit; we have no duties toward their framers. . . . In giving the Articles a Catholic interpretation, we bring them into harmony with the Book of Common Prayer.[60]

By revealing this attitude of Newman towards the BCP through his statements referring to portions of the Thirty-nine Articles we wanted to give only a small sample of his theological misinterpretation of the BCP.

Today it is fashionable, particularly in ecumenical theology, to use Biblical terms but to fill them with another meaning. This occurs to a large degree in the exegesis of a political and social-revolutionary theology which takes its orientation from "contextuality."[61]

B. FRUIT OF THE OXFORD MOVEMENT IN THE NINETEENTH AND AT THE START OF THE TWENTIETH CENTURIES

1. THE BCP FURNISHED WITH LUSTRE LEADS TO REVIVAL

We affirmed in Section A that The Oxford Movement had a great love for the BCP of 1662 and wanted also to preserve it without external changes. Its misinterpretation of the English book of liturgy in a Catholic sense and the Anglo-Catholic literature required a lengthy period of incubation before the theological consequences intended by the exponents of Tractarianism became visible and conspicuous.

Since The Book of Common Prayer found great acknowledgment among High-Churchmen due to Newman's Catholic interpretation they therefore propagated it among rural and urban congregations. For many committed High-Churchmen it was of great concern that a renewal should take place among the church people through a truly spiritual life.

Many Anglo-Catholics possessed no spiritual discernment in regard to those theological switches which had been thrown by Newman, Keble, and Pusey. Most had mainly a vision of a spiritual renewal through ceremonial embellishments of the liturgy which came to its realization chiefly in the second phase of The Oxford Movement, in so-called ritualism.

There were many ritualists who were well-acquainted with the figure of John Wesley and who wanted to learn from him. They could learn from Wesley how people can become renewed in a spiritual way. Wesley thought highly of the prayer book and the sacrament of holy communion. As Dieter Voll has demonstrated, High Church features[62] were characteristic of Wesley. These High Church elements in Wesley's theology led many Tractarians to think highly of the great revivalistic preacher of the eighteenth century.

It is probable that Wesley received the essential impulses for a revivalistic theology from The Book of Common Prayer. We want to introduce a few High Church theologians who in a revivalistic sense promoted a spiritual renewal in their congregations wholly in accordance with the spirit of the BCP.

a. Robert Aitken (1800-1873)

This pastor of Pendeen (Cornwall) emphasized in his sermons the necessity for conversion. At the same time he laid great store upon the frequent taking of the sacrament. Of interest are his lay missions with associated prayer meetings organized by him in the schoolhouses of various places. C. Bodington reported on these prayer meetings based on his own memory:

> Here it was, where the last effort would be made for the persuasion of the individual souls for a conscious union with Christ and to bring them to an open declaration of conversion and a firm belief in their salvation. Among the congregation continuous free prayers would be uttered and hymns sung while the missionary and his collaborators, priest and laiety, men and women, moved among the kneeling figures and urged them to surrender to the firm assurance to share their experience and to confirm the acceptance of their salvation.[63]

b. Richard Twigg (1825-1879)

Twigg was active as a slum-pastor in Wednesbury. He intensified the liturgical life through daily matins or Morning Prayer and Evening Prayer.

He nursed the liturgy given in the BCP with much care. For that reason he was accused before the local bishop with being a ritualist.

D. Voll wrote of Twigg:

> Each Sunday morning at 6 a.m. steel and mine workers met at the pastor's office for a prayer meeting and to prepare for the following celebration of the sacraments.[64]

The same author says in reference to the sermons:

> Twigg's sermons are models of evangelical preaching in the old style. They are, using the modern term, fundamentalistic; they preach a clear-cut Gospel: "Think upon death, the last judgment, heaven and hell and on eternity—think thereon, that you are a sinner, a dying sinner, and still unsaved—and pray that before death cuts you down you may have made your peace with God!"[65]

Twigg encouraged the members of his congregation in confirmation class to practice free prayer.

c. George Howard Wilkinson (1833-1907)

He belongs among the most prominent figures of High Church pietism. Wilkinson occupied the office of bishop in Truro. Prior to achieving this honourable position, Wilkinson had worked successfully among the coal miners. He saw as one of his main functions the organization of great evangelizations for which the parish of Bishop Auckland with its 12,000 souls offered him ample opportunity. Much is known of the particulars about Wilkinson's preparation for an evangelization or lay mission.

Wilkinson involved the core of his congregation in regular prayer and in active missionary work. One can understand from the following memorandum of Wilkinson how his staff of coworkers recruited from the core of his congregation were to behave during an evangelization:

> Keep an eye out for souls that have been touched. . . . Pray during the meeting. When I say it, go and kneel by a soul. Help him to speak to God. Repeat what is in the sermon. . . . Push no one toward the faith; give yourself time. Tell what the Lord has done.[66]

Wilkinson also had much to do in his London parish with alcoholics and prostitutes. For that reason he sought to reach the people through street sermons. However, he arranged his approach to the destitute in the street in a dignified High Church-like way, for a ceremonial procession of the choir marched ahead with the processional cross in the lead.

D. Voll tells us pertinently how very strongly Wilkinson kept the interests of a living congregation at heart:

> As though against a rigid church tradition of protestant stamp he provided step by step room for free prayer and for a sacramental life. Evening after evening his church was open for prayer meetings in accordance with the evangelical tradition; and morning after morning he celebrated Holy Communion at the altar. In that way Wilkinson confined himself strictly to the formulas of the common prayer book. . . . Early and late the goal of his pastoral duties was the conversion of individual men to the beginning of a new life in the body of Christ.[67]

For Wilkinson the BCP is but the necessary outgrowth of the Biblical and church message.

d. Arthur H. Stanton (1839-1913)

This priest was for much of his life the assistant pastor at St. Alban's. He concentrated in particular upon the working population. His special merit is that he knew how to articulate what the other evangelical High-Churchmen took as a matter of course. This meant a fellowship of believers regardless of denomination. Thus Stanton said in an address to the young candidates for holy orders at Oxford:

> Instruct not your church members therein, to be Church of England— instruct them therein to have love for the Lord! . . . The disarray of the Church of God is there so that we do not ascribe too much importance to the outer conditions of its existence.[68]

Stanton wrote in a letter to a Benedictine:

> All who love and revere the Redeemer must find one another in Him.[69]

D. Voll says also with justice:

> Stanton's heart beat warmer for the nonconformists than for Rome.

Stanton had no inhibitions, preaching even to nonconformist congregations.[70]

However he was by conviction a confession-hearing and celebrating priest at St. Alban's where evangelical sermons and fiery revivalistic hymns belonged as a matter of course to the services.

2. THE OXFORD MOVEMENT LEADS TO THE FORMATION OF MONASTIC BROTHERHOODS AND SISTERHOODS

a. The Community of the Epiphany in Truro

It was the important clergyman George Howard Wilkinson (1833-1907) who because of his High Church evangelical conscience was the founder of a sisterhood, namely the Community of the Epiphany in Truro.[71]

In his book *The Silent Rebellion* A. M. Allchin referred pointedly to the connexion between the Wesleyan revivalistic spirit and the foundation of monastic communities within the Church of England when he wrote:

> The conversion of 1738 revolutionized the Wesleys' methods and outlook, but it left the substance of their faith not radically altered, as their hymns and the books which they published show. Their aim was christian perfection, they spoke much of prayer without ceasing. Much of the longing for christian holiness, the desire to preach the gospel to the poor, the practice for more and frequent communion, which in the 19th century found expression in the religious communities, in the 18th century went into the methodist movement.[72]

The sisters of the Community of the Epiphany observe the divine offices, besides which they organize retreats for visitors for spiritual strengthening. The sisters teach Sunday school in the neighborhood and also maintain an old people's home. The sisters also take particular care to make intercessory prayer based on concerns which are shared with the sisterhood by those outside. An important financial help for the sisterhood is the manufacture of the host for holy communion.

b. The Society of St. John the Evangelist[73]

The principal founder of this brotherhood was R. M. Benson. His concern was especially to win clergymen so that they might live together under monastic rules and let themselves be equipped for missionary work in the working class district of Oxford. Benson succeeded in carrying out his plan. The celibate clergy of the Society of St. John the Evangelist (Cowley Fathers) tried in an evangelistic way to call people of the lower class to follow Jesus at a time when R. M. Benson's spirit had still a powerful influence. In addition the "Cowley Fathers" considered it their duty to receive students so that they could during their period of study live under spiritual rule. The principal objective of the society of St. John the Evangelist was formulated as follows:

> The object of the Society of St. John the Evangelist was, "to seek that sanctification to which God in his mercy calls us, and in so doing to seek, as far as God may permit, to be instrumental in bringing others to be partakers of the same sanctification."[74]

Over one hundred monastic-like brother and sister communities came into existence within the Church of England due to the animation of The Oxford Movement.[75] The two communities mentioned are typical in their concept of most of the other monastic-like communities. The light of the Gospel has been carried in a Biblical sense to the people and into the schools through the undertaking of these Anglican monastics. These "religious communities" have again placed on a pedestal important aspects of Christian living: a sanctified way of life, readiness for sacrifice in service to one's neighbors, a disciplined prayer life from the point of view of laud, worship, and intercession as well as spiritual studies. Fellowship played a significant role in those cloisters.

3. QUESTIONS AND CONCLUSIONS

Since it is established that John Wesley had a high regard for The Book of Common Prayer, is it not then likely for that reason that he with his revivalistic attitude is a product of this common prayer book of the year 1662? Hasn't John Wesley, in the office of a megaphone, simply proclaimed with power the substance of the BCP of 1662 to the common people?

Those High-Churchmen who relied on Wesley have discovered in his "method" of the spiritual life a practical discipline and they must have noted that a usable discipline is provided in Morning and Evening Prayer for one's devotional life, which could be extended to the seven traditional offices of the monastic tradition.

Because of the propaganda of the leading Tractarian theologians designed to keep the prayer book unaltered and to protect its liturgy, the Word of God which is so strongly integrated in the BCP of 1662 had an opportunity to have an impact on the nation. The BCP as one of the most important factors for establishing order in the English church was bound to bring forth its fruit even if Tractarianism was to be the instrument for a temporary strengthening of the liturgy book in a very critical situation in the nineteenth century. Dieter Voll addresses this point when he says:

> Time and again the evangelical appeal makes good its penetration—although not with polemics against the regulations of the church but much more often as a result of these regulations![76]

The High Church movement with its emphasis on the church as a juridical entity had its significance as long as the right interpretation was there. The revivalistically oriented theologians whom we have briefly introduced also understood the church as a juridical entity which to some extent draws externally a line of demarcation within which the true congregation of Jesus can develop under legal protection while this external framework should also hold together the true congregation.

Despite the many positive aspects of The Oxford Movement we should not forget that through the theology of Newman, Keble, and Pusey, whose features[77] we have already sketched, dangerous points of departure were created which provided provocation for a later continuation. That revival in a Biblical sense could come into existence through The Oxford Movement despite these features with their dangerous points of departure is what we desire to explain. We should not forget that the Tractarian Movement wanted to preserve The Book of Common Prayer as a factor of order for the sake of unity. Nevertheless a liturgical book with its emphasis on Biblical-Reformation theology had to bring forth its good fruit in accordance with the principle of Isaiah 55:10-11, that God's Word does not return void. The High Church theologians especially stressed the liturgies with those elements which accord with the criterion of the "Consensus Quinquesaecularis." That this liturgy of the BCP is at the same time very Biblical was for the High-Churchmen merely an accident. Holy Scripture placed on a pedestal in the BCP is not the principal unifying factor, but rather those liturgical elements[78] contained in the common prayer book which accord with the "Consensus Quinquesaecularis." We encounter here a principle which we want to call the "cut flower principle." Cut flowers bloom and are beautiful for a certain amount of time but after a few days they wither away in contrast to potted plants which keep their roots and therefore bring forth new buds.

The Book of Common Prayer with its Biblical content could still bring forth fruit because it was placed on a pedestal by the High-Churchmen of the nineteenth century. But in the long run The Book of Common Prayer could not maintain its high position because the roots of the prayer book, i.e., Holy Scripture, had been attacked through unbiblical interpretation. From that point of view we must look upon the revival of that time within The Oxford Movement as a kind of cut flower, a bud, produced by the evangelistic spirit within the BCP, which, although it bloomed for a while was destined to wither because its animating evangelistic spirit had been detached from its roots in "Sola Scriptura" and "Scriptura sui ipsius Interpres."

In the next section we undertake the task of sketching the further development of Anglo-Catholic theology based on the statements of its proponents.

C. CHARLES GORE AND *LUX MUNDI* AS WELL AS WILLIAM TEMPLE COMPOSE THE SYNTHESIS

1. INTRODUCTORY REMARKS

The points of departure provided by the Tractarians in their theology led to a further development of their doctrines by certain prominent theologians who understood themselves as advocates of the Anglo-Catholic heritage. The most significant figure among those theologians was Charles Gore who was the first principal of the library of Anglo-Catholic literature which had been erected in honor of Pusey. This library is the famous "Pusey House" situated in Oxford which was founded in the eighties of the last century.

Charles Gore located a number of outstanding theologians of the Tractarian persuasion who then began to write theological essays within the continuity of the High Church doctrine. Gore brought these essays together in a well-known and very influential collected volume under the title of *Lux Mundi*,[79] which was published in 1889. The most important contributors to *Lux Mundi* were H. S. Holland, A. Moore, J. R. Illingworth, E. S. Talbot, and R. C. Moberly. These theologians delineated and developed the following structural elements of Anglo-Catholicism, of which we only name a few of the most important: a strong emphasis on incarnation, the idea of development, tradition, and the church as an organizational-sacramental unity.

Prior to *Lux Mundi* Tractarians had set forth an antithesis with respect to The Book of Common Prayer in such a way that they disassociated themselves from the Reformation thinking of the common prayer book.

Lux Mundi on the other hand composes a synthesis in the sense that The Book of Common Prayer is retained with its Anglo-Catholic interpretation but now as a new factor is added the affirmation of the historical-critical method. It was understood that the Reformation[80] was to be given credit for this historical-critical method. We leave undecided whether or not this coincides with the facts. As has been previously mentioned, Tractarians vehemently opposed Biblical criticism.

2. SEVERAL EXAMPLES OF THE CONTINUATION OF TRACTARIAN TRACES IN *LUX MUNDI*

The theological opinions expressed in *Lux Mundi* had an impact upon Anglican spirituality for more than half a century and created new points of departure which led to extreme positions. These further extreme positions ultimately became the factors which triggered an attempt at a radical revision of The Book of Common Prayer.

In his book *From Gore to Temple* Michael Ramsey writes pointedly about the authors and propagandists of the ideas of *Lux Mundi*:

> They were men of synthesis, who could enable many to be "glad because they were at rest." Here were seen to be united the piety and churchmanship of the Tractarians and the critical spirit. . . . Here was the use of contemporary philosophy and a faith drawn from the Bible and the Fathers. . . . Here was a religion marked by the otherworldly spirit, which soon led to the creation of the Community of the Resurrection, no less than the alert social conscience which created the Christian Social Union.[81]

Some conceptions reference incarnation should be briefly treated.

a. Incarnation and Development

Incarnation and development are looked upon in *Lux Mundi* as having a close connexion with each other. J. R. Illingworth sees incarnation as the most central world historical event. The incarnation as a presupposition to the atoning death of Jesus is rejected by *Lux Mundi* theologians. Thus Illingworth writes the following as a criticism of the Reformation conception:

> The Reformers, from various causes, were so occupied with what is now

called Soteriology, or the scheme of salvation, that they paid but scant attention to the other aspects of the Gospel . . . and the religion of the incarnation was narrowed into the religion of the atonement.[82]

The main point of the coming of Jesus is thus not the reconciliation of man to God, but much more the consecration of the whole universe to God. Illingworth thinks that the Church Fathers saw the incarnation in that perspective:

They realized that redemption was a means to an end, and that end the reconsecration of the whole universe to God.[83]

Since the incarnation consecrates the universe, in a way therefore all the developments within this world are also sanctified. He has in mind all the different areas like politics, philosophy, theology, ethics, economics, etc. To generalize, Illingworth says:

We can conceive no phase of progress which has not the Incarnation for its guiding star.[84]

R. C. Moberly in his essay "The Incarnation as the Basis of Dogma" states that the church is the continuation of Jesus' incarnation. The dogma created by the church must be so structured that it adapts itself to the world. Therefore Moberly can say a sentence of great consequence:

The Church of Christ is balanced, harmonious, all-embracing, all-adjusting.[85]

In this "Complexio Oppositorum" which is expressed in the term "all-embracing" in the quotation above, there is enormous field.

Michael Ramsey comments on this incarnation theology of the theologians of *Lux Mundi* as follows:

Furthermore, the doctrine of the Incarnate Christ as the Logos gave a constant impulse towards relating the incarnation, wherever possible, with contemporary movements in thought or social progress.[86]

b. Church and Tradition

Charles Gore emphasizes the external visibility of the church. The church isn't held together only through the Holy Spirit but instead chiefly through external institutions. To these absolutely necessary external institutions belong, among other things, apostolic succession and the continuity with the old undivided church. In Gore's opinion it is peculiar to the catholicity of the English church to promote the organizational reunion of the different Christian denominations into the one undivided church. Gore calls this "Christian reunion." One of the most important factors for the reunion of Christian churches must be the acknowledgment of the apostolic succession. One is born into the true catholic church in which baptism is indispensable.

3. CONTINUATION OF THE THEOLOGY OF *LUX MUNDI* THROUGH WILLIAM TEMPLE

William Temple (1881-1944) became one of the most influential theologians of the Church of England after the First World War. As Archbishop of Canterbury he was taken very seriously by the generation of theologians of his time. Temple confessed that Charles Gore was one of his most important theological teachers. Temple took over the strong emphasis on the doctrine of incarnation as modified by Gore, and developed it further. The process philosophy of Hegel had a strong impact on Temple's thinking.[87] Therefore he could make utterances of great import like perhaps those in his work, *Nature, Man and God*, where he says:

> Unless all existence is a medium of revelation, no particular revelation is possible. . . . Either all occurrences are in some degree revelations of God, or else there is no such revelation at all.[88]

When Temple says "there are no revealed propositions" and "it is incorrect to speak of revealed truths,"[89] then indeed we have here clear points of departure for a pluralistic-relativistic theology.

It is William Temple who endorsed Gore's idea of the necessity for a reunion of the divided Christian denominations into the one undivided church and who also took the first steps in that direction. Temple belonged to the most important cofounders of the ecumenical council of which he became first president of the provisional board. Temple was a master of the theological synthesis. His brilliancy in original thinking and thinking devoted to the world added a lot to bring his church along the "broad way."

4. THE BCP OF 1927/28[90]

We do not intend to inquire deeply into this prayer book. But this much should be said that the Tractarian theology of the early phase as well as of the late phase and the modern continuation of Anglo-Catholicism in the spirituality of *Lux Mundi* gave the impetus toward a prayer book of synthesis. By 1927 a point had been reached that a prayer book could be presented which was very similar to the BCP of 1549. However Parliament did not accept this prayer book of compromises.

D. THE ANGLO-CATHOLIC ELEMENTS CONVERTED THROUGH JOHN ROBINSON INTO A RADICALLY MODERNISTIC THEOLOGY, AS BACKGROUND TO THE EXPERIMENTAL LITURGIES AND THE ASB 1980

SOME IMPORTANT CHARACTERISTICS OF ROBINSON'S THEOLOGY

One can draw a straight line which runs from the fathers of Anglo-Catholicism to *Lux Mundi* and William Temple to Robinson. Robinson often refers back in his theological works to Temple. In order to sketch the most important features of the Robinson theology we rely on the following works: *The New Reformation? On Being the Church in the World, Honest to God,* and *Liturgy Coming to Life.*

In addition to the Anglo-Catholic background in Robinson's theology, one should not underestimate the influence of Bonhoeffer and Tillich. We now take up the task of sketching some Anglo-Catholic features of the Robinson development.

a. The Incarnation and Its Consequences

In *Liturgy Coming to Life* Robinson expresses ideas which draw from the incarnation of God's Son consequences with a very great impact. Thus he writes:

We forget the offence to the old religion contained in the very name "Holy

254

> Communion," the KOINONIA HAGION, "the making common of the holy." To the Jews that meant the desecration of the holy: to the Christian it meant the sanctification of the common. Such was the difference which the incarnation had made, when God himself had called all things holy; and it is this difference of which the sacraments are the standing embodiment and reminder. But for this reason they remain, or should remain, a standing offence to any mentality that would still like to drive a wedge between the holy and the common.[91]

The incarnation sanctifies the whole present world because Jesus has entered this world. The incarnation is for Robinson the consecration of the world and therefore any difference between the profane and the sacred no longer exists. Robinson sees in the incarnation the duty to secularize the Christian liturgy, especially holy communion. Why? Because the incarnate Logos presents itself in the communion service in the very worldly signs of bread and wine and thereby gives the call for action in the world and for the world. Jesus gave the task for the action with the words: "This do in remembrance of me."[92] Jesus enters this world because, according to Robinson, the horizontal dimension is central. The sacred which is embodied in Jesus has to dissolve itself in the world like salt in order to change a world accepted by God and sanctified through the incarnation, in the sense of the realization of more human structures. This becomes clear in Robinson's own words:

> The Holy Communion is the great workshop of the new world, where the "we who are many" are recreated as the true, the new community in Christ.[93]

Robinson becomes even clearer when he writes:

> The Eucharist, as the Christian action from which all other Christian action flows, is the most political act to which the Church sets its hand. As we expressed it at the end of our Communion Manual, "The sharing of bread, concluded now sacramentally, must be continued socially—and hence economically and politically."[94]

In order to let the holy communion liturgy become effective as the "great workshop of the new world" a desecration needs to take place in the sense that the phenomenology of the sacred and the supernatural is annulled. This happens in this wise, that an ordinary meal takes place in a secular room with cups and plates instead of chalice and paten:

> Nevertheless, it is only by some such symbol that we may recognize that the barrier has been broken down in our own minds, that the Holy Meal is

the Common Meal, and that this Common Meal is continuous with every other common meal. Indeed, so powerful is the psychological barrier built up by centuries of thinking of the Holy Communion primarily as a "service" rather than a meal, that vast numbers of people, I am convinced, are simply not going to "see" this at all, until they see the Eucharist taken from time to time out of the sanctuary altogether and "done" on the kitchen table, if necessary with ordinary cups and saucers.[95]

Robinson sees something proper in that communicants should use the strength given them in the eucharist in the form of love and respect for their fellow men also during a secular common meal. But Robinson overlooks the distinction made by Paul between the eucharist and ordinary food. Annulment of the sacred[96] phenomenology leads very easily to the loss of its challenging character as a sign of the proclamation of the Good News which the sacrament should be. What is meant is that challenge or impulse which, thanks to the sacred demarcations, makes one aware of the difference between the divine and the fallen earthly realm. Indeed Robinson has in mind the salvation of this world and the relevance of the Gospel for this earth by means of liturgy. Robinson can even speak of the evangelistic function of liturgy:

I have insisted that liturgy, true and relevant worship, lies at the very heart of its evangelistic task, and that the Holy Communion is the creative centre of the whole life of the people of God.[97]

Robinson can also write:

It is the Holy Communion supremely that the Gospel is shown forth: liturgy is the heart of evangelism.[98]

But Robinson has an essentially different understanding of evangelization from what has been understood under the traditional sense of that term. Evangelization is essentially that mission which promotes the conversion to the world and undertakes its consecration through social action. The catalyst for the consecration of the world is the eucharist liturgy:

Now if the Eucharist is thus the heart and hub of social action, the point where this world is taken and consecrated, broken and restored for God and his kingdom and where the Church itself is renewed as the agent of the Christian revolution, then we must learn again what the early Church meant when it spoke naturally of "doing the Eucharist."[99]

It is the world as a collective of human beings who have to be changed and become revolutionized in their structures. This does not refer

256

to individual men separated from God, who need to grasp the proffered salvation in Jesus due to his atoning death through penance and the act of a living faith. According to Robinson the church is not seen as a fellowship of single believing individuals but as a given corporation in which one becomes incorporated through baptism. Because of that conception Robinson[100] reaches a negative attitude toward The Book of Common Prayer, especially with respect to the Holy Communion Service. This is individualistic and pietistic and has nothing to do with this world. Robinson's question is: what can work a positive impression on the outside and what can demonstrate a Gospel in action which challenges and changes the kingdoms of this world? The Holy Communion Service of The Book of Common Prayer of 1662 isn't able to make such an impression on the outsider. Thus J. A. T. Robinson then writes:

> If, as a layman, one really wanted to show men the Gospel in action, the manner by which the kingdoms of this world were being challenged and reduced by the transforming power of God and his Christ, would one immediately point them to the sacrament of Holy Communion as administered in one's own Church? Would this be one's working model of the Gospel? That was the question I found myself asking. . . . In fact, I began to realize with dismay that anyone looking at the typical "Anglican eight o'clock"[101] of my own tradition might naturally suppose that this was how I understood the Gospel. It was, in fact, about the last embodiment of it to which I should have wished to point them. For there could hardly be anything that would strike them as more individualistic, more pietistic, more unrelated to the stuff and muck of the world where the redemption is meant to be taking place."[102]

In addition Robinson objects that the traditional Book of Common Prayer concentrates in a one-sided way on the atoning death of Christ:

> The Prayer Book liturgy is indeed, seriously inadequate, focusing attention solely on Calvary and its propitiation for sin.[103]

For Robinson the healing of society and the world doesn't happen through a conversion and change of single individuals, but the healing occurs through an act of the collective which is the church as a corporate entity. In this connexion, with Robinson the term "corporate" plays an immense role. Robinson's doctrine of the incarnation has a decisive influence with regards to the sacraments. The incarnation is most of all relevant for this earthly life and therefore the sacraments are the extended arm of the church, which is the continued incarnation of Christ, and its instrument for changing the world.[104] One should not ignore the fact that

Robinson seldom speaks of the self-activity of the Biblical Word which changes human hearts by the witness of Holy Scripture. Therefore the eucharist with its corporate structure is more than the Word and possesses a world-changing power:

> Yet of all earthly things upon which we can be engaged the Eucharist is the most practical. Do we really want a new and better world? Then this is the great solvent of the old, transforming it by divine alchemy into the new.[105]

With respect to participation in holy communion nothing is said about one's personal condition of faith nor of the danger that one can take the eucharist also to his own judgment. Although Robinson does not rely in reference to holy communion on a power in the sense of an "Ex opere Operato"—he is very critical about medieval Catholicism—nevertheless this "Ex Opere Operato" essentially is there when he says:

> The forces of the risen life are released, and a hang-dog collection of men becomes galvanized into the new community of the Body of Christ.[106]

It isn't God's Word which creates the church, but rather the eucharist.

> The Eucharist is that which creates, and constantly recreates, the Church.[107]

b. Development

We have already noted in the early phases of Tractarianism the idea of the potential for development within God's Word and the dogma.[108] In *Lux Mundi* there is even to be found some sympathy for the Darwinian theory of evolution. The theory of development then is to be applied not only to the Word of Scripture and dogma but also to men as "homo sapiens" and "homo faber."

In his book *The New Reformation?*[109] Robinson makes the point that the process of coming of age has set in among men and due to this state of having come of age God is no longer necessary as a presupposition for our thinking. Robinson expresses this as follows: "God is intellectually superfluous,"[110] which means that God is not necessary for the solution of our questions in regard to the meaning of life. In order to survive morally, in order to keep our emotions in balance, God can be eliminated as a factor of comfort. According to Robinson it can be said that "God is emotionally dispensable."[111] In order to provide ethics with a foundation one can easily do without God, which Robinson expresses in the following way: "God is morally intolerable."[112]

The influence of Bonhoeffer is obvious here, but also the development concept which presents man of the period of the Reformation as being childish in contrast to the secularized man of the modern age. Robinson explains what he means by a man who has come of age when he writes:

> Man is discovering that he no longer needs God or religion. He finds that he can stand on his own feet without having to refer constantly to Daddy in the background or to run to Mummy's apron-strings.[113]

For Robinson it is naive to rely upon the providence of God and to receive from his hands burdens such as sicknesses. For Robinson such thinking leads to irresponsibility vis-à-vis the world. In this connexion Robinson quotes The Book of Common Prayer of 1662 and criticizes its theodicy:

> Most traditional theodicy, so far from justifying the ways of God to man, has the effect of strengthening atheism. "Whatever your sickness is," the priest is instructed to say in the seventeenth-century Anglican Book of Common Prayer, "know certainly that it is God's visitation." Who could speak like that today? Atheism has done its purifying work. . . . One of the liberating effects of secularization is that this idea of causation has at any rate been discredited.[114]

The coming of age of man is the result of a development. A mankind come of age desires secularization according to Robinson. Only secularization can bring man to the point of devoting his entire time to the renewal of the world.

We can see now how, according to Robinson, secularization is to be understood in detail. Man who has come of age desires a new Reformation. Robinson sketches the old Reformation in the following way:

> There lies the difference. The old Reformation revolved around Luther's agonized question and his triumphant liberating answer: "By faith alone!" It released to men the gracious God. It began from revelation, and centered characteristically in the doctrine of election. And this for that age was the pure gospel. As the Thirty-Nine Articles put it, ecstatically: "The godly consideration of Predestination, and our Election in Christ, is full of sweet, pleasant, and unspeakable comfort" (Article XVII).[115]

And now Robinson displays the progress of modern man who is approaching maturity, in which he reveals the point of departure for the New Reformation:

> For the fact remains that to larger and larger members of our generation this

259

is simply not gospel,[116] it evokes no sense of good news, however purely the Word is preached and however duly the Sacraments are administered. And a Church which is identified with this function becomes progressively more irrelevant. For the world is not asking "How can I find a gracious God?" It is asking "How can I find a gracious neighbor?"[117]

For Robinson this changed situation has to be taken very seriously. This situation is man's belief in the horizontal line. Therefore Robinson confesses:

Fundamentally I believe that we can and must accept this new starting-point. In other words we must recognize the fact that Man's question is in the first instance about man and not about God.[118]

As a first order of business a Biblically disciplined theology is not striven for, but rather, an anthropology detached from Scripture. From such a presupposition the church can no longer proclaim absolute truth. Therefore Robinson denies the church the right to issue catechisms. The new Reformation has to propagate a church which takes upon itself an agenda with the subjects under discussion those required by the world and not by the Bible. In short, the house of God is not the church but instead the world.

We let these ideas of Robinson speak for themselves:

Once again, the house of God is not the Church but the world. . . . What happens if we really take seriously the fact that the world must be allowed to "write the agenda" (not the minutes!), and that the Church must take shape round the needs of the world?[119]

Catechisms which originated within the old Reformation church contradict men who have come of age:

I doubt if the New Reformation will produce any catechisms, for the whole assumption on which they rest is being undermined. It is not the Church which puts its question and waits to hear its answers returned to it. It is the world that puts the questions—and refuses to accept any prefabricated answers.[120]

For Robinson solidarity with modern man is very important from the point of view of the incarnation. An adaptation of the church to the self understanding of the so-called modern and matured man is an act of compassion, according to Robinson. According to Robinson's concept God is for the secularized and horizontally oriented modern man an experience of an I-thou relationship consisting of human encounters. Thus Robinson writes:

The man who finds himself compelled to acknowledge the reality of God, whatever he may call him or however he may image him, is the man . . . who is met by the same grace and the same claim that he recognizes in the I-Thou relation with another person. It may come to him through nature, through the claims of artistic integrity or scientific truth, through the engagements of social justice or of personal communion.[121]

In order to offer a legitimate place to men who have unclear ideas about God and whose ideas contradict the Reformation confessions, obviously a church with a pluralistic understanding of truth is demanded. Such a church needs to have an openness and a room for the "Complexio Oppositorum." Robinson calls this church of the new Reformation "the latent church." He picks up a definition from Tillich which is characteristic of the new church conception. Robinson writes, quoting Tillich:

> The latent Church is an indefinite historical group which within paganism, Judaism or humanism actualizes the New Being, while the manifest Church is a definite historical group in which the New Being is actualized directly and manifestly.[122]

Commenting on Tillich, Robinson now goes further:

> In its latent form of existence it may not be organized, it may not be able to say "Lord, Lord," and within it the pure Word of God is certainly not preached nor the Sacraments duly ministered. And yet it may be nearer the truth to view it as the latent Church than as the godless world.[123]

With these explanations we wanted to present in cursory fashion the ideological conception of the so-called matured and secularized man as Robinson sees him. As a result this "maturity" and secularization has to be understood as the outcome of a development from bottom to top.

c. Demythologizing for the Purpose of Concentrating on the World

Robinson is of the opinion that a demythologizing needs to take place with respect to the heavenly world. A hope for life after death does not belong to the essentials of the Bible. The kingdom of God is first of all a reality of the here and now, although only in a symbolic way. According to Robinson the Bible is interpreted in the correct way if one discerns between the present and the coming eon. The coming eon is nothing less than the renewal of the world which is taking place already, in the here and now. Heaven as a gathering place of all the ones saved by faith who are waiting in an intermediate state until the "new heaven and the new earth" comes is for Robinson irrelevant. But isn't this conception of a heavenly reality in the sense of the hereafter as the abode for the redeemed ones until the coming of the new heaven and the new earth Biblical doctrine, as well as Hell which is the eternal abode for the lost?[124]

It is significant that Robinson gives a horizontal interpretation to Biblical statements that are intended to be understood in a vertical sense, which is in his opinion legitimate demythologizing. From this viewpoint it follows that Philippians 3:20 would be thus interpreted by him:

> For preaching the Gospel in the categories in which Jesus himself preached it is preaching the Gospel of the Kingdom, of the sovereign rule of God over the whole range of human life. And it is this kingdom, or commonwealth, of which Christians are the citizens and ambassadors of "this world."[125]

Robinson gives Marxism credit when he says:

> Indeed the Marxist, with no belief in an after-life, is in a real sense closer to the biblical outlook than the Christian who pins everything upon it.[126]

His theology which is completely devoted to this world stands in the closest connexion with his anthropological starting point, that the immortality of the soul is nonsense. Robinson puts forward the following:

> Again, contrary to what is usually supposed, the doctrine of the immortality of the soul, properly speaking, finds no place in the Old Testament or the New.[127]

In connexion with this question it is especially helpful to consider Calvin's Biblically oriented discussion respecting the immortality of the soul.[128] Also consult the Heidelberg Catechism XXII:57.

Another conception of redemption also arises closely connected with the demythologizing of heaven by way of reducing it to a mere entity[129] of the here and now. The salvation of the soul is therefore nonsense and totally irrelevant. Conversion and salvation according to Robinson has to be understood as a social event:

> It is clear that neither mass conversion nor the saving of a man put and apart from his environment is nowadays possible or desirable . . . it is not possible because economically and socially it is only as a person and to become a person that today he can be saved if he is to be saved at all. This means that conversion must be, through and through, a community affair. For a man becomes a person when he discovers himself in the I-Thou relation of community, and in actual experience grasps with the

total response of his being that he has been made for, and has his centre in, other persons.[130]

According to Robinson, if the world as a secularized society has to give with its imaginations and propositions for solving its problems an agenda with the subjects under discussion to the church then conversion can mean nothing else than solidarity with the world and adaptation to the world with its potpourri of ideological, political, and ethical opinions.

For Robinson the earthly death is not an essential factor in the life of a Christian. It is not a warning to prepare oneself in order that one can meet his redeemer and saviour in a state of faith. In a derogatory way Robinson says:

> And traditional Protestant thought . . . has gone even further and held that at death a man passes beyond the need even of purgation or prayer. If he is among the elect he is at once made fit for communion with Christ; if he is not, he is out. Now few people, I suspect, really believe this today. . . . But the Bible never says that a man must be brought to Christ before he dies, or else.[131]

The fate of man according to Robinson is not decided before the end of this earthly life.[132]

Robinson becomes very clear in his demythologizing interpretation of the Last Judgment. This occurs in this life. The Last Judgment takes place continuously but it does not take place at a particular point in history where God holds a general settling of accounts, where the departed are also included. No; the Last Judgment is a continuous reality and occurs in the horizontal realm through one's fellowmen. Thus Robinson can say:

> In his mercy he judges us in this world not by confronting us with himself but by confronting us with our neighbour. . . . He comes to meet us in the neighbour, in the one whose sole claim upon us is simply that he is man—in the starving, the destitute, the suffering. Christ wills to judge us through them, to let them be our judges.[133]

Robinson states unequivocally:

> We must demythologize the Day of Judgement if we are to begin to commend it as a category of relevance to our world.[134]

The Last Judgment has already occurred through the coming of Jesus. Therefore the incarnation of Jesus is to be equated with the "Last Judgment":

> We have allowed ourselves to forget that the truth of the Last Judgement, as of every other Christian doctrine, is ultimately nothing else but the truth of the Incarnation.[135]

To let men become our judges means in its ultimate consequences that we have turned ourselves over to a reign of terror of an atheistic humanism which judges us without any mercy. Peter Beyerhaus shows us in his book *Aufbruch der Armen*[136] what it means, with its terrible consequences, to let ourselves be judged by the concepts of the political, economic, and ethical ideologies.

This conception of the "Last Judgment" also brings with it a demythologizing of the return of Christ.

Just as the fall of man was no historical event, just so the coming again of Christ has nothing to do with any historical event for which one should wait. Thus Robinson holds to the following opinion:

> A deeper understanding of biblical revelation indicates, surely, that it is just as mistaken to see the Parousia as a single datable event of future history as it is to see the Fall as a single datable event of past history.[137]

The coming again of Christ also occurs, according to Robinson, not as an event here from the heavenly world where Jesus apparently dwells. It is an event which happens in various ways time and again in the here and now. Thus Robinson says:

> What are we watching for? It is pious humbug to say that we are watching for the Second Coming, if when the Lord comes, as the New Testament interpretation of the fall of Jerusalem makes clear, in what often seem purely secular and political issues, in those signs of the present time which Jesus said his contemporaries could not read. . . . Everywhere, at any moment, Jesus comes in. That is what the doctrine of the Second Coming is concerned to assert.[138]

Another area which in accordance with Robinson needs demythologizing and secularizing is ethics. The demythologizing consists in a change from heteronomy to autonomy. The determining factor for ethical action is the situation of the moment, and not the question of the will of God. We want to let this be said in Robinson's own words:

> Love alone, because, as it were, it has a built-in moral compass, enabling it to "home" intuitively upon the deepest need of the other, can allow itself to be directed completely by the situation. It alone can afford to be utterly open to the situation, or rather to the person in the situation, uniquely and for his own sake . . . it is able to embrace an ethic of radical responsiveness, meeting every situation on its own merits, with no prescriptive laws.[139]

By way of summary we want to keep in mind the following in reference to Robinson's theology: the incarnation doctrine is used for the justification of secularization and demythologizing, while the theology is converted into anthropology. Secularization and demythologizing as well as the changing of theology into anthropology has one great goal: the radical conversion to the world. The mature man needs no supernatural or heavenly comfort. His task is only in this world and its society, which should be totally humanized.

The Biblical view of the world with its transitoriness and the concentration on the eternal and imperishable goals through the peace of God in a personal justification by faith is an anachronism of the man who has not matured.

Robinson uses and reflects Biblical terms regularly in such a way that these Biblical terms are given a horizontal trend. The world therefore is not a place where we walk as pilgrims in order to come afterwards by faith to the sight of eternal glory. For Robinson the goal of life is the transformation of this earth. There is no goal beyond this earthly life for which one should strive in obedience to prescriptive commands.

With this theology one shouldn't be astonished that the book *Honest to God* was welcomed as atheistic propaganda in the Communist East. Robinson also prides himself on the fact that his book *Honest to God* has been received with joy by Hindus and Buddhists.[140]

Following right along the line of Robinson there came into existence a collection of essays of a radically modernistic theology, the so-called *Soundings*, which Alec Vidler edited in 1962. Bishop Robinson and the *Soundings* may be seen as the trigger for the proclamation and popularizing of modern theology.

Peter Staples gives in his studies on the Church of England in the years 1961-1980 very great credit to the influence of Robinson and the *Soundings*. Let us give heed to the statement of Peter Staples:

> "Soundings" marks the surfacing of the debate about the New Theology and the New Morality amongst the English intellectuals. It was the Honest to God Debate, however, that carried these discussions into virtually every English household in which the daily papers are read. Furthermore, the proponents of these new ideas seemed to be standing orthodox christian theology on its head and turning the Church inside out.[141]

The experimental liturgies and The Alternative Service Book 1980 are unthinkable without this theological background of the Anglo-Catholic Movement and its further development in a combination with modern ideology.

E. EXPERIMENTAL LITURGY SECOND SERIES AND SERIES 3

Among the three alternative eucharistic experimental liturgies, known as First Series, Second Series, and Series 3, the First Series is still the closest to the traditional Book of Common Prayer. We intend to limit our research in the experimental liturgies to the eucharistic services and to concentrate on Second Series[142] and Series 3.[143]

The experimental liturgies mentioned are the immediate predecessors of The Alternative Service Book 1980.

1. PARTIAL ELIMINATION OF REFORMATION SUBSTANCE

a. Introductory Rubric

The introductory rubric with its urgent warning not to participate in the communion in the event of unsettled quarrels or of an unrepented dissolute manner of living, is lacking in both liturgies.

b. Ten Commandments

The Ten Commandments appear in both forms simply as optional matter in the Appendix.[144]

c. Nicene Creed

In Series 3 the Nicene Creed is expressed in the first person plural and no longer in the first person singular as is still the case in the BCP.[145]

d. Twenty Offertory Verses

The twenty offertory verses[146] are lacking in both liturgies.

e. Prayer for the Church Militant

The Prayer for the Church Militant is abbreviated in both liturgies, though chiefly in the Second Series.[147] We will go into the differences in the lit-

urgies later on. In the Second Series as in the third formula[148] the theme
of this prayer is preserved in part.

The following points are however lacking in these alternative liturgies:

(1) The mention of Holy Scripture as the datum point in the prayer for
    the unity of the church.
(2) The prayer for the clergy, that they through their life and doctrine
    set forth God's true and lively Word.
(3) The prayer for the congregation that it might receive God's Word
    with meek heart and due reverence.
(4) The express petition for the power of sanctification.

We compare the BCP in the above-mentioned points with the formulas in the Second Series and Series 3:

BCP[149]	Second Series[150]	Series 3[151]
	Under (1)	
"And grant, that all they that do confess thy holy Name may agree in the truth of *thy holy Word* and may live in unity and godly love."	"Grant that we who confess thy name may be united in thy truth, live together in love, and show forth thy glory in the world."	"Strengthen your church to carry forward the work of Christ; that we and all who confess your name may unite in your truth, live together in your love, and reveal your glory in the world."
	Under (2)[152]	
"Give grace, o heavenly Father, to all Bishops and Curates, that they may both by their life and doctrine set forth thy true and *lively Word* . . ."	lacking	lacking

Under (3)[153]

"And to all thy people give thy heavenly grace; and especially to this congregation here present; that with meek heart and due reverence; they may hear, and receive *thy holy Word;*"   lacking   lacking

Under (4)[154]

"truly serving thee in holiness and righteousness all the days of their life."   lacking   lacking

f. Exhortations

The exhortations which occupy such an important place in the BCP are missing from both alternative communion services.

g. The Confessions in Both Formulas

The confessions of both formulas are substantially shorter than those of the BCP. The confession in the Second Series[155] is especially terse. The following points found in the traditional BCP are not present in the confessions of the Second Series and Series 3:

(1) The conception of God as judge.[156]
(2) The conception of sin as lese-majesty towards God.[157]
(3) The idea of sin as the innate condition of men[158] which provokes the wrath of God.

Comparison of the BCP with the alternative formulas may clarify this:

BCP	Second Series[159]	Series 3[160]
	Under (1)[161]	
"Almighty God, Father of our Lord Jesus Christ, Maker of all things, *Judge of all men.*"	lacking	lacking
	Under (2)[162]	
"We acknowledge . . . our manifold sins and wickedness . . . which we most grievously have committed . . . against thy *Divine Majesty,* . . ."	lacking	lacking
	Under (3)[163]	
"Provoking most justly *thy wrath* and *indignation* against us."	lacking	lacking

h. Preface

The Preface[164] with its important feast day variations is substantially enlarged in both formulas.[165] Series 3 has added to the Preface more variations which correspond to certain feast days. Series 3 has provided the following variations in Prefaces over and above that in the BCP:

(1) Proper Preface for Advent
(2) Proper Preface for Epiphany
(3) Proper Preface for Holy Week
(4) Proper Preface for Saints Days
(5) Proper Preface for consecration of a church[166]

i. Consecration Prayer

The Prayer of Consecration introduces an anamnesis[167] in both forms.

269

Such was lacking in the BCP of 1662 but was present in the BCP of 1549. The Anamnesis in the Second Series reads:

> Wherefore, O Lord, with this bread and this cup we make the memorial of his saving passion, his resurrection from the dead, and his glorious ascension into heaven, and we look for the coming of his kingdom.[168]

In the Prayer of Consecration[169] in Series 3 the following epiclesis[170] is present:

> Grant that by the power of your Spirit these gifts of bread and wine may be to us his body and his blood.

j. Liturgical Matter after Consecration Prayer

In order that the congregation might be understood as a corporative-sacramental entity the liturgical passage after the Prayer of Consecration amounts to a new liturgical creation, which characterizes both experimental liturgies. Here is the wording of the Second Series:

> We being many are one bread, one body, for we all partake of the one bread.[171]

> The wording in Series 3 is very similar.[172]

k. Agnus Dei

The Second Series[173] and Series 3[174] reintroduce the Agnus Dei.

l. Both Alternative Closing Prayers

Both alternative closing prayers in the Second Series and in Series 3 are, compared with the BCP, markedly altered and abbreviated.

The following points are noteworthy:

BCP of 1662[175]
First alternative
closing prayer

Second Series[176]
First alternative
closing prayer

Series 3[177]
First alternative
closing prayer

1st: Petition for acceptance of the sacrifice of praise and thanksgiving.
2nd: Petition for forgiveness of sins based on the merit of Jesus and on faith in his blood sacrifice as well as a request to participate in the achievements of Jesus thanks to his passion.
3rd: Offering of body and soul as a living sacrifice to God.
4th: Request for grace and heavenly benediction.
5th: request for the acceptance of service to God with the understanding of one's own sinfulness and the inadequacy of one's own merits.
6th: Doxology from Romans 11:36.

1st: Thanks to Almighty God because he nourishes his guests with the body and blood of Jesus.
2nd: Thanks in that participation in the communion makes one a part of the body of Christ.
3rd: Petition for perpetual living membership in the congregation.
4th: Petition for good works.
5th: Doxology.

1st: Thanks to the heavenly Father in that he has brought men home by his Son.
2nd: Proclamation that Jesus through death and life has revealed the love of the Father and has opened the door to eternal life.
3rd: Petition for life in the strength of the resurrection.
4th: Request for light for the world through those illuminated by the Holy Ghost.
5th: Request for steadfastness in the hope laid hold of, so that all children of God may live to laud the name of God.

BCP of 1662[178] Second alternative closing prayer	Second Series[179] Second alternative closing prayer	Series 3[180] Second alternative closing prayer
1st: Thanks that all those have been nourished with the spiritual foods of his body and blood, who have received these holy mysteries in the proper attitude.	1st: Presentation of body and soul as a living sacrifice.	1st: Thanks that they have been nourished through the body and blood of Jesus.
2nd: Thanks that God has revealed his kindness by means of the holy communion.	2nd: Petition to be sent out into the world possessed of the power of the Holy Ghost.	2nd: Presentation of body and soul as a living sacrifice.
3rd: Thanks that all who have enjoyed the communion in the proper attitude are taken into the fellowship of all the faithful.	3rd: Petition to live and work to the glory of God.	3rd: Petition to be sent out into the world possessed of the power of the Holy Ghost.
4th: Thanks that one is heir to eternal life due to the merit of Jesus because of his costly death and suffering.		4th: Petition to live and work to the glory of God.
5th: Petition to the heavenly Father for the necessary help of his grace to remain within this fellowship of the faithful and to lead in accordance with God's decree a life of good works.		
6th: Doxology.		

m. Closing Benediction

The closing benediction in the Second Series and in Series 3 is identical to that in the canonical BCP. However Series 3 furnishes a succession of alternative closing benediction prayers[181] which can be used on important feasts of the church year.

2. THE MOST IMPORTANT DIFFERENCES IN RESPECT TO FORM IN THE TWO LITURGIES MENTIONED AS COMPARED WITH THE CANONICAL BCP

(a) After the opening collect, which accords with that in the BCP, there follows in Series 3 the *Kyrie Eleison,*[182] whereas this is optional in the Second Series. In place of the Kyrie the Ten Commandments can also be inserted there. In the BCP, on the contrary, the Decalogue follows the opening collect as an obligatory part.

(b) In Series 3 the *Gloria*[183] follows immediately after the Kyrie. In the Second Series the Gloria[184] follows the opening collect in those cases where neither the Kyrie nor the Decalogue is used. In the BCP one or both of the prayers for the government follow the Ten Commandments.

(c) *The Collect for the Day* comes immediately after the Gloria in both alternative liturgies.

(d) In harmony with the BCP the lessons follow the collect for the day. The difference however lies in the fact that both experimental liturgies provide in addition to the Epistle and Gospel a *lesson from the Old Testament.* In the Second Series as well as in Series 3 there are present at the conclusion of the lessons *responses* which do not occur in the canonical BCP. Thus the congregation in Series 3 responds after the reading of the Old Testament and the Epistle: "Thanks be to God." After the proclamation of the lesson from the Gospel the response reads: "Glory to Christ our Saviour." When the priest has finished with the lesson from the Gospel the congregation joins in with: "Praise to Christ our Lord."[185]

(e) The *Creed* following the lesson differs in Series 3 from that in the BCP. The latter states the Creed in the first person singular: "I believe in . . ." Series 3 expresses the Nicene Creed in the *first person plural:* "We believe in . . ."[186]

(f) In place of the twenty offertory sentences taken from Holy Scripture in the BCP, following the Creed, we find in the alternative forms the

Prayer for the Church Militant, which differs considerably from that in the BCP. The Second Series and Series 3 *split this prayer*[187] *up themati-cally arranged in different sections so that after each pause the congre-gation speaks the following response: "Lord, in your mercy hear our prayer."*

(g) Since the space for the exhortations is lacking *the Prayer for the Church Militant and the confession move very close together* in the alter-native communion formulas.[188]

(h) In Series 3 the *Four Comfortable Words* from Matthew 11:28; John 3:16; 1 Timothy 1:15; and 1 John 2:1 *precede the confession.* Imme-diately after the absolution is found the "Prayer of Humble Access."[189] In the Second Series the "Prayer of Humble Access" comes after the Four Comfortable Words.

(i) *The Preface with Sanctus* is attached to that liturgical element which is typical of both alternative forms,[190] which proclaims the unity of the body of Christ by virtue of baptism. In the BCP we find the Preface with Sanctus just before the "Prayer of Humble Access."

(j) In Series 3 *the courtly terms of address to God* such as "thee," "thou," and "thy" are rejected. "You" and "your" are used instead.

3. INTERPRETATION OF THE ABOVE-MENTIONED DIFFERENCES BETWEEN THE BCP 1662 AND THE ALTERNATIVE LITURGIES SECOND SERIES AND SERIES 3

a. Introductory Rubric, Exhortations, Confession, and Closing Prayers[191]

One does not find in Second Series or Series 3 any introductory rubric[192] referring in an admonitory way to the danger of an unrepentant attitude or which refers to the fact that holy communion is only offered to those who have reconciled themselves with their enemies. This can be seen as disdain for the concept of man's sinful fall. The exhortations which in the BCP of 1662 bring one face to face with man's guilt in respect to God in an uncompromising and energetic way are likewise missing. The con-fessions of sin are abbreviated, which becomes particularly noticeable in the deletion of the following concepts: missing is the conception of God as a judge, sin as an insult to the majesty of God, and sin as a characteristic of man. In the concluding prayer there is even a failure to mention sin.

The matters referred to indicate how uncomfortable is the Reformation emphasis on the sinful downfall of man. No longer present is any boldness to confront the autonomous and secularized man with this hard and disturbing reality. According to Robinson's contention[193] man is no longer interested in a "gracious God." This according to Robinson is to be evaluated as a positive fact; for it expresses a higher step in the development toward maturity.[194] Hence Reformation doctrine is no longer relevant.

A God who takes sin seriously is also after all a judge who has to punish insults directed against his majesty. But if one follows Robinson a supernatural God exists no more. Man who has come of age has done away with him. He is no longer the judge of a single individual. This God is to be identified as something which happens within the human relationship and therefore sin is guilt in respect to man. Man becomes then the judge of man.[195]

The exhortative element which we also find so often in Holy Scripture naturally has to be eliminated based on the point of view of the presuppositions mentioned above of the self-understanding of a mankind which has "come of age." Exhortation implies that man cannot be considered to be spiritually mature, but needs a challenge from a heteronomous side for his self-examination and penance because of his addiction to sin. Hence the lack of exhortations is intimately connected with a rejection of the Reformation conception of sin. Exhortations presuppose that man needs to be told what he has to do and what he has to believe. The man who "has come of age" apparently knows himself, knows what he should do, and what he should not do.

Since a new understanding of salvation has arisen and a different conception of conversion, any emphasis on the sin of individuals is irrelevant; if death is not the wages of sin but supplies a biological necessity, and if there is no eternal glory in the sense of the "many mansions in My Father's house," to which you enter through confession of sin, penance, and a personal decision of faith by obedience to the Word of God, why should one speak any more of sin? If, as Robinson states, conversion to Jesus prior to death is, according to the Bible, unnecessary[196] and if the individual fate is not determined after physical death, then sin and death are not to be taken seriously. In view of the transiency of this world that which spurs man to set his "affections on things above" (in the words of Colossians 3:1-2) is precisely fear of the sin which would prevent him from seeing the living God face to face.

Because fear of the consequences of sin leads to a vertical orientation and therefore conversion to the world is hindered, sin in the individual and ontological sense is mentioned as little as possible, and collective guilt is emphasized the more.

In a collection of different essays with the title *Towards a Modern Prayer Book* criticizing the alternative services J. I. Packer writes generally about the Second Series (but which also applies well to Series 3):

> The Book of Common Prayer is widely censured these days for the fulness and intensity of its public confessions of sin, as if there was something morbid about them . . . ; but the matter was never disputed till very recently—the theological and pastoral purpose of these poignant utterances is to highlight in the worshippers' minds and hearts the wonder and glory of free forgiveness through the cross of Christ. The lower we are made to go in knowing ourselves as sinners, the higher shall we rise in joy when assurance of God's pardon breaks in. To play down the sinfulness of sin is to obscure the greatness of grace, and to invite a shallow, superficial devotion and experience. This is in reality the highroad to formalism. . . . Historically, of course, we owe it to our Reformers, not to their earlier models, that the theme of sin and forgiveness is so powerfully expressed in the Prayer Book.[197]

It is significant that Packer puts his critical remarks about the conception of sin in the Second Series in writing under the following title:

"The momentousness of our sin and of God's forgiveness is played down."

b. The Twenty Offertory Verses, Prayer for the Church Militant, and the Four Comfortable Words[198]

Why are the twenty offertory verses drawn from Scripture lacking in Second Series and Series 3?

These offertory sentences[199] demonstrate by example the principle of "Scriptura sui ipsius Interpres." The self-interpretation of the Bible contradicts that modernistic thinking which welcomes the conception of evolution and thereby becomes a passport for arbitrary exegesis.[200]

In the prayer for Christ's church militant here on earth[201] it is obvious how very greatly the Word of God is held up in the BCP of 1662 as the Truth as well as a guiding principle for life and doctrine. The congregation is besought to hear and receive God's Word with adequate humility and respect. In Second Series and Series 3 this prayer for the church militant is present in a decidedly altered form in which in comparison with the BCP of 1662 the failure to extol God's Word is very marked. The intention is to eliminate the Reformation "Sola Scriptura." As early as the old Tractarian Movement there was a tendency to put tradition[202] above the Word of Scripture. Opinions differ in the understanding of Scripture. Therefore as a prerequisite for a reunion of the denominations into "Una Sancta" the principle to be proclaimed is not "Sola Scriptura" but instead "Consensus Quinquesaecularis."[203]

The four "comfortable words," as the quotations from Matthew 11:28; John 3:16; 1 Timothy 1:15; and 1 John 2:1 are called, refer by their arrangement to "Scriptura sui ipsius Interpres." The "comfortable words" contain the truth that men lost through sin may find salvation through the atoning death of Jesus.

Second Series does not use the "comfortable words" but Series 3 contains them.

c. Decalogue

The Ten Commandments appear purely as an optional choice in the annexes to both liturgies. What is the special reason for this? According to Robinson it is a property of the man who has come of age to be autonomous. Absolute ethical rules are no longer relevant for an autonomous man. The determining factor is love which has to judge the situation of the moment and make an ethical decision based thereon.[204]

J. W. Charley comments on this transfer of the Ten Commandments to an annex in Second series as follows:

> A striking omission from the Introduction is the Ten Commandments. Not even the summary of the Law, which the 1928 Book provided as an alternative, gets a mention. . . . Does this omission reflect the aversion to the very idea of law, so prevalent today? . . . Yet any tendency to play down the nature of man's offence only removes the backcloth against which redemption is seen most clearly for what it really is.[205]

d. Preface and Consecration[206]

The expansion of the Preface with five additional variations for advent, epiphany, Lent, saints' days, and dedication of a church reveals an adaptation to the Roman missal which in the edition before the Second Vatican had already far more variations in its preface than did the BCP of 1662.[207]

This expansion is to be seen as an ecumenical gesture in the liturgical area in order to make an eventual merger into a world church easier.[208]

The Anamnesis within the consecration prayer of both alternative liturgies is to be seen in connexion with the process of adaptation to the Latin tradition and the epiclesis introduced in Series 3 also documents the connexion with the Eastern Church tradition.[209]

This adaptation to the Latin as well as to the Eastern tradition reveals the process of promoting the principle of "Consensus Quinquesaecularis." The reintroduction of the Agnus Dei must also be seen in this connexion, although it is a Biblical liturgical pearl.

After the prayer of consecration the congregation answers by way of proclamation: "Though we are many, we are one body, because we all share in one bread."[210]

Here is expressed a very important concept which Robinson emphasizes in his writings time and again: the dimension of the corporate. This idea had a very strong impact on liturgical reform and implies the following: the eucharist creates a church where, independently of any individual's attitude, the people are, so to speak, drawn together in a body corporate, namely into the professed body of Christ. Questions concerning sound doctrine and the proper individual attitude are irrelevant. Robinson's statement found on page 258 herein which is of great importance, bears repeating:

> The forces of the risen life are released, and a hang-dog collection of men becomes galvanized into the new community of the Body of Christ.[211]

This strong emphasis on the corporate dimension can be clearly noted in the creed where is found in Series 3 "We believe . . ." instead of "I believe . . ."[212]

Where the tradition of the "Consensus Quinquesaecularis" becomes the standard one can easily justify the "We believe . . ." The "I believe . . ." expresses the importance of the individual's faith and refers clearly to the fact that every individual is responsible for himself before God with his faith. Individual faith never means that arbitrariness in respect to conceptions of faith is tolerated. What we want to express is that there shouldn't be anything like a collective faith which frees people from a personal decision or lets the individual be absorbed in collective pluralistic-modernistic ideas. The individual needs first of all to be brought into line by the Word of God and to let himself be disciplined in his faith and not by a collective, even if this latter calls itself the Church or the Body of Christ. The Reformation concern in the "I believe . . ." arises from the fact that every individual has to make a personal step to faith and that no substitution is possible in this respect. Fellowship is only possible in the true sense of the word where men have turned their lives over to the Lord through a conscious act of faith and have listened to the Word so that everyone lets himself be touched by the Word and offers himself in the service of this Word.

e. Interpretation of the Formal Dissimilarities

The sequence of Kyrie-Gloria-collect of the day is in harmony with the structure of the Roman eucharistic liturgy[213] and with all those liturgies which adhere strictly to the structure of the Occidental-Latin holy communion tradition. Introduction of this sequence in Second Series and Series 3 is again clearly an ecumenical gesture. Preface and Sanctus link up in an uninterrupted way with the prayer of consecration in the alternative formulas by which the unity of the canon and hence an openness with reference to the pre-Reformation situation is acknowledged. That which R. C. D. Jasper established with reference to the Reformation handling of the canon was in no way to find any support in the liturgical reform of the Holy Communion Service:

> At the Reformation the abolition of the canon was almost an article of faith with the Reformers.[214]

It was also intended with respect to form to do away with everything which might be a symbol of the clear witness of the Reformation in order to support the strongly desired ecumenical breadth.

The annulment of the courtly forms of address such as "thee," "thou," and "thy" in Series 3 reflects in unmistakable fashion those tendencies toward secularization popularized by John Robinson, which are also to be found distinctly expressed by Harvey Cox[215] and James Pike.[216]

Robinson sees God not as a supernatural force but as an event in the affairs of mankind. From this it is understandable that special forms of reverence are irrelevant.

In closing, the opinions of W. M. Brett and V. E. Watson which were carried in the quarterly *The Anglican Catholic* in a long article critical of the anti-sacral concepts in Series 3 may follow:

> To a large number of people the use of "you," in addressing God, savours of familiarity, even after hearing it for several years. Man needs to be taught,

and to be lifted to a higher sphere, where there is mystery and spirituality. "Thee" and "Thou," words hallowed by centuries of usage, may no longer be part of common speech, but is "common speech" suitable in addressing the Omnipotent, Omniscient, Omnipresent God? Should there not be deepest reverence in our approach to Him . . . ? How can this awe and reverence be expressed? Certainly not with the informality with which we address our neighbour today. "Thee" provides a way of distinguishing God from all others, even so we approach Him as a loving Father.[217]

F. THE ALTERNATIVE SERVICE BOOK 1980: DISCUSSION OF SEVERAL LITURGIES

1. INTRODUCTORY REMARKS

As was observed in reference to the experimental liturgies, these would be unthinkable without Tractarianism, *Lux Mundi*, and the modernistic theology of Robinson and his adherents. The same applies to The Alternative Service Book[218] that sprouted as the fruit of the experimental liturgies. Many of the facts stated with regard to the experimental liturgies are repeated in our analysis. We are not dealing here simply with a provisional alternative as was the case with the experimental liturgies, but with a definitive alternative which possibly might become the new "canonical" prayer book.

2. MORNING PRAYER[219]

a. Survey of Liturgical Components

1. Declaration on the meaning of the service[220]
2. A Biblical sentence which is to be taken from a given selection[221]
3. A freely chosen hymn
4. Sentence from 1 John 1:8-9 as a transition to the confession[222]
5. Confession[223] or a selection from alternative confessions[224]
6. Absolution[225]
7. Opening sentences with the Little Gloria[226]
8. Venite (Ps. 95) or Jubilate (Ps. 100) or an Easter anthem on Easter[227]

9. The psalm for the appointed day[228]
10. First lesson, taken from the Old Testament[229]
11. Congregation speaks a response[230]
12. Benedictus (Luke 1:67-79) or Benedicite (Apocryphal annex from Daniel 3) or the hymn "Great and Wonderful"[231]
13. Second lesson from New Testament[232]
14. Congregation speaks a response[233]
15. Opportunity for sermon[234]
16. Te Deum or Gloria in Excelsis, for Lent (Saviour of the World)[235]
17. The Apostles' Creed[236]
18. Lord, have mercy (Miserere)[237]
19. Lord's Prayer[238]
20. Closing sentences[239]
21. Collect of the day[240]
22. Collect for peace[241]
23. Collect for grace[242] or an alternative
24. State prayers as well as freely selected prayers[243]
25. Benediction[244]

b. Observations Respecting the Most Important Liturgical Components Mentioned in Survey (a) and Their Interpretation

Reference 1: Declaration on the Meaning of the Service

We have come together as the family of God in our Father's presence to offer him praise and thanksgivings, to hear and receive his holy word, to bring before him the needs of the world, to ask his forgiveness of our sins, and to seek his grace, that through his Son Jesus Christ we may give ourselves to his service.

Noteworthy is the fact that this Morning Prayer brings immediately upon the outset a reflection upon the meaning of the service. In the BCP 1662 we find right at the beginning a collection of Biblical texts[245] which have as a theme the depravity of man. The recognition of the total indebtedness of man in regard to God is the overture in the traditional Morning Prayer in its opening sentences. However in ASB 1980, in its opening declaration upon the meaning of the service, the forgiveness of sins as an important purpose first appears near the close. The order in this declaration on the meaning of the service with reference to the matters mentioned is: an offering of praise and thanksgiving, listening to the word of God, reviewing the needs of the world, then the plea for forgiveness of sins.

Packer refers to a very important point when he comments on the missing references to man's depravity in the opening sentences of Morning and Evening Prayers in the Second Series, which Series exercised an influence on the corresponding formulas in the ASB 1980:

> Similarly, the aim of the penitential introduction, with confession and absolution, which was prefixed to Morning and Evening Prayer in 1552, was to show that Christian praise and prayer spring from knowledge of the remission of sins, and by bringing us that knowledge afresh every time we met in church to make us "heartily rejoice in the strength of our salvation" on each occasion.... Unhappily, for whatever reason, modern revisions of the Prayer Book have regularly toned down this emphasis.[246]

Reference 2: A Biblical Sentence Which Is to Be Taken from a Given Selection

The sentences provided on page 47 in ASB 1980 for Morning Prayer say nothing about sin. In the additional selection of Biblical sentences provided for one's own selection on pages 37-42 are found only a few sentences which have sin among their contents. There is a further point to be noted, that only one sentence may be chosen, as compared with the BCP 1662 where one may choose several from the given collection of sentences. Since all the opening sentences in the Morning and Evening Prayer of the BCP of 1662 speak about sin, the principle of "Scriptura sui ipsius Interpres" receives expression there in a fine way. Where one can only use one single sentence from the Bible no chance is given for the self-interpretation of the Bible to function. Praise and worship is the theme in the general sentences given on page 47. Within the context of a self-interpretation of Holy Scripture adoration is only possible for that person who has become aware of his own inadequacy and sinfulness.

Reference 5: Confession or Choice of Alternative Confessions

We introduce the general confession found on pages 48-49 in Morning Prayer in The Alternate Service Book 1980:

Almighty God, our heavenly Father, we have sinned against you and against our fellow men, in thought and word and deed, through negligence, through weakness, through our own deliberate fault. We are truly sorry and repent of all our sins. For the sake of your Son Jesus Christ, who died for us, forgive us all that is past; and grant that we may serve you in newness of life; to the glory of your name. Amen.

Comparison with the confession in the BCP of 1662[247] reveals some essential differences. The weakness of the confession in Morning Prayer of the ASB 1980 doesn't consist in that which is written but rather in that which remains unwritten and one becomes especially aware of this through a comparison with the BCP of 1662.

The ASB 1980 knows nothing of the concept that sin consists of the rebellious schemes of man.

The ASB 1980 has nothing to say to us about what sin is, namely the transgression of the law.[248]

Nor do the alternative confessions of sin[249] which are given for a choice mention that sin exists in lawlessness, in the violation of divine rules. The BCP of 1662 aptly expresses the essence of sin when it speaks of the rebellion against God's prescriptions: "We have offended against thy holy laws."

The very important Reformation emphasis on the fact that man is separated from God and lost is also lacking. The confession in the BCP of 1662 shows us this fact with its picture of the lost sheep: "We have erred, and strayed from thy ways like lost sheep." The total depravity of man is suppressed in all the confessions in ASB 1980. How clear in this respect is that of the BCP of 1662 with its concise expression which is so much to the point: "there is no health in us."

In ASB 1980 it says simply: "We are truly sorry and repent of all our sins." The BCP of 1662 handles the matter concerning the confession of sin with greater pedagogical wisdom where it makes the protection and restitution of a state of grace dependent on confession and repentance as a prior condition: "Spare thou them, O God, which confess their faults. Restore thou them, that are penitent." The BCP 1662 holds to the opinion that the service might also be attended by unconverted nominal Christians who need to be made aware of the conditions for the obtaining of salvation. In ASB 1980 the opinion is not held that there exists any such difference between faithful and unfaithful, which is strictly consistent with the incorporation thinking wherein every baptised person automatically belongs to the body of Christ.

When it says at the close of the confession in the ASB 1980: "And grant that we may serve you in newness of life," this "newness of life" is not defined as it is in the BCP of 1662 where it calls for a "godly," "righteous," and "sober" life.

The first alternative confession:[250]

> Almighty God, our heavenly Father [1], we have sinned against you and against our fellow men [2], in thought and word and deed [3], in the evil we have done and in the good we have not done, through ignorance, through weakness, through our own deliberate fault [4]. We are truly sorry, and repent of all our sins [5]. For the sake of your Son Jesus Christ, who died for us [6], forgive us all that is past [7]; and grant that we may serve you in newness of life [8] to the glory of your name. Amen. [9]

This confession introduces two new aspects that it is sinful to fail to do good as well as to act in ignorance. [4] This incorporates an important aspect of the 1662 confession in Morning Prayer, namely the failure to do what we ought to do.

Second alternative confession:[251]

> Almighty God, our heavenly Father [1], we have sinned against you [2], through our own fault [3], in thought and word and deed, and in what we have left undone [4]. For your Son our Lord Jesus Christ's sake, forgive us all that is past [5]; and grant that we may serve you in newness of life to the glory of your name. Amen. [6]

In the confession above is found as a new aspect one's own responsibility for sin [3].

Third alternative confession:[252]

> Father eternal, giver of light and grace [1], we have sinned against you and against our fellow men [2], in what we have thought, in what we have said and done [3], through ignorance, through weakness, through our own deliberate fault [4]. We have wounded your love, and marred your image in us (5). We are sorry and ashamed [6], and repent of all our sins [7]. For the sake of your Son Jesus Christ, who died for us (8), forgive us all that is past [9]; and lead us out from darkness to walk as children of light. Amen. [10]

This brings to light the following new aspects: the Father is eternal, he is the giver of light and grace [1]. Men have wounded his love and marred God's image [5]. Also new is the petition that God lead men out of darkness so that they can walk as children of light [10].

We note then that the most important Reformation substance is suppressed in the general confession of ASB 1980. Even the additional aspects of the alternative confessions are not able to balance out this lack.

Reference 6: Absolution

Almighty God, who forgives all who truly repent, have mercy upon you, pardon and deliver you from all your sins, confirm and strengthen you in all goodness, and keep you in life eternal; through Jesus Christ our Lord.

We intend to mention only the most important points which reveal a change in substance as compared with the BCP of 1662.[253]

The idea that sin leads to the soul's death is lacking in the ASB 1980 absolution. This though is stated unequivocally in the BCP 1662: "who desireth not the death of a sinner." Although one reads in the ASB 1980 that God forgives all who truly repent it is not clear of what repentance consists. The expression "who forgives all who truly repent" is too general. Repentance has to do with conversion and a decided faith. This is clearly expressed in the BCP 1662 where it says: "He pardoneth and absolveth all them that truly repent, and unfeignedly believe his holy gospel." To conversion and repentance belongs an attachment to God's Word, which again clearly reveals the Reformation line. The very important plea to the Holy Ghost to lead one in a life pleasing to God based on a true repentance, is lacking.

How weak is the expression "confirm and strengthen you in all goodness" compared with the BCP of 1662 with its statement: "Wherefore let us beseech him to grant us true repentance, and his holy Spirit, that those things may please him, which we do at this present."

There is also danger of a purely horizontal soteriology in the expression "and keep you in life eternal" as contrasted with the expression in the absolution of the BCP 1662 "so that at the last we may come to his eternal joy." The difference between faith and seeing is not expressed.

Assuredly eternal life begins here and now, an idea also clearly present in the BCP 1662. This "eternal life" however in fellowship with Jesus is still hidden and must be tested in struggles and temptations as well as in great tribulation. The expression in the BCP 1662 "so that at the last we may come to his eternal joy" takes seriously the pilgrimage character of this earthly life and points out with the words "at last" that the state of perfection beyond death is still to come. On the other hand by the expression "keep you in life eternal" it is possible to understand something limited purely to the here and now, such perhaps as acting in accordance with the spirit of Jesus and following his example.

Reference 7: Opening Sentences with the Minor Gloria

It is noteworthy that these opening sentences contain only praise. In the BCP 1662 though a supplication for God's saving help is also an important part of the opening sentences, in order to express the transitoriness of man and his total dependency on God:

> O God make speed to save us.
> O Lord make haste to help us.

Reference 11: The Congregation Speaks a Response

In answer to the Old Testament lesson the congregation speaks the words: "Thanks be to God." This response may serve for overcoming monotony.

Reference 12: Benedictus or the Benedicite, Omnia Opera or the Hymn Great and Wonderful

In contrast to the BCP 1662 we have here three alternatives.

Reference 14: Response of the Congregation

After the New Testament lesson the congregation can again answer in order to overcome monotony with the response "Thanks be to God."

Reference 15: Opportunity for the Sermon

An improvement contrasted with the BCP 1662 is the rubric which provides opportunity for a sermon after the New Testament lesson.

Reference 16: Te Deum or Gloria in Excelsis (For Lent, Saviour of the World)

New is the alternative of the Gloria in Excelsis in place of the Te Deum. The Gloria in Excelsis is lacking in the traditional Morning and Evening

Prayer. Here is a clear change in contrast to the BCP 1662, where the Benedictus or Psalm 100 follows the New Testament lesson.

Reference 20: Closing Sentences

Show us your mercy, O Lord; [1]
and grant us your salvation. [2]
O Lord, save the Queen, [3]
and teach her counsellors wisdom. [4]
Let your priests be clothed with righteousness; [5]
and let your servants shout for joy. [6]
O Lord, make your ways known upon the earth; [7]
let all nations acknowledge your saving power. [8]
Give your people the blessing of peace; [9]
and let your glory be over all the world. [10]
Make our hearts clean, O God; [11]
and renew a right spirit within us. [12]

Comparison with the closing sentences in Morning Prayer in the traditional BCP[254] discloses the following:

Reference [4] it says in the BCP of 1662:

And mercifully hear us when we call upon thee.

Reference [7] it says in the BCP of 1662:

O Lord, save thy people.

Reference [8] it says in the BCP of 1662:

And bless thine inheritance.

Reference [10] it says in the BCP of 1662:

Because there is none other that fighteth for us, but only thou, O God.

Reference [12] it says in the BCP of 1662:

And take not thy holy Spirit from us.

The remaining sentences [1], [2], [3], [5], [6], and [9] correspond in general with the contents of the above.

There is no great change in substance here.

Nevertheless the omission of "because there is none other that fighteth for us" is noteworthy. This sentence aptly expresses the Reformation-

Biblical doctrine of the helplessness of man without God. Also the sentence "and take not thy holy Spirit from us" refers clearly to the fact that even a person possessed of faith must never boast and become self-sufficient; for the danger that the Holy Spirit might be grieved is great.

Reference 21: Collect for the Day

In conformity with the Morning Prayer of the BCP 1662 the collect for the day follows the response to the closing sentences.

Reference 22: Collect for Peace

The collect for peace in the ASB 1980 occupies the same position as that in the Morning Prayer of the traditional BCP. However certain differences in the text may be observed:

ASB 1980	BCP of 1662
"O God, the author of peace and lover of concord, [1] to know you is eternal life, [2] to serve you is perfect freedom. [3] Defend us your servants from all assaults of our enemies; [4] that we may trust in your defence, [5] and not fear the power of any adversaries [6] through Jesus Christ our Lord. Amen." [7]	"O God, who art the author of peace and lover of concord, [1] in knowledge of whom standeth our eternal life, [2] whose service is perfect freedom; [3] Defend us thy humble servants in all assaults of our enemies; [4] that we, surely trusting in thy defence, [5] may not fear the power of any adversaries, [6] through the might of Jesus Christ our Lord. Amen." [7]

In clause [2] the collect for peace of ASB 1980 differs considerably from that in the BCP 1662. "In knowledge of whom standeth our eternal life" (1662) places its stress more on eternal life in the sense that whether the soul is to be saved or not is something to be revealed in the future. "To know you is eternal life" on the contrary expresses a current condition of salvation.

In clause [4] the collect for peace in the edition of 1662 has the addition "thy humble servants," whereas it doesn't say "defend from" but "defend us . . . *in* all assaults of our enemies."

In clause [5] it says in the edition of 1662 "surely trusting" instead of simply "that we may trust."

In clause [7] the collect for peace in the BCP of 1662 introduces the phrase "through the might" in order to characterize Jesus more particularly.

Moreover in the ASB 1980 there is lacking any designation of this collect as a "Collect for Peace," as was the case in the BCP of 1662.

Reference 23: Collect for Grace

The collect for grace in the ASB 1980 occupies the same position as that in the Morning Prayer of the traditional BCP. There are a few differences in the texts:

ASB 1980	BCP OF 1662
"Almighty and everlasting Father, [1] we thank you that you have brought us safely to the beginning of this day. Keep us from falling into sin or running into danger; [3] order us in all our doings;[4] and guide us to do always what is right in your eyes; [5] through Jesus Christ our Lord. Amen." [6]	"O Lord, our heavenly Father, Almighty and everlasting God, [1] who hast safely brought us to the beginning of this day; [2] Defend us in the same with thy mighty power; [3] and grant that this day we fall into no sin, neither run into any kind of danger; [4] but that all our doings may be ordered by thy governance, [5] to do always that is righteous in thy sight; [6] through Jesus Christ our Lord. Amen." [7]

In contrast to the ASB 1980 the edition of 1662 introduces in clause [1] a more detailed characterization of God through the expressions "O Lord" and "heavenly." In [3] the text of 1662 voices the petition that God might provide defence throughout the day with his mighty power. This petition is lacking in the ASB 1980 edition. That which appears in the BCP of 1662 under [4] is introduced in the ASB 1980 in an abbreviated form under [3]. Under [5] is found in the traditional edition the request that the doings of men might be ordered by God's governance. The ASB 1980 shortens this petition by omitting governance. That which appears in the traditional edition under [6] is found in ASB 1980 under [5] with the exception of the two important terms "righteous" (1662) and "right" (ASB

1980), which do not express the same thing theologically. Here also the designation "Collect for Grace" is lacking in the ASB 1980.

As an alternative to the Collect for Grace the ASB 1980 introduces in addition the following prayer which is missing in the BCP 1662:

> Eternal God and Father, you create us by your power and redeem us by your love: guide and strengthen us by your Spirit, that we may give ourselves in love and service to one another and to you; through Jesus Christ our Lord. Amen.[255]

Reference 24: State Prayers and Freely Selected Prayers

There is a certain dissimilarity with reference to the sequence of the state prayers in comparison with the BCP of 1662. The prayer which comes at the beginning of the state prayers in the BCP of 1662, namely "A Prayer for the Queen's Majesty," is lacking in the ASB 1980. In place of this prayer the ASB 1980 introduces a new prayer.[256] The two following prayers agree essentially with those in the BCP of 1662. The names however are lacking.[257]

The rubric in the ASB 1980[258] gives for the close of Morning Prayer the opportunity to make a free selection. Prayers may also be freely spoken. Three forms are given for selecting the closing prayer,[259] of which the first form corresponds to the benediction just at the close of the traditional Morning Prayer. The "Prayer of St. Chrysostom" found in the Morning Prayer of 1662 following the state prayers is missing in the morning service in the ASB 1980.

Reference 25: Prayers of Benediction[260]

The ASB 1980 Morning Prayer gives for selection two prayers of benediction for the conclusion of the service. The first is the benediction of Aaron, the second benediction is a new creation of the ASB 1980 with the following wording:

> The love of the Lord Jesus draw you to himself, the power of the Lord Jesus strengthen you in his service, the joy of the Lord Jesus fill your hearts; and the blessing of God almighty, the Father, the Son, and the Holy Spirit, be among you and remain with you always. Amen.[261]

Balance Sheet

In the declaration of the meaning of the service placed right at the beginning[262] a tendency is to be noted toward autonomous rather than theonomous thinking. Man comes first in his evaluation of the service, and not the admonition of God's Word to beware of the guilt separating him from God. Man is principally seen as being able to have fellowship with God. Therefore the text places laud and praise in the foreground while confession and absolution appear as quantité négligeable. It is not the attitude of the listening man letting himself be told about his situation which comes first; it is rather the homo iudicans who places himself in the first rank. Therefore it is consequent that this man placing himself in the foreground cannot tolerate any exhortation. All that which we have heard from Robinson in regard to man having come of age[263] is clearly reflected in the Morning Prayer of the ASB 1980.

In the confession and absolution one can notice a shifting of the conception of guilt in the direction of understanding sin first of all as something being done unto man rather than unto God.

The offer of alternatives for the confessions or prayers needs to be seen as connected with the modern phenomenon of pluralism with its palette of various attitudes of thinking. Alternatives take this fact of pluralism into consideration in the dogmatic liturgical area. The second alternative confession[264] can be prayed by representatives of strongly divergent theological conceptions because it demarcates almost nothing and leaves a lot open.

It is strange for the formula of the absolution in ASB 1980 that repentance and penance are seen according to the Gospel as a relation of obedience to the revealed Word of God and that this relation of obedience is a condition for the reception of forgiveness. It is also a matter of impossibility with these modern absolutions to see the death of a sinner in the case of disobedience towards the Gospel and therewith we come again to Robinson for whom the reception of grace is not dependent on forgiveness and on the correct Biblical understanding of God.[265]

Clear binding directions for faith in the sense of "no other gospel" are according to Robinson "irrelevant." Therefore catechisms need to be rejected.[266]

The absolution in the BCP 1662 is an encouragement to sanctification through holding out the prospect of eternal glory ("so that at the last we may come to his eternal joy"). Eternal life in the sense of seeing the Lord face to face in contrast with mere faith becomes an important moti-

291

vation for sanctification. In the ASB 1980 the absolution leaves it open whether eternal life is also a reality beyond the grave or if it is only a reality in the here and now. In any case the mode of expression in ASB 1980 leaves sufficient room for representatives also of a horizontal theology.[267]

With reference to the closing sentences it seems to me that the absence of such an important phrase as "because there is none other that fighteth for us"[268] which is to be seen in the context of peace in the BCP of 1662, is connected with the peace movements and peace demonstration which received so much support from the established churches. Is it perhaps intended by the elimination of the clause "because there is none other that fighteth for us" to express the idea that peace is something that can be achieved by man's own strength on the basis of the elimination of unjust social and economic structures which provoke aggression? A theology which is sold to secularized thinking will certainly have much trouble with this closing sentence which implies that only God can fight for us, and no other person.

It is noteworthy with respect to the closing prayers that they have no name as is the case for example in the BCP of 1662 where they are called the "Collect for Peace" and the "Collect for Grace." But the closing prayers in ASB 1980 bear a strong resemblance to those in the BCP 1662.

Could the suppression of these names have a connexion with the idea that it is intended to avoid letting the reader be provoked to compare the corresponding prayers in the traditional prayer book?

In the collect for peace in the edition of 1980 the horizontal dimension of the life eternal is especially stressed, when it reads: "To know you is eternal life" in comparison with the passage in the BCP of 1662: "in knowledge of whom standeth our eternal life." Significant also is the difference between "defend us . . . from all assaults of our enemies" (ASB 1980) and "defend us . . . in all assaults of our enemies" (BCP 1662). The conception of peace in the ASB 1980 refers to an understanding of peace which believes in the possibility of the total overcoming of war. The petition in the BCP 1662 takes the direction that one can experience the protection of God in the midst of all the warlike confrontations. The BCP 1662 looks at it in a realistic way, that war belongs to a fallen world. We as human beings are not able totally to avoid it, for there are only signs of the peace of God possible here.

The question is raised: why does the ASB 1980 in its collect for grace omit the passage which in the corresponding prayer in the BCP 1662 reads as follows: "Defend us in the same with thy mighty power"? "Mighty power" means omnipotence. Manifestly this plea for the protection of God through his omnipotence is therefore not possible for the ASB 1980 because one wishes particularly to take into consideration the sensibilities of modern men.

The secularized man thinks about God—to the extent he intellectually still accepts him as existent—in deistic categories. From a deistic point of view one can hardly speak of God's "mighty power."

When it reads in the ASB 1980 in clause (4) "order us in all our doings" there is a weakening compared with the wording in the BCP of 1662 where it says: "but that all our doings may be ordered by thy governance." The latter text reveals much more lucidly that our human actions must occur under the guiding sovereignty of God. The second to last clause in ASB 1980 "and guide us to do always what is right in your eyes" contrasts with the expression used in the BCP of 1662 where it says: "to do always that is righteous in thy sight." The term "righteous" means in a Biblical-Reformation sense the justice which is acknowledged by God, and so this theological term presupposes that injustice is inherent in the nature of man. When a question of relevance is put forward as is particularly true for today it is understandable that the Biblical-Reformation doctrine of justification is not proclaimed; then the autonomous man who stands up for situation ethics in the Robinsonian sense can only become guilty in respect to his fellow man, but not against the living God. How can man insult God or fall into disgrace with him if his commandments are not in the final analysis binding? Therefore a rehabilitation with respect to God is superfluous.

Why is the state prayer which in the BCP of 1662 is entitled "A Prayer for the Queen's Majesty" omitted? This prayer[269] stands out through addressing God with a strong hymnal accent while the conception of the absoluteness of the Biblical God is expressed; "O Lord our heavenly Father, high and mighty, King of kings, Lord of Lords, the only Ruler of princes."

The proclamation of the absoluteness of the Biblical God is no longer workable for an ecclesiastical theology which has allowed itself to be influenced through the phases of rationalism, existentialism, nihilism (God is dead), as well as through political-radical and syncretistic theology of an eastern cast.

The above-mentioned factors should partially explain the elimination of this prayer. With Robinson, who has exercised in the closing years of the twentieth century the greatest influence on the English church, we find in a more or less scintillating way, rationalism,[270] existentialism,[271] nihilism,[272] and syncretism.[273]

We do not want to go into Evening Prayer because it has the same structure as Morning Prayer. The distinctions consist merely in the different hymns and prayers.

3. THE ORDER FOR HOLY COMMUNION RITE A[274]

a. Survey of Liturgical Components

Preparation

1. Selection of a suitable sentence which is spoken by the congregation; hymn to be sung by congregation or a psalm to be sung[275]
2. Priest's greeting to congregation and congregation's answer[276]
3. Opening collect[277]
4. Decalogue or summary of the Decalogue[278]
5. Transitional passage to the confession[279]
6. Confession[280]
7. Absolution[281]
8. Kyrie Eleison[282]
9. Gloria in Excelsis[283]
10. Collect for the day[284]

Ministry of the Word

11. Lesson from Old Testament with congregation's answer[285]
12. Possible lesson from the Psalms[286]
13. Lesson from New Testament (Epistle) with congregational answer[287]
14. Congregational song or psalm[288]
15. Gospel lesson with congregation's answer[289]
16. Sermon[290]
17. Nicene Creed[291]
18. Intercessions and prayer of thanks[292] (with alternatives)

The Ministry of the Sacrament

19. Prayer of humble access[293] (with alternatives)
20. Proclamation of the peace with congregation's answer and mutual exchange of a sign of peace[294]
21. Hymnic words at the placing of the bread and wine on the altar[295]

22. Hymnic words at the taking of the collection[296]
23. Congregational hymn[297]
24. Presentation of the bread and wine[298]
25. Eucharistic prayer (with alternatives)[299]
26. The Lord's Prayer[300]
27. Words for the breaking of bread[301]
28. Agnus Dei[302]
29. Words of invitation[303] (with alternatives)
30. Words of distribution with the communicant's answer[304] (with alternatives)
31. Singing of hymns during the distribution[305]
32. Special prayer of the priest in the event more bread and wine is needed[306]

After Communion

33. A suitable sentence and a hymn[307]
34. Concluding prayer of thanks and intercession of the priest[308]
35. Concluding prayer of thanks of the congregation (with alternative)[309]
36. Benediction by the priest (with alternative)[310]
37. Response of the congregation[311]

There are still two alternative sequences of liturgical elements of Holy Communion Rite A: 1-3, then instead of 4-7 there follows immediately 8-18 and after 18 follows 4 and John 3:16. As an alternative one can use the four "Comfortable Words"[312] from the BCP 1662. Afterwards follow 6 and 7 and 19-37 or this variant where one uses a part of the sequence of the traditional prayer book.[313] We do not intend to discuss the last variant.

b. Observations Respecting the Most Important Liturgical Components Mentioned in Survey (a) and Their Interpretation

Reference 4: Decalogue or Summary

Instead of using the Decalogue one need employ simply the summary of the Ten Commandments. The summary never is a real substitute for the Ten Commandments. The danger of considering it a real substitute is great. With this one could easily slip into the situation ethics of Robinson where love relieves one of obedience to absolute standards.[314]

Reference 5: The Transitional Words to the Confession

The text employs as transitional words John 3:16. But one must be made aware of a suppression of great consequence:

Namely, there is lacking in this passage "God so loved the world, that He gave His only Son Jesus Christ" the important attribute "begotten." By eliminating this "begotten"[315] the supernatural dimension of Jesus can be suppressed. Of even greater consequence however is the omission of the conditional clause "that whosoever believeth in Him should not perish." Universalistic tendencies reveal themselves in this elimination.[316]

Reference 6: Confession

What we have said about the confession in the "Alternative Services" Second Series and Series 3 should be noted.[317]

Reference 7: Absolution

It should be observed that the absolution here in contrast to the same matter in the BCP 1662 omits the following important wording: "and true faith turn unto him." The elimination of the wording "hath promised forgiveness of sins to all that . . . with true faith turn unto him" is understandable from the point of view of a dynamic conception of truth where a judgment about the correctness or falseness of faith is an impossibility from the outset. The expression "true faith" presupposes that a correct faith exists and therefore also an absolute truth. There is no such thing as believers or unbelievers according to the conception of this absolution, which becomes understandable when we consider the influence of Robinson. The latter emphasizes the point that the world doesn't let itself be told what is to be believed and what is not. And one must give in to this world, to adjust himself to it.[318] From the point of view of such presuppositions, which are proclaimed by Robinson, only a relativistic pluralism has the right to exist, in which clear positions of faith based on unequivocal statements of faith constitute an affront.

Reference 8-10: Kyrie and Gloria as Well as Collect for the Day

Take into consideration what has been said in our work on pages 279-80.

Reference 17: Nicene Creed

This follows the sermon here whereas in the traditional prayer book the preaching follows the Creed. The question arises whether this changed position of the Creed is meant as a statement that the preaching is not to be constrained by the basic Biblical truths contained in the Creed. The Creed preceding the sermon is like a warning that the preaching has to be submitted to the substance of the Creed.[319]

Reference 18: Intercessions and Thanksgivings: The Great Intercessory and Thanksgiving Prayer[320]

Whereas in the BCP 1662 the sermon is followed by a selection from the twenty given offertory Biblical verses, the great intercessory and thanksgiving prayer follows the Nicene Creed in ASB 1980. This intercessions and thanksgivings prayer is a modification of the traditional prayer in the BCP for the church militant.

On the following pages we set out by way of contrast the great intercessions and thanksgivings prayer of ASB 1980 and the prayer for the church militant from the BCP of 1662.

The Intercession ASB 1980	The Prayer for the Church Militant Here in Earth BCP 1662
[1] Let us pray for the Church and the world, and let us thank God for his goodness. [2] Almighty God, our heavenly Father, you promised through your son Jesus Christ to hear us when we pray in faith. [3] Strengthen N our bishop and all your Church in the service of Christ; that those who confess your	[1] Almighty and everliving God, [2] who by thy holy Apostle hast taught us to make prayers, and supplications, and to give thanks, for all men; [3] We humbly beseech thee most mercifully (to accept our alms and oblations, and) to receive these our prayers, which we offer unto thy Divine Majesty; [4] be-

name may be united in your truth, live together in your love, and reveal your glory in the world. [4] Bless and guide Elizabeth our Queen; [5] Give wisdom to all in authority; [6] and direct this and every nation in the ways of justice and of peace; [7] that men may honour one another, and seek the common good. [8] Give grace to us, our families and friends, and to all our neighbours; [9] that we may serve Christ in one another, and love as he loves us. [10] Comfort and heal all those who suffer in body, mind or spirit . . . ; give them courage and hope in their troubles; [11] and bring them the joy of your salvation. [12] Hear us as we remember those who have died in the faith of Christ . . . ; according to your promises, grant us with them a share in your eternal kingdom. [13] Rejoicing in the fellowship of (N and of) all your saints, we commend ourselves and all Christian people to your unfailing love.

seeching thee to inspire continually the universal Church with the spirit of truth, unity, and concord: [5] and grant, that all they that do confess thy holy Name may agree in the truth of thy holy Word, [6] and live in unity, and godly love. [7] We beseech thee also so to save and defend all Christian Kings, Princes, and Governors; and specially thy Servant Elizabeth our Queen; [8] that under her we may be godly and quietly governed: [9] and grant unto her whole Council, and to all that are put in authority under her, that they may truly and indifferently minister justice, to the punishment of wickedness and vice, and to the maintenance of thy true religion, and virtue. [10] Give grace, O heavenly Father, to all Bishops and Curates, that they may both by their life and doctrine set forth thy true and lively Word, and rightly and duly administer thy holy Sacraments: [11] And to all thy people give thy heavenly grace; and specially to this congregation here present; that with meek heart and due reverence, they may hear, and receive thy holy Word; [12] truly serving thee in holiness and righteousness all the days of their life. [13] And we most humbly beseech thee of thy goodness, O Lord, to comfort and succour all them, who in this transitory life are in trouble, sorrow, need, sickness, or any other adversity. [14] And we also bless thy holy

Name for all thy servants departed this life in thy faith and fear; [15] beseeching thee to give us grace so to follow their good examples, that with them we may be partakers of thy heavenly kingdom: [16] Grant this, O Father, for Jesus Christ's sake, our only Mediator and Advocate. Amen.

ASB 1980

First: The start at [1] is the call to pray for church and world and to offer thanks for God's goodness. Reference to God as the principal of the apostle who teaches us to pray and give thanks is *omitted.*

Second: In [2] the text states that the Almighty and heavenly Father hears the prayers of faith through Jesus Christ.

This statement is *omitted.*

Third: At [3] is a request for the strengthening of the bishop and the church in the service of Christ. The petition has the further content that all believers in God join together on the grounds of divine truth and also live together in love and make the glory of God manifest in the world.

This more particular definition of truth as God's Word is *lacking.*

BCP of 1662

First: The start at [1] and [2] is the invocation to God, wherein the text appeals for prayer and thanksgiving to God who commissioned the apostle to teach this kind of prayer.

This statement is *lacking.*

Second: In [3] the text contains a humble supplication for the merciful acceptance of the prayers directed to the divine Majesty.

Third: One finds partly the same aspects under the references [4] to [6] as in the left column. However the following important differences must be noted: The left column speaks in [3] of the plea for strength for the church in the service of Jesus. In our text here it speaks of a plea for the continued inspiration of the Church through the spirit of truth, unity, and concord.

Of special importance however is now this that the text in reference to the requested unity in the truth

299

Fourth: In [4] to [7] is found the petition for a blessing upon Queen Elizabeth and for wisdom for the whole government. The petition includes moreover the prayer that God might lead all nations in the ways of justice and peace, that men honour one another and seek the common good.

Any aspect of salvation with eschatological undertones is missing. How the kingdom is to be ruled is *unmentioned.* There is no passage relating to how the wisdom requested for the government should appear. There is thus *omitted* any specification that the government should carry out its governmental authority without regards for persons and through punishment meted out against corruption and dissoluteness. The statement that the type and method of government is evidence of the true religion is *omitted.*

Fifth: In [8] and [9] is found the request for God's blessing for one's own family, friends, and neighbours so that each through his behaviour towards the others may serve Christ and pass on his love.

Various aspects as found in the right column are *omitted:* it *omits* the petition for the bishop relating to establishing Biblical ethics and dogmatics. The request for proper administration of the sacraments is *omitted.* It *omits* the request that the

defines this truth more particularly: It is the truth of God's Word.

Fourth: From [7] to [9] is the plea that God save all Christian kings, princes, and other rulers, especially Queen Elizabeth. The text explains how men who are under the queen should be ruled: namely, in a godly and quiet way. All who have received authority from the queen should exercise it in truth and without esteem of person that wickedness and vice might be punished so as to maintain true religion and virtue.

Fifth: From [10] to [12] we find the request that the heavenly Father bless bishops and curates in such a way that they through the example of life and doctrine might set forth the true and living Word of God and administer the sacraments in a proper form. Furthermore it is prayed that everyone and especially the present congregation might with meek heart and reverence hear and accept the divine Word so that they can serve the congregation receive the grace to listen to and receive God's Word and then also to live this Biblical Word in sanctification.

Sixth: In [10] and [11] we find a petition for help and healing for those suffering in body and soul. Also asked for is courage and hope as well as the joy of divine salvation. Lacking also is the characterization of this earthly life as being transient.

Seventh: In [12] and [13] is found a request similar to that in the right column. However there is a distinction between death "in the faith of Christ" and death "in thy faith and fear." The first, in the left column and hence "in the faith of Christ," can be understood as the subjective genitive or as the objective genitive. The second, in the right column and thus "in thy faith and fear" means the same faith as Jesus has taught. This has consequences in the interpretation. The characterization of Jesus as sole mediator and advocate is *lacking*.

Lord all the days of their lives in holiness and righteousness.

Sixth: In [13] the request for comfort and help follows for those who in this transitory life are in trouble, sorrow, need, and sickness. References to courage, hope, and joy are *lacking*.

Seventh: From [14] to [16] comes an honouring of the holy name of God for all those servants who have departed this life in a Biblical faith and a Biblical fear. A request is made for grace to follow the good example of the departed faithful so that one might be a partaker in the heavenly kingdom. Might the heavenly Father grant this request for the sake of Jesus Christ who is sole mediator and advocate.

Because the great intercessions and thanksgivings prayer as a modification of the prayer for the church militant is almost identical with that in Series 3, we refer to what is said in our work on pages 276-77. On pages 297 to 301 in our work we have brought out additional points which require interpretation:

Reference First

Why is there lacking right at the beginning any reference to God as the principal of the apostle in teaching intercessions and thanksgivings, in contrast to the BCP 1662? This may be in connexion with the fact that in the hermeneutical discussions of the twentieth century the human aspect of the Biblical Word stands in the foreground, wherein this human side of God's Word is readily compared with the earthen vessel. And this vessel is fragile. From such a point of view it is not at all possible to understand the apostles as spokesmen of God with direct instructions from above.

Reference Second

Why is the humble petition for the gracious acceptance of the prayers directed to the divine Majesty missing in contrast with the BCP 1662?[321] It is a characteristic of the ASB 1980 that the usage of supplicatory petitions is there lacking. The most plausible explanation for this seems to me that it is due to the theology of "mankind having come of age" which has been adopted from Robinson.

According to Robinson, the idea of applying to God in a humble way stands in opposition to "the man having come of age." The autonomous man no longer knows what to do with theonomy. Robinson expresses this attitude clearly in his opinion on an often-repeated personal experience:

> Each time I go to London Airport I am met by a large notice, greeting me with the assurance: "BOAC takes good care of you." What are we to make of this declaration of secular providence? . . . When first I flew, I used to indulge in additional "cover" for those tense thirty seconds of take-off as one waits to see whether the plane will make it and leave the ground. Did my prayer in the gap—when somehow a little supernatural "lift" would always be welcome— do credit to my trust in God? I think not. I suspect that this is where a Christian ought to be a practical atheist—and trust the pilot.[322]

Reference Third

The 1662 version of the BCP speaks of unity in the sense of an agreement with the truth of Holy Scripture. Why is this definition lacking in the ASB 1980 and why does one speak only of divine truth? Has this perhaps something to do with the fact that a world church can be realized much easier through manipulation when one relies on the "Consensus Quinquesaecularis" rather than on an appeal to God's Word which merely causes divisions?

Reference Fourth

Why is the plea for salvation in an eschatological sense in regards to the Queen missing though clearly expressed in the BCP 1662? Why is the important assertion that Queen and government should serve in their work the maintenance of the true religion missing from the ASB 1980?

The conception of salvation as an eschatological reality for single individuals also, in the sense of a redemption of souls, has become irrelevant in Robinson's theology[323] which has become so influential in the English church.

That which produced the elimination of the statement that the Queen and government should serve the purpose of maintaining the true religion should be sought in connexion on the one side with the syncretistic points of departure of Robinson[324] and on the other side with the tendencies disavowing the absolute pretensions of the Christian faith at the World Mission Conference at Bangkok 73.[325] Prominent Anglicans like Father Murray Rogers[326] and Archbishop George Appleton[327] are convinced representatives of a syncretistic theology. One shouldn't underestimate the influence of the important Catholic theologian Karl Rahner with his thesis of an "anonymous Christianity" in the non-Christian religions,[328] which was championed also by Tillich and as a disciple thereof by Robinson.

Not to be forgotten is the World Council of Churches which exercises its influence in regard to the significance of other religions for Christianity through Stanley Samartha, H. J. Margull, M. M. Thomas, and many others.[329]

Reference Sixth

Why is the reference towards its end to the transitoriness of one's earthly life missing from this prayer with its plea for the sick and heavy laden? A theology oriented in a secular and horizontal direction tries to avoid the thought of transitoriness because the idea of transitoriness can animate one's hope for a better life in the hereafter and just this could paralyse the engagement to improve one's situation in this world.[330] In the ASB there is assuredly a prayer for courage, hope, and joy. It remains unclear whether this means primarily courage and hope for this world or in addition for the life after this earthly existence.

Reference Seventh

Why does the text use the term "in the faith of Christ" in its plea for participation in the glory for those who died believing in Christ as contrasted with the expression in the BCP where in the corresponding place it says "in thy faith and fear"? "In the faith of Christ" leaves open to which Christology one adheres. Faith in the sense of one's own opinion about Christ could be understood. This possibility has to be offered by a church[331] committed to relativistic pluralism.

In contrast, how clear is the text in the BCP 1662 with its expression "in thy faith and fear," which would have our faith as a thinking about God and Christ limited by that which Jesus himself teaches.

Reference 19: Prayer of Humble Access and Its Alternative

This prayer as contrasted with the corresponding one in the BCP 1662 reveals an important difference: the petition made towards the end is missing, that the sinful bodies should be cleansed through the body of Jesus and the souls washed through his precious blood:

> That our sinful bodies may be made clean by his body, and our souls washed through his most precious blood.[332]

According to the teaching in Romans 7:23-24 we all have to wear a body of death which is seen in the closest connexion with the law of sin working in our members.

The absence of the cleansing power of the blood of Jesus in this prayer could support the conception of the liberal school which rejects the atoning death of Jesus. It is very understandable not to speak of the "sinful body." The conversion to the world particularly promoted at the end of the 1960s of this century includes also the liberation of the body in the sense of an affirmation of the principle of pleasure. The BCP 1662 implies with the expression "sinful bodies" a realistic Biblical thinking which sees an inclination to uncontrolled instincts. Most interesting and noteworthy is the alternative which speaks of the cleansing power of Jesus and even that "the whole company of Christ may sit and eat in your kingdom." This new point of view could indeed be interpreted in an eschatological rather than in an innerworldly sense.

The Alternative clearly expresses the creed of pluralism.

Reference 20: Proclamation of the Peace, with Alternatives

The text refers to Ephesians 2:14 where it says that Christ is our peace. The proclamation moreover emphasizes reconciliation with God into one body. "He has reconciled us to God in one body by the cross." In the alternative proclamation of peace one finds the affirmation that all present constitute the body of Christ due to their baptism: "In the one Spirit we were all baptized into one body." Special peace proclamations are provided for Advent, Christmas, Epiphany, Lent, Easter, Ascension Day, Pentecost, and saints' days. In the traditional BCP there follows after the Prayer for the Church Militant the exhortations,[333] then, instead of peace proclamations, come confession and absolution and then immediately the "Prayer of Humble Access."

To the extent that one disposes of oneself, one belongs automatically to the body of Christ.[334] Therefore the declaration can follow "Let us then pursue all that makes for peace and builds up our common life." The expression "pursue all that makes for peace" seems to give support to the peace movements which understand peace as something which can be somewhat manufactured through structural changes in the political and economical and pyschological fields.

Reference 25: Eucharistic Prayer, with Three Alternatives

First Eucharistic Prayer

Worthy of note is the essentially different sequence in the BCP 1662 where the eucharistic prayer is immediately preceded by the four comfortable words.

After a hymn by the congregation the priest takes the bread and the cup in his hands and immediately thereafter one of the four eucharistic prayers follows. The following responsive sentences form the prelude to this prayer: "The Lord be with you."

> And also with you.

or

> The Lord is here.
> His Spirit is with us.
>
> Lift up your hearts.

We lift them to the Lord.

Let us give thanks to the Lord our God.
It is right to give him thanks and praise.

In comparison with the BCP of 1662 it is striking that the Preface and Sanctus compose together with the prayer of consecration a unity which is not interrupted by the prayer of humble access. The Preface portion is substantially longer than in the traditional BCP.

BCP 1662	ASB 1980
"It is very meet, right and our bounden duty, that we should at all times, and in all places, give thanks unto thee, O Lord, Holy Father, Almighty, Everlasting God."	"It is indeed right, it is our duty and our joy, at all times and in all places to give you thanks and praise, holy Father, heavenly King, almighty and eternal God, through Jesus Christ your only Son our Lord."
If no Preface expressly designated for Christmas, Easter, Ascension Day, Whitsunday, or Trinity follows, the conclusion of the Preface occurs forthwith with the words: "Therefore with Angels and Archangels, and with all."	For he is your living Word; through him you have created all things from the beginning, and formed us in your own image. Through him you have freed us from the slavery of sin, giving him to be born as man and to die upon the cross; you raised him from the dead and exalted him to your right hand on high. Through him you have sent upon us your holy and life-giving Spirit, and made us a people for your own possession.

The Preface portion of the first eucharistic prayer of the ASB 1980 reveals the following additional aspects:

Jesus is the living Word of God; through this living Word the heavenly Father has created all things; he has created us in his image and freed us from the slavery of sin; through Jesus God has sent us his life bestowing Spirit and made us his people who are his possession.

ASB 1980 has many more variable portions of the Preface[335] than has the BCP of 1662. In the latter there are just five variable parts of the Preface while the ASB 1980 reveals twenty-one of them. The Roman Missal[336] contains however substantially more variable parts of the Preface than the ASB 1980.

Consecration part in the BCP[337]

[1] Almighty God, our heavenly Father, who of thy tender mercy didst give thine only Son Jesus Christ to suffer death upon the cross for our redemption; [2] who made there (by his one oblation of himself once offered) a full, perfect, and sufficient sacrifice, oblation, and satisfaction, for the sins of the whole world; [3] and did institute, and in his holy Gospel command us to continue, a perpetual memory of that his precious death, until his coming again; [4] Hear us, O merciful Father, we most humbly beseech thee; [5] and grant that we receiving these thy creatures of bread and wine, according to thy Son our Saviour Jesus Christ's holy institution, in remembrance of his death and passion, may be partakers of his most blessed Body and Blood: [6] who in the same night that he was betrayed, took Bread; and, when he had given thanks, he brake it, and gave it to his disciples, saying, Take, eat, this is my Body which is given for you: [7] Do this in remembrance of me. [8] Likewise after supper he took the Cup; and, when he had given thanks, he gave it to them, saying, Drink ye all of this; for this is my Blood of the New Testament, which is shed for you and for many for the remission of sins: Do this, as oft as ye shall drink it, in remembrance of me. Amen.

Consecration part in the ASB[338]

[1] Accept our praises, heavenly Father, through your Son our Saviour Jesus Christ; [2] and as we follow his example and obey his command, grant that by the power of your Holy Spirit these gifts of bread and wine may be to us his body and his blood; [3] Who in the same night that he was betrayed, took bread and gave you thanks; [4] he broke it and gave it to his disciples, saying, Take, eat; this is my body which is given for you; [5] do this in remembrance of me. [6] In the same way, after supper he took the cup and gave you thanks; he gave it to them, saying, Drink this, all of you; this is my blood of the new covenant, which is shed for you and for many for the forgiveness of sins. [7] Do this, as often as you drink it, in remembrance of me. [8] Christ has died:

Christ is risen:

Christ will come again.[339]

[9] Therefore, heavenly Father, we remember his offering of himself made once and for all upon the cross, and proclaim his mighty resurrection and glorious ascension. [10] As we look for his coming in glory, we celebrate with this bread and this cup his one perfect sacrifice. [11] Accept through him, our great high priest, this our sacrifice of thanks and praise; [12] and as we eat and drink these holy gifts in the

presence of your divine majesty, renew us by your Spirit, inspire us with your love, [13] and unite us in the body of your Son, Jesus Christ our Lord. [14] Through him, and with him, and in him, by the power of the Holy Spirit, with all who stand before you in earth and heaven, we worship you, Father almighty, in songs of everlasting praise:

[15] Blessing and honour and glory and power be yours for ever and ever. Amen.[340]

BCP of 1662

First: The introduction from [1] to [3] expresses God's goodness through the once and sufficient sacrifice of Jesus for the redemption of men from their sins. It is obligatory, according to the mandate of the Gospel, to commemorate again and again what God has let it cost himself for our redemption. As is said in [1], this act of salvation is of his "tender mercy."

Second: Immediately after this humble approach the text introduces [4] and [5] that God might give a hearing and might bestow upon the faithful a share in his body and blood by the receiving of the gifts of bread and wine in memory of his death and suffering. The expression "most humbly beseech thee" indicates in connexion with the foregoing that it refers in the

ASB of 1980

First: In [1] the introduction to the prayer of consecration is not a petition but a command that laud and praise of the churchgoers should be accepted of the Father through Jesus Christ.

The humble approach through the proclamation of the unfathomable grace of God, which consists of the price paid for sins, is *omitted.* The following concept is *omitted:* full, perfect, and sufficient sacrifice, oblation, and satisfaction.

Second: In [2] the epiclesis is already upon us as a consecration formula.

consecration prayer to a continuation and even an augmentation of the "Prayer of Humble Access." The consecrating form of the epiclesis is lacking.

Third: The proceedings on the institution follow at the end of this long introductory on the remembrance of the sacrificial death of Jesus.

An anamnesis is *lacking.*

An allusion to the coming again is *lacking.*

The supplication that the praise and thanks be taken as a sacrifice is *lacking.*

Third: Immediately after the epiclesis follows, in [3] to [7], the institution and the words belonging thereto.

Fourth: This is something new: in the middle of the consecration prayer the congregation at [8] takes the floor and proclaims the death, the resurrection, and the coming again of Christ.

Fifth: An anamnesis is encountered at [9].

Sixth: The text at [10] speaks of the wait until his coming again.

The declarations made in the right column under [11] to [13], and [14] are *lacking.*

Seventh: At [11] to [13] we find the concern that God may accept praise and thanks as a sacrifice. There follows the entreaty that God renew and inspire with his love and unite the churchgoers in the body of Christ. In [14] the text states that mankind worships the almighty Father together with the militant and triumphant church in singing eternal praises, by virtue of the Holy Spirit.

Second Eucharistic Prayer[341]

The introductory responsive sentences are the same as in the first eucharistic prayer. The Preface part is likewise identical assuming that no special Preface provided for a special feast day must be used. Differences arise first in the consecration part.[342] The text speaks right at the beginning of the acceptance of praises in the sense of a sacrifice. The epiclesis is attached immediately thereto. Thereafter follow the words of institution. Further on in the course of the text, after the words spoken by the congregation "Christ has died—Christ is risen—Christ will come again," there follows the anamnesis, which reveals few changes.

Thus the text specifies that it is a matter of resurrection *from the dead* and ascension *into heaven*.

The imperiously expressed appeals aim at other gifts. Thus grace and heavenly blessing are requested as well as nourishment through the body and blood of Christ "that we may grow into his likeness" and thus through a unity in the Spirit to become a living temple to the glory of God. The closing doxology is similar.

Third Eucharistic Prayer[343]

The Preface portion contrasts considerably with the first and second eucharistic prayers. The text exhibits the following new aspects:[344] Jesus Christ as the living Word, through whom all things have been created; the sending of Jesus as saviour and expression of the great goodness of God; Jesus as the Word who through the Holy Spirit clothed himself in a body and walked up and down on earth among men; Jesus as the one who, on the cross, opened wide his arms for men and put an end to death through his death; Jesus revealed the resurrection by rising to new life.

In the consecration portion the text emphasizes at the beginning that God is the source of all holiness. After the epiclesis and the words of institution there follows the anamnesis in which the text stresses the emotional side in the sense of the rejoicing over resurrection, ascension, and the coming again. Toward the end one encounters the request that all churchgoers who participate in the communion might, with all the saints and hence with the church triumphant, offer praise to God.

Fourth Eucharistic Prayer[345]

The Preface portion as its principal new aspect emphasizes Jesus as the high priest who has redeemed us from our sins and made us a royal priesthood. The consecration portion conforms strongly to that of the BCP of 1662.[346] The difference consists chiefly in the existence of an epiclesis which appears later inside the consecration part than in the other three eucharistic prayers. That portion designated for the words of institution is identical with the corresponding parts of the other eucharistic prayers. The text following the anamnesis reveals a striking conformity with the first alternative closing prayer[347] of the BCP of 1662.

We now intend in resumé to define these four eucharistic prayers vis-à-vis the BCP, wherein the following features in particular stand out:

All these eucharistic prayers reveal an *unbroken canon* without any Reformation deletions, which means: preface and consecration portions are not separated one from the other nor are the epiclesis and anamnesis omitted. The requests brought before God are delivered in an imperative form: accept ..., renew us ..., hear us ..., fill us ..., nourish us ..., grant that ..., send the Holy Spirit. ... On the other hand, in the traditional BCP the characteristic form of requests is this: "We most humbly beseech thee ..." In addition, the accumulation of adjectives, so typical of the BCP, in the sense of attributes for a more detailed characterization of particular substantives[348] is to a large extent lacking.

The question presents itself to us: why does the ASB 1980 offer four eucharistic prayers? Is an important enrichment of the substance gained thereby? One can admit that as contrasted with the BCP 1662 some additional elements have been brought in which could be understood as an enrichment. These are chiefly in the third eucharistic prayer with its utterances about Christ. But the question is whether these additional utterances have on the whole really any important effect or do these additional statements instead simply do homage to the principle of supply and demand in a pluralistic sense.

The first and third eucharistic prayers in the ASB 1980 have obvious similarities to the second eucharistic prayer in the new Roman Missal.[349] It is noteworthy that the new Roman Missal is distinguished by having four eucharistic prayers.[350] Our four eucharistic prayers not only have an unbroken canon with epiclesis in common with those in the new Roman Missal, but also those sentences which are spoken by the congregation after the words of institution: "Christ has died: Christ is risen: Christ will come again."

The explanation for this harmony with the Roman Missal or for the similarities to the Roman Catholic liturgy can be best understood by those efforts which are intended to prepare for a reunion[351] with the Roman Catholic Church. A defense of the Reformation thinking, as for example the broken canon and the rejection of an epiclesis, has to be declared null and void in favour of a spirituality which needs to be created, a spirituality for the merger of the different denominations into a unified world church.

The anamnesis in the second eucharistic prayer[352] is well suited to be used by clergy oriented toward the theologically orthodox who tend a congregation which is conservative in a Biblical sense. The resurrection and the ascension are defined more exactly while room is left in the other anamnesis for a spiritual interpretation of the passion, resurrection, and ascension.

Reference 27: Words upon the Breaking of Bread

We break this bread to share in the body of Christ. Though we are many, we are one body, because we all share in one bread.

The words that are used for the breaking of the bread declare that every partaker of the holy communion belongs to the body of Christ independently of the situation as to whether the communicant has Biblical faith or not. The conception which stands behind these words for the breaking of bread reveals an ecclesiological understanding containing universalistic tendencies with which it is easiest to integrate a pluralistic society into the church. Exhortations with the warning not to receive holy communion to one's own judgement, as is the case in the BCP 1662,[353] are naturally unnecessary from the point of view of universalistic presuppositions.[354]

Reference 29: Words of Invitation

The words of invitation "draw near with faith" do not stand here in the closest connexion with the confession and absolution as in the BCP 1662. In the latter the "draw near with faith" occurs in the context of a personal confession and repentance while in the ASB 1980 it remains unclear what is the context of its "draw near with faith."[355]

Reference 30: Words of Distribution, with Alternative

In the first word of distribution the text avoids any allusion to the dichotomic structure of man when it reads: "The body of Christ keep you in eternal life. The blood of Christ keep you in eternal life." Or simply: "The body of Christ. The blood of Christ."

One will probably make concessions to those theological trends which doubt or reject the doctrine of the immortality of the soul as one finds it in the early church and in historic Protestantism.[356]

The text of the alternative words of distribution which is identical with the words of distribution in the BCP 1662, creates, in a pluralistic sense, room for an early church and historic Reformation interpretation with its conception of the dichotomy of man.[357]

Reference 36: Benediction (with Alternatives)

It is not by chance that there are twenty alternatives available for a benediction. Although these forms of benediction are not subject to challenge on a doctrinal basis they nevertheless underline in a symbolic way a commitment to pluralism.

4. APOLOGETICAL REFLECTIONS

The goal of the ASB 1980 and the preceding experimental liturgies consists of the following matters:

This new liturgical book should unite men and their manifold ideas and also to a certain degree meet a secularized society halfway. This man who is now a part of a pluralistic society needs to be taken seriously. This man should be integrated into a corporate body which the world finds credible. This corporate body is however only credible when it strives after an organizational unity in which the world in its disorientation and variety of contradictory ideas sees itself confirmed in the sense of an empathy. To this belongs a proclamation of humane structures. This implies that man is not understood as a depraved being but rather that an appeal will be made to the good in him. It would be inhuman to let one's self be told what is good and what is not. He, the man who has come of age, makes the decision what is or is not valid for him. Therefore it would be an unreasonable imposition to present truth to him in an apodictic way in the form of a catechetic statement. Modern man, having come of age, is rubbed the wrong way if he has to be exposed to exhortations. He, the modern man having come of age, is honoured if for instance one leaves as many statements in the liturgy as possible open or in suspense in regards to their answers. The alternatives express for him in a creditable way that he is able to choose the right things for himself.

The great influence with reference to the English church which Peter Staples ascribes to the theological organ of modern ideas, the *Soundings*, consists in the language of J. W. Montgomery of the following:

> Soundings stresses from beginning to end the tentativeness, uncertainty and indefiniteness of Christian truth.[358]

It is this spirituality coming from and being spread by *Soundings* and Bishop Robinson which together with the spirit of the Geneva ecumenism is reflected in the ASB 1980.

Only the best was desired for modern man: to accept and integrate him in such a way that he has to give up as little as possible. The alternatives in the ASB 1980 which can't be surveyed any more make it impossible to attach roots and feel at home in this liturgical book. But this is just what is wanted. Whoever can set his roots in a liturgy thanks to clear unequivocal Biblical statements such as are in the BCP 1662 and come to a firm conviction cannot be won to a commitment to the building of a worldwide unified church of a pluralistic character. He would resist for the sake of bearing witness to the truth. This creates division. The English church which is so devoted to the Geneva ecumenism must close its eyes to a recognition of this which Fritz Grünzweig formulates in the following way in reference to this ecumenical mentality:

> It is obvious that ecumenical literature hardly speaks of the fact that the Gospel also has a character of bringing about division.[359]

The Alternative Service Book may have certain improvements compared with the BCP 1662 in regard to the active involvement of the congregation but nevertheless from the standpoint of substance it can never measure up to the traditional Book of Common Prayer. Alternatives in a pluralistic sense which lack an unequivocal character contradict the revivalistic substance which to such a large degree is present in the BCP 1662 and which can nourish people spiritually. Without this unequivocal character there can be no revival and without clear Biblical substance no one will feel called to make a decision.

ASB 1980 may have taken some elements of the traditional BCP into consideration, but these liturgical elements of the prayer book of 1662 appear like erratic blocks. The objectives of the ASB 1980 and of the BCP 1662 differ. The BCP wants to call men out of the world in order to build

a fellowship of believers. ASB 1980 seems, based on the rites dealt with, to want to make the Reformation null and void through a great opening in relation to a spirituality of the Complexio Oppositorum where instead of decisions on one's faith there is a striving for Una Sancta. The last sentence finds its confirmation in a statement made by Archbishop Runcie (Archbishop of Canterbury) on the occasion of the fifth meeting of the "Anglican Consultative Council" in the year 1981:

> It is our vocation as Anglicans to seek for our extinction by working for the restoration of the one great universal church, the coming church.[360]

That this Church of England which is engaged to a special degree in the ecumenical movement isn't untouched by the theological trends of the World Council of Churches and will not be untouched in the future is shown by the enthusiasm in respect to the last full gathering of the ecumenical council in the Canadian port of Vancouver in the year 1983. Peter Beyerhaus who was in Vancouver as an observer, writes in his theological report on this sixth full gathering:

> The stubbornly pursued goal of the champions of the World Council of Churches is and will remain a one world church for a humanity unified across all existing boundaries into One World.[361]

Beyerhaus remarks in an emphatic way that those elements succeeded in the celebrated "Lima Liturgy" in Vancouver which we established as a strong tendency in ASB 1980 as well as in the experimental liturgies:

> The first celebration of the "Lima Liturgy" on August 31 was particularly remarkable, in which a majority of the 3500 participants received communion while the functioning clergymen under the leadership of Archbishop Runcie flanked by two female pastors represented the various denominational traditions. In this order of service which was structured according to the theological views of the previously mentioned declaration of convergence[362] the elements of the Lord's supper which hitherto were appraised in a controversial way were harmoniously joined together in a complementary manner and provided the congregation an experience of a catholic intensity never before experienced. . . . The question which arises is the following: Should the liturgical event in its in the last analysis super-rational essence bridge over the controversies of a divided Christianity which couldn't be overcome either in a doctrinal way nor through a common world engagement of ideologically loaded programs of activity? Exactly the confession of sin in the Lima Liturgy makes plain this suspicion: the ecumenical congregation called according to the Lord's prescription for his mercy

upon the sins of the Christians, who have erected walls of separation, including some between the different religions![363]

The ASB 1980 couldn't be understood without the tendencies of the World Council of Churches and Anglo-Catholic theology. In the present phase we have to conclude that not only has the World Council of Churches had an influence on the Anglican church but also the Anglican church has had an impact on the World Council of Churches, i.e., there is an interaction.

The great goal of the revision of the liturgy is the merger of the various denominations into a worldwide and organizationally visible single church. This is stated with an alarming clarity by the famous Oxford scholar G. D. Kilpatrick in his book *Remaking the Liturgy*:

> Liturgical revision is not a device for perpetuating the distinctive features of sixteenth-century Anglicanism and it should have in mind not only English-speaking Christianity but also the reunion of Christendom as a whole.[364]

In order to understand the ideological presuppositions of the ASB 1980 it is important to know that this new liturgical book wants to be first of all humane and this involves the great endeavour to pick modern man up where he is through a language adapted to him. The liturgy has to be, from the point of view of language, relevant for the present-day man and herewith we have arrived at a semantic problem.

Andor Gomme refers to the fact that a peculiar religious language is necessary in order to express spiritual matters in an adequate way. God as the totally Other One should have a language appropriate to him through which one can honour him. The heterogeneity of the language used to express a Biblical-religious content can become an impulse for someone to reflect and also become a challenge not to mix up the secular and the religious areas in a pantheistic way. With the aid of a heterogeneous language one can also find recuperation for his soul which is exhausted by everyday life and its worldly problems.

Based on the analysis of Andor Gomme the fact is that the English of the King James Version expresses with an astonishing clarity the meaning of the original Hebrew and Greek texts of Holy Scripture except for a few inaccuracies. Just because this English, not being the ordinary language of the people of those days, might contrast with the common language, one could memorize Biblical passages much easier. We let Andor Gomme speak to us:

The "vulgar" tongue into which the Bible was translated in the succession of versions culminating in 1611 was not ordinary speech; it wasn't even the ordinary literary English of the day insofar as there was such a thing. What the translators from Wycliff onwards did was to create a religious language within English: not a technical jargon like the language of biochemistry, say, but still a special creation for a special purpose: a language in which it was possible to think and talk about God. Why should we be surprised that this language is often strange and sometimes difficult? It is not easy to read the truth about God: one cannot expect to do it in the language proper for ordinary events of the day; for the truth about God is not ordinary in this sense.[365]

The language of the King James Version which is also used in The Book of Common Prayer is a language shaped by Reformation thinking. During more than three centuries this language mediating the Biblical substance was able to nourish and edify spiritually millions of people. The explanation for this is provided by Andor Gomme when he writes:

But the language of the Authorized Version proved itself—uniquely in the history of English—as fully up to its task as is humanly possible: an astounding task after all—to speak the word of God. It was not, to repeat an essential point, the ordinary language of the day, though it was contemporary English.[366]

David Martin argues in respect to epistemology and semantics, which are used to justify the modern metamorphosis of the BCP, in the following way: he makes the point that at the time of Cranmer the people had far less education than the people of this century. Human beings of today are able to fill out complicated tax forms as well as follow sophisticated commentaries on television. The cultural horizon has been widened a lot. Still, all this knowledge and information of today may not be sufficient to understand the speech and contents of The Book of Common Prayer. We let David Martin speak to us:

From 1549, the year when Cranmer first prepared the Book of Common Prayer, till 1949, most of our ancestors received little or no education and during that time Cranmer's little book was "understanded of the people." However, since 1949 a greater number of people have been educated . . . at the same time there has been a continuing evolution in methods which are designed to enrich our sensibilities and to extend our cultural horizons. The result is that the "little Book of Common Prayer" and that large miracle, the Authorized Version of the Bible, together by universal consent the crown and glory of our language, are now declared "difficult" and "misleading." . . . Meanwhile we are all apparently able to fill out income tax forms, and even to read the complicated leaflets which accompany them. . . . But not it seems, the Book of Common Prayer.[367]

David Martin demonstrates clearly that the reproach of irrelevance directed at The Book of Common Prayer because of its extreme conception of sin is not justified. Why should men who know from history about Auschwitz and the Gulag Archipelago not be able to understand what the sentences in the confession in The Book of Common Prayer want to say? Are sentences like "there is no health in us" or "we . . . are heartily sorry for our misdoings; the remembrance of them is grievous unto us; the burden of them is intolerable" not of the highest relevance?[368]

Martin asks the very legitimate question, how then do we treat fine arts and creations of musical genius. It is a matter of course to preserve valuable paintings and where necessary to restore them with the utmost care. In the interpretation of great musical compositions it is not legitimate to change them. He gives as an example a fugue by J. S. Bach. Consider how many people are spiritually enriched by listening to Bach's music: no one ventures to say "this is not timely therefore this music shouldn't be played any more."

David Martin lets it become clear how this is to be explained and so he makes the following convincing statement: Everything of a classical nature, be it in the field of architecture, painting, music, or literature, contains something timeless. It will always appeal to men time and again. He refers particularly to the language of liturgy and to the music therein. Thus he writes in this connexion:

> The big secret is that really great and inspired writing becomes "classical" and remains so! Bach's fugues, though written in the musical colloquialisms of his day, are classical for ever. The same can be applied, mutatis mutandis, to religious and liturgical literary composition. The secret of liturgy (and of Scripture in liturgical use) is its ability to become classical. . . . One of the unique features of the English "Reformation"—i.e., of the history of the Church of England—is the fact that it coincides with a climax in the history of English prose. . . . The King James Bible, the BCP and what we today associate with the name of Cranmer are lasting monuments to this accidental (or providential?) conjunction.[369]

I ask myself: Is it not a great privilege to worship the living God with a liturgy whose language has opened up the Bible for a whole nation? It is in fact the language of the Reformation which in an almost flawless form has prepared the way for the 1662 edition of the BCP through the King James Version. After all, it is the language through which re-vivalism was kindled.

Simply because the liturgy of the BCP of 1662 was able to nourish and edify people for centuries it expresses stability in the midst of a world of change, caprice, and uncertainty. Something of the static character of truth, which isn't subject to change like the wind, can break through in such a liturgy. Bryan Thwaites alludes to these thoughts when he asks the question:

> And how modern is modern?—for idiomatic usage is changing remarkably rapidly nowadays. Contrariwise: is there not much to be said for a liturgy which, in its constancy, matches the eternal and unchanging nature of God Himself?[370]

The warning of David Martin which he repeats among his students time and again is to be taken seriously:

> I spend much time explaining to my students that the definition of today's relevance is tomorrow's antiquated irrelevance.[371]

We ask in an urgent way: Is it necessary to revise The Book of Common Prayer of 1662 substantially or even to replace it by a new liturgy? Are there really linguistic-semantic and theological as well as epistemo-logical problems in connexion with secularization to justify such mea-sures as a substantial as well as formal liturgical reform?

We want to receive the answer from G. E. Duffield. Duffield sees the chief problem in the spiritual darkening of hearts. Epistemological dif-ficulties in respect to the Prayer Book cannot be solved through linguis-tic-semantic as well as theological adaptations. And this on the whole is connected with the fact that the Prayer Book 1662 is Holy Scripture in li-turgical form:

> The reason is not far to seek. Christian people are concerned that others, both inside the Church and outside, should understand better. Why is it that they do not understand? After all, education is at a higher level than ever before. . . . Is the problem just one of language? If so, it could be solved by a panel of English experts. Is it an intellectual problem? Is it that people simply cannot grasp the meaning intellectually, that it is too difficult for them? Some Christians believe that this is the problem; but the Bible has another explanation. Paul told the Corinthians that men did not believe be-cause the God of this world (the devil) had blinded them (2 Cor. 4:4). The battle is spiritual, and the devil seeks to prevent men understanding. They are dead in trespasses and sins . . . until the Spirit of God brings life and re-

news them (Eph. 2). . . . The whole thoughtworld of the Bible is foreign to them, because they do not comprehend the things of the Spirit. This analysis is nothing new; it is simply taking seriously what the Bible says about man in his natural unregenerate state (1 Cor. 2:14).[372]

Duffield has observed that in living congregations with Bible studies criticism of the prayer book is rather rare. So he concludes:

> This suggests that the "unintelligibility" of the Prayer Book is a symptom of ignorance of the Bible rather than a disease in itself. . . . The modern failure is not the failure of Bible translations and Prayer Book language but the failure of the modern church in its preaching and teaching ministry. The problem of intelligibility, we must insist, is not intellectual nor linguistic, but basically spiritual. And the only proven answer is in the power of the Spirit to enlighten the heart and mind, and on the human level in the patient long-term teaching and exposition of biblical faith.[373]

Now there are passages in the Bible and also in the Prayer Book which one doesn't understand at the first attempt. Would it not be proper to simplify such passages so that they would become immediately understandable without any explanation?

Duffield's answer seems to me to be the right one when he emphasizes that the churchgoer needs to take the trouble to understand what has been heard and read. Otherwise one would arrive quickly at that point where one would not consider attendance at a church service as something worthwhile:

> The outsider cannot expect to grasp everything first time. If he could, he might conclude there was little need to come back! With the real outsider, we may have to start a long way off and gradually teach him biblical ideas.[374]

In respect to difficult passages Bryan Thwaites clearly shows that the many repetitions of liturgical points have the purpose of providing time for contemplation precisely in relation to the difficult passages. In this connexion he criticizes the very short formulas in the ASB 1980:

> Is brevity—no, not the soul of wit; is brevity an end in itself? Or: Does not repetition, either of words and phrases or of ideas, give the mind time to grasp and contemplate the meaning? . . . Is there no room for subtlety and allusion?[375]

The most central and crucial reason why the Prayer Book 1662 should continue to exist is due to the fact—and this cannot be stressed too greatly—that this precious liturgy is a product of Holy Scripture itself.

Therefore we want to let the warning of Peter Newman Brooks have a strong impact when he tells us:

> For make no mistake about it, the Book of Common Prayer is a very holy thing. To shelve it altogether, as if it were some kind of embarrassing report of a select committee of inquiry, would be as absurd as it would be to shelve Holy Scripture itself, to abandon the very quarry, the bedrock, whence the liturgy was itself originally hewn. No, the English liturgy of 1662 must always remain an alternative to any new collection. And it must be a real alternative—not some kind of compromise in the tradition of the imagined "via media Anglicana," or a mere early morning alternative in a side chapel.[376]

For our discovery that the BCP 1662 appeals with its revivalistic substance most of all to the heart and feeling of man, we find a confirmation by Peter Newman Brooks. To take The Book of Common Prayer away from the church people would be a pastoral affront; for the experimental liturgy and the ASB 1980 are not able to nourish and uplift the soul to the extent of the BCP 1662. A pluralistic mentality with its uncertainty does not offer man a real ministry to his soul. In a time of spiritual isolation and disorientation it is most important to stand at the barricades in defence of The Book of Common Prayer 1662. The warning of Peter Newman Brooks may have its impact, when he writes:

> What wisdom there is in such a context of pastoral concern! For make no mistake about it, stewardship in this vital matter of the Book of Common Prayer primarily relates to matters of the heart and soul. It is certainly for such considerations that Cranmer's masterpiece remains of the greatest comfort, providing consolation and hope today just as it has done down the long corridor of time.[377]

APPENDIX ON THE EXPLANATION OF
LITURGICAL TERMS

1. INTROIT

This was initially the song upon the entrance of the clergy into the church prior to the beginning of mass. Today the introit in the liturgies assimilated to the Western rite (Lutheran and Old Catholic formulas) comes after the congregation's action of penance. As a rule the introit consists of one or two verses from the Psalms. The so-called minor doxology, a formula for the glorification of the Trinity, closes the introit: "Glory be to the Father, and to the Son, and to the Holy Ghost; as it was in the beginning, is now, and ever shall be, world without end. Amen." The congregation often speaks this little antiphon as a reply after the choir has sung the verse of the introit. The first word of the introit has in many places become the name of the particular Sunday such as "Laetare," "Jubilate," "Cantate," etc.

The formula of the introit has indeed been known since the fifth century.[1]

2. AGNUS DEI

This song, "Lamb of God, which taketh away the sins of the world, have mercy upon us," is based on John 1:29. As a liturgical formula it is borrowed from the Syrian Church. Pope Sergius I introduced the "Agnus Dei" into Western liturgy in the seventh century. In eucharistic liturgies of a Western character the "Agnus Dei" is sung shortly before the receiving of holy communion.[2]

3. THE CANON

In the Roman liturgy it is understood as that combination of short prayers which are offered in connexion with the consecration of the elements. Most of these prayers remain the same. The following portions constitute the canon: the "Sursum Corda," with the attached "Sanctus," a petition for the acceptance of the offering of bread and wine, a prayer for the living and a prayer for the offering, then the words of institution, next the anamnesis, again a prayer for the gracious acceptance of the offering, further a petition for the fruitful taking of the sacrament, memorial of the dead and the saints, finally again two doxologies. Ambrosius mentions the basic elements of the eucharistic canon in his work "De Sacramentis" (circa A.D. 378). These elements have been included in the Gelasian and Gregorian sacramentaries of theseven7th century and have been traditional up into the twentieth century.[3]

4. PREFACE WITH SURSUM CORDA

The Preface is the opening prayer of thanks in the canon. It includes the "Sursum Corda" and the great thanksgiving prayer which then merges into the "Sanctus." A summons ushers in the great prayer of thanks: "Lift up your hearts [Sursum Corda]." Then comes the summons: "Let us give thanks unto our Lord God." The congregation replies: "It is meet and right so to do." Then comes the great prayer of thanksgiving in which homage is paid to God the Father. In it the prayer mentions the hierarchy of angels as an illustration of the proper way to worship God.

The Preface with Sanctus became an important part of the Alexandrian liturgy just before the Nicene Council toward the end of the third century. The Preface in its original form had been taken from that liturgy into the Syrian Church and in the fifth century into the Latin. Probably the Eastern Popes Zosimus, Hormisdas, and Sergius I were the intermediaries. There were Greek, Syrian, and Egyptian monasteries in Rome where the Eastern liturgies were well cultivated.[4]

5. SANCTUS

The prayer of thanks in the Preface merges into the great praise of the angels as it is mentioned in Isaiah 6:3: "Holy, holy, holy, is the Lord of hosts: the whole earth is full of his glory."

The closing portion appended to the Sanctus is called "Benedictus," since this passage from Matthew 21:9b in the Vulgate version opens with Benedictus.[5]

6. ANAMNESIS

The anamnesis is that portion toward the close of the canon in which the most important historical events of salvation are mentioned in a representational sense, such as the passion, resurrection, and ascension.[6]

7. EPICLESIS

The epiclesis is that prayer in the canon which implores the descending of the Holy Spirit upon the elements of bread and wine for the consecration of the same. These epicleses are chiefly a peculiarity of the Eastern liturgies. The Gallic rite took up the epiclesis in the West. From there it was taken into the Sarum missal which constituted the principal model for the BCP of 1549.[7]

8. THE MAJOR GLORIA[8]

This hymn begins with the song of the angels in Luke 2:14. In the East the Gloria was expanded. This doxology was already known in the transition period between the fourth and fifth centuries in Egypt, Syria, and Asia Minor. In the Codex Alexandrinus (about A.D. 400) the major Gloria is found as an annex to the Psalter. The Gloria belonged originally in the ecclesiastical tradition of the East to the morning office. St. Hilary of Poitiers (died 368) imported this great doxology toward the end of the fourth century into the Latin-Western tradition. The major Gloria was already an ingredient of the divine service of mass under Pope Symmachus (498-514).[9]

9. MISERERE OR KYRIE ELEISON

The Miserere follows immediately after the introit in eucharistic liturgies of the Western type. The Miserere is primarily the answer of the congregation to the litany. This answering cry of "Lord, have mercy upon me" stems from the liturgies used in Jerusalem and Antioch in the fourth century. A litany with the antiphonal Kyrie Eleison was received into the liturgy of the mass during the pontificate of Pope Gelasius (492-504). Under Pope Gregory the Great (590-604) the litany was eliminated and there remained only the antiphon, "Kyrie Eleison, Christe Eleison."[10]

10. TE DEUM LAUDAMUS

This hymn is also known under the name "Ambrosian Song of Praise." To be sure, Ambrose of Milan (died 397) is not the author of this hymn. Certain hymnologists ascribe it to Niketa of Remesiana (340-414). This hymn was taken in the sixth century into the canonical hours and specifically at the beginning of lauds. The Te Deum consists of three parts: 1. A praising of God with its attached doxology; 2. A hymn to Christ; 3. The closing portion with some verses from the Psalms.[11]

BIBLIOGRAPHY

A. SOURCES

The First and Second Prayer Books of King Edward VI, Every Man's Library No. 448, London 1968.

The Book of Common Prayer 1559, John E. Booty, ed., The University Press of Virginia, Charlottesville 1976.

The Book of Common Prayer, Pocket Book Edition, Oxford, 1969.

Alternative Services: Second Series, An Order for Holy Communion, Cambridge 1966/1967.

An Order for Holy Communion, Alternative Services Series 3, Margate 1970/1971.

The Alternative Service Book 1980, London 1980.

Missale Sarum, edited by J. Wickham Legg, Oxford 1966.

Missale Romanum, Edition VIII juxta Typicam Vaticanam, Regensburg, 1923.

Lateinisch-Deutsches Volksmessbuch, edited by U. Bomm, Einsiedeln 1961.

Deutsches Messbuch I & II, Regensburg 1975.

Breviarum Romanum, Regensburg 1961.

The Saint Andrew Daily Missal, St. André-near Bruges 1951.

The Sunday Missal, London 1975.

Martin Bucer, *Censura*, translated by E. C. Whitaker, Alcuin Club Collections No. 55, Mayhew-McCrimmon 1975.

Martin Bucer, *Loci Communes*, ed. by D. F. Wright, Appleford 1972.

Martin Bucer, *De Regno Christi*, edited by François Wendel, Gütersloh 1955.

Heinrich Bullinger, *The Second Helvetic Confession 1566*, edited by Arthur C. Cochrane, London 1966.

Heinrich Bullinger, *De Testamento seu Foedere Dei Unico*, Zurich 1534.

John Calvin, *Institutes of the Christian Religion*, ed. by J. T. McNeill, translated by F. L. Battles (2 vols.) London and Philadelphia 1960.

Cranmer's Works, vols. I and II, ed. for the Parker Society by John E. Cox, Cambridge 1844-1846.

The Remains of Edmund Grindal, ed. by W. Nicholson, Cambridge 1843.

R. Hooker, *Of the Laws of Ecclesiastical Polity*, Oxford 1874.

John Hooper, *Early Writings*, Cambridge 1843.

John Hooper, *Later Writings*, Cambridge 1852.

Ludwig Lavater, *De Ritibus et Institutius Ecclesiae Tigurinae*, Zurich 1559.

Petrus Martyr, *Defensio Doctrinae Veteris et Apostolicae de Sacrosancto Eucharistiae Sacramento*, Zurich 1559.

Petrus Martyr, *In Selectissimam S. Pauli Priorem ad Corinth*. Epistolam . . . Commentarii doctissimi . . . , Tiguri ex officina Christ, Zurich 1551.

Petrus Martyr, *In Epistolam S. Pauli ad Romanos* . . . , Basilea apud Petrum Per nam 1558.

[The citations from the above works of Martyr are chiefly taken from the *Veritas Sacramenti* of Salvatore Corda, Theol. Verlag Zurich 1975. Adequate page references to these Latin works of Vermigli are to be found there. Other citations are taken from *The Visible Words of God* by J. C. McLelland, Edinburgh 1957.]

Original Letters relative to the English Reformation, Vols I and II, Cambridge 1847 and 1856.

Zurich Letters, 1558-1579, Parker Society, Cambridge 1842.

Huldrych Zwingli, *In catabaptistarum strophas elenchus*, Zurich 1527.

B. SECONDARY LITERATURE

Karl Adam, *Das Wesen des Katholizismus*, 4th Edition, Munich 1927.

A. M. Allchin, *The Silent Rebellion—Anglican Communities*, 1845-1900, London 1958.

M. W. Anderson, *Peter Martyr, A Reformer in Exile*, Niewkop, 1975.

P. F. Anson, *The Call of the Cloisters—Religious Communities and Kindred Bodies in the Anglican Communion*, London 1964.

Karl Barth, *Dogmatik III*, 2, Zurich 1948.

Karl Barth, *Gesetz und Evangelium*, Zollikon 1961.

R. T. Beckwith, ed., *Towards a Modern Prayer Book*, Appleford/Abingdon 1966.

Peter Beyerhaus, *Bangkok 73, Anfang oder Ende der Weltmission*, Bad Liebenzell 1973.

Peter Beyerhaus, *Aufbruch der Armen*, Bad Liebenzell 1981.

Peter Beyerhaus, "Vancouver: Schwerpunkte und Konsequenzen," *DIAKRISIS*, Bielefeld September 1983.

C. Bodington, *Devotional Life in the 19th Century*, London 1905.

J. C. Bowmer, *The Sacrament of the Lord's Supper in Early Methodism*, London 1951.

Josef Braun, *Der Christliche Altar*, Munich 1924.

Josef Braun, *Die Liturgische Gewandung in Occident und Orient nach Ursprung und Entwicklung, Verwendung und Symbolik,* 1907.

W. M. Brett, "A Critique of the Series 3 Communion Service," *The Anglican Catholick,* vol. 8, no. 33, 1978.

Stella Brook, *The Language of The Book of Common Prayer*, Oxford 1965.

G. W. Bromiley, *Thomas Cranmer, Theologian*, New York 1956.

F. Büchsel, "μονογενῳ," *Theologische Wörterbuch zum Neuen Testament* (Th.W.N.T), vol. IV, Stuttgart 1942. Translated and edited by Geoffrey Bromiley, Grand Rapids, 1979-1982.

Kuno Bugmann, *Kirche und Sakramente,* Einsiedeln 1945.

Heinrich Bullinger, *Das Zweite Helvetische Bekenntnis*, Zurich 1967.

Heinrich Bullinger (1504-1575), *Collected Essays on the 400th Anniversary of His Death*, vol. I, Zurich 1975.

Edward Cardwell, *A History of Conferences and other proceedings connected with the Revision of THE BOOK OF COMMON PRAYER* ... Oxford 1849, republished Ridgeway, N.J. 1966.

C. S. Carter, *The English Church in the Seventeenth Century,* London 1909.

O. Chadwick, *The Mind of the Oxford Movement*, London 1963.

Joseph Chambon, *Der Puritanismus,* Zollikon-Zurich 1944.

A. C. Cochrane, ed., *Reformed Confessions of the 16th Century*, Philadelphia 1966.

C. H. Colette, *The Life, Times and Writings of Thomas Cranmer*, London 1887.

Patrick Collinson, *Archbishop Grindal*, London 1979.

Patrick Collinson, *The Elizabethan Puritan Movement*, London 1967.

Patrick Collinson, "The Reformer and the Archbishop," *Journal of Religious History,* VI (1970)

James H. Cone, "Schwarze Theologie und Schwarze Befreiung," in Basil

Moore, editor, *Schwarze Theologie in Afrika, Dokumente einer Bewegung*, Göttingen 1973.

G. Cope, article on "Gestures," "Postures," and "Vestments" in the *Dictionary of Liturgy and Worship*, edited by J. G. Davies, London 1974.

Salvatore Corda, *Veritas Sacramenti*, Zurich 1975.

Jack Warren Cottrell, "Is Bullinger the Source for Zwingli's Doctrine of the Covenant?" See *Zürcher Beiträge zur Reformationsgeschichte, Heinrich Bullinger 1504-1575, Collected Essays on the 400th Anniversary of his Death*, vol. I, Zurich 1975.

Harvey Cox, *The Seduction of the Spirit*, London 1974.

Harvey Cox, *The Secular City*, New York 1966.

F. C. Cross, *The Oxford Movement and the Seventeenth Century*, London 1963.

Oscar Cullmann, "Oekumenismus im Lichte des Biblischen Charisma Begriffs," in *Theologische Literaturzeitung*, 1972.

J. G. Davies, *A Dictionary of Liturgy and Worship*, London 1974.

H. Davies, *Worship and Theology in England*, vol. I, Princeton, N.J. 1970.

Charles Davis, *A Question of Conscience*, New York 1967.

Peter Day, *Capsule Report*, Consultation on Church Union (CoCU), Denver 1971.

Henrici Denzinger, *Enchiridion Symbolorum*, Freiburg 1946.

Leslie Dewart, *The Future of Belief*, New York 1966.

Gregory Dix, *The Shape of the Liturgy*, Glasgow 1947.

J. P. Donnelly, *Calvinism and Scholasticism in Vermigli's Doctrine of Man and Grace*, Leiden 1976.

J. Dowden, *The Workmanship of the Prayer Book*, London 1904.

G. E. Duffield, *The Work of Thomas Cranmer*, Philadelphia 1965.

G. R. Dunstan, *The Artifice of Ethics*, London 1974.

Gerhard Ebeling, *Aufsatz die Rechtfertigung der historisch-kritischen Methode betreffend*, in ZThK 1950.

H. Eels, *Martin Bucer*, New York 1971.

Joseph Fletcher, *Situation Ethics: The New Morality*, Philadelphia 1966.

Joseph Fletcher, *Moral Responsibility: Situation Ethics at Work*, Westminster 1967.

Christina Garrett, *The Marian Exiles*, Cambridge 1938, reprinted 1966.

M. J. Gaxiola, "Salvation Today: A Critical Report," in R. Winter, ed., *The Evangelical Response to Bangkok*, Pasadena 1973.

G. Gloege, article on "Biblizismus," *RGG* vol. I, 1957.

Charles Gore, *Lux Mundi, A Series of Studies in the Religion of the Incarnation*, London 1889.

W. Jardine Grisbrooke, article on "Cathedral Offices," "Anaphora," and "Kyrie" in *Dictionary of Liturgy and Worship*, ed. by J. G. Davies, London 1974.

Fritz Grünzweig, article "Welteinheit durch Kircheneinheit?" in *Reich Gottes oder Weltgemeinschaft?* edited by Peter Beyerhaus and Walter Künneth, Bad Liebenzell 1975.

W. Haller, *The Rise of Puritanism*, Philadelphia 1972.

A. E. Harvey, *Martin Bucer in England*, Marburg 1906.

Friedrich Heiler, *Der Katholizismus*, Munich 1923.

Sergius Heitz, *Der Orthodoxe Gottesdienst*, Mainz 1965.

Karl Heussi, *Kompendium der Kirchengeschichte*, Tübingen 1928.

C. Hopf, *Martin Bucer and the English Reformation*, Oxford 1946.

G. Huelin, "Peter Martyr and the English Reformation," London University Ph.D. thesis, London 1955.

W. Hugelshofer, "Zum Porträt des Petrus Martyr Vermilius," *Zwingliana* V (1930), pp. 127-29.

P. E. Hughes, *Theology of the English Reformers*, London 1965.

Kurt Hutten, *Seher, Grübler und Enthusiasten*, Stuttgart 1968.

G. Itti, *Dans quelle mésure Bucer est-il piétiste?*

E. Jammers, "Ambrosianischer Lobgesang" and "Introitus" in *RGG*, vols. I and III, 1957/1959.

R. C. D. Jasper, article on the "Canon" in the *Dictionary of Liturgy and Worship*, ed. by J. G. Davies, London 1974.

Markus Jenny, *Die Einheit des Abendmahlsgottesdienst*, Zurich 1968.

E. M. Jung, "On the Nature of Evangelism in 16th Century Italy."

W. Jung, *Liturgisches Wörterbuch*, Berlin 1964.

John Keble, *Sermons for the Christian Year*, I-XI, London/Oxford 1875-1880.

John Keble, "A sermon, preached at the Cathedral Church of Winchester, September 27, 1836," London 1837.

Max Keller-Hüschemenger, *Die Lehre der Kirche in der Oxford bewegung, Struktur und Funktion*, Gütersloh 1974.

G. D. Kilpatrick, *Remaking the Liturgy*, London 1967.

M. G. King, *Foxe's Book of Martyrs*, Old Tappan, N.J. 1975

E. Koch, *Die Theologie der Confessio Helvetica Posterior, Beiträge zur Geschichte und Lehre der Reformierten Kirche*, vol. XXVII, Neukirchen 1968.

E. W. Kohls, *Das Wort Gottes hat alles gehandelt*, Lahr 1983.

E. W. Kohls, *Luther oder Erasmus*, vol. I, Basel 1972.

E. W. Kohls, *Mein Bibelkatechismus zum Alten Testament, zum Neuen Testament und zur Kirchengeschichte,* Marburg 1983.

Helmut Kressner, "Schweizer Ursprünge des Anglikanischen Staatskirchentums," dissertation, Gütersloh 1953.

W. Künneth, *Fundamente des Glaubens,* Wuppertal 1974.

August Lang, *Puritanismus und Pietismus,* Neukirchen 1941.

Ludwig Lavater, *De ritibus et institutis Tigurinae,* Zurich 1559, ed. 1702.

D. H. Lawrence, *Lady Chatterly's Lover,* London 1972.

J. B. Lightfoot, ed., *The Apostolic Fathers,* Grand Rapids 1973.

E. A. Litton, *Introduction to Dogmatic Theology,* London 1960.

G. W. Locher, *Huldrych Zwingli in neuer Sicht, Zehn Beiträge zur Theologie der Zürcher Reformation,* Zurich 1969.

G. W. Locher, *Streit unter Gästen,* Zurich 1972.

G. W. Locher, *Zwingli's Einfluss in England und Schottland,* Zwingliana vol. XIV, book 4, 1975.

Walter Lotz, *Das Hochzeitliche Gewand,* Kassel 1949.

H. J. Margull and St. Samartha, *Dialog mit andern Religionen, Material aus der ökumenischen Bewegung,* Frankfort 1972.

David Martin, *A Sociology of English Religion,* New York 1964.

A. J. Mason, *Thomas Cranmer,* London 1898.

Wilhelm Maurer, *Gesammelte Aufsätze,* vol. I, Göttingen 1970.

J. C. McLelland, *The Visible Words of God,* Edinburgh 1957.

Philipp McNair, *Petrus Martyr in Italy, An Anatomy of Apostasy,* Oxford 1967.

B. Moeller, "Reichsstadt und Reformation," *SVRG* no. 180, 1962.

J. Moltmann, "Gemeinschaft in einer geteilten Welt," *Beiheft zur ökumenischen Rundschau* no. 23, Utrecht 1972.

H. Montefiore, *Awkward Questions on Christian Love,* London 1964.

J. W. Montgomery, *The Suicide of Christian Theology,* Minneapolis 1975.

Brian Morris, ed., *Ritual Murder,* Manchester 1980.

E. F. K. Müller, *Die Bekenntnisschriften der Reformierten Kirche,* Leipzig 1903.

Charles Neil, *The Tutorial Prayer Book,* London 1963.

J. H. Newman, *The Via Media of the Anglican Church,* vol. I, *Lectures of the Prophetical Office of the Church,* London 1891.

J. H. Newman, *Tracts for the Times, Remarks on Certain Passages in the Thirty-Nine Articles,* London 1841.

J. H. Newman, *An Essay on the Development of Christian Doctrine,* London 1914.

W. Nijenhuis, *Traces of a Lutheran Eucharistic Doctrine in Thomas Cranmer,* Ecclesia Reformata, Studies on the Reformation, Leiden 1972.

Walter Nitsch, "Emanuel Swedenborg und sein geschichtlicher Einfluss bis in unsere Zeit," *Bibel und Gemeinde,* Waldbronn, April-June 1983.

E. R. Norman, *Church and Society in England 1770-1970,* London 1976.

J. I. Packer, *Introduction to the Work of Thomas Cranmer,* Appleford 1964.

James Pike, *What Is This Treasure?* New York 1966.

C. E. Pocknee, article on "Altar Hangings," "Altar Rails," and "Reredos" in *A Dictionary of Liturgy and Worship,* ed. by J. G. Davies, London 1974.

C. E. Pocknee, article on "The Sacrament of Sacrifice" in *The Anglican Catholick,* vol. 7, no. 31, 1977.

C. E. Pocknee, article on "The English Reformers and the Mass," in *The Anglican Catholick,* vol. 6, no. 27, 1976.

A. F. Pollard, *Thomas Cranmer and the English Reformation,* London 1904.

G. R. Potter, *Zwingli,* Cambridge 1976.

O. Procksch, article on "Die Verwendung des Heiligkeitsbegriffs im Alten Testament," *Theol. Wörterbuch zum Neuen Testament,* vol. I, edited by Gerhard Kittel, Stuttgart 1933.

Procter and Frère, *New History of The Book of Common Prayer,* London 1949.

G. E. Pruett, "A Protestant Doctrine of the Eucharistic Presence," *Calvin Theological Journal,* vol. X, no. 2, 1975.

Karl Rahner, *Das Christentum und die nichtchristlichen Religionem,* Schriften zur Theologie V, Einsiedeln 1962.

B. Rainbow, *The Choral Revival in the Anglican Church,* London 1970.

M. Ramsey, *From Gore to Temple,* London 1960.

C. C. Richardson, "Cranmer and the Analysis of Eucharistic Doctrine," *The Journal of Theological Studies* XVI/2, 1965.

C. C. Richardson, *Zwingli and Cranmer on the Eucharist, Cranmer dixit et contradixit,* Evanston 1949.

A. L. Richter, *Die Evangelischen Kirchenordnungen des 16. Jahrhunderts,* Weimar 1846.

Jasper Ridley, *Thomas Cranmer,* Oxford 1966.

Otto Riecker, "Das evangelistische Wort," Heidelberg 1935 (dissertation).

J. A. T. Robinson, *Honest to God,* London 1965.

J. A. T. Robinson, *On Being the Church in the World*, London 1960.

J. A. T. Robinson, *The New Reformation?* London 1965.

J. A. T. Robinson, *Liturgy Coming to Life*, London 1960.

E. G. Rupp, *Studies in the Making of the English Protestant Tradition*, Cambridge 1947.

G. W. E. Russel, *Arthur Stanton—A Memoir*, London 1917.

Werner Schilling, *Heiliges Abendmahl oder Feierabendmahl?* Lahr-Dinglingen, 1980.

Martin Schmidt and Wilhelm Jannasch, *Das Zeitalter des Pietismus*, Bremen 1965 (Dieterich Collection vol. 271).

Martin Schmidt, article on "England," in *RGG* II, 1958.

Martin Schmidt, article on "Presbyterianer," in *RGG* V, 1961.

H. J. Schulz, *Symbolik des Orthodoxen Christentums*, Stuttgart 1962.

R. L. Schuyler, *Cardinal Documents in British History*, Princeton 1961.

Wigand Siebel, "Origenismus in der Katholischen Kirche," in *DIAKRISIS*, Bielefeld, February 1982.

C. H. Smyth, *Cranmer and the Reformation under Edward VI*, London 1926.

W. Solowjew, *Die Erzählung vom Antichrist*, Lucerne 1946.

R. C. Sproul, *Explaining Inerrancy: A Commentary*, Oakland 1980.

C. H. Spurgeon, *Twelve Sermons on Soul-Winning*, London.

Peter Staples, *The Church of England 1961-1980*, Utrecht-Leiden 1981.

W. P. Stephens, *The Holy Spirit in the Theology of Martin Bucer*, Cambridge 1970.

R. Stupperich, article on "Bucer," in *RGG* I, 1957.

K. Sturm, "Die Theologie Peter Martyr Vermigli's während seines ersten Aufenthalts in Strassburg 1542-1547, ein Reformkatholik unter den Vätern der Reformierten Kirche," *Beiträge zur Geschichte und Lehre der Reformierten Kirche*, vol. XXXI, Neukirchen 1971.

William Temple, *Nature, Man and God*, London 1934.

William Temple, *Revelation, A Symposium*.

Edith Thomas, *Das Gotteshaus*, Kassel 1964.

M. M. Thomas, *Beiheft zur Oekumenischen Rundschau*, no. 24, Geneva 1973.

W. H. Griffith Thomas, *The Catholick Faith*, London 1911.

W. H. Griffith Thomas, *The Principles of Theology, an Introduction to the Thirty-Nine Articles*, London 1930.

Istvan Tökés, "Bullinger's hermeneutische Lehre," in *Heinrich Bullinger (1504-1575), Collected Essays on the 400th Anniversary of His Death*, vol. I, Zurich 1975.

G. M. Trevelyan, *A Shortened History of England,* London 1971.

Evelyn Underhill, *Worship,* London 1962.

Paul van Buren, "The Dissolution of the Absolute," *Religion in Life,* XXIV, Summer 1964.

Dieter Voll, *Hochkirchlicher Pietismus,* Munich 1960.

H. E. Weber, *Reformation, Orthodoxie und Rationalismus,* Darmstadt 1937-1951.

O. Weber, *Grundlagen der Dogmatik,* vols. I and II, Neukirchen 1955.

G. Weiss-Stähelin, article on "Vermigli," in *RGG* VI, 1962.

W. M. S. West, *John Hooper and the Origins of Puritanism,* Zurich 1955.

W. M. S. West, *A Study of John Hooper with Special Reference to his Contact with Henry Bullinger,* Zurich 1953.

E. C. Whitaker, *Martin Bucer and the Book of Common Prayer,* Great Pickering 1975.

Benjamin Whitehead, *Church Law, Being a concise Dictionary of Statutes, Canons, Regulations . . . ,* London 1911.

Ralph Winter, ed., *The Evangelical Response to Bangkok,* Pasadena 1973.

Kurt von Wistinghausen, *Der Neue Gottesdienst,* Stuttgart 1965.

William Wordsworth, *The Ecclesiastical Sonnets,* Oxford 1973.

D. F. Wright, *Martin Bucer,* Appleford 1972.

C. PERIODICALS

Beihefte zur Oekumenischen Rundschau.

Beiträge zur Geschichte und Lehre der Reformierten Kirche Bibel und Gemeinde.

Calvin Theological Journal.

DIAKRISIS.

Die Religion in Geschichte und Gegenwart (RGG) 1957-1962.

Journal of Theological Studies.

Religion in Life.

Religious News Service (New York).

Schriften des Vereins für Reformationsgeschichte (SVRG).

Soundings, Cambridge 1962.

The Anglican Catholick

The British Critic.

The Journal of Ecclesiastical History (JEH).

The Journal of Religious History.
Theologische Literaturzeitung (ThLZ).
Theologische Wörterbuch zum Neuen Testament (ThWNT) 1933-1974.
Zeitschrift für Theologie und Kirche (ZThK).
Zwingliana.

D. PATRISTIC AND MEDIEVAL LITERATURE

Augustine, *De Civitate Dei* VI, 12 (The City of God), translated by D. B. Zema and G. G. Walsh, in *The Fathers of the Church,* vol. 6, p. 337, Washington 1977. See p. 313 in our work, reference to note 351.

Augustine, *De Doctrina Christiana,* lib. 3,28. See an English translation in Saint Augustine, *On Christian Doctrine,* translated by D. W. Robertson, Jr., New York 1958, p. 102. See p. 93, second quotation, in our work which refers to this work of Augustine.

Augustine, *In Joan.*, Tract 25, *Bibliothek der Kirchenväter* vol. 11, *Bibliothek der Kirchenväter,* Munich 1911. See page 119 in our work.

Cyril of Jerusalem, Catechesis XVIII, 26, in *The Fathers of the Church,* vol. 64 [vol. 2, p. 134], Washington 1970. See pp. 184-85 in our work.

Eusebius Emissenus, *Sermo de Eucharistia*; Cranmer gives no closer reference for his citation from Eusebius. See p. 119 in our work.

Hieronymus, *In Hieremiam*, chap. 8. The passage cited by Cranmer is not to be found in the German translation in the *Bibliothek der Kirchenväter.* See pp. 91-92 in our work. The second quotation in note 16 is from Hieronymus.

John Chrysostomos, *De Lazaro,* Sermons 3 and 4, also the 35th. Homilies on Genesis 14. The passages cited by Cranmer are not to be found in the German translation of the *Bibliothek der Kirchenväter.* See p. 93 in our work. The last quotation refers to a quotation from Chrysostom.

John Gerson, *De auferibilitate Papae,* edition of L. E. Dupin, 5 volumes, Antwerp 1706. Cranmer gives no precise reference.

Ignatius of Antioch, *Epistle to the Smyrnaeans 8*, translated by J. B. Lightfoot, in *The Apostolic Fathers,* p. 84, Grand Rapids 1973. See p. 184, first quotation, in our work.

Origin, *De oratione XXX, 3,* translated by J. J. O'Meara, in *Ancient Christian Writers,* vol. XIX, pp. 131-32, New York 1954.

Panormitan; Cranmer cites this teacher in the medieval church but gives no closer reference.

Theodoret of Kyrus, *Eranistes seu Polymorphus*; Cranmer cites Theodoret but gives no closer reference.

Vincent of Lérins, "Commonitories" chap. 2, in *The Fathers of the Church*, vol. 7, p. 270, translated by R. E. Morris, Washington 1970. See p. 184 in our work.

John Calvin, *Institutes of the Christian Religion* IV,1,2, 2 vols. London and Philadelphia 1960. See pp. 186-87.

Greek Liturgies, *Bibliothek der Kirchenväter,* vol. 5, Munich 1912. See Apostolic Constitutions. Cf. p. 216 in our work, reference to note 330.

CLOSING SUMMARY

This work has made it its business to present The Book of Common Prayer 1662 as a unity of liturgy and the awakening of faith in which the following apologetical concerns constantly find expression: Up to the present no liturgy has been used in the Anglican church which can compare with the BCP of 1662. Therefore the preservation of this liturgical book is of great importance.

To understand the secret of why this unity of liturgy and revival or awakening of faith functions is in fact the main concern of this composition.

The awakening of faith with the purpose of glorifying God through worship is the chief purpose of Holy Scripture.

This work now tries to prove that unity of liturgy and revival is only realized where Holy Scripture is given unlimited room in the liturgy. This is not the case with the BCP of 1549 which is still permeated with many Catholic elements. In the prayer books of 1552 and 1662 the Reformation principle of "sola scriptura" has succeeded, with its special puritanical emphasis, in bringing the Bible with its offer of salvation in a propagandizing way to the churchgoer.

Is the BCP of 1662 anything other than God's Word, which has been arranged artistically in a liturgical form?

With the discussion of the experimental liturgies and The Alternative Service Book 1980 the evidence should establish that by reducing Biblical materials in the liturgy in favour of ecumenical[1] elements, unity of ritual and revival is lost. The danger then is that such a liturgy becomes representative of a church in the sense of an ideologically oriented organization which holds its members together through a festive frame.

Where "pura doctrina" is a "cantus firmus" in the liturgy, there the power is present for building up a congregation.

There is a value of uniqueness in the fact that a liturgical book under a Reformation-puritanical premise comprehends in a Biblically disciplined way the legitimate elements of the early church, the Middle Ages, Protestantism, and, most of all, an anticipation of pietism. This is indeed also the legitimate "Via Media." Therefore, may The Book of Common Prayer of 1662 be preserved still for many generations for the awakening of faith and edification!

NOTES

NOTES TO PREFACE

1. This abbreviation, here and elsewhere in this work, refers to The Book of Common Prayer.

2. The term "revival" occurs here and there with Peter Martyr. See p. 28 in our work.

3. Cf. Martin Schmidt and Wilhelm Jannash, *Das Zeitalter des Pietismus*, Bremen 1965, pp. xxvii-xxix.

4. The term "puritanism" was already existent in 1567. Cf. W. Haller, *The Rise of Puritanism*, p. 378, under 3. We limit the term "puritanism" to Hooper puritanism.

5. See "Walter Nitsch, Emanuel Swedenborg und sein geschichtlicher Einfluss in unserer Zeit," in *Bible und Gemeinde*, April-June 1983, pp. 162-73.

6. See *RGG*, vol. IV, Tübingen 1960, article on W. Löhn by G. Merz, p. 427.

7. Ibid., vol. III, Tübingen 1959, article on Claus Harms, p. 76.

8. See pp. 326-36 in this work.

9. Hooper, although not brought in from abroad by Cranmer for he was a native, nevertheless exercised a great influence over the archbishop.

10. This abbreviation, here and elsewhere in this work, refers to The Alternative Service Book 1980.

NOTES TO CHAPTER I

1. See *The First and Second Prayer Books of Edward VI*, Everyman's Library, Letchworth 1968, pp. 21ff.

2. Ibid., pp. 28ff.

3. Ibid., pp. 212ff.

4. Ibid., pp. 231ff.

5. Ibid., pp. 236ff.

6. Ibid., pp. 242ff.

7. Ibid., pp. 247ff.

8. Ibid., pp. 252ff.

9. Ibid., pp. 259ff.

10. Ibid., pp. 266ff.

11. Ibid., pp. 269ff.

12. Ibid., pp. 278ff.

13. Ibid., pp. 280ff.

14. Ibid., pp. 293ff.

15. Ibid., pp. 303ff.

16. Ibid., pp. 313ff.

17. Procter and Frère, *New History of the BCP*, London 1949, pp. 5-9. See also Karl Heussi, *Kompendium der Kirchengeschichte*, 6th edition 1928, pp. 123-24.

18. Procter and Frère, *New History of the BCP*, pp. 9-14.

19. See Appendix. p. 323, No. 3.

20. Procter and Frère, *New History of the BCP*, pp. 15-18. One of the most important persons who was responsible for the realization of the Sarum missal and breviary was a certain Osmond (1085). Richard Poore, Bishop of Salisbury, worked as compiler of the Sarum book of liturgy at the beginning of the thirteenth century. In this respect see Charles Neil, *The Tutorial Prayer Book*, p. 635.

21. Charles Neil, *The Tutorial Prayer Book*, p. xxi.

22. Cf. also *RGG*, vol. III, p. 240. See article on Hermann v. Wied. Also illuminating is the recently published work of Geoffrey Cuming, *The Godly Order*, London 1983, pp. 1-25. Specifically for Hermann von Wied see pp. 68ff.

23. Procter and Frère, *New History of the BCP*, pp. 25-38. For a more detailed orientation on the elements used in the BCP and drawn from "Hermann's Consultation" I refer to G. Cuming, *The Godly Order*, pp. 81ff.

24. Jasper Ridley, *Thomas Cranmer*, pp. 7-24.

25. Ibid., pp. 40-43.

26. Cf. G. W. Locher, *Zwingli's Einfluss in England und Schottland*, p. 190.

27. Since Zwingli exercised his chief influence on Hooper as the initiator of puritanism we speak also of Zwinglian-puritanical spirituality.

28. W. Nyenhuis, *Traces of a Lutheran Eucharistic Doctrine in Thomas Cranmer*, pp. 1-22.

29. G. W. Locher, *Zwingli's Einfluss in England und Schottland*, pp. 193-94 (translated here).

30. See J. Ridley, *Thomas Cranmer*, pp. 382-411.

31. Ibid., especially bottom of p. 402 and p. 403.

32. See p. 1 in our work.

33. See BCP of 1662, Pocket Book Edition, Oxford University Press, pp. 339-49.

34. Ibid., pp. 677-87.

35. Ibid., pp. 411-616.

36. Ibid., pp. 77-86.

37. Ibid., pp. 617-32.

38. The BCP of 1549 is meant.

39. Cf. G. Cuming, *The Godly Order*, pp. 91ff.

40. See p. 8 in our work.

41. Short hymnic sentences of supplication or praise, to which the congregation makes response during the liturgy.

42. This refers to the so-called "Little Gloria," a doxology or an assembled unit of sentences of praise: "Glory be to the Father, and to the Son, and to the Holy Ghost," etc.

43. See Appendix, p. 325, No. 10.

44. The hymn spoken by Zechariah in Luke 1:67-79.

45. See Appendix, p. 325, No. 9.

46. Short prayers selected for the appropriate day of the church year.

47. The hymn spoken by Mary in Luke 1:46-55.

48. The hymn spoken by Simeon in Luke 2:29-32.

49. This is the confession with absolution in the last hourly prayer of the monastic daily services, and in the missal.

50. Cf. O. Weber, *Grundlagen der Dogmatik*, vol. I, pp. 609-10. Cf. also Thomas Aquinas, *Summa Theologica* II, 1, 85, 2.

51. Cf. First and Second Prayer Books of Edward VI, pp. 212-30.

52. Cf. *The Saint Andrew Daily Missal*, St. André-Near Bruges 1951, pp. 969-78. Cf. also *The Sunday Missal*, London 1975, pp. 33-48. Cf. chiefly also G. Cuming, *The Godly Order*, pp. 91-107.

53. See Appendix, p. 323, No. 4.

54. See Appendix, p. 324, No. 5.

55. See Appendix, p. 324, No. 6.

56. See Appendix, p. 322, No. 1.

57. See Appendix, p. 322, No. 2.

58. *First and Second Prayer Books of King Edward VI*, p. 222.

59. Ibid., p. 222.

60. Ibid., p. 222.

61. Ibid., p. 223.

62. Ibid., p. 223.

63. Godparents answer as representatives of the baptized infant.

64. Ibid., p. 241.

65. Ibid., p. 241.

66. Ibid., p. 264.

67. Ibid., p. 279. Cf. the rubric there at the very bottom.

68. All the deletions from the Sarum books of liturgy which Cranmer made in the compilation of the BCP of 1549 are found lucidly set forth by Charles Neil in *The Tutorial Prayer Book*. Of particular interest also are the deletions from the Sarum mass which resulted in the eucharistic liturgy of the BCP of 1549. Note in particular pp. 259-61 of the above cited book.

NOTES TO CHAPTER II

1. Compare as a supplement to this section A: G. E. Pruett, "A Protestant Doctrine of the Eucharistic Presence," *Calvin Theological Journal*, 1975.

2. *RGG*, Vol. VI, article "Vermigli" by G. Weiss-Staehlin, p. 1361 (translated here).

3. Chiefly the important works by Salvatore Corda and M. W. Anderson. See bibliography, pp. 327, 329.

4. Compare chiefly pp. 154ff. of this work.

5. The term "revivalistic" is to be understood in the sense of the definition at pp. xxviii and xxix in our work.

6. Peter Martyr, on 1 Corinthians 11:17, quoted from J. C. McLelland, *The Visible Words of God*.

7. Cf. S. Corda, *Veritas Sacramenti*, p. 23.

8. Cf. E. M. Jung, "On the Nature of Evangelism in 16th Cent. Italy," *The Journal of The History of Ideas* XIV, no. 1, Jan. 1953.

9. Ibid., p. 522.

10. Ibid., p. 520.

11. Ibid., p. 520.

12. Ibid., p. 520.

13. Ibid., p. 523.

14. Ibid., p. 524.

15. Ibid., p. 523.

16. Ibid., p. 523.

17. S. Corda, *Veritas Sacramenti,* pp. 22-23, 35, and 40.

18. Cf. M. W. Anderson, *Peter Martyr, a Reformer in Exile,* pp. 133-35.

19. Ibid., p. 133.

20. Cf. the opening rubric in the Communion of the Sicke of 1549 in *The First and Second Prayer Books of King Edward VI,* p. 266.

21. Cf. M. W. Anderson, *Peter Martyr, a Reformer in Exile,* p. 134.

22. Cf. BCP of 1662 in the Pocket Book Edition of the Oxford University Press, pp. 386ff. In the opening rubric there is no longer present anything concerning the distribution of the laid aside bread (the host) which had already been consecrated at the Sunday communion service.

23. S. Corda, *Veritas Sacramenti,* p. 134.

24. The complete title to this 1559 published work reads *Defensio Doctrinae Veteris et Apostolicae de Sacrosanto Eucharistiae Sacramento.*

25. Ibid., p. 763. "And therefore this change in the bread, of whatever nature it may be, is directed towards that great goal, that it bring forth and create to the extent possible our own transformation."

26. S. Corda, *Veritas Sacramenti,* p. 178.

27. Cf. J. C. McLelland, *The Visible Words of God,* p. 76.

28. Ibid., p. 77.

29. Ibid., p. 84.

30. Cf. what is said on p. 119 in our work.

31. S. Corda remarks thereon: "Celestial matters, in Vermigli's basic convictions, are never united with terrestrial objects—as sacred as these may be." S. Corda, *Veritas Sacramenti,* p. 152.

32. Peter Martyr, *Defensio,* p. 656. "We admonish our people that they, being animated by visible symbols, bring their souls away from them to heaven."

33. See first quotation on p. 118 of this work.

34. This conception is within the Zwinglian tradition.

35. S. Corda, *Veritas Sacramenti,* p. 152.

36. Cf. the second quotation on 117 of this work.

37. S. Corda, *Veritas Sacramenti,* p. 153.

38. By "general ritual of holy communion" is meant that divine service formula which is intended for a congregation assembled in church in contrast to the communion of the sick. Cf. BCP of 1552, *The First and Second Prayer Books of Edward VI,* pp. 377-93.

39. BCP of 1662, pp. 693ff.

40. BCP of 1552, cited above, pp. 382-86.

41. Cf. A. Beesley, "An Unpublished Source of the Book of Common Prayer: Peter Martyr Vermigli's 'Adhortatio ad Coenam Domini Mysticam,'" pp. 83-88.

42. See G. Cuming, *The Godly Order, Texts and Studies Relating to The Book of Common Prayer,* London 1983, p. 87.

43. BCP of 1552, *The First and Second Prayer Books of Edward VI*, Letchworth 1968, pp. 385-86.

44. Ibid., pp. 377-93.

45. Ibid., pp. 377-78.

46. See pp. 48ff. and p. 124 in our work.

47. Martyr had a desire to mediate between the Reformed and the Lutheran theology.

48. M. W. Anderson, *Peter Martry, A Reformer in Exile*, p. 296.

49. Cf. Karl Barth's view of the Law and the Gospel. See K. Barth, *Gesetz und Evangelium*, 3rd edition, 1961, p. 13.

50. Cf. points 1-6 on pp. 125-26 of our work.

51. Cf. E. F. K. Mueller, *Die Bekenntnisschriften der Reformierten Kirche*, p. 511.

52. Cf. H. Bullinger, *Das Zweite Helvetische Bekenntnis*, chap. X, p. 43. Zwingli is important in this connexion. See G. W. Locher, *Huldrych Zwingli in neuer Sicht*, Zurich 1969, pp. 117-23. Cf. Heinrich Bullinger, *The Second Helvetic Confession of 1566*, Ch. X, ed. by C. Cochrane, London 1966, pp. 240ff. See also G. W. Locher, *Bullinger und Calvin Probleme des Vergleichs ihrer Theologien*, Zurich 1975.

53. M. W. Anderson, *Peter Martyr, a Reformer in Exile*, p. 149. Cf. also Griffith Thomas, *The Principles of Theology*, pp. 236-57.

54. See pp. 15-18 in our work.

55. The BCP of 1552 is chiefly meant.

56. *Zurich Letters, 1558-1579*, ed. for Parker Society, Cambridge 1848, p. 45.

57. Ibid., pp. 53-54. Letter of November 5, 1559.

58. Ibid., p. 55.

59. M. W. Anderson, *Peter Martyr, a Reformer in Exile*, pp. 347ff.

60. Ibid., p. 148.

61. Cf. *RGG*, vol. I, article on M. Bucer by R. Stupperich, pp. 1453-57.

62. Cf. pp. 3 and 4 in our work. "Hermann's Consultation" is a Reformation church order for Cologne on which Bucer and Melanchthon collaborated. Since Hermann von Wied in his position as Elector gave the commission for the drafting, one speaks of it as "Hermann's Consultation."

63. Cf. C. Hopf, *M. Bucer and the English Reformation*, pp. 58ff.

64. Cf. E. C. Whitaker, *M. Bucer and the Book of Common Prayer*. In this book is also found the English translation of Martin Bucer's *Censura*.

65. Ibid., p. 14. Cf. *The Second Helvetic Confession* I,1: "The preaching of the Word of God is the Word of God." See translation by A. C. Cochrane, London 1966, pp. 224ff.

66. Ibid., p. 14.

67. Ibid., p. 14. This view is important for the Reformed and is foreign to the Roman Catholic rite, which is an action within itself and outside itself in front of the invisible world (ex opere operato).

68. The term "sacral" will be defined later. See pp. 195-96 in our work.

69. Cf. *The First and Second Prayer Books of King Edward VI*, p. 212.

70. E. C. Whitaker, *M. Bucer and the BCP*, p. 18.

71. A brief historical summary in reference to the origin of this service is found in Charles Neil, *The Tutorial Prayer Book*, p. 489.

72. BCP of 1662, pp. 401-10.

73. Cf. E. C. Whitaker, *M. Bucer and the Book of Common Prayer*, pp. 130 and 132.

74. Cf. *First and Second Prayer Books of King Edward VI*, pp. 229-30.

75. Cf. E. C. Whitaker, *M. Bucer and the Book of Common Prayer*, pp. 20 and 22.

76. Ibid., pp. 28 and 30.

77. Cf. *The First and Second Prayer Books of King Edward VI*, pp. 236-41.

78. E. C. Whitaker, *M. Bucer and the Book of Common Prayer*, p. 94.

79. Cf. *The First and Second Prayer Books of Kind Edward VI*, p. 241.

80. Cf. BCP of 1662, p. 329.

81. E. C. Whitaker, *M. Bucer and the Book of Common Prayer*, p. 96.

82. The *First and Second Prayer Books of King Edward VI*, pp. 247-51.

83. Cf. E. C. Whitaker, *M. Bucer and the Book of Common Prayer*, p. 102.

84. Ibid., pp. 104 and 106.

85. Cf. *The First and Second Prayer Books of King Edward VI*, p. 230.

86. Cf. E. C. Whitaker, *M. Bucer and the BCP*, p. 30.

87. Ibid., p. 30.

88. Cf. BCP of 1662, p. 320. Cf. *The First and Second Prayer Books of Edward VI*, p. 392.

89. Cf. E. C. Whittaker, *M. Bucer and the BCP*, pp. 50 and 52.

90. Cf. Calvin, Inst. III,2,16, "Certainty of faith." Cf. Calvin, *Institutes of the Christian Religion*, III,2,16, ed. by J. T. McNeill, trans. by F. L. Battles (2 vols.), London & Philadelphia 1960, pp. 561-62.

91. Cf. E. C. Whitaker, *M. Bucer and the BCP*, p. 52.

92. Ibid., p. 52.

93. Cf. BCP of 1662, p. 302.

94. Cf. *The First and Second Prayer Books of King Edward VI*, p. 222.

95. Cf. that said at p. 10, bottom, and p. 11, top, in this work.

96. Cf. E. C. Whitaker, *M. Bucer and the BCP*, pp. 58 and 60.

97. Ibid., pp. 66 and 68.

98. Ibid., pp. 106 and 108.

99. Ibid., p. 144.

100. This refers to the prayer of humble access. Cf. *The First and Second Prayer Books of King Edward VI*, p. 225.

101. E. C. Whitaker, *M. Bucer and the BCP*, p. 144.

102. Ibid., p. 14.

103. This term salvation is the matter under discussion in Chap. IV in the treatment of exhortations at pp. 172ff. in our work.

104. M. Bucer, *Common Places (Loci Communes)*, The Courtenay Library of Reformation Classics, p. 211.

105. Ibid., p. 202.

106. Ibid., p. 105.

107. Ibid., p. 208.

108. Ibid., pp. 218-21.

109. *The First and Second Prayer Books of King Edward VI*, pp. 227 and 390. Cf. also BCP of 1662, p. 316.

110. M. Bucer, *Common Places (Loci Communes)*, p. 223.

111. The Bible plan which leads through the entire Bible in one year exists in all three principal editions.

112. Cf. C. Hopf, *Martin Bucer and the English Reformation*, pp. 228-30.

113. M. Bucer, *De Regno Christi*, p. 25 (translated).

114. Ibid., p. 25 (translated).

115. Cf. *Journal of Religious History*, VI, p. 308, article by Patrick Collinson, "The Reformer and the Archbishop," Cf. also B. Moeller, "Reichstadt und Reformation," *SVRG* no. 180, 1962.

116. M. Bucer, *De Regno Christi*, p. 70 (translated).

117. Ibid., p. 143 (translated).

118. G. Itti, *Dans quelle mésure Bucer est-il piétiste?*

119. E. Troeltsch, *Die Soziallehren der Christlichen Kirchen.*

120. August Lang, *Puritanismus und Pietismus.*

121. D. F. Wright, *M. Bucer,* Courtenay Library of Reformation Classics, p. 30.

122. Constantine Hopf, *M. Bucer and the English Reformation,* p. 58.

123. Cf. *RGG,* vol. V, article on the Puritans by M. Schmidt, pp. 722-23.

124. Ludwig Lavater whom Hooper encountered in Strasbourg described in his 1559 published booklet *De ritibus et institutis Tigurinae* the decorations as well as the divine service rites of the Reformed Church of Zurich, with which Hooper was acquainted. See the edition of 1702 of the above-mentioned work, p. 19.

125. W. M. S. West, *John Hooper and the Origins of Puritanism,* Zurich, p. 12.

126. See Ludwig Lavater's *De ritibus et institutis Tigurinae.*

127. See *Early Writings of Bishop Hooper,* Cambridge 1843, pp. 436, 439, and 441.

128. Ibid., p. 488.

129. Ibid., p. 19.

130. One of the great antipodes of this puritanical perception is Richard Hooker (1554-1600), one of the most important of the Anglican canonical theologians. Hooker holds the view in his principal work that in questions of liturgy and church equipment the Bible is not alone authoritative, but also common sense and tradition. See R. Hooker, *Of the Laws of Ecclesiastical Polity,* book II, ch. V.7, Oxford 1874, p. 308.

131. This manuscript found in the Bodleian Library, Oxford, is published by K. Hopf in the *Journal of Theological Studies,* XLIX, July-October 1943, p. 196.

132. This refers to the book dedicated to Henry VIII, *De Scripturae Sanctae autoritate, certitudine, firmitate, et absoluta perfectione,* Zurich 1538.

133. See W. M. S. West, *A Study of John Hooper with Special Reference to his Contact with Henry Bullinger,* Zurich 1953, p. 101.

134. Ibid., p. 98.

135. See Istvan Tökés, "Bullinger's hermeneutische Lehre," in *Heinrich Bullinger (1504-1575): Collected Essays on the 400th Anniversary of his Death,* Zurich 1975, vol. I, p. 185.

136. John Hooper, *Later Writings,* Cambridge 1852, p. 120.

137. See E. Koch, *Die Theologie der Confessio Helvetica Posterior,* Neukirchen 1968. *Beiträge zur Geschichte und Lehre der Reformierten Kirche,* vol. XXVII, p. 43.

138. See John Hooper, *Early Writings,* p. 255.

139. W. M. S. West, *A Study of John Hooper with Special Reference to his Contact with Henry Bullinger,* p. 111.

140. "Limits and bounds" means the Ten Commandments.

141. John Hooper, *Early Writings,* p. 259.

142. The rudiments of this federal theology are found in Zwingli's *In catabaptistarum strophas elenchus,* Zurich 1527, pp. 414-24 in vol. III of the Zwingli edition of Schuler and Schultess, 1828-1842. With Bullinger the systematic development of the federal theology is found in *De Testamento seu Foedere Dei Unico,* Zurich 1534.

On the question of the source of federal theology reference is made to the following essay: Jack Warren Cottrell, "Is Bullinger the Source for Zwingli's Doctrine of the Covenant?" This essay is to be found in *Zürcher Beiträge zur Reformations geschichte, Heinrich Bullinger, 1504-1575, Collected Essays on the 400th Anniversary of his Death,* vol. I, pp. 75-83. See principally W. M. S. West, *A Study of John Hooper with Special Reference to his Contact with Henry Bullinger,* pp. 112-16.

143. Word of God or the law of God are interchangeable concepts to Hooper.

144. See John Hooper, *Later Writings,* p. 361.

145. See John Hooper, *Early Writings,* p. 76.

146. Ibid., p. 88.

147. Ibid., p. 32.

148. Ibid., pp. 340 and 341.

149. Ann Warcop had through material help made herself particularly useful to those who had to flee from England under Bloody Mary. See Christina Garrett, *The Marian Exiles,* Cambridge 1938, reprinted 1966, p. 35.

150. John Hooper, *Later Writings,* p. 604.

151. See W. M. S. West, *A Study of John Hooper with Special Reference to his Contact with Henry Bullinger,* p. 138.

152. See John Hooper, *Early Writings,* p. 144.

153. Ibid., p. 173.

154. John Hooper, *Later Writings,* pp. 589 and 590.

155. W. M. S. West, *A Study of John Hooper with Special Reference to his Contact with Henry Bullinger,* pp. 222 and 223.

156. W. M. S. West, *John Hooper and the Origins of Puritanism,* Zurich 1953, p. 23.

157. See p. 51 in our work.

158. Ibid., pp. 52.

159. Ibid., pp. 68ff.

160. Ibid., pp. 74-76.

161. See p. 54 in our work.

162. Martin Micronius was pastor of the Netherlands refugee congregation in London and a good friend of Hooper.

163. *Original Letters Relative to the English Reformation,* ed. by the Parker Society, Cambridge 1847, vol. II, p. 557.

164. John Butler was the Commissioner of Calais appointed by Cranmer.

165. Thomas Blaurer belonged to that South German Reformation which advocated the Reformation chiefly in Constance, howbeit unsuccessfully.

166. *Original Letters,* vol. II, pp. 635-36.

167. Ibid., p. 662. John Burcher was an English Zwinglian who had a close contact with Bullinger.

168. Hooper delivered these Lenten sermons in February/March 1550.

169. Ibid., pp. 559-60.

170. Ibid., pp. 415-16. Cf. also letter of Micronius to Bullinger, pp. 566-67. John ab Ulmis was a committed German student at Oxford who had a strong inclination toward Zwinglianism.

171. *Original Letters,* vol. I, Cambridge 1856, p. 73.

172. Ibid., vol. II, p. 560.

173. Ibid., vol. I, p. 93.

174. Ibid., pp. 71-72.

175. Ibid., p. 77.

176. Ibid., vol. II, p. 500.

177. Ibid., vol. I, pp. 23-24.

178. Ibid., vol. II, p. 503.

179. Hooper spent three months with Cranmer in Lambeth Palace from January until March 1552. See Jasper Ridley, *Thomas Cranmer,* p. 315.

180. *Original Letters,* vol. II, p. 580.

181. Ibid., p. 580.

182. *Later Writings of John Hooper,* Cambridge 1852, p. 160.

183. *Early Writings of John Hooper,* Cambridge 1843, p. 485.

184. *Later Writings of John Hooper*, p. 168.

185. Ibid., p. 173.

186. Ibid., p. 173.

187. Ibid., p. 161.

188. Ibid., p. 171.

189. Ibid., p. 170.

190. Ibid., p. 171.

191. The terms "innovation" and "renovation" are as a matter of fact identical with the term "rebirth" or "being born again."

192. *Later Writings of John Hooper*, p. 174.

193. Ibid., p. 174.

194. Ibid., p. 175.

195. William Haller, *The Rise of Puritanism*, Philadelphia 1972, p. 92.

196. See pp. 51-53 of our work.

197. *Later Writings of John Hooper*, p. 167.

198. *Early Writings of John Hooper*, p. 509.

199. Ibid., p. 456.

200. Ibid., p. 458.

201. Ibid., p. 71.

202. Cf. p. 52 in our work where we find the connexion between sanctification and the Decalogue.

203. *Early Writings of John Hooper*, p. 72.

204. *Later Writings of John Hooper*, p. 175.

205. *Early Writings of John Hooper*, p. 482.

206. Ibid., p. 483.

207. W. Haller, *The Rise of Puritanism*, p. 117.

208. The term "godly behaviour" is identical with sanctification to the extent that the accent lies on ethics.

209. W. Haller, *The Rise of Puritanism*, p. 120.

210. Spenser is a very famous puritan.

211. W. Haller, *The Rise of Puritanism*, pp. 120 and 122.

212. The "Injunctions" is an admonitory writing by Bishop Hooper to the clergy of his diocese in the year 1551.

213. *Later Writings of John Hooper*, pp. 137-38.

214. *Early Writings of John Hooper*, p. 344.

215. Ibid., p. 451.

216. Ibid., p. 465.

217. *Later Writings of John Hooper*, p. 131.

218. Cf. W. Haller, *The Rise of Puritanism*, pp. 194, 197-98, 235, 337.

219. See pp. 49 and 50 in our work.

220. *Early Writings of John Hooper*, p. 542.

221. Ibid., p. 549.

222. Ibid., p. 534.

223. Ibid., pp. 536-37.

224. Ibid., p. 537.

225. *Later Writings of John Hooper*, p. 160.

226. Ibid., pp. 561 and 562.

227. See pp. 64-68 in our work.

228. W. Haller, *The Rise of Puritanism*, p. 97.

229. *Early Writings of John Hooper*, p. 449.

230. Ibid., p. 449.
231. Ibid., p. 468.
232. Ibid., p. 495.
233. See p. 53 in our work.
234. *Later Writings of John Hooper,* p. 582.
235. Ibid., p. 581.
236. See p. 53 in our work.
237. *Later Writings of John Hooper,* p. 602.
238. Ibid., p. 604.
239. W. Haller, *The Rise of Puritanism,* p. 149.
240. See pp. 53 and 54 in our work.
241. *Early Writings of John Hooper,* p. 26.
242. Ibid., p. 139.
243. See p. 54 in our work.
244. *Later Writings of John Hooper,* p. 40.
245. Ibid., pp. 52-53.
246. Ibid., p. 42.
247. In the BCP of 1552 is found the new expression "church militant," which was lacking in the BCP of 1549. Is Hooper's Influence behind this? Cf. also *The Second Helvetic Confession XVII,* ed. by A. C. Cochrane, London 1966, p. 262.
248. Ibid., pp. 42-43.
249. Ibid., pp. 73-74. Cf. also *The Second Helvetic Confession XVII,* p. 263.
250. Ibid., p. 87.
251. Ibid., p. 87.
252. *Early Writings of John Hooper,* p. 183.
253. Ibid., p. 85.
254. *Later Writings of John Hooper,* p. 130.
255. W. Haller, *The Rise of Puritanism,* p. 176.
256. Ibid., p. 216.
257. Ibid., p. 63.
258. See p. 77 under (4) in our work.
259. W. Haller, *The Rise of Puritanism,* p. 62.
260. Ibid., p. 119.
261. See p. 53 in our work.
262. *Early Writings of John Hooper,* p. 340.
263. Ibid., p. 340.
264. W. Haller, *The Rise of Puritanism,* p. 128.
265. *Early Writings of John Hooper,* p. 496.
266. Ibid., pp. 496-97.
267. Ibid., p. 459.
268. Ibid., pp. 468-69.
269. W. Haller, *The Rise of Puritanism,* p. 34.
270. *Early Writings of John Hooper,* p. 486.
271. Ibid., p. 435.
272. Ibid., p. 513.
273. Ibid., p. 437.
274. Ibid., p. 497.
275. Ibid., p. 459.
276. W. Haller, *The Rise of Puritanism,* p. 140.
277. S. Corda, *Veritas Sacramenti,* p. 152.

NOTES TO CHAPTER III

1. *Cranmer's Works*, vols. I and II, ed. for the Parker Society by John Edmund Cox, Cambridge 1844-1846.

2. See pp. 67-70 in our work.

3. Bucer's influence in England began appreciably earlier than 1549. He had already begun to exert an influence in England from the Continent by the end of the thirtieth year of the sixteenth century.

4. Hooper exercised his greatest influence in the years 1549-1553 after his return from Switzerland.

5. Cf. *RGG*, vol. I, p. 1211, article by P. H. Vogel on European translations of the Bible other than German.

6. Cf. Preface to the "Great Bible" of 1540, *Cranmer's Works* II, p. 119.

7. Ibid., pp. 120 and 121.

8. Ibid., p. 120.

9. Ibid., p. 121.

10. Cf. *RGG*, vol. I, article on Fundamentalism by G. Gloege, pp. 1262-63.

11. Cf. *Cranmer's Works* II, p. 121.

12. Ibid., p. 10.

13. Ibid., p. 13.

14. Ibid., p. 19.

15. Ibid., pp. 36-37.

16. Ibid., pp. 43 and 44. Cranmer here produces two quotations from well-known Church Fathers. The first stems from Chrysostom from the fourth homily *De Lazaro*; the second from Hieronymus from his Commentary on Jeremiah 8.

17. Ibid., pp. 190 and 191. This is a quotation from a short work of Cranmer bearing the title "A sermon concerning the time of rebellion," written in 1548/1549.

18. Ibid., p. 419. This is a quotation from a letter of Cranmer to King Edward VI in the year 1548.

19. Ibid., p. 420.

20. Ibid., pp. 449 and 450. This is a quotation from a letter of Cranmer to Bloody Mary in the year 1555.

21. Ibid., p. 17. This deals with a quotation of Cranmer from Augustine's *De Doctrina Christiana*, Bk. 3, Chap. 28.

22. Ibid., p. 17. This refers to a quotation from Chrysostom, 35 Hom. on Gen. 14.

23. Ibid., p. 21.

24. Ibid., p. 77. Here we have a quotation from the minutes of the significant assertions of Cranmer preserved in his discourse of 1534 on the authority of popes and general councils (substance of a speech about the year 1534 on the authority of the pope and of general council).

25. Cf. *The First and Second Prayer Books of King Edward VI*, London 1968, pp. 327-46.

26. Thomas Cranmer, *Reformation Classic II*, The Sutton Courtenay Press, p. xxiii.

27. One should compare the last citation on p. 89 of this work. (Moreover it would be worthwhile to enquire exhaustively into the concept of Scripture in the BCP as the root of the indeed typical fundamentalism of Anglo-Saxon theology.)

28. Essential material on Cranmer's theology of the Word consists of the 1547/1548 composed "A Confutation of unwritten Verities," the 1548/1549 written "A Sermon concerning the time of rebellion" as well as the letters from the late forties and the middle fif-

ties. Only the quotations from the foreword to "The Great Bible" are earlier. Cranmer's statements on the theology of the Word coincide in time with the period of the influence of Hooper who pled the validity of the Word with vehemence. See pp. 67-73 of our work. The inference is obvious that Hooper influenced Cranmer.

29. For the theme of catholicity see pp. 184-90 in this work.

30. Cf. Gregory Dix, *The Shape of the Liturgy,* p. 672.

31. Cf. BCP of 1552 in *The First and Second Prayer Books of Edward VI,* pp. 347-48.

32. A synoptical table of the arrangement of the liturgical units of Morning Prayer is found on pp. 8 and 9 of this work. The Morning Prayer of 1549 is referred to in that table, thus the Morning Prayer of the first Edwardian prayer book, from which these twelve opening quotations of Scripture are missing.

33. See what is said on p. 94 of our work about the self-interpretation of the Bible.

34. Cf. BCP of 1552 in *The First and Second Prayer Books of Edward VI,* p. 348.

35. Ibid., pp. 348 and 349.

36. Ibid., p. 349.

37. Ibid., p. 349.

38. Ibid., pp. 349-50.

39. See note 42, chapter 1. Cf. BCP of 1552 in *The First and Second Prayer Books of Edward VI,* pp. 350-51.

40. Ibid., p. 350. See also Appendix under No. 10, p. 325 of this work.

41. Cf. *The First and Second Prayer Books of Edward VI,* p. 353.

42. Ibid., p. 353.

43. Ibid., p. 354.

44. Ibid., p. 354 See also Appendix, No. 9, p. 325 of this work.

45. BCP of 1552 in *The First and Second Prayer Books of Edward VI,* p. 354. Cf. the placement of the first Lord's Prayer, p. 349.

46. Namely, the twelve Bible quotations, exhortation as well as confession with absolution. Ibid., pp. 347-49.

47. Namely, all that mentioned in (3)-(9).

48. *The First and Second Prayer Books of Edward VI,* pp. 354-55.

49. Ibid., pp. 377-93. Cf. also the summary on pp. 120-21 of this work.

50. BCP of 1552 in *The First and Second Prayer Books of Edward VI,* p. 377.

51. Ibid., pp. 377-79.

52. This is Calvinism.

53. In this there is also a petition for forgiveness, viz., for mercy.

54. Cf. *The First and Second Prayer Books of Edward VI,* pp. 380-81.

55. Ibid., p. 382.

56. "Offering" is best understood as making a contribution.

57. *The First and Second Prayer Books of Edward VI,* p. 382.

58. Ibid., p. 382.

59. Ibid., p. 382.

60. Ibid., pp. 382-86.

61. Ibid., pp. 382-84.

62. Ibid., p. 382.

63. Ibid., p. 383.

64. Ibid., pp. 384-85.

65. Ibid., p. 384.

66. Ibid., p. 385.

67. Ibid., pp. 385-86.

68. Ibid., p. 386.

69. Ibid., pp. 386-87.

70. Ibid., p. 387.

71. Ibid., pp. 387 and 388.

72. Ibid., pp. 388-89.

73. Ibid., p. 389. Cf. also the revealing study by G. Cuming, *The Godly Order, Texts and Studies Relating to The Book of Common Prayer,* London 1983, pp. 110-22.

74. Ibid., p. 389.

75. Ibid., p. 389.

76. Ibid., pp. 389-90.

77. Ibid., pp. 390-91.

78. Homilies of Salvation, Faith and Good Works, *Cranmer's Works* II.

79. Ibid., p. 130.

80. See p. 111, top, in our work.

81. *Cranmer's Works* II, pp. 131-32.

82. See *The First and Second Prayer Books of Edward VI*, p. 390.

83. *Cranmer's Works* II, pp. 132-33.

84. Forgiveness is meant.

85. BCP of 1552 in *The First and Second Prayer Books of Edward VI*, p. 389.

86. *Cranmer's Works* II, p. 135.

87. Ibid., p. 136.

88. BCP of 1552 in *The First and Second Prayer Books of Edward VI*, pp. 377-79.

89. Ibid., pp. 380-81.

90. *Cranmer's Works* II, p. 136.

91. *Cranmer's Works* I, p. 15.

92. BCP of 1552 in *The First and Second Prayer Books of Edward VI*, p. 390. Cf. *The Second Helvetic Confession XXI*, pp. 283ff.

93. *Cranmer's Works* I, pp. 38-39.

94. There comes to mind what an important role the analogy method plays with Peter Martyr. See p. 21 in our work. Cranmer's predilection for analogies becomes more understandable in connexion with his close association with Martyr.

95. Ibid., pp. 40-41.

96. BCP of 1552 in *The First and Second Prayer Books of Edward VI*, p. 389.

97. *Cranmer's Works* I, pp. 41-42.

98. Ibid., pp. 43 and 45. (This deals with the Reformed handling of "Manducatio Impiorum.")

99. BCP of 1552 in *The First and Second Prayer Books of Edward VI*, p. 385.

100. A more precise definition of "revivalism" and "puritanism" is found on pp. xxviii-xxxi at the beginning of our work.

101. *Cranmer's Works* I, p. 71. Cf. also Hch. Bullinger, "Confessio Helvetica Posterior," Zwingli Verlag Zurich 1967, Ch. XXI, p. 111. Cf. *The Second Helvetic Confession, XXI*, pp. 286ff.

102. *Cranmer's Works* I, p. 118.

103. Cf. the Anglican dogmatist E. A. Litton, *Introduction to Dogmatic Theology,* where one reads on p. 409: "The true consecration was the living faith of the partakers."

104. On questions of a memorial one should compare G. W. Locher, *Streit unter Gästen*, pp. 10-11.

105. *The First and Second Prayer Books of Edward VI*, p. 389.

106. Martyr's influence should not be forgotten. See p. 20 in our work where Martyr's views on transformation or conversion are the subject.

107. *Cranmer's Works* I, p. 271.

108. See on pp. 22-23 of our work what Martyr has to say about "Sursum Corda," about the uplifting of the heart.

109. BCP of 1552 in *The First and Second Prayer Books of Edward VI*, p. 387.

110. This is typical of Zwinglian and Calvinistic thinking.

111. *Cranmer's Works* I, p. 131.

112. See Appendix, p. 322, No. 1.

113. See Appendix, p. 322, No. 2.

114. See Appendix, p. 324, No. 8.

115. See p. 121 in our work and note there in the table of the communion liturgy of 1549 the numbers 14-19 and in the table of the communion liturgy of 1552 the numbers 17-22.

116. The collect for the day is a short prayer keyed to the church year.

117. Admonition for the proper attitude and preparation for taking communion.

118. That liturgical element within the canon which contains the calling down of the Holy Spirit upon the communion elements.

119. That liturgical portion of the canon in which the remembrance of Jesus' death, resurrection, and ascension occurs.

120. Cf. Kuno Bugmann, *Kirche und Sakramente,* pp. 45ff.

121. Cf. *The First and Second Prayer Books of Edward VI*, p. 223.

122. See pp. 36-37 in our work.

123. See *The First and Second Prayer Books of Edward VI*, pp. 380-81.

124. See Hooper's third quotation on p. 72 of our work.

125. See *The First and Second Prayer Books of Edward VI*, pp. 392-93.

126. Ibid., pp. 347-48.

127. See pp. 24-25 in our work.

128. See *The First and Second Prayer Books of Edward VI*, pp. 382-86.

129. Ibid., pp. 377-79.

130. For more details on the Hooper covenant and Decalogue theology see pp. 51-53 in our work.

131. Based upon a comparison with many communion liturgies I have come to the conclusion that the placing of the Decalogue in the BCP of 1552 in the communion liturgy is unique. Cf. A. L. Richter, *Die Evangelischen Kirchenordnungen des 16. Jahrhunderts,* Weimar 1846, pp. 141, 258, 288. Cf. also M. Jenny, *Die Einheit des Abendmahlsgottesdienst,* Zurich 1968, pp. 22, 41, 57, 85, 92, 97, 112ff., 116ff., 119, 122ff., 123, 132, 133ff.

132. *The First and Second Prayer Books of Edward VI*, p. 377.

133. Ibid., p. 212.

134. See p. 72 in our work.

135. *Cranmer's Works* II, pp. 524-25.

136. The BCP of 1549 is meant.

137. *Cranmer's Works* II, p. 525.

138. See *The First and Second Prayer Books of Edward VI*, p. 347. See the second rubric at the top.

139. Ibid., p. 212, rubric No. 4.

140. See pp. 49-50 and 72 in our work.

141. Cf. Calvin, *Institutes of the Christian Religion,* II,7,6, 2 Vols. London and Philadelphia 1960, pp. 354-55.

142. Sanctissimum means the elements of bread and wine made especially holy through consecration.

143. Cf. J. G. Davies, *A Dictionary of Liturgy and Worship,* p. 113.

144. See pages 279 and 311 in our work.

NOTES TO CHAPTER IV

1. *Foxe's Book of Martyrs,* ed. by Marie Gentert King, Old Tappan, N.J. 1975.

2. For the "Act of Uniformity" see Robert Livingston Schuyler, *Cardinal Documents in British History,* Princeton 1961, pp. 59ff.

3. The ideas of Grindal are meant.

4. The revivalistic concept is present in Martyr and Bucer but without any special emphasis on the puritanical aspects, whereas it is with John Hooper that the term "revivalistic-puritanical" chiefly holds true.

5. For Grindal's sojourn on the continent cf. P. Collinson, *Archbishop Grindal,* London 1979.

6. In this connexion see the revealing dissertation of Helmut Kressner with the title "Schweizer Ursprünge des Anglikanischen Staatskirchentums," Gütersloh 1953. Kressner points out Zwingli's crucial influence upon Archbishop John Whitgift through Wolfgang Musculus and Rudolf Gualter. John Whitgift stood in high favour with Elizabeth I.

7. See *The Remains of Edmund Grindal,* ed. by W. Nicholson, Parker Society, Cambridge 1843, p. 202.

8. Ibid., p. 202.

9. Ibid., pp. 249-50.

10. See Patrick Collinson, *Archbishop Grindal,* p. 60.

11. See p. 129, at the middle, in our work.

12. See the list on pp. 55 and 56 in our work.

13. See p. 54 in our work.

14. See p. 123, the last citation (Black Rubric) in our work.

15. See Edward Cardwell, *A History of Conferences and Other Proceedings connected with the Revision of The Book of Common Prayer from the Year 1558 to the Year 1690,* Oxford 1849, republished in Ridgeway, N.J. 1966, pp. 18-41.

16. See Patrick Collinson, *Archbishop Grindal,* p. 87.

17. See John E. Booty, ed. *The Book of Common Prayer 1559,* Charlottesville, Va. 1976, pp. 5-323.

18. See *The Remains of Edmund Grindal,* p. 211.

19. See Patrick Collinson, *Archbishop Grindal,* pp. 112-16.

20. Ibid., p. 179.

21. Ibid., p. 129.

22. See *The Remains of Edmund Grindal,* p. 147.

23. See Patrick Collinson, *Archbishop Grindal,* pp. 207 and 234.

24. See G. R. Potter, *Zwingli,* Cambridge 1976, pp. 223-24.

25. See also *RGG,* vol. V, 1961, article by R. Pfister with the title "Prophezei," p. 638. Cf. also G. W. Locher, *Huldrych Zwingli in neuer Sicht,* Zurich 1969, pp. 51-54.

26. Patrick Collinson, *Archbishop Grindal,* p. 212.

27. Ibid., p. 234.

28. *The Remains of Edmund Grindal,* p. 376.

29. Ibid., p. 377.

30. Ibid., p. 378.

31. Ibid., p. 379.

32. Ibid., p. 386.

33. Ibid., pp. 386-87.

34. See J. E. Booty, *The BCP of 1559,* pp. 48 and 339.

35. *The Remains of Edmund Grindal,* p. 207.

36. Patrick Collinson, *The Elizabethan Puritan Movement*, London 1967.

37. Patrick Collinson, *Archbishop Grindal*, pp. 289 and 290.

38. Ibid., p. 291.

39. Cf. Joseph Chambon, *Der Puritanismus*, quoted from the top of p. 102 retranslated from the German. Taken from Burrage, *The Early English Dissenters*, vol. I: *History and Criticism*, vol. II: *Illustrative Documents*, Cambridge 1912.

40. C. S. Carter, *The English Church in the Seventeenth Century*, London 1909, pp. 11ff.

41. See Edward Cardwell, *A History of Conferences and other proceedings connected with the Revision of The Book of Common Prayer*, Oxford 1849. On pages 121-212 are found all the important details of the Hampton Court Conference.

42. C. S. Carter, *The English Church in the Seventeenth Century*, p. 12.

43. See Edward Cardwell, cited above, pp. 130-31.

44. See C. S. Carter, *The English Church in the Seventeenth Century*, p. 13.

45. Cf. *RGG*, vol. V, article on "Presbyterianism" by M. Schmidt, pp. 542-43.

46. Cf. *The First and Second Prayers Book of Edward VI*, p. 407.

47. Edward Cardwell, *A History of Conferences . . .* , p. 187.

48. Ibid., pp. 194-95.

49. This contribution of the puritans in having initiated the translation of the Bible into the "King James Version" is of enormous spiritual and cultural importance.

50. G. M. Trevelyan, *A Shortened History of England*, London 1971, p. 287.

51. Anglicans were forbidden the use of The Book of Common Prayer. Cromwell issued in 1655 an edict in which the use of the BCP was strictly prohibited. See C. S. Carter, *The English Church in the Seventeenth Century*, p. 48.

52. Ibid., p. 43.

53. See Joseph Chambon, *Der Puritanismus*, quotation on p. 156, top.

54. Ibid., p. 156.

55. Cf. G. Cuming, *The Godly Order*, London 1983. See therein chap. 8, "The Savoy Conference," pp. 142-52.

56. See Edward Cardwell, *A History of Conferences . . .* , p. 284.

57. See pp. 140-41 in our work.

58. See E. Cardwell, *A History of Conferences . . .* , pp. 314-35.

59. See p. 141 in our work.

60. See The Book of Common Prayer 1662 in the Pocket Book Edition of Oxford University Press 1969, pp. 82-85.

61. Cf. G. Cuming, *The Godly Order*, London 1983, chap. 7, "The Anglicanism of John Cosin," pp. 123-39. Cuming throws light primarily on Cosin's High Church side.

62. BCP 1662, p. 302.

63. Ibid., p. 314.

64. Cf. *RGG*, vol. II, p. 477, article on "England" by M. Schmidt.

65. See pp. 10 and 122 in our work.

66. Cf. BCP of 1662, pp. 37-38.

67. See p. 163 under 4.a. in our work.

68. See BCP of 1662, p. 37.

69. Ibid., p. 38.

70. Ibid., p. 38.

71. "To acknowledge and confess our manifold sins and wickedness" [3].

72. See p. 164 under 4.b. in our work.

73. See BCP 1662, p. 38, and page 152 above, the clause designated [4].

74. See p. 82 under 5.b. in our work.

75. Cf. G. Cuming, *The Godly Order*, p. 58.

76. Ibid. See also pp. 76-80 under 4.i. in this work

77. We have not examined the important aspect of laud and praise in Hooper's sermons. Typically however they end with laud and praise.

78. See pp. 67ff. under 4.d. in our work.

79. Ibid., p. 73 under 4.e. It is interesting how in the songs of the revivalistic movement as well as in those of orthodoxy and pietism the soul plays a big role. In Charles Wesley's hymns (1707-1788) the word "soul" is used countless times. Cf. *The Hymnbook*, published by the Presbyterian Church in the United States: hymns 47:3; 216:1; 362:3; 423:2; and many others.

80. See p. 81 under 5.a. in our work.

81. See BCP of 1662, p. 39.

82. On the question of descriptiveness cf. pp. 83-84 under 5.c. in our work.

83. See p. 84 under 5.e. in our work.

84. Ibid, pp. 68-70, under 4.d.(1).

85. In this absolution is found genuine Reformation wording. This is indicated in the absence of the "absolvo te" which is typical of the Roman-Catholic wording of a confession, whereas in the Lutheran sphere the phrase "by authority of the promise I pronounce..." is often found in use in absolutions.

86. Cf. BCP of 1662, pp. 39 and 40.

87. See *Predigten von C. H. Spurgeon*, vol. I, Hamburg 1869, pp. 282 and 430.

88. See pp. 65 and 66 under 4.c. in our work.

89. Ibid., p. 82 under 5.b.

90. Ibid., p. 74 under 4.g.

91. Matins is the first of the daily offices either spoken or sung by monks in choir prayer in accordance with Western tradition. Cf. *Breviarum Romanum*, 1961, p. 580. See chiefly p. 8 in our work.

92. BCP of 1662, p. 40.

93. Ibid., p. 41. Cf. also *Breviarum Romanum*, p. 580, as well as p. 8 in our work.

94. BCP of 1662, p. 42.

95. See p. 8 in our work.

96. See Appendix, No. 10, p. 325, in our work.

97. The rubric applying to the Old Testament lesson is instructive in that it requires that God's Word be read with expression and audible to everyone. The Word of Scripture in this is to be contrasted in particular with the other liturgical elements. See BCP of 1662, p. 42.

98. BCP of 1662, p. 43.

99. Ibid., p. 43.

100. Ibid., p. 43.

101. See p. 202 in our work.

102. Compare what is said about Francis de Quinonnes in reference to the lessons from the Old Testament and the New Testament. See p. 4 in our work reference thereto. In the Roman breviary the longer Biblical lessons occurred only in Matins. All other offices were accustomed only to the so-called "capitulum," which simply quoted two or three verses from the New Testament. It would take us too far afield to go into the recently effected first revision of the Roman breviary.

103. Cf. BCP of 1662, pp. 46 and 47. The Benedictus is an important liturgical element within lauds in the Roman as well as in the Sarum breviary. Cf. the *Breviarum Romanum*, p. 585, lower.

104. Cf. J. G. Davies, *A Dictionary of Liturgy & Worship*, p. 156.

105. As a supplement to note 91 on p. 157 in our work you are referred to the fact that it deals with the Roman breviary which was essentially that of Pius V from the year 1568, with some changes resulting from revisions. This breviary has thus been in use up until the seventies of the twentieth century.

106. These litany-like sentences appearing just before the Lord's Prayer are called "the Lesser Litany."

107. See BCP of 1662, pp. 49-52.

108. Charles Neil, *The Tutorial Prayer Book*, pp. 108-9.

109. For a short orientation on these responsive closing sentences or versicles with reference to liturgical history, see the exposition on p. 8 in our work.

110. See BCP of 1662, p. 49.

111. Cf. pp. 82 and 114 in our work.

112. The following Bible quotations were used in the composition of these versicles: Ps. 85:7, versicles [1] and [2]; 1 Sam. 10:24 and Ps. 20:9, versicles [3] and [4]; Ps. 132:9, versicle [5]; Ps. 28:9, versicles [7] and [8]; Ps. 51:10 and 11, versicles [11] and [12].

113. See the table at p. 8 in our work.

114. This is found in the lauds of the Sarum breviary. See BCP of 1662, p. 50.

115. See *The First and Second Prayer Books of King Edward VI*, pp. 27 and 355.

116. See BCP of 1662, p. 50.

117. See pp. 68-70 under 4.d.(1) in our work.

118. See BCP of 1662, p. 49.

119. J. Dowden, *The Workmanship of the Prayer Book*, pp. 219 and 220.

120. See BCP of 1662, p. 51.

121. Ibid., pp. 51 and 52.

122. Ibid., p. 52.

123. In the offices of the Roman breviary the close consists of the well-known form of prayer for the dead: "Fidelium animae per misericordiam Dei requiescant in pace. Amen."

124. BCP of 1662, pp. 53 and 54.

125. Ibid., pp. 54 and 55.

126. Ibid., pp. 55 and 56.

127. Ibid., p. 57. The Magnificat is also an important constituent of the Roman vespers together with the Nunc Dimittis.

128. Ibid., p. 59.

129. Ibid., pp. 61 and 62.

130. Ibid., p. 62.

131. Scrupulously accurate liturgical history commentaries on the exhortation, confession, and absolution by Charles Neil are to be found in his *Tutorial Prayer Book*, pp. 93-98.

132. See the confiteor with absolution in the compline, the last office of the day. This confiteor because of its formality lacks the power of a personal commitment and a speaking from the heart. Cf. *Breviarum Romanum*, pp. 594 and 595.

133. Cf. BCP of 1662, pp. 293-321.

134. These alternative formulas are known under the title "An Order for Holy Communion," Series 1, 2, 3, London 1966, 1967 (thus they have not existed very long).

135. Cf. BCP of 1662, Pocket Book Edition, Oxford University Press, p. 293. In this edition the opening rubric has been revised in the sense of being reduced. For that reason in this special case we rest on the authority of the BCP in the Pocket Book Edition of Cambridge University Press, p. 141. The printing is of a newer date. Generally in these liturgical pocket book editions no date is given. Probably the edition stems from the beginning of the 1960s.

136. Cf. p. 76 under 4.i.(3) and p. 78 under 4.i.(7) in our work.

137. Ibid., p. 68 under 4.d.(1).

138. This refers to the missal based on the revision of Pope Pius V in the year 1570. Cf. *Saint Andrew Daily Missal,* St. André near Bruges 1951. The new missal also, *The Sunday Missal* from the year 1975, knows no such rubric.

139. See *Saint Andrew Daily Missal,* St. André near Bruges, 1951, p. 951.

140. In the new book of the mass which appeared in 1975 in the Collins Liturgical Publication, this opening ceremony of the "Asperges Me" is modified.

141. Cf. BCP of 1662, p. 294.

142. Ibid., pp. 294-96. In connexion with the proclamation of the Ten Commandments it should again be recalled that this placement of the Decalogue at the beginning of the communion service is due to John Hooper.

143. Cf. p. 68 under 4.d.(1) in our work.

144. Cf. BCP of 1662, pp. 296 and 297.

145. The term "governor" was already found in the holy communion service of 1549. But it might have been possible under the influence of the monarchs James I and Charles II for the term "head" to have found favour. That this did not occur may perhaps be ascribed to puritanical influence.

146. The romantic restoration in Germany in the nineteenth century saw the monarch as the representative of God just as did the Reformation.

147. Cf. BCP of 1662, pp. 297 and 298.

148. Ibid., pp. 298-301.

149. See pp. 106-7, 122, bottom, and 123, top, in our work.

150. Ibid., p. 76 under 4.i.(3).

151. Ibid., p. 74 under 4.g.

152. Cf. BCP of 1662, pp. 301-3.

153. Ibid., p. 302, top.

154. Ibid., p. 302, middle.

155. In this connexion see the distinguished Word theology associated with Hooper and Cranmer. See pp. 67-73 under 4.d. and pp. 89ff. under 1. and 2. in our work.

156. Cf. BCP of 1662, p. 302.

157. See pp. 68ff. under 4.d.(1), in our work.

158. Cf. BCP of 1662, p. 302.

159. See p. 74 under 4.g. in our work.

160. Cf. BCP of 1662, pp. 302-3.

161. Hooper speaks of a firm belief in one's salvation only through Holy Scripture. See p. 73 under 4.e. in our work.

162. Cf. BCP of 1662, pp. 303-8. See also pp. 107 and 108 in our work.

163. See p. 82 under 5.b. in our work

164. BCP of 1662, pp. 303-5.

165. See pp. 152-54 in our work.

166. BCP of 1662, p. 303.

167. See p. 83 under 5.c. in our work.

168. BCP of 1662, p. 303.

169. See pp. 65 and 66 under 4.c. in our work.

170. Hymn book of the Evangelical-Reformed Church of German-speaking Switzerland, p. 530, Hymn 265 (freely translated here).

171. BCP of 1662, p. 304.

172. See p. 73 under 4.f. in our work.

173. BCP of 1662, p. 304.

174. Ibid., pp. 304 and 305.

175. Ibid., p. 305.

176. Ibid., p. 305.

177. Ibid., p. 306.

178. Ibid., p. 306.

179. See p. 84 under 5.e. in this work.

180. BCP of 1662, p. 306.

181. Ibid., pp. 307 and 308.

182. Ibid., p. 307.

183. See p. 81 under 5.a. in our work.

184. You are reminded of what has been said about repetitions as an element of style, on p. 84 under 5.e. in our work.

185. BCP of 1662, p. 307.

186. See p. 81, second to last quotation under 5.a. in our work.

187. BCP of 1662, pp. 307-8.

188. Ibid., p. 308.

189. Ibid., p. 308.

190. Ibid., p. 309. This confession stems from "Hermann's Consultation." Cf. p. 4 in our work. For more detailed information on the liturgical history I direct you to G. Cuming, *The Godly Order, Texts and Studies Relating to the Book of Common Prayer*, London 1983, pp. 81-90.

191. See p. 66 under 4.c., quotation at top in our work.

192. Cf. 2 Cor. 5:17; Eph. 4:23-24; Col. 3:10; John 3:3.

193. *The Saint Andrew Daily Missal*, p. 955. The confession in the modern *Sunday Missal* of 1975 does not differ importantly from the Latin-English *The Saint Andrew Daily Missal* from 1951 prior to the Second Vatican. For the confession in the new book of the mass see *The Sunday Missal*, London 1975, pp. 22 and 23.

194. Cf. *The Sunday Missal*, cited above, pp. 22 and 23.

195. Under the Ordinarium one understands the invariable portion of the text of the mass. Under Proprium de Tempore one understands the varying parts appropriate to the days of the church year such as intercessions, lessons, hymnal pieces, etc.

196. BCP of 1662, p. 310. These "Comfortable Words" are taken from "Hermann's Consultation." See p. 4 in our work. Cf. also G. Cuming, *The Godly Order, Texts and Studies relating to the Book of Common Prayer*, London 1983, p. 80.

197. See BCP of 1662, pp. 314-15.

198. See p. 117, the second quotation from Cranmer, in our work.

199. Ibid., p. 116, quotation from Cranmer at bottom.

200. BCP of 1662, pp. 315-16. At the beginning of the prayer it is clearly stressed that it deals with a sacrifice of praise and thanksgiving: "We thy humble servants entirely desire thy fatherly goodness mercifully to accept this our sacrifice of praise and thanksgiving."

201. BCP of 1662, pp. 316-17. The first prayer of thanksgiving is more Zwinglian, the second more Calvinistic-Buceristic.

202. See p. 117, the second quotation from Cranmer, in our work.

203. Ibid., p. 78 under 4.i.(7).

204. Ibid., p. 54, first full quotation at top, and all quotations beginning mid-page 79 and on to top, p. 80.

205. See pp. 40 and 78 in our work.

206. Cf. BCP of 1662, p. 317.

207. Ibid., pp. 317-18.

208. The revivalistic substance is meant.

209. See J. B. Lightfoot, ed. *The Apostolic Fathers, Epistle of St. Ignatius to the Smyrnaeans,* ch. 8, Grand Rapids 1973, p. 84.

210. See *The Fathers of the Church,* vol. 7, Vincent of Lérins, Commentaries Ch. 2. Trans. by R. E. Morris, Washington 1970, p. 270.

211. See *The Fathers of the Church,* vol. 64, Cyril of Jerusalem, Catechesis XVIII, 26, Washington 1970, vol. 2, p. 134.

212. See what has been said with reference to John Hooper, principally the quotation from Hooper's works on p. 49, middle, in our work.

213. See *Cranmer's Works,* vol. I, p. 13.

214. Ibid., p. 46.

215. Ibid., p. 71.

216. Ibid., p. 34.

217. Ibid., p. 93.

218. Ibid., p. 354. In this connexion one should not forget Hooper's position.

219. Ibid., p. 366.

220. See Calvin, *Institutes of the Christian Religion* IV, 1, 2, ed. by J. T. McNeill, London and Philadelphia 1960, p. 1014. One should also take note of the title to *The Second Helvetic Confession* of Heinrich Bullinger, where it reads: "Confession and simple explanation of the orthodox faith and the *catholic* doctrine of the pure Christian religion." The edition issued in German is published by the Zwingli Verlag 1966. See therein p. 9. See A. C. Cochrane, ed., *The Second Helvetic Confession of 1566,* London 1966.

221. BCP of 1662, p. 4.

222. See pp. 8 and 9 in our work.

223. BCP of 1662, p. 298.

224. Ibid., p. 316.

225. The idea of "catholic" here comes close to puritan understanding. See also *The Second Helvetic Confession,* Ch. XVII, ed. by A. C. Cochrane, London 1966, p. 261.

226. BCP of 1662, p. 637.

227. Ibid., p. 653.

228. Ibid., p. 701. Cf. also Confessio Augustana Art. 7.

229. See Appendix, p. 324, No. 5.

230. Strictly speaking there is no Lady Day in the BCP of 1662. The feast of February 2 is well named "The Purification of St. Mary the Virgin," but the collect for it makes mention of the presentation of Jesus in the Temple. Likewise there is the feast of the 25th of March called "The Annunciation of the Blessed Virgin Mary." Only Jesus is spoken of in the collect. See in the BCP of 1662, pp. 259-60 and 264.

231. See Art. XX in The Thirty-nine Articles.

232. See BCP of 1662, p. 302.

233. This understanding of catholicity is one of the most important contributions of the puritans. See also *The Second Helvetic Confession,* Ch. XVII, p. 261.

234. Cf. pp. 79-80 in our work with special reference to the two supporting quotations. Family prayers were a particular concern in puritanism. The fact that the BCP was useful as a formula for household devotions is chiefly to be ascribed to puritan influence.

235. H. Davies, *Worship and Theology in England,* vol. I, pp. 36-37.

236. Quite definitely there are theologians who give expression to the belief that the long-range objective of an ecumenical effort must consist in an organizationally evident worldwide church. Thus Peter Day says in the "Capsule Report" of the Consultation on Church Union (CoCU) in Denver, Colorado, 26-30 Sept. 1971, the following: "We declare with renewed conviction that the Gospel demands an organizational union. As Christians

who share this one Gospel we can no longer justify our institutionalized separation from each other."

M. M. Thomas writes in the *Beiheft zur Oekumenischen Rundschau Nr. 24,* Geneva 1973, pp. 13ff. (translated here): "I once heard in a staff discussion how C. I. Itty made the remark that the council should set the year 2000 as the goal to realize the unity of the church and should carry out its program on the basis of a countdown. . . . His observation was in my opinion nevertheless really justified. We must set ourselves a, in many respects, historical goal in time if our union is not to run the risk of losing its dynamic."

Jürgen Moltmann writes in the *Beiheft zur Oek. Rundschau Nr. 23,* Utrecht 1972, in the article "Gemeinschaft in einer geteilten Welt," pp. 51ff. (translated here): "We should also consider here whether the loyalty binding one ᴛo one's own denomination must not more and more give way to solidarity with the ecumenical Christendom."

237. Oscar Cullmann, "Oekumenismus im Lichte des biblischen Charisma begriffes," *Theologische Literaturzeitung,* 97, 1972, no. 11, p. 817.

238. Cf. C. C. Richardson, *Zwingli and Cranmer on the Eucharist, Cranmer dixit et contradixit,* Evanston 1949.

239. W. Nyenhuis, *Traces of a Lutheran Eucharistic Doctrine in Thomas Cranmer,* Leiden, 1972.

240. Cf. C. E. Pocknee, "The Sacrament of Sacrifice," in *The Anglican Catholick,* vol. 7, no. 31, Autumn 1977, pp. 5ff. Cf. also C. E. Pocknee's "The English Reformers and the Mass" in *The Anglican Catholick,* vol. 6, no. 27, Autumn 1976, pp. 12ff.

241. Cf. pp. 149-50 above, in our work.

242. G. W. Locher, *Streit unter Gästen,* pp. 7 and 13.

243. The Reformed tradition united within itself presbyterian and puritanical thinking.

244. Walther Künneth, *Fundamente des Glaubens,* p. 170 (translated).

245. Cf. *Theological Dictionary of the New Testament,* ed. by Gerhard Kittel, vol. I, article by O. Procksch, "The Use of the Term Holiness in the Old Testament," translated and ed. by G. W. Bromiley, Grand Rapids 1978-1982, pp. 89ff.

246. Cf. also 1 Cor. 14:26; Col. 3:16-17; 1 Tim. 2:8-10; Heb. 3:6; 1 Pet. 2:4-5; Rev. 5:8-10.

247. This discotheque bears the name "The Boston Tea Party."

248. Cf. Harvey Cox, *The Seduction of the Spirit,* London 1974, pp. 156-58.

249. The candles were located on the borders of the bathing pool.

250. See H. Cox, *The Seduction of the Spirit,* pp. 207-9.

251. Ibid., p. 205.

252. In reference to Cox see (4), p. 199 of this work.

253. It is significant that Harvey Cox generally doesn't speak at all of the sinful downfall of man which requires pardon and purging in order to be permitted to approach the Holy God. Cf. also what J. I. Packer says in regards to the confession in his criticism of the experimental liturgy Second Series. This is to be found in *Towards a Modern Prayer Book,* ed. by R. T. Beckwith, Appleford 1966, p. 83.

254. See BCP of 1662, p. 40.

255. Ibid., p. 40.

256. Ibid., p. 41.

257. Ibid., p. 41.

258. See p. 340, note 42, in our work. See also in the BCP of 1662, p. 42, the rubric at the top.

259. See Appendix, p. 324. Cf. also BCP of 1662, pp. 42 and 43.

260. See p. 340, note 44, in our work.

261. See BCP of 1662, pp. 47 and 48.

262. Ibid., p. 57.

263. The interpretation here of the text of the Psalms is based on that of the King James Version.

264. See J. G. Davies, *Dictionary of Liturgy and Worship*, article "Postures" by G. Cope, p. 315. This facing to the east is practiced chiefly in those churches where the congregation is seated to the south and north of the choir stalls. This applies principally to cathedrals.

265. BCP of 1662, pp. 293-321.

266. Ibid., p. 294.

267. See p. 200 under c.(1), first, in our work.

268. BCP of 1662, p. 294. See also p. 167 in our work.

269. BCP of 1662, pp. 294-96.

270. Ibid., pp. 298-301.

271. Ibid., pp. 303-8.

272. Ibid., p. 303.

273. Ibid., p. 310.

274. Ibid., pp. 310-11. See also Appendix, p. 324, No. 5 in our work.

275. See BCP of 1662, p. 313.

276. Ibid., p. 314.

277. Ibid., pp. 314 and 315.

278. Ibid., p. 317.

279. The Thirty-nine Articles of the Anglican prayer book are highly appreciated by conservative low churchmen; they are almost hated by the Anglo-Catholics.

280. See "Ecclesiastical Sonnets" in *Wordsworth's Poetical Works*, ed. by Thomas Hutchinson, Oxford 1973, p. 349.

281. Ibid., pp. 349 and 350.

282. Ibid., p. 351.

283. Ibid., p. 354.

284. Cf. Stella Brook, *The Language of the BCP*, Oxford 1965.

285. Cf. BCP of 1662, pp. 40 and 56.

286. During school vacations the boys' choirs are on leave. Cf. BCP of 1662, pp. 42, 48, and 58.

287. Ibid., pp. 42, 46, 47, 48, 57, 58, and 60.

288. Ibid., pp. 38 and 54.

289. Ibid., pp. 39, 55, and 56.

290. Ibid., pp. 39, 40, 55, and 56.

291. Ibid., pp. 40 and 56. Cf. also p. 340, note 41, in our work.

292. Ibid., pp. 40, 41, 56, and 57. Cf. p. 340, note 42, in our work.

293. Ibid., pp. 41, 42, 47, and 58 in the BCP of 1662.

294. Ibid., pp. 42-47, and 57-60.

295. See Appendix, p. 325, No. 10 (Te Deum) in our work; the Benedictus is the hymn spoken by Zechariah in Luke 1:67-79.

296. Ibid., p. 340, notes 47 and 48.

297. See BCP of 1662, pp. 48 and 60.

298. Ibid., pp. 49 and 60. Cf. also Appendix, p. 325, No. 9 in our work.

299. See BCP of 1662, pp. 49 and 61.

300. Cf. J. G. Davies, *A Dictionary of Liturgy and Worship*, article on "Gestures" by Gilbert Cope, pp. 185-89.

301. Cf. *Ancient Christian Writers*, New York 1954, Origenes, De Oratione XXX, 3, transl. by J. J. O'Meara, pp. 131 and 132.

302. BCP of 1662, pp. 39-40.

303. Ibid., pp. 49-52.

304. Ibid., pp. 55-56 and 61-64.

305. Ibid., pp. 294-97.

306. Ibid., p. 309.

307. Ibid., p. 40. Cf. also p. 340, note 42, in our work.

308. Ibid., p. 48.

309. Ibid., pp. 56 and 60.

310. Ibid., p. 297.

311. See B. Rainbow, *The Choral Revival in the Anglican Church,* 1970.

312. E. Pusey was the chief founder of the High Church movement in England during the nineteenth century. The reintroduction of the eucharistic vestments as well as the processionals of vested choirs are due to him.

313. BCP of 1662, p. 36.

314. *The First and Second Prayer Books of King Edward VI,* p. 212.

315. See Charles Neil, *The Tutorial Prayer Book,* London 1963, pp. 78-89. See also W. H. Griffith Thomas, *The Catholick Faith,* London 1911, pp. 430-41.

316. The "Ornaments Rubric" is found in the first quotation on p. 213 in our work and on p. 36 in the BCP of 1662.

317. See Griffith Thomas, *The Catholick Faith*, London 1911, p. 438.

318. Ibid., p. 438.

319. Ibid., p. 434.

320. That clause from the Act of Uniformity is meant which we have quoted above.

321. See Griffith Thomas, *The Catholick Faith*, p. 434.

322. Ibid., p. 438.

323. An admirable brief historical review of vestments and their usage is found in J. G. Davies, *A Dictionary of Liturgy and Worship,* in the article "Vestments" by Gilbert Cope, pp. 365-83.

324. Ibid., p. 376.

325. See Karl Heussi, *Kompendium der Kirchengeschichte,* Sec. 123, d-i. pp. 416 and 417.

326. See J. G. Davies, *A Dictionary of Liturgy and Worship,* p. 366.

327. Ibid., p. 370.

328. Ibid., pp. 372 and 373.

329. Ibid., pp. 368 and 369.

330. Cf. Book VIII of the *Apostolischen Konstitutionen,* chiefly the rubric on the preface. *Bibliothek d. Kirchenväter,* vol. V, p. 43.

331. See *Symbolik des Orthodoxen u. Orientalischen Christentums,* Stuttgart 1962, article by H.-J. Schulz, pp. 27 and 28.

332. A good description of the liturgical garments in the Eastern catholic tradition is found in the *Bibliothek der Kirchenväter,* vol. 5, "Griechische Liturgien," pp. 304-6.

333. Ibid., p. 208 (translated).

334. Ibid., p. 209 (translated).

335. Ibid., p. 209 (translated).

336. *Missale Romanum,* Edition VIII, 1923.

337. Ibid., p. (42). Orationes dicendae cum sacerdos induitur sacerdotalibus paramentis (Rubric).

338. Ibid., p. (42). "Make me white, O Lord and purify my heart that being made white through the Blood of the Lamb, I may relish eternal joys."

339. Ibid., p. (42). "Give me back, O Lord, the stole of immortality which I have lost

through the prevarication of the first father: And in however an unworthy state I approach your holy mystery, may I nevertheless acquire eternal joy."

340. Ibid., p. (42). "Lord, You have said: My yoke is sweet and my burden easy: Make that I may be able to carry this burden in this way that I can win your grace."

341. Cf. also the extensive work by J. Braun, *Die Liturgische Gewandung in Occident und Orient nach Ursprung und Entwicklung, Verwendung und Symbolik*, 1907. See also Walter Lotz, *Das Hochzeitliche Gewand*, Kassel 1949. Cf. moreover Edith Thomas, *Das Gotteshaus*, chapter "Kirchengewand und Amtstracht," Kassel 1964. See also Kurt von Wistinghausen, *Der Neue Gottesdienst*, Stuttgart 1965, chapter on clerical vestments, pp. 38-47.

342. The new righteousness received in Jesus through the indwelling of the Holy Ghost brings about the gift of the glorified resurrection body based on the assertion in Romans 8:11.

343. See W. H. Griffith Thomas, *The Catholick Faith*, p. 432.

344. See 2 Chronicles 5:11-13.

345. The antependium is a decorative linen cloth which hangs down from the communion table. Cf. in regard thereto J. G. Davies, *A Dictionary of Liturgy and Worship*, article "Altar Hangings" by C. E. Pocknee, pp. 6 and 7.

346. A good summary reference interior furnishings is found in *The Tutorial Prayer Book* of Charles Neil, p. 89. The BCP of 1662 has only minimal references with regard to the interior appointments of the church room. In order to prevent arbitrariness binding regulations came into existence which can be found in the standard work *Church Law*, by Benjamin Whitehead, London 1911, under the chapter, "Ornaments."

347. See footnote 345, above.

348. Ibid., pp. 146-47. See what William Laud has said thereon.

349. See J. G. Davies, *Dictionary of Liturgy and Worship*, article by C. E. Pocknee, p. 333.

350. Famous reredos representations with crucifixions are found in the cathedrals of Oxford, Winchester, St. Albans, but countless modest village churches have such depictions.

351. See pp. 50 and 51 above in our work. That type of reredos where the Ten Commandments, the Lord's Prayer, and the Creed are present requires no niche.

352. See Benjamin Whitehead, *Church Law*, London 1911.

353. This is typical of Zwingli's understanding of holy communion.

354. Thus C. E. Pocknee says with justice in connexion with the altar-like aspect of the communion table in respect to the eucharist service: "Today we should prefer to say that the sacrifice of Christ recalled in the Eucharist is the whole of his atoning work culminating in the cross, resurrection, and ascension." See J. G. Davies, *Dictionary of Liturgy and Worship*, p. 6.

355. See pp. 124-25 in our work.

356. Cf. J. Braun, *Der Christliche Altar*, vol. II, pp. 270-75.

357. Ibid., vol. I, Chap. 6, pp. 750-55.

358. Incense is only found in High Church circles.

359. Processions with a crucifer marching in front of the choir have gained a vogue in Morning and Evening Prayer as well as in communion services also in the low churches with their frequent evangelical alinement. The description above is of course based on services in a cathedral since they are at their most impressive there.

360. See p. 340, note 42, in our work.

361. See p. 219; see also note 342 on p. 363, in our work.

362. Cf. BCP of 1662, p. 303.

363. The BCP of 1662 provides during the offertory no ceremonial removal of the

napkins covering the chalice. But there is also no rubric forbidding it. There exists here a certain freedom in reference to administering the liturgy.

364. See BCP of 1662, p. 311.

365. Evensong is sung by a liturgically vested choir daily except in school vacation. During the school vacation Morning and Evening Prayer are only spoken.

366. Cf. J. G. Davies, *Dictionary of Liturgy and Worship,* article "Cathedral Office" by W. Jardine Grisbrooke, pp. 124 and 125.

367. See pp. 128-48 in our work.

368. Cf. E. W. Kohls, *Luther oder Erasmus,* vol, 1, Fr. Reinhardt Verlag, Basel 1972, pp. 159-67. See also vol. II, pp. 183ff. See also by the same author *Mein Bibelkatechismus zum Alten Testament, zum Neuen Testament und zur Kirchengeschichte,* Marburg 1983, pp. 19 and 33ff. Also informative is E. W. Kohls, *Das Wort Gottes hat alles gehandelt,* Lahr 1983.

369. To the authors of the Chicago Declaration, which emphasized so strongly the self-interpretation and the self-effectiveness of the Bible, belong among others E. P. Clowney, Norman L. Geisler, J. I. Packer, H. Hoehner, R. C. Sproul. The Chicago Declaration with its nineteen articles is commented upon by R. C. Sproul in the publication *Explaining Inerrancy: A Commentary,* Oakland 1980. Of particular importance in our connexion are Articles XVII and XVIII on pp. 37 and 38.

370. Wilhelm Maurer, *Gesammelte Aufsätze,* vol. I, *Reformation und Mission,* p. 176 (translated).

NOTES TO CHAPTER V

1. A broad survey of The Oxford Movement in respect to origin and development is found in O. Chadwick's *The Mind of the Oxford Movement,* London 1963.

2. Cf. F. C. Cross, *The Oxford Movement and the Seventeenth Century,* London 1963.

3. Cf. G. M. Trevelyan, *A Shortened History of England,* p. 339.

4. Ibid., p. 472.

5. Declaration on the inspiration of the Word of God, and the Eternity of Future Punishment, by Clergymen of the United Church of England and Ireland, Address to the Archbishops and Bishops of the United Church of England and Ireland, June 1, 1864.

6. See M. Keller-Hüschemenger, *Die Lehre der Kirche in der Oxford-bewegung,* Gütersloh 1974, p. 55.

7. Ibid., pp. 60ff.

8. See J. H. Newman, *The Via Media of the Anglican Church,* vol. I, Lectures of the prophetical Office of the Church, London 1891, p. 29.

9. See J. H. Newman, *Tracts for the Times, Remarks on Certain Passages in the Thirty-nine Articles,* London 1841, p. 11.

10. See M. Keller-Hüschemenger, *Die Lehre der Kirche in der Oxford-bewegung,* p. 79.

11. Ibid., p. 81.

12. See J. H. Newman, *The Via Media of the Anglican Church,* vol. I, Lectures of the Prophetical Office of the Church, p. 158.

13. Cf. M. Keller-Hüschemenger, cited above, p. 245.

14. See M. Keller-Hüschemenger, *Die Lehre der Kirche in der Oxford-bewegung,* pp. 101 and 103.

15. John Keble, "A sermon, preached at the Cathedral Church of Winchester, September 27, 1836," London 1837, p. 73.

16. See *The British Critic*, Vol. XXXII, 1842, p. 389.

17. Cf. M. Keller-Hüschemenger, *Die Lehre der Kirche in der Oxford-bewegung*, p. 70.

18. J. H. Newman, *An Essay on the Development of Christian Doctrine*, London 1914, p. 65.

19. Ibid., p. 63.

20. Ibid., p. 62.

21. Ibid., p. 186.

22. Cf. Karl Adam, *Das Wesen des Katholizismus*, p. 14, Munich 1927 (translated).

23. Cf. H. Denzinger, *Enchiridion Symbolorum*, Freiburg im Br. 1947, 2011.

24. See M. Keller-Hüschemenger, *Die Lehre der Kirche in der Oxford-bewegung*, pp. 114-15.

25. Ibid., p. 125.

26. Ibid., p. 129.

27. Ibid., p. 138 (translated).

28. Ibid., p. 168.

29. Ibid., p. 195 (translated).

30. Ibid., p. 182.

31. Ibid., p. 219.

32. Ibid., p. 221.

33. See Ph. E. Hughes, *Theology of the English Reformers*, pp. 44ff.

34. See John Keble, *Sermons for the Christian Year*, XI, Sermon XXIII on "The Holy Eucharist the Crown and Centre of Christian Worship," London/Oxford, 1875-1880.

35. M. Keller-Hüschemenger, *Die Lehre der Kirche in der Oxford-bewegung*, p. 155 (translated). We see here a genuine Eastern Church element.

36. Ibid., p. 156.

37. Ibid., p. 157.

38. Ibid., p. 153.

39. Ibid., p. 157.

40. See John Keble, *Sermons for the Christian Year*, III, p. 404, Sermon XL.

41. See M. Keller-Hüschemenger, *Die Lehre der Kirche in der Oxford-bewegung*, p. 244.

42. Ibid., p. 247.

43. When we speak of the Greek Church, this is identical with the Eastern Church, which embraces the Russian, Armenian, Syrian, and Coptic churches.

44. M. Keller-Hüschemenger, *Die Lehre der Kirche in der Oxford-bewegung*, pp. 252-53.

45. Tractarians of the later phase around the middle of the nineteenth century are called ritualists because they often decorated divine services with late medieval ritual.

46. See M. Keller-Hüschemenger, *Die Lehre der Kirche in der Oxford-bewegung*, p. 253.

47. *The British Critic, Quarterly Theological Review*, and *Ecclesiastical Record*, vol. XXVII 1840, p. 249.

48. J. Keble, *Sermons for the Christian Year*, I, Sermon XXXIV, p. 346.

49. See p. 231, last quotation, in our work. Article VI is to be found in the BCP of 1662 in the Pocket Book Edition, Oxford University Press, p. 694.

50. Ibid., p. 702.

51. See J. H. Newman, *Tracts for the Times, Remarks on Certain Passages in the Thirty-nine Articles*, London 1841, p. 25.

52. Ibid., p. 26.

53. Ibid., p. 24.

54. Ibid., p. 37.

55. Ibid., p. 42.

56. BCP of 1662, p. 710.

57. Cf. J. H. Newman, *Tracts for the Times, Remarks on Certain Passages in the Thirty-nine Articles*, London 1841, p. 78.

58. Ibid., p. 78.

59. BCP of 1662, p. 701.

60. Cf. J. H. Newman, *Tracts for the Times, Remarks on Certain Passages in the Thirty-nine Articles*, London 1841, p. 80.

61. Cf. Peter Beyerhaus, *Aufbruch der Armen*, Bad Liebenzell 1981, pp. 48-54 ("Kontextualität").

62. Cf. Dieter Voll, *Hochkirchlicher Pietismus*, Munich 1960, pp. 28ff.

63. Cf. C. Bodington, *Devotional Life in the 19th Century*, 1905, p. 86.

64. Dieter Voll, *Hochkirchlicher Pietismus*, Munich 1960, p. 45 (translated).

65. Ibid., p. 45 (translated).

66. Ibid., p. 50 (translated).

67. Ibid., p. 51 (translated).

68. G. W. E. Russel, *Arthur Stanton—A Memoir*, London 1917, pp. 253 and 222.

69. Ibid., p. 281.

70. Dieter Voll, *Hochkirchlicher Pietismus*, p. 88.

71. Cf. Peter Anson, *The Call of the Cloisters*, London 1964, pp. 457ff.

72. Cf. A. M. Allchin, *The Silent Rebellion—Anglican Communities*, 1845-1900, London 1958, p. 33.

73. See Peter F. Anson, *The Call of the Cloisters*, pp. 72ff.

74. Ibid., p. 79.

75. The book of Peter F. Anson provides a survey of the most important brother and sister communities in the Anglican Church.

76. Cf. Dieter Voll, *Hochkirchlicher Pietismus*, p. 58.

77. See pp. 229-43 in our work.

78. See on pp. 8-9 and 121 of our work descriptions of Morning Prayer and the Holy Communion Service with their matching liturgical elements.

79. The full title is *Lux Mundi, A Series of Studies in the Religion of the Incarnation*, ed. by Ch. Gore, London 1889.

80. Gerhard Ebeling had the conviction that the historical-critical method was to be seen as in the closest connexion with the Reformation doctrine of justification. See Gerhard Ebeling's *Aufsatz in der ZThK* 1950, pp. 41ff.

81. Michael Ramsey, *From Gore to Temple*, London 1960, p. 11.

82. See *Lux Mundi*, "The Incarnation and Development," p. 183.

83. Ibid., p. 183.

84. Ibid., p. 214.

85. Ibid., p. 272.

86. M. Ramsey, *From Gore to Temple*, p. 27.

87. Ibid., p. 151.

88. William Temple, *Nature, Man and God*, p. 306.

89. William Temple, *Revelation, A Symposium*, p. 107.

90. For more detailed information on the BCP 1927/28 one should consult

G. Cuming, *The Godly Order, Texts and Studies Relating to The Book of Common Prayer*, London 1983. See in particular Chap. 10, "Towards the 1928 Prayer Book," pp. 168-80.

91. J.A.T. Robinson, *Liturgy Coming to Life*, London 1960 p. 39. I. R. Thompson ascribes to Robinson an enormous influence in reference to today's liturgical thinking. In the collection of essays called *Ritual Murder* I. R. Thompson in his composition "The other liturgical Revolution" writes the following: "Now this idea—that God is to be encountered in the commonplace—was the central feature of a well-known book . . . a book, moreover which continues to exercise an enormous influence on liturgical thinking. I refer of course, to John Robinson's *Honest to God*," p. 156.

92. See Luke 22:19.

93. J.A.T. Robinson, *Liturgy Coming to Life*, p. 37.

94. Ibid., p. 26.

95. Ibid., p. 42.

96. Cf. that said on the "Sacral Aspects" at pp. 195ff. in our work.

97. J.A.T. Robinson, *Liturgy Coming to Life*, p. 17.

98. Ibid., p. 11.

99. Ibid., p. 22.

100. Robinson totally overlooks that the Gospel contained in the BCP has also a character of separation so that the great masses do not turn to the Biblical message. "The little flock" which receives the Good News is Biblical. Robinson however wants to have a BCP with which you can have a big impact upon the world without requiring that the world change itself in respect to an individual rebirth in the Biblical sense.

101. By the term "Anglican eight o'clock" is meant the Holy Communion Service which in Anglican churches takes place generally in the early morning at 8:00 A.M.

102. Ibid., p. 11.

103. Ibid., p. 23.

104. See p. 238 in our work.

105. J. A. T. Robinson, *Liturgy Coming to Life*, p. 71.

106. Ibid., p. 73.

107. Ibid., p. 74.

108. See pp. 233ff. in our work.

109. J. A. T. Robinson, *The New Reformation?* London 1965.

110. Ibid., p. 107.

111. Ibid., p. 110.

112. Ibid., p. 112.

113. Ibid., p. 110.

114. Ibid., p. 114.

115. Ibid., p. 33.

116. With "this is simply not gospel" Robinson means that which is understood as gospel in the Reformation of Luther.

117. J. A. T. Robinson, *The New Reformation?* p. 33.

118. Ibid., p. 34.

119. Ibid., p. 92.

120. Ibid., p. 81.

121. Ibid., p. 117.

122. Ibid., p. 47.

123. Ibid., pp. 47 and 48.

124. Cf. Luke 16:19-31; 23:39-43; 2 Corinthians 5:1-10; 12:1-4; Matthew 6:19-20; John 14:1-3; Hebrews 11:8-16; 13:14; Revelation 7:9-17.

125. J. A. T. Robinson, *On Being the Church in the World*, London 1960, p. 19.

126. Ibid., p. 13.

127. Ibid., p. 13.

128. See Calvin, *Institutes of the Christian Religion*, I, 15, 2 vols., London and Philadelphia 1960, pp. 184-86. Cf. also Augustine, *De immortalitate animae* (The Immortality of the Soul), translated by Ludwig Schopp, in *The Fathers of the Church*, vol. 4, Washington 1977, pp. 15-47. See also The Heidelberg Catechism XXII, 57 (1563) in *Reformed Confessions of the 16th Century*, ed. by A. C. Cochrane, Philadelphia 1966, p. 315.

129. We do not deny in our work that the kingdom of God has also a dimension of the here and now, but I reject this unbiblical shifting of proportions wherein the vertical as the dominant is converted into a horizontal line.

130. J. A. T. Robinson, *On Being the Church in the World*, p. 28.

131. Ibid., pp. 130-31.

132. One should not forget what Hebrews 9:27 tells us.

133. J. A. T. Robinson, *On Being the Church in the World*, pp. 141-42.

134. Ibid., p. 144.

135. Ibid., p. 144.

136. See Peter Beyerhaus, *Verlag der Liebenzeller Mission*, Bad Liebenzell 1981.

137. See J. A. T. Robinson, *On Being the Church in the World*, p. 149.

138. Ibid., pp. 152 and 155.

139. J. A. T. Robinson, *Honest to God*, London 1963, p. 115.

140. See J. A. T. Robinson, *The New Reformation?* pp. 12-13.

141. See Peter Staples, *The Church of England 1961-1980*, p. 53.

142. Second Series, An Order for Holy Communion, printed in Great Britain at the University Printing House, Cambridge 1966.

143. An Order for Holy Communion, Alternative Services Series 3, printed in Great Britain by Eyre & Spottiswoode Ltd., Margate 1971.

144. See Second Series, p. 13, and Series 3, pp. 30 and 31.

145. Series 3, p. 9, "We believe in one God."

146. See p. 106 in our work. Also see in the BCP, pp. 298-301.

147. Second Series, pp. 3 and 4.

148. Series 3, pp. 10-13.

149. BCP of 1662, p. 302.

150. Second Series, p. 4.

151. Series 3, p. 11.

152. BCP of 1662, p. 302.

153. Ibid., p. 302.

154. Ibid., p. 302.

155. Second Series, p. 5.

156. See 2 Cor. 5:10; Heb. 9:27.

157. See Ps. 2; 90:9; Rev. 6:15-17.

158. See Ps. 14; Rom. 3:23.

159. Second Series, p. 5.

160. Series 3, p. 15.

161. BCP of 1662, p. 309.

162. Ibid., p. 309.

163. Ibid., p. 309.

164. See Appendix, p. 323, No. 4.

165. Cf. Second Series, p. 7, and Series 3, p. 18.

166. Series 3, pp. 19 and 20. Cf. BCP of 1662, pp. 311-12.

167. See p. 352, note 119, in our work.

168. Second Series, p. 9.
169. Series 3, p. 21.
170. See p. 352, note 118 in our work. Moreover the epiclesis is a typical element tending toward the Catholic.
171. Second Series, p. 9.
172. Series 3, p. 23.
173. Second Series, p. 9.
174. Series 3, p. 24.
175. BCP of 1662, pp. 315-16.
176. Second Series, p. 11.
177. Series 3, p. 27.
178. BCP of 1662, pp. 316 and 317.
179. Second Series, p. 11.
180. Series 3, p. 27.
181. Ibid., pp. 28 and 29.
182. Ibid., pp. 6 and 7.
183. Ibid., p. 7.
184. Second Series, p. 1.
185. Series 3, p. 8.
186. Ibid., p. 9. Series 3 here follows the form of the early church.
187. See in Second Series pp. 3 and 4, and in Series 3, pp. 10-13.
188. See in Second Series, p. 5, and in Series 3, p. 15.
189. Series 3, p. 16.
190. Series 3, p. 16; Second Series, p. 6.
191. See pp. 266, 268, and 270 in our work.
192. There is a special edition of Series 3, Mowbrays, London 1973l, with a brief commentary preceding the individual liturgical parts furnished by George Reindorp, Bishop of Salisbury.
193. See pp. 259-60 in our work.
194. Ibid., pp. 258-59. Cf. also pp. 233ff.
195. Ibid., pp. 263-64.
196. Ibid., p. 263, first full quotation.
197. R. T. Beckwith, ed., *Towards a Modern Prayer Book*, Sutton Courtenay Appleford/Abingdon 1966, p. 83.
198. See pp. 266-68 in our work.
199. Cf. BCP 1662, pp. 298ff.
200. See pp. 232ff. in our work.
201. BCP 1662, pp. 298ff. See also pp. 266-67 in our work.
202. See pp. 232ff. in our work.
203. Ibid., pp. 235, 238, and 239.
204. See p. 264 in our work. In addition to Robinson, Joseph Fletcher, Alec Vidler, and James Pike had a wide influence on the "New Morality."
205. Cf. R. T. Beckwith, ed., *Towards a Modern Prayer Book*, p. 64.
206. See pp. 121 and 269-70 in our work as well as pp. 311ff. in the BCP of 1662.
207. Cf. *The Sunday Missal*, London 1975, pp. 60-68, 111, 123-24, 129, 130, 738, 742, 745, 748, 749, 757, 766, 770, 776, and 780. These pages contain the various prefaces in today's Roman missal.
208. Cf. p. 360 note 236 in our work.
209. See Sergius Heitz, *Der Orthodoxe Gottesdienst*, Matthias Grünewald Verlag, Mainz 1965 p. 243.

210. See Second Series, p. 9. Almost identical in Series 3, p. 23.

211. J. A. T. Robinson, *Liturgy Coming to Life*, p. 73.

212. Cf. H. Denzinger, *Enchiridion Symbolorum*, 1957 No. 86, p. 41.

213. See *The St. Andrew Daily Missal*, pp. 951ff. Cf. also *The Sunday Missal*, pp. 22-25.

214. See J. G. Davies, *A Dictionary of Liturgy & Worship*, article on "Canon" by R. C. D. Jasper, p. 113.

215. Harvey Cox, *The Secular City*, chapter on "To Speak in a Secular Fashion of God," New York 1966.

216. James Pike, *What Is this Treasure?* New York 1966.

217. *The Anglican Catholic*, the quarterly gazette of the Anglican Society, vol. 8, no. 33, Spring 1978, p. 15.

218. The Alternative Service Book 1980, Cambridge University Press.

219. Ibid., pp. 47-60.

220. Ibid., p. 48.

221. Ibid., pp. 37-42, and 47.

222. Ibid., p. 48.

223. Ibid., pp. 48-49.

224. Ibid., pp. 165-66.

225. Ibid., p. 49.

226. Ibid., p. 49.

227. Ibid., pp. 49ff.

228. Ibid., p. 51.

229. Ibid., p. 52.

230. Ibid., p. 52.

231. Ibid., pp. 52-54.

232. Ibid., p. 55.

233. Ibid., p. 55.

234. Ibid., p. 55.

235. Ibid., pp. 55-57.

236. Ibid., pp. 57-58.

237. Ibid., p. 58.

238. Ibid., p. 58.

239. Ibid., p. 59.

240. Ibid., p. 59.

241. Ibid., p. 59.

242. Ibid., p. 60.

243. Ibid., p. 60.

244. Ibid., p. 107.

245. BCP 1662, pp. 37 and 38.

246. See R. T. Beckwith, ed., *Towards a Modern Prayer Book*, p. 84.

247. See p. 154 in our work.

248. 1 John 3:4.

249. See ASB 1980, pp. 165-66. Cf. also the commentary given by Gordon Tayler in his composition "The Book of Common Prayer as a repository of doctrine" in the book *Ritual Murder*, edited by Brian Morris, Manchester 1980, pp. 41-43.

250. ASB 1980, p. 165.

251. Ibid., p. 165.

252. Ibid., p. 166.

253. See p. 155 in our work and see ASB 1980, p. 147 (absolution).

254. See BCP 1662, p. 49.

255. Cf. ASB 1980, p. 60.

256. Ibid., p. 103. See BCP of 1662, pp. 50-51.

257. The designation for the state prayers is given in the BCP of 1662 as follows: "A Prayer for the Queen's Majesty," "A Prayer for the Royal Family." Additionally, but not as a part of the state prayers, comes "A Prayer for the Clergy and People."

258. ASB 1980, p. 60.

259. Ibid., p. 107.

260. Ibid., p. 107.

261. Ibid., p. 107.

262. Ibid., p. 48.

263. See p. 259 in our work.

264. Cf. Alternative Service Book 1980, p. 165.

265. See pp. 259-60 in our work.

266. Ibid., p. 260.

267. Ibid., p.. 262.

268. Ibid., p. 287.

269. Cf. BCP 1662, p. 50.

270. See Robinson's rationalistic explanations of the "Last Judgment" and the "Return of Christ" on pp. 263-64 in our work where demythologizing is strongly emphasized.

271. In our discussions on the "Last Judgment" and the "Return of Jesus" on pp. 263-64 we find also existentialistic thought structures of a Bultmann-Heideggerian stamp.

272. See pp. 258-59 in our work where Robinson welcomes the theological conception of the man come of age who doesn't need God any more.

273. See p. 261, first full quotation, in our work.

274. ASB 1980, pp. 119-73.

275. Ibid., p. 119.

276. Ibid., p. 119.

277. Ibid., p. 119.

278. Ibid., pp. 120 and 161-64.

279. Ibid., p. 120.

280. Ibid., pp. 120-21 and 165-66.

281. Ibid., p. 121.

282. Ibid., p. 121.

283. Ibid., pp. 121-22.

284. Ibid., p. 122.

285. Ibid., p. 122.

286. Ibid., p. 122.

287. Ibid., p. 122.

288. Ibid., p. 122.

289. Ibid., p. 123.

290. Ibid., p. 123.

291. Ibid., pp. 123-24.

292. Ibid., pp. 124-25 and 166-69.

293. Ibid., pp. 128 and 170.

294. Ibid., pp. 128-29.

295. Ibid., p. 129.

296. Ibid., p. 129.

297. Ibid., p. 129.

298. Ibid., p. 130.

299. Ibid., pp. 130-32 and 133-41.

300. Ibid., p. 142.

301. Ibid., p. 142.

302. Ibid., pp. 142-43.

303. Ibid., pp. 143 and 172.

304. Ibid., pp. 143 and 150.

305. Ibid., p. 143.

306. Ibid., p. 144.

307. Ibid., p. 144.

308. Ibid., p. 144.

309. Ibid., pp. 145 and 173.

310. Ibid., pp. 145 and 159.

311. Ibid., p. 145.

312. Cf. BCP of 1662, p. 310 and ASB 1980, pp. 126ff.

313. ASB 1980, pp. 146-53.

314. See on p. 265 the quotation at the bottom in our work.

315. By suppressing this "begotten" the door and gate are opened for a humanistic understanding of Christology. Cf. in this connexion the article on "μονογεηϭ" by F. Büchsel in *Th.W.N.T.*, vol. IV, chiefly p. 749. Cf. the same article by F. Büchsel in the *Theological Dictionary of the New Testament*, trans. and ed. by Geoffrey Bromiley, vol. IV, pp. 737ff., Grand Rapids 1979-1982.

316. Cf. Wigand Siebel, "Origenismus in der Katholischen Kirche," *DIAKRISIS*, Bielefeld, Februar 1982, pp. 8-10.

317. See pp. 274-76 in our work.

318. See second full quotation on p. 260 in our work.

319. Cf. Gordon Tayler in his essay "The Book of Common Prayer as a repository of doctrine," published in *Ritual Murder*, ed. by Brian Morris, Manchester 1980, p. 42.

320. See pp. 124-25 in ASB 1980.

321. The statement of Geoffrey Cuming in his book *The Godly Order* in the chapter "Cranmer at Work" is of interest, pp. 56-57.

322. J. A. T. Robinson, *The New Reformation?* p. 111.

323. Cf. what is said on p. 262 of our work.

324. Ibid., p. 261, first full quotation.

325. Cf. the informative analysis of Peter Beyerhaus, *Bangkok 73, Anfang oder Ende der Weltmission?* Bad Liebenzell 1973.

326. See M. J. Gaxiola, article "Salvation Today: A Critical Report," edited by Ralph Winter in *The Evangelical Response to Bangkok*, Pasadena 1973, p. 70.

327. See *Religious News Service* (Foreign Service) for June 6, 1974.

328. Cf. K. Rahner, *Das Christentum und die nichtchristlichen Religionen*, Schriften zur Theologie V, 1962, pp. 136-58.

329. Cf. H. J. Margull and St. J. Samartha, *Dialog mit andern Religionen: Material aus der ökumenischen Bewegung*, Frankfort 1972.

330. See p. 262 in our work.

331. In order to justify pluralism Robinson quotes in an approving way Albert van den Heuvel: "Let those who can still stand the heat of the day with their traditional confessions of faith do so, but let them rejoice in those who are for the total rethinking of all they know." See *The New Reformation?* p. 99.

332. See BCP 1662, p. 313.

333. The exhortations are lacking in the communion service of ASB 1980.

334. Through the efficacy of baptism one belongs so to speak to the body of Christ automatically.

335. See ASB 1980, pp. 154-58.

336. See note 207 on p. 370 of this work.

337. BCP of 1662, pp. 313-14.

338. ASB 1980, pp. 131-32.

339. These words are spoken by the congregation.

340. These words are spoken by the congregation.

341. See ASB 1980, pp. 133-35.

342. Ibid., pp. 134 and 135.

343. Ibid., pp. 136-38.

344. Ibid., p. 136.

345. Ibid., pp. 139ff.

346. BCP of 1662, pp. 313-14.

347. Ibid., pp. 315-16.

348. See p. 153 in our work.

349. See *Sunday Missal,* Collins Liturgical Publications, London 1975, pp. 37 and 38.

350. Ibid., pp. 33-48.

351. The new "Liturgie der Evangelisch-Reformierten Kirchen in der Deutschsprachigen Schweiz," Volumn III, Holy Communion, Bern 1983, points in this direction. The formula for the mass of the Roman Church is integrated herein while the epiclesis and canon have been restored.

352. See ASB 1980, pp. 133-35.

353. See BCP 1662, p. 307.

354. Revealing for a conception of the eucharist which is not Biblical, but which is emphasized more and more in the established denominations, is the documentation of Werner Schilling in his book *Heiliges Abendmahl oder Feierabendmahl?* Telos-Taschenbuch No. 280, 1980, pp. 23-30 and 109-14.

355. It is of great significance that the "Black Rubric" is missing from all the formulas of the ASB for holy communion. Why? Should pluralism go so far that a magical sacramentalistic understanding in respect to bread and wine should also have place in the sense of an adoration of the consecrated host in the tabernacle? This practice has already existed for a long time in the Anglo-Catholic wing of the Anglican church and one has to support this practice of course through the elimination of the "Black Rubric."

356. The anthropological monism of Karl Barth has great consequences. See *Kirchliche Dogmatik* III,2, pp. 450ff.

357. Cf. Augustine, *De Civitate Dei* VI, 12 (The City of God), trans. by D. B. Zema and G. G. Walsh, in *The Fathers of the Church,* vol. 6, Washington 1977, p. 337.

358. Cf. J. W. Montgomery, *The Suicide of Christian Theology,* Minneapolis 1970, p. 52.

359. Cf. Fritz Grünzweig, "Welteinheit durch Kircheneinheit?" in *Reich Gottes oder Weltgemeinschaft,* edited by Walter Künneth and Peter Beyerhaus, Telos-Dokumentation, No. 900, 1975, p. 164.

360. *Religious News Service,* September 28, 1981, New York, p. 5.

361. Cf. Peter Beyerhaus, "Vancouver: Schwerpunkte und Konsequenzen," *DIAKRISIS,* September 1983, p. 40 (translated).

362. The Declaration of Convergence is the same thing as the Declaration of Lima of the year 1982 where a harmony of the hitherto controversial conceptions of baptism, holy eucharist, and holy orders is claimed.

363. Ibid., p. 40 (translated).

364. G. D. Kilpatrick, *Remaking the Liturgy,* London 1967, p. 9.

365. Andor Gomme, "The New Religious English," in *Ritual Murder,* ed. by Brian Morris, p. 77.

366. Ibid., p. 84.

367. Cf. David Martin, "A Plea for our Common Prayer," in *Ritual Murder,* ed. by Brian Morris, p. 11.

368. Ibid., p. 12.

369. Ibid., pp. 16-17.

370. Cf. Bryan Thwaites, "A College Sermon," in *Ritual Murder,* ed. by Brian Morris, p. 142.

371. Cf. David Martin, "A Plea for our Common Prayer," in *Ritual Murder,* ed. by Brian Morris, p. 16.

372. See G. E. Duffield, "The Language of Worship" in *Towards a Modern Prayer Book,* ed. by R. T. Beckwith, p. 69.

373. Ibid., pp. 70-71.

374. Ibid., p. 71.

375. See Bryan Thwaites, "A College Sermon," in *Ritual Murder,* ed. by Brian Morris, p. 142.

376. P. N. Brooks, "Stewardship in the Great Tradition," in *Ritual Murder,* ed. by Brian Morris, p. 149.

377. Ibid., p. 151.

NOTES TO THE APPENDIX

1. Cf. *RGG,* vol. III, article by E. Jammers, pp. 796-97. See also J. G. Davies, *A Dictionary of Liturgy and Worship,* "The Chants of the Proper of the Mass," p. 130.

2. Cf. Gregory Dix, *The Shape of the Liturgy,* p. 523.

3. Cf. J. G. Davies, *A Dictionary of Liturgy and Worship,* article by R. C. D. Jasper, pp. 112-13.

4. Cf. Gregory Dix, *The Shape of the Liturgy,* pp. 537ff.

5. Ibid., pp. 537ff.

6. Cf. J. G. Davies, *A Dictionary of Liturgy and Worship,* article by W. Jardine Grisbrooke, p. 15.

7. Ibid., pp. 15-16.

8. The major Gloria should be distinguished from the minor Gloria. See p. 340, note 42, in our work.

9. Cf. Gregory Dix, *The Shape of the Liturgy,* p. 456.

10. Cf. J. G. Davies, *A Dictionary of Liturgy and Worship,* article by W. Jardine Grisbrooke, p. 209.

11. Cf. *RGG,* vol. 1, article by E. Jammers, under the title "Ambrosianischer Lobgesang," pp. 306-7.

NOTE TO CLOSING SUMMARY

1. Ecumenical is here to be understood negatively as that spiritual attitude which adopts the major worldwide trends of pluralism, socialism, humanism, pacifism, etc.

Index

Aarau, 55, 132
Aaron, 217
Abel, 56
absolution, 100, 109, 114, 121, 125, 155, 163, 178-80, 200, 205, 211, 212, 280, 285, 291-292, 294, 296, 312
"Absolvo Te," 155 n. 85
Act of Uniformity (1559), 129, 132, 137, 214-215
Adam, 64
Adam, Karl, 234
"Adhortatio ad Coenam Domini Mysticam," 24
adiaphora, 50, 72, 85, 86, 132
adoration, 210-17, 282
Aelmer, 131
Agnus Dei, 10, 120-21, 299, 350
Aitken, Robert, 244
alb, 213, 216-18
Alexandrian liturgy, 323
Allchin, A.M., 247
Alleine, 84
altar, 121-26, 150, 196, 197, 219, 224
altar rail, 147, 212, 221, 226
Alternative Service Book 1980 (See: ASB 1980)
Ambrose of Milan, 325
Ambrosian Song of Praise (See: Te Deum Laudamus)
Ambrosius, 242, 323
anabaptists, xxx, 47
Analogia Entis, 22

anamnesis, 9, 269, 278, 309-10, 324
Anderson, M.W., 24, 28
Anglican, xxv, xxvii, 192, 215-16, 218, 220, 222-23, 225, 229-30, 232, 234, 236, 237-38, 243, 248, 251, 303, 315-16, 337
Anglican Consultative Council, 315
Anglo-Catholicism (See: Anglo-Catholic Movement)
Anglo-Catholic Movement, xxxv, 214, 219, 222, 232, 234, 238-39, 243, 250-51, 254-55, 265, 312 n. 355, 316
Anniversary of the coronation of the monarch, 7
Anointing of the sick, 3, 11
Anson, Peter F., 248 n. 75
antependium, 220
Antioch, 325
antiphonal, 3
Apocrypha, 139, 141
Apostles' Creed, 8, 103, 159, 203, 221-22, 281
"Apostolic Church," 240
apostolic succession, 53, 236, 237, 253
apostolic symbol (See: Creed)
Archbishop George Appleton, 303
Aristotelian (See: Aristotle)
Aristotle, 13, 85
Article VI, 231
ASB 1980, xxv, xxxv, 229, 265, 280-321, 337

Ash-Wednesdaye, 1, 31
Asia Minor, 324
atonement, 172, 252
Attyn, 55
Augustine, xxv, 2, 93, 118, 119, 241
Augustinism (See Augustine)
Auschwitz, 318
authorized version of the Bible (See: King James Version)

Bach, J. S., 318
baldachin, 222
Banks, 55
baptism, 47, 98, 119, 136, 141, 146, 159, 184, 208, 216, 237 253, 257, 305
baptism, adult, 7, 146
baptism, child, 11, 33
baptism, private, 1, 3
baptism, public, 1, 3, 4, 146
Baptists, 196
Barrow, Henry, 137-38
Barthelot, 56
Basle, 56, 130
Baxter, Richard, 136, 143, 145
BCP, xxvii n. 1, xxviii, xxxi, xxxvi, 14, 26, 29, 34, 43, 47, 71, 78, 85, 86, 94, 99, 113, 118, 119-21, 125-27, 143 n. 51, 145, 146, 149-51, 187-94, 200, 206-9, 227, 228, 240, 243-46, 248-51, 257, 266-70, 273, 276, 317-18, 321
BCP 1549, xxxiv, 1, 3, 4, 7-12, 18-20, 24, 29, 31, 34, 37, 39, 85, 89, 120-22, 125-26, 129, 131, 150, 161, 213, 254, 270, 324, 337
BCP 1552, xxxiv, 3, 4, 6, 7, 9, 10, 12, 13, 20, 24, 29, 31, 34, 36, 47, 63, 87, 98, 105, 120-21, 123-27, 131, 141, 147, 150, 161, 183, 214, 337
BCP 1559, 128, 129, 131, 136, 137, 139, 141, 146, 213-14
BCP 1662, xxv, xxvii, xxviii,xxxiv, xxxv, 3, 4, 7, 9, 10, 20, 24, 29, 31, 34-38, 98, 127, 128, 136, 141, 193, 200, 201, 214, 219-22, 227-29, 240, 248,

259, 267-74, 276, 277, 281, 283-85, 287-93, 295-314, 318-21, 337-38
BCP 1927/1928, 254
Beaumont, 55
Bedford, Earl of, 55-56
Beesley, Alan, 24
Bellarmine, 242
Benedicite Omnia Opera, 158, 202, 281, 286
benediction, 8, 121, 163, 273, 281, 290, 295, 313
Benedictus, 8-9, 103, 113, 159, 202, 211, 281, 286, 324
Benson, R.M., 247
Bentham, 55
Beyerhaus, Peter, 315-316
Bible, xxx, 1, 5, 14-16, 21-26, 29, 32, 36, 39-43, 45, 50, 51, 52, 53, 54, 67-68, 70-77, 80, 82-84, 88-97, 99, 102-3,106-9, 114-16, 122-26, 128-29, 133-35, 137-39, 141, 152-53, 157, 159-60, 162-65, 168-71, 173-74, 180, 185, 189-90, 192, 194, 196, 199, 205, 207, 211, 217, 219, 221-25, 227, 228, 230-37, 239-43, 248, 249, 251, 258, 260-61, 263, 267-68, 273, 275, 276-79, 282, 285, 291, 294, 298-302, 306, 310, 316-21, 337
Bishop (See: Consecration of Bishop)
Bishop Auckland (Parish of), 297
"Black Rubric," 123, 131, 146, 312 n. 355
Blaurer, Thomas 59
Bloody Mary (See: Queen Mary)
Blumhart, Johann Christoph, xxx
bodily real presence, 22
Bodington, C., 244
Bonhoeffer, 254, 259, 309
"Book of Common Order" (Scotch), 140, 148
Daniel, Book of, 158-159
"Book of Sports," 142
born again, 41, 44, 46, 66, 116-117, 145, 182
Boston, 197
Brandenburg, 4

Brett, W.M., 279
breviary, 3-4, 7, 157, 159, 163, 164-65
British church, 2
"British Critic, The," 232
Brooks, Peter Newman, 321
Browne, Robert, 94, 137
Bucer, Martin, xxix, xxxiv, 4, 7, 12-14, 19, 28-47, 60, 85-89, 120, 122-23, 126, 129, 149, 151, 181 n. 201, 183, 194
Bullinger, H., 6, 14, 25, 48, 50, 52, 54-57, 59-63, 123, 129, 131, 133, 136, 148, 187 n. 220
Burcher, John, 55, 59
burial, 1, 3, 146, 216
Butler, John, 59

Calvin, John, 4, 93, 119 n. 110, 158, 182, 184, 186-187, 189, 191-192, 220, 228, 236, 239, 262
Calvinistic (See: John Calvin)
Cambridge, 5, 6, 29, 60
canon, 9, 110, 120-122, 125-126, 150, 279, 311, 323
canons of colour (See: colour canon)
Canterbury, 6, 27, 71-72, 133-134, 138, 142, 151, 253, 315
"Caroline divines", 149, 229-230
Carter, C.S., 139
Carter, John, 79
Cartwright, 140
Carvell, 55
cassock, 146, 215-216, 219
catechism, 1, 3, 34, 51, 141, 184, 291
Catherine of Aragon, 5
Catherine of Braganza, 144
Catholic (See: Roman Catholic)
catholic, 184-90
Catholic Emancipation Act, 230
Catholicism (See: Roman Catholicism)
catholicity, 184, 188-90, 253
censer, 225
Censura, 12, 18, 28-29, 32, 38
Chambers, 55
"Character Indelebilis," 19, 21, 35
Charles I (See: King Charles I)

Charles II (See: King Charles II)
Charles V, 5
Charley, J.W., 277
chasuble, 216-18
Cheke, John, 19, 55, 129
Chicago, 228
"Chicago Declaration," 228
choir, 40, 212, 215
choir stall, 223-24
Christ (See: Jesus Christ)
"Christ and His Office," 76
Christ Church College, Oxford, 14, 24
Chrysostom (See: St. John Chrysostom)
Church Fathers, 47, 94, 97, 126, 185, 216, 240-41, 251-52
"Church Law," 220 n. 346, 221
"Church Militant," 77
Church of England, xxvii, xxviii, 26, 71, 132-33, 187, 213-14, 231, 247-48, 253, 265, 315, 318
church windows, 223
Cistercian Order, 48
Civil War, 136, 143, 147-49
Cleeve Abbey, 48
closing prayers, 111, 113, 188, 211, 270, 274, 290, 292
closing sentences, 104-5, 160, 211, 281, 287, 292
closing versicles, 160
Clowney, E.P., 228 n. 369
Cockroft, 55
Codex Alexandrinus, 324
Codex Iuris Canonici, 28
Cole, 55
collect for the day, 8-9, 120, 161, 169, 273, 288, 294, 297
collect for grace, 9, 161, 281, 289-90, 292
collect for the king, 120
collect for peace, 8-9, 161, 281, 288-89, 292
collect of purity (See: opening collect)
Collinson, Patrick, 45, 133, 136
Cologne Church Agenda, 4
Colonna, Vittoria, 15, 17

colour canon, 216, 220

comfortable words, 109, 121, 205-6, 276-77

coming of age, 54, 258-60, 275, 291, 293 n. 272, 302, 313

commination, 31, 208-9

Commonwealth, 144

communion, 1, 4, 9-10, 19-24, 32, 37-38, 72, 76, 79, 85, 98, 105, 107, 110, 113-15, 118, 119-20, 123-25, 131-32, 136, 139, 141, 147, 149-50, 165-67, 172-75, 177, 179, 182-83, 186, 188, 191-94, 204, 211-13, 216, 218-19, 222, 225-27, 237, 244, 246-47, 249 n. 78, 254-58, 266, 274, 278, 294-95, 312

communion rail (See: altar rail)

communion of the sick, 1, 4, 19-21

communion table, 220-22

Community of the Epiphany, 247

compline, 8, 9, 10, 11, 163, 187

Confessio Augustana, 189 n. 228

confession, 100-01, 109, 114, 121, 125, 152-55, 163, 165, 178-80, 193, 200, 205, 210, 212, 224, 268, 274-75, 280, 282-84, 291, 294, 296, 312

confirmation, 1, 4, 34, 136, 139, 141, 208

confiteor, 9, 179

"Confutation of Unwritten Verities, A," 90

congregation, 190-91

consecration of bishops, 1, 3, 188

consecration prayer, 10, 37-38, 110-11, 121, 123, 125, 180, 226, 277-79, 308-11

consecration section with words of institution, 9, 226, 323

"Consensus Quinquesaecularis," 235, 238-41, 249, 277-78, 302

conversion, 99, 118-19, 156, 178

Contarini, 20

Cope, 213, 216

Corda, Salvatore, 18, 20-21, 23, 85

Cosin, John, 145-46, 148, 214

Council of Trent, 241

court, 56

Coventry, 66

"Cowley Fathers" (See: Society of St. John the Evangelist)

Cox, 131

Cox, Harvey, 197-200, 199

Cranmer, Thomas, xxv, xxxiv, 4-8, 12-14, 18, 22, 24-26, 28-29, 48, 59, 60-61, 85-87, 88-98, 105, 112-19, 122-26, 151, 158, 162, 183-86, 189, 194, 222, 232, 317-18, 321

"Cranmer's Bible," 89

Creed, 8, 34, 51, 53, 58, 78, 106, 120, 141, 147, 159, 169, 186, 188, 203, 211-12, 221, 226

Cromwell, Oliver, 136, 143-44, 149

Cullman, Oscar, 192

Cyprian, 241

Cyril of Jerusalem, 184-85, 189

Darwinian theory of evolution, 258

Day, 56

Day, Peter, 192 n. 236

deacons (See: Ordering of deacons) Decades, 61

Decalogue (See: Ten Commandments)

"Declaration of the Ten Commandments, A," 80

"Defense of the True and Catholic Doctrine of the Sacrament of the Body and Blood of our Saviour Christ, A," 115

Defensio, 15, 20

"De Lazaro," 89, 92 n. 16

demythologizing, 261-65, 293 n. 270

"De Regno Christi," 46-47, 86

"De Sacramentis," 323

development, 233-35, 250-51, 258-59, 261

Devil, 174, 319

Dix, Gregory, 98

Dod, John, 69

doxology, minor, 8 n. 42, 102, 145, 202, 210, 212, 224, 286, 310, 322, 324 n. 8

Duffield, G.E., 319-20

Durham, 56, 145-46, 214

Durham Prayer Book, 147-48

Eastern Church, 193, 216-17, 217 n. 331, 235-36, 238 n. 35, 238-39, 278, 322-23
Ebeling, Gerhard, 251 n. 80
"Ecclesiastical Sonnets," 206
Ecclesiola in Ecclesia, 182
Ecumenicity (See: Ecumenism)
Ecumenism, 191-92
Edward VI (See: King Edward VI)
Egyptian, 323
Elizabeth I (See Queen Elizabeth I)
Ely, Bishop of, 12, 29
England, xxxv, 5, 14, 27, 29, 48, 55-57, 59, 71, 81, 88, 128-30, 343, 140, 142, 165, 214, 227
epiclesis, 10, 278, 309-11, 324
Episcopal (See: Episcopalianism)
Episcopalian (See: Episcopalianism)
Episcopalianism, xxxiv, 136-38, 142-45, 147, 150
epistle, 106, 120, 169, 212, 223, 294
Epistle to the Romans, 15, 21, 25-26
epitrachelion, 217-18
Erasmus, 5
Esalen Institute, 198-99
Esay (See: Isaiah)
eucharistic prayer, 295, 305, 309-11
eucharistic service or liturgy (See: communion)
eucharistic vestments, 12, 125, 131-32, 136, 146, 213-14, 219
Eusebius Emissenus, 119
evangelical (See: evangelism)
Evangelisch-Reformierten Kirchen (Swiss), 311 n. 351
evangelism, 16-17, 142, 151, 153, 154-55, 158, 163, 172, 183, 220, 224 n. 359, 246-47, 250, 256
evangelistic, evangelization (See: evangelism)
Evening Prayer, 1, 8-9, 98, 105, 113-14, 124, 145, 163-65, 172, 183, 187, 190, 201, 203-04, 207, 210-12, 215, 226-27, 244, 248, 282, 286-87, 294

Evensong, 1, 203-04, 215, 224, 227
exhortations, 24, 100-01, 107-08, 113, 117, 121, 124-25, 152-54, 163, 172-77, 179, 205, 210, 224, 226, 268, 274-75, 291, 312, 313
"ex opere operato," 11, 115-16, 181, 196, 239, 258
Experimental Liturgy, 266, 321, 337
Experimental Liturgy First Series, 266
Experimental Liturgy Second Series, 266-74, 276-77, 279
Experimental Liturgy Series 3, 266-74, 276-79

Faber, 5
faith, xxv, 15, 66, 68, 76, 80, 82-83, 85-86, 91, 97-120, 126, 128, 156, 158-59, 172-73, 176-77, 179, 180, 182, 185, 187, 190, 192, 194, 196, 222, 227, 231, 235, 237, 241, 245, 257-59, 261, 263, 265, 275, 279, 285, 288, 291, 296-99, 301, 320, 337
fascinosum and tremendum, 199, 207, 208, 224-25, 228, 268-69
Fathers (See: Church Fathers)
fellowship, 40, 78, 182
Fiesole, 13
finitum capax infiniti, xxx
First Corinthians, 15, 21, 24
Flaminio. 15, 17
Fletcher, Joseph, 277 n. 204
Fliedner, Pastor, 46
font, 224
forgiveness, 152, 155, 156, 159, 167, 179, 219, 291
Foxe, 56
Francke, August, 46
Flanders, 5
Frankfort, 55, 130, 132
Friedrich, Casper David, 207
Friedrich, John, of Saxony, 5
Froude, R. H., 230-231, 238
fulness, 236
fundamentalism, 90, 96, 97, 169, 185, 231, 245

fundamentalistic (See: fundamentalism)
funeral (See: burial)
Fytz, Richard, 137

Gallic rite, 324
Gardiner, Stephen, 15, 185
Geisler, Norman L., 228 n. 369
Gelasian and Gregorian Sacramentaries, 323
Gelasius (Pope), 325
Geneva, 54, 132, 148, 314
Geneva liturgy, 133
Germanos of Constantinople, 217
Germany, 5, 129, 231
gestures, 196, 211, 213
Gloria in Excelsis, 8, 111, 120-21, 183, 188, 206, 212, 273, 281, 286, 294, 297, 324-25
Gloria, Little (See doxology, minor)
Gloucester, 60, 62-63
Gloucester, Bishop of, 50, 60
Godparents, 11
Golden Chaine, 66
Gomme, Andor, 316
Gonzago, Giulia, 17
Goodrich (See Ely, Bishop of)
Gore, Charles, 250-53
Gospel, 106, 120, 169, 212, 294
grace, 51, 98-112, 122, 161-62, 170, 176, 182, 275, 281, 292, 310
gradual, 2
"Great and Wonderful", 281, 286
Greek Church (See: Eastern Church)
Greenham, 82
Greenwood, John, 137
Gregory the Great, Pope, 2, 325
Gregory of Nazianzen, 242
Grindal, Edmund, 27, 56, 129-38, 149, 169
Grünzweig, Fritz, 314
Gualter, 55-56
Guest, 131
Gulag Archipelago, 318

Haddon, 55

Hadleigh Conference, 229-30
Hahn, Michael, xxx
Hales, 55
Haller, William, 66, 69, 73, 75, 79, 82, 83
Hampton Court Conference, 139-41, 145-46, 214
Harms, Claus, xxx
Hegel, 253
Heidelberg Catechism, 262
hell, 69, 74, 245, 262
Henrietta Marie, 142
Henry VIII, 5-6
Hereford Cathedral, 2
"Hermann's Consultation," 29, 180 n. 196
Hieronymus, 92 n. 16
High Church, 144, 146, 149, 151, 203, 213, 213 n. 312, 215, 219-20, 230, 236, 244-47, 249-50
High-Churchism, 150
High-Churchman, 142, 144, 149-50, 213, 229-30, 243, 246, 248, 249
Hilles, 56
historical-critical method, 251
Hoehner, H., 228 n. 369
Holland, H. S., 250
Holy Ghost, 10, 22, 33, 36, 42-43, 46, 65-66, 68, 77, 85, 90, 93, 105, 116, 155, 160, 167, 174, 176, 186, 188, 192, 195-96, 199, 204-5, 219 n. 342, 231, 237, 285, 287, 310, 324
Holy Mystery (See: Mystery)
Holy Scripture (See: Bible)
Holy Spirit (See: Holy Ghost)
"Homilies of salvation, faith, and good works," 112-13
"Homily in time of pertilence," 64-65, 67, 73
"Homily of the true, lively and christian faith ...," 114
Hooker, Richard, 50 n. 130
Hooper, A., 55
Hooper, Anne (wife of John Hooper), 74
Hooper, John, xxix, xxxi, xxxiv, 6-7,

12-13, 25, 28, 48-55, 57-84, 86-89, 120, 123-26, 128-29, 131, 136-37, 149-51, 153, 155, 167 n. 142, 169, 172 n. 161, 183, 221

Hopf, Constantine, 47

Hormisdas, 323

Horn, 55, 56

Horne, 131

Humphrey, 55, 56

Iconoclasm, 17, 143

Iconoclastic (See: Iconoclasm)

Ignatius of Antioch, 184

Illingworth, J.R., 250-52

Incarnatio Christi, 21

Incarnation, 237-38, 250-52, 254-55, 257, 260, 263, 265

incense, 196, 203, 224

independency, 132, 137-38, 141-42

independentism (See: independency)

independent (See: independency)

indulgences, 241

infallibility, 91

"Injunctions," 70, 133

Innocent III, 220

intercessions, 8

intercessory and thanksgiving prayer, 294, 297-305

introductory quotations, 99, 151

introductory sentences (See: introductory quotations)

introit, 120, 322

Introitus, 10, 120

invitation to confession, 109, 177

invitation to sanctification, 121

invocation of the saints, 241-42

Ireland, 132

Irish Church Reform Bill, 230

Iron Curtain, 187

Isaiah, 74

Italian evangelism, 18

Italian revival movement, 17

Italy, 5

James I (See: King James I)

Itti, Gerard, 46

Jasper, R.C.D., 279

Jeremiah, 92 n. 16

Jerusalem, 184-85, 189, 264, 325

Jesus Christ, 10, 18-19, 25, 35-38, 42-43, 46-47, 49, 51-54, 57, 59, 61, 65-66, 68, 72, 74-76, 83, 98, 105-6, 108, 110-19, 122-23, 135, 137-38, 140, 155-56, 159, 161-163, 173, 175-182, 186-87, 189, 192-95, 219, 221-22, 225-26, 228, 237-39, 244, 246, 252, 255, 257-58, 263-64, 271-73, 278, 281, 283, 285, 288-90, 296-98, 304, 307-8, 310-12, 325

Jesus College, Cambridge, 5

John the Baptist, 159

Jewel, John, 27, 55-56, 129, 131

Jonah, 48, 60, 64, 68, 72-74, 74, 81-84, 155

Jonas (See: Jonah)

Jubilate Deo, 159

Judas, 174

Jung, E.M., 15, 18, 26

justification, 98, 112-13, 122, 237, 251 n. 80, 293

Keble, John, 230-31, 232, 234, 238, 240, 244, 249

Keller-Hüschemenger, M., 231, 235, 236, 237

Kelly, 55

Kilpatrick, G.D., 316

King Charles I, 142, 146, 149

King Charles II, 144, 149-50, 221

King Edward VI, 44, 49, 54, 59-61, 63, 67-69, 86-87, 92 n. 18, 128-30, 137, 213-14, 221

King James I, 140-41

"King James Version," 141, 316-19

kneeling, 12, 72, 123, 132, 136, 139, 141, 146, 200, 206, 211-12

Knox, John, 123, 148

Koch, Ernest, 50

Kohls, E.W., 228

Külling, Samuel, 228

Künneth, W., 194
Kyrie Eleison, 8, 120, 211, 273, 294, 297, 325

Lady Days, 189
Lambeth Palace, 14, 24-26, 63
Lang, August, 46
Langhern, 55
Lasco, 63
Laski, John, 6-7, 13
Latimer, H., 128
Latin (See: Roman Catholic)
Laud, William (Archbishop) 142-43, 146, 147, 221
lauds, 8-10, 156, 160, 187, 325
lectern, 223
lectionary, 2
Lérins, 184, 189
lesser litany, 159 n. 106
lesson from New Testament, 8
lesson from Old Testament, 8
Letter to the Romans (See: Epistle to the Romans)
Lever, 55-56
"Lima Liturgy," 315
litany, 1
liturgical cloths, 213, 220
liturgical linen (See: liturgical cloths)
liturgical vestments, 49-50, 139, 213
"Liturgy, The," 208
Locher, G.W., 7, 193
"Loci Communes," 41
Löhe, Wilhelm, xxx
London, 55-56, 59-60, 63, 129-30, 132, 145, 245
Lord's Prayer, 8-9, 31, 51, 101, 104, 111, 120-121, 141, 157, 159-60, 167, 181, 200, 204, 210-12, 221-22, 281, 295
Lucca, 13
Luke 19:10, 64
Luther, 4, 14, 85, 228, 237, 259
Lutheran, xxx, 155 n. 85, 191, 193-94, 236, 239, 322
"Lux Mundi," 250-54, 258, 280

Magnificat, 8, 164, 203, 211
Manducatio Impiorum, 22
Manton, 140
manual, 3
Margull, H.J., 303
marriage (See: matrimony)
Marian exile(s), 54-55
Martin, David, 317-18
Martyr, Peter (See: Peter Martyr Vermigli)
Mary (mother of Jesus), 10
Mary (Queen Mary) (See: Queen Mary)
mass, 2, 32, 179-80, 216, 325
Master, 55
matins, 1, 8, 156-57, 187, 244
matrimony (marriage), 1, 3, 139, 141, 146, 209, 216
Matthew, 75
Matthew 18:20, 19
Matthew Bible (See: "The Great Bible")
Maurer, Wilhelm, 228
McLelland, J.C., 22
Methodism, 25
Micronius, Martin, 59-61, 63
Middle Ages—High Scholastic Tradition, 12
Millenary Petition, 138-39, 145
Miserere, 104, 281, 325
missal, 2, 166, 179 n. 193, 180 n. 194, 218, 277, 306, 311
Moberly, R.C., 250, 252
Moltman, Jürgen, 192 n. 236
monastic communities, 247
Montgomery, J.W., 314
Moore, A., 250
Morison, 55
Morning Prayer, 1, 8-9, 98-99, 103, 112-13, 124, 145, 151, 159, 163-64, 172, 183, 187, 190, 200-01, 203, 207, 210-13, 215, 226, 244, 248, 249 n. 78, 280, 284, 286-91, 294
Moses, 69
Mueller, Georg, 46

Mullins, 55
"mysterium" (See: mystery)
mystery, 150, 193, 205-6, 226, 232

Naples, 13, 15, 18
Nettesheim, Cornelius Agrippa von, 5
Newman, J.H., 230-31, 238, 240-44, 249
New Testament, 232-33, 264
New Testament lesson, 8, 103, 159, 202, 281, 287, 294
Nicene Council, 323
Nicene Creed, 188, 266, 273, 294, 297
Niketa of Remesiana, 325
1977 BCP (USA), xxv
Nineteenth Article, 189
Noah, 77, 79
nonconformist, 246
none, 8
Norwich, 56, 145
notices, 120, 169
Novalis, 207, 209
Nunc Dimittis, 8, 164, 211
Nürnberg, 4, 5
Nyenhuis, W., 6

Oakeley, F., 240
Oath of Supremacy, 137
Oberlin, xxx
Oetinger, Christoph, xxx
offertory texts, 115
offertory verse, 121, 125, 169
oil, 11
Old Catholic, 322
Old Testament lesson, 8, 102-3, 202, 212, 273, 281, 286, 294
opening collect, 24, 105, 120, 167, 204, 212, 294
opening sentences, 101, 157, 163, 210, 286
Ordering of Deacons, 1, 3, 188
Ordering of Priests, 1, 3, 188
Ordinarium, 180
ornaments, 214-15
"Ornaments Rubric," 214-15

Orthodox Church (See: Eastern Church)
Osiander, 5
Osiander's Church Agenda, 4
Oxford, 6-7, 14-15, 25, 56, 60, 60 n. 170, 221 n. 350, 246-47, 250, 316
Oxford Movement, 216, 220, 229-31, 233-39, 243, 247-50

Packer, J.I., 95, 228 n. 369, 282
Padua, 13
Palmer, W., 230
Parker, Archbishop, 129
Parkhurst, John, 27, 55-56
Parliament, 142-43, 213-14, 254
Parliament of Saints, 143
"Pastoral Character," 208
patristic, 184, 189
Paul (the apostle), xxix, 69,75, 186, 256
Perceval, A.P., 230
Perkins, William, 66
Peter (the apostle), xxix, 52
petition for the power of sanctification, 267
pews, 223
phelonian, 217-18
pietism, xxix, 154 n. 79, 171, 177-78, 182, 245, 257, 338
pietist, pietistic (See: pietism)
Pike, James, 277 n. 204, 279
Pilkington, 55-56
Pius X (pope), 234
"Plaine and Familiar Exposition of the Ten Commandments, A," 69
pluralistic-relativistic theology, 253
pluvial, 216
Pocknee, C.E., 222 n. 354
Poland, 14
Pollanus, Valeranus, 7, 12-13
Ponet, 55
pontifical, 3
Possy, 14
Pownall, 55
praise, 158
prayer for communion with the saints, 9, 10

prayer for the acceptance of the sacrifice, 9-10
prayer for the blessed receiving of the sacraments, 9
prayer for the church militant, 37, 106-07, 121, 125, 147, 170, 172, 189, 205, 226, 266, 276-277, 297, 301
prayer for the clergy, 267
prayer for clergy and people, 162
prayer for the congregation, 267
prayer of dismissal, 160
prayer for the ecclesia militans (See: prayer for the church militant)
prayer of humble access, 110, 121, 206, 294, 304
prayer for the king or queen, 162, 290, 293
prayer for the living and dead saints, 9, 10, 36, 122
prayer for the royal family, 162
prayer of St. Chrysostom, 162, 290
prayer of thanks, 121
prayer of thanks with anamnesis, 121
prayers of thanksgiving, 146, 181
prayers for those at sea, 7
prayers for various concerns, 7
predestination, 25
Preface, 121, 226, 269, 277, 306, 309-10
preface to the BCP, 187
Preface with Sanctus, 9, 109, 121, 189, 206, 279, 306-07, 323
Preface with Sursum Corda, 323
presbyterian (See: presbyterianism)
presbyterianism, 137, 139, 140-45, 193
priests (See: Ordering of Priests)
prime, 8, 159-60
processing (See: procession)
procession, 212-13, 224, 226
proclamation of the peace, 294, 305
"prophesyings," 133-36
Proprium de Tempore, 180 n. 195
protestant, xxvii, 126, 128-29, 133, 338
protestantism (See: protestant)
psalm, 44, 85, 190, 203, 212, 224
Psalm 95 (Venite), 8, 102, 157, 159,

201, 280
Psalm 100 (Jubilate), 103, 202, 280, 287
Psalter, 7, 44
Puetie, 55
pulpit, 223
pura doctrina, xxix-xxxi, xxxv, 68, 71-72, 86-87, 151, 184, 200, 337
"pura ecclesia," 50
pura vita, xxx-xxxi, 67, 68, 87, 151
"pure congregation," 138
purgatory, 73, 241
Purification of Women, 1, 3, 11, 209
puritan(ical) (See: puritanism)
puritanism, xxvii-xxxi, xxxiv, 48, 54, 57, 66-67, 69-72, 75, 79-82, 86-87, 118, 126, 129-30, 132-37, 139, 144-51, 166, 168 n. 145, 170, 183, 188 n. 225, 190 n. 233, 190 n. 234, 191, 193-94, 208, 227-28, 230, 239, 337-38
purus cultus, xxx, xxxi, 48, 49, 67, 71-72, 85, 87, 151, 184, 200
Pusey, E.B., 213, 230-31, 238, 244, 249, 250
Pusey House, 250

Queen Elizabeth I, 15, 27, 55, 56, 128-29, 132, 134-35, 137, 138, 214-15
Queen Mary, 14, 27, 53, 53-55, 128-29, 133, 137
Quinonnes, Francis de, 4

Rahner, Karl, 303
Railton, 55
Ramsey, Michael, 252
Reading of the Gospel, 147
rebirth, 15, 35, 178
Reformation, xxviii-xxix, xxxiv, 6, 12, 14, 28, 29, 47-48, 59, 62, 85, 98, 120, 122, 126-32, 136, 149-50, 153, 155, 164-65, 169 n. 146, 184-85, 189, 209, 222, 228, 231, 239, 240, 249-51, 258-61, 266, 275, 277-79, 284-85, 287, 293, 311, 313, 315, 318, 337-38
Reformed, 14, 48 n. 124, 85, 130, 193-94, 221, 224, 237

Reindorp, George, 274 n. 192
remembrance of the dead, 10, 36, 37, 171-72
Reniger, 55
repentance, 52, 66, 152-56, 172, 179, 200, 283, 291
reredos, 221-22
Restoration, 144, 149, 221
revival (See: revivalism)
revivalism, xxvii-xxxi, 57, 86-87, 118, 120, 127, 129, 143, 149, 151-56, 158, 161-66, 168-74, 176-83, 190, 194, 207, 228, 244, 246, 248-49, 314, 319, 321
revivalistic (See: revivalism)
Reynolds, Dr., 139
Reynolds, Bishop, 145
Richter, Ludwig, 207
Ridley, Nicholas, 12, 128
ring exchange, 139, 147
ritualism (See: ritualists)
ritualists, 239 n. 45, 244-45
Robinson, John, xxxv, 254-65, 255 n. 91, 277-79, 291, 293, 295-96, 302-3, 314
Rogers, Father Murray, 303
Roman breviary (See: breviary)
Roman Catholic, 122, 149, 158, 181, 192-93, 196, 207, 219, 222, 224, 229-30, 231, 233-36, 238-39, 241, 242-43, 279, 303, 311
Roman Catholicism, 144, 207, 238-39
Roman missal (See: missal)
romantic, 206-7
romanticism, 162, 169
Rome, 246,
Rome, Bishop of, 242
Rose, H.J., 229
royalism, 137, 138, 147, 149
royalistic (See: royalism)
royalist (See: royalism)
rubric, 123-124, 131, 146, 158, 165, 169, 200, 211, 212-14, 220-21, 226 n. 363, 266, 274, 286, 290
Rump Parliament, 143
Runcie, Archbishop, 315

sacral, 195-200, 217, 220, 224, 227
sacrality (See: sacral)
sacramentary, 2
sacrament, 119, 237, 244, 255, 257, 260, 261, 298, 312
sacristan, 215
Sadoleto, 17
St. Albans, 221 n. 350, 246
St. Hilary of Poitiers, 324
St. John Chrysostom, 89, 92 n. 16, 93, 119, 162
St. Paul (See: Paul)
St. Paul's, 132
Salisbury, 2, 56, 274 n. 192
Salisbury Cathedral, 2, 4
Salkyns, 55
salvation, 16, 65, 66, 90-91, 95, 102, 103, 110, 118, 122, 149, 153, 156, 158, 163-64, 171, 179, 195, 196, 201, 217, 222, 225-27, 232, 244, 252, 257, 262, 275, 277, 283, 300, 303, 337
Salvation Army, 196
Samartha, Stanley, 303
Sampson, 55, 56
sanctification, 18, 51-52, 57-58, 68-69, 86, 140, 155-56, 161, 164, 166-67, 171, 196, 199, 227, 248, 255, 292
sanctuary light, 223
Sanctus, 9, 323, 324
Sandys, Edwin, 27, 55-56, 129
Sarum breviary, 2-3, 7-9, 12 n. 68, 156-59, 163-64, 191
Sarum missal (See: Sarum breviary)
Satan, 64, 117, 158, 174
Saviour of the World, 281
Savonarola, 13
Savoy Conference, 144-148, 214
Savoy Palace (See Savoy Conference)
Schaeffer, Francis, 228
Schlegel, the brothers, 207
Scholastic tradition, 9, 12
Scory, 131
Scotch-Irish church, 2
Scotland, 146
Scottish church, 142
Scottish Prayer Book of 1637, 146, 148

"Scriptura Sui Ipsius Interpres," 97, 228, 231, 250, 276, 282
Scripture (See: Bible)
Second Helvetic Confession, 30 n. 66, 115 n. 92
Second Series, 266-77, 282, 296
Second Vatican, 122, 179, 218, 277
Septuagint, 159
Sergius I (Pope), 322-23
Series 3, 266-280, 296, 301
sermon, 120, 122, 125, 169, 212, 281, 286, 294, 297
"Sermon concerning the time of rebellion, A" 92 n. 17
Seventeenth Article, 25
Sext, 8
Sheldon, Bishop, 145
sign of the cross, 12, 123, 139, 141, 146
Simeon, 164
sin, xxix, 98-105, 107-14, 117, 119, 126, 152-53, 173-74, 175, 177-81, 218, 238, 245, 268, 275-76, 281-85, 296, 304, 306-8
sinfulness (See: sin)
sin-grace-faith, 102-5, 107-8, 110, 112-13, 126
sinner (See: sin)
sitting, 212-13
Smith, 82
Smyrna, 184
Society of St. John the Evangelist, 247-48
"Sola Fide," 237
"Sola Scriptura," xxix, 129, 222, 229, 234, 250, 277, 337
"Soli Deo Gloria," 16, 155, 157, 228
soul, 73
"Soundings," 265, 314
Sowerby, 55
Spalatin, 5
Spencer, 55
Spener, P. J., 182
Spenser, 70
spirituality, 224
Spitzweg, 207

Sproul, R.C., 22875 n. 369
Standing, 212
Stanton, Arthur H., 246
Staples, Peter, 265, 314
state prayers, 281, 290
sticharion, 218
stole, 216-17
Strasbourg, 14, 18, 28, 55, 130
Stuart, House of, 144
surplice, 146, 214-15, 219
Sursum Corda, 9, 121, 323
Sutton, 55
Switzerland, 61, 88 n. 4, 132
Symmachus (Pope), 325
Syrian church, 322-23

Taakaas, Istvan, 50
Talbot, E.S., 250
Taverner, 55
Te Deum Laudamus, 8, 158, 202, 211, 281, 286, 325
Temple, William, 250, 253-54
Ten Commandments, 25, 34, 50-53, 57-58, 67-69, 105, 115, 120, 124-25, 141, 167, 205, 212, 221-22, 266, 273, 277, 294-95
terce, 8
Test Act, The, 230
"Testimonium Internum Spiritus Sancti," 93, 97
thanksgiving of women after childbirth (See: Purification of Women)
Theodoret of Cyrrus, 119
Thirty-nine Articles, 4-25, 189, 207, 231, 241, 243
Thomas, M.M., 192 n. 236, 303
Thomas, W.H. Griffith, 214, 219
Thompson, I.R., 255 n. 91
Thwaites, Bryan, 319-20
Tillich, 254, 261
Tractarian (See: Tractarian Movement)
Tractarian Movement, xxxv, 215, 229,231-32, 235-37, 239-40, 243-44,248, 250-51, 258, 277, 280
"Tracts for the Times, The," 229-30
Travers, 140

Trevelyan, G.M., 142
"triers," 143
Troeltsch, Ernst, 46
"True Marks of Christ's Church, The"
    137
Truro, 245, 247
Turks, 5
Turner, 56
Turpin, 55
twelve Biblical opening quota-
    tions,124, 164
twenty offertory sentences, 106, 122,
    205. 266, 276, 297
Twigg, Richard, 244-45

Ulmis, John ab, 60
universal apostolic church, 194

Valdes, Juan, 13, 15, 18
Vancouver, 315-16
van den Heuvel, Albert, 304 n. 331
veneration of pictures and relicts,241
Venite (See: Psalm 95)
Verbum Visibile, 24, 98, 265, 267
Vermigli, Peter Martyr, xxix, xxxiv,4,
    5, 12-15, 18-28, 60, 62, 84-87,120,
    124, 126, 128, 149, 183, 194
versicle, 121
vespers, 8, 163, 187, 227
vested choir, 220
vestments, 124-25, 141, 196, 214-19
"via media," xxxv, 338
Vidler, Alec, 265, 277 n. 204
Vincent of Laarins, 184, 189
visitation of the sick, 1, 4, 11, 208
Voll, Dieter, 244-46, 249
Vox Patrum, 185
Vulgate, 44

Warcop, Ann, 53, 75
Ward, W.G., 232
Watson, V.E., 279
Wells, 56
Wesley, John, 244, 247

Wesleyan (See:John Wesley)
West, W.M.S., 48, 51-52, 57
Western Church, 216, 324
western rite, 322
Westminster Confession, 140, 142
Westminster Synod, 142
Whitby, Synod of, 2
Whitehead, 55, 131
Whitehead, Benjamin, 221
Whitgift, John, 138, 162
Wiburn, 56
Wied, Hermann von, 4
Wilford, 55
Wilkinson, George Howard, 245-46
Winchester, 56, 221 n. 350
Withers, 56
Worcester, 56, 63
Word (See: Bible)
Word of Scripture (See: Bible)
words of distribution, 114, 117, 121,
    125, 180, 206, 295, 312-13
words of institution, 9, 19, 125, 206,
    323,
words of invitation, 121, 295, 312
World Mission Conference at "Bang-
    kok 73," 303
Wordsworth, William, 208-9
World Council of Churches, xxxv, 303,
    315-16
Worms, 130
Wright, D.F., 47
Wycliff, 317

York, 56, 133
York Cathedral, 2

Zinzendorf, Nikolaus Ludwig von,
    173, 177
Zosimus, 323
Zurich, 6, 14, 48-50, 54, 59, 88, 133,
    136 102, 150, 153
Zwingli, 4, 6 n. 27, 48, 52, 54, 57, 119
    n. 110, 123, 133, 148, 181n. 201,
    191-93, 222 n. 353, 236